Legacy of Violence

Legacy of Violence

Lynch Mobs and Executions in Minnesota

John D. Bessler

University of Minnesota Press
Minneapolis • London

Parts of this book were previously published in John D. Bessler, *Death in the Dark: Midnight Executions in America* (Boston: Northeastern University Press, 1997); copyright 1997 by John D. Bessler; reprinted with permission of Northeastern University Press. Other sections of the book were previously published in John D. Bessler, "The 'Midnight Assassination Law' and Minnesota's Anti–Death Penalty Movement, 1849–1911," *William Mitchell Law Review* 22 (1996): 577; reprinted with permission.

Published by the University of Minnesota Press
111 Third Avenue South, Suite 290
Minneapolis, MN 55401-2520
http://www.upress.umn.edu

Printed in the United States of America on acid-free paper

Library of Congress Cataloging-in-Publication Data

Bessler, John D.
  Legacy of violence : lynch mobs and executions in Minnesota /
John D. Bessler.
    p. cm.
Includes bibliographical references (p.) and index.
  ISBN 0-8166-3810-1 (alk. paper)
  1. Lynching—Minnesota—History. 2. Capital
punishment—Minnesota—History. 3. Executions and
executioners—Minnesota—History. I. Title.
  HV6462.M6 B47 2003
  364.1′34—dc21
                                    2003008002

The University of Minnesota is an equal-opportunity educator and employer.

12 11 10 09 08 07 06 05 04 03   10 9 8 7 6 5 4 3 2 1

For my brothers

The ultimate weakness of violence is that it is a descending spiral, begetting the very thing it seeks to destroy. . . . Returning violence for violence multiplies violence, adding deeper darkness to a night already devoid of stars.

—Martin Luther King Jr.

Contents

Acknowledgments

Few human endeavors require more endurance than writing a book, except perhaps climbing Mount Everest, trekking across Antarctica, running for public office, or living in the same household as a book's author. I ran the Twin Cities Marathon in 1987—a feat that took over four hours—but the months spent training to do that literally pale in comparison to the time needed to write a book. After spending hundreds of hours researching, drafting, and continually revising a book-length manuscript, it becomes hard to convince oneself that a piece of writing is truly finished and should be let go into the world. For me, though, the time clearly had come to do just that.

The seed for *Legacy of Violence* was planted in 1991, when I stumbled across an obscure Minnesota Supreme Court case from 1907 in which the *St. Paul Pioneer Press* attacked the constitutionality of a Minnesota gag law passed in 1889. That law, dubbed the "midnight assassination law" by its contemporaries, required that executions be conducted "before the hour of sunrise" and within a jail or "an enclosure which shall be higher than the gallows." It expressly forbade newspapers, on pain of criminal prosecution, from printing any details of state-sanctioned executions beyond the fact that the executions were "duly executed according to law." The discovery of this tidbit of American legal history led to what can only be described as a fortuitous chain of events, culminating with the publication of this book.

The book's odyssey started in earnest in 1994 when I began writing an article about the history of Minnesota's "midnight assassination law" and the state's anti–death penalty movement. The fruits of my historical research were published in 1996 in an article in the *William Mitchell Law Review*, and portions of my discoveries also found their way into my first book, *Death in the Dark: Midnight Executions in America*, published by Northeastern University Press in 1997. Both the law journal and Northeastern University Press have graciously permitted me to reprint text here needed to tell this story. The person most responsible for this book's publication, however, is Todd Orjala, acquisitions editor at the University of Minnesota Press.

I met Todd when I was writing my first book, and a letter that I received from him out of the blue in 1999 quite literally launched this project. Todd sent me a copy of *Minnesota's Twentieth Century: Stories of Extraordinary Everyday People*, an award-winning title he shepherded to publication, and drew my attention to a chapter on the lynchings of three African American circus workers in Duluth in 1920. Todd then asked if I was interested in writing a book about the history of Minnesota's death penalty. I was. A book contract was signed in the year 2000, and a publication date was set for 2003—a dozen years after I ran across the nearly forgotten Minnesota Supreme Court case from the past century's first decade.

If books, once published, have a life of their own, it is clearer than ever to me that so too do books' origins. I owe a debt of gratitude to Todd Orjala for suggesting that this book be written, and to Douglas Armato, the director of the University of Minnesota Press, for sending this project to the presses. The book would not be on bookshelves today if not for their commitment to this story from the start and the hard work and backing of everyone at the Press. I also need to thank the many librarians, writing mentors, and friends—people like Fred Bauman, Bruce Beddow, Bill Everts, and Deborah Keenan—who willingly gave of their time as I researched, wrote, and rewrote the manuscript. The book is a better one for their efforts.

A special thanks goes to Malcolm MacKenzie, the grandson of

the author of the bill that outlawed capital punishment in Minnesota. Malcolm invited me to the MacKenzie clan tent at Macalester College's Scottish Country Fair on a beautiful day in May to learn more about his grandfather, George MacKenzie. Malcolm later sent me his grandfather's unpublished autobiography, photographs, and a copy of the typewritten, anti–death penalty speech that his grandfather delivered at the state capitol in 1911. These materials were instrumental to the telling of this story.

Many thanks to Heidi Bakk-Hansen, Jane Engh, Michael Fedo, Craig Grau, Mary Keirstead, Bud Lawrence, Michael Mello, Jim Moore, and Daardi Sizemore. These individuals gave me valuable insights on this project, as did the capable staffs of the Minnesota Historical Society and the Library of Congress, who tracked down hard-to-find sources. Michael Fedo's book *The Lynchings in Duluth* opened a much-needed dialogue about racial prejudice and violence in the nation's past, and it is my hope that my reexamination and retelling of that story will do that as well. Nan Wynn, the site manager of the Lincoln Tomb in Springfield, Illinois, sent information that worked its way into my manuscript, as did Sandra Peck at the Tuskegee Institute, and Lori Bessler, my sister-in-law, who works for the Wisconsin Historical Society. Sincere thanks, too, to all of them.

It helps when writing a book to work in the company of writers. I am blessed to work at a law firm with some of the best, and I have been privileged to get to know many more in Hamline University's M.F.A. program. The gifted fiction and nonfiction writers and the poets and playwrights I have met have been a constant source of inspiration throughout this project's completion. I am especially grateful for the helpful feedback on portions of the manuscript I received from Julie Landsman, Shannon Lynch, Nora Murphy, Nancy Sather, and Zachary "Lex" Taylor. The many students I have taught at the University of Minnesota Law School over the years also have influenced my thinking on America's death penalty. I only hope that through my annual spring semester seminar on capital punishment I have been able to return the favor.

I would be especially remiss if I did not thank my parents, Bill and Marilyn Bessler. They tirelessly culled through microfilmed newspapers, boxes of old records, photo archives, and President Abraham Lincoln's letters and speeches to help me gather needed information. My mother spent days at a time at the Minnesota History Center helping me piece together this story, and my father, with his lifelong interest in Lincoln and Native American culture, found many valuable nuggets of information for me. I will never be able to repay their love and devotion. Finally, a heartfelt thanks to Amy and Abigail, my wife and daughter, who encourage and nurture—and on a continual basis, selflessly indulge—my writing life. They have enriched my life more than I will ever be able to tell them, try as I do, in words.

Introduction

The cornerstone for Minnesota's state capitol building, designed by famed architect Cass Gilbert, was laid in 1898. The white marbled dome, set on a St. Paul hilltop, was modeled on Michelangelo's dome for the cathedral of St. Peter in Rome. As state officials quibbled over what artwork to commission for the capitol's interior, another, weightier debate—over the death penalty—was raging among the state's legislators. In nearly every legislative session from 1891 to 1905, when the new statehouse was finally completed, Minnesota lawmakers sought to abolish capital punishment, with Representative George MacKenzie authoring the bill that did just that in 1911. The MacKenzie law would make the 1906 botched hanging of William Williams in St. Paul the last state-sanctioned execution to take place within Minnesota's borders.[1]

This book tells the nearly forgotten story of that hard-fought struggle in a midwestern state—Minnesota—between death penalty proponents and those opposed to death as a form of punishment. It is a story about convicted killers and murder victims and the people who made life-ending decisions, from military tribunals and President Abraham Lincoln—in the case of the largest mass hanging in U.S. history—to lynch mobs, judges, juries, and the state's governors. The state's executions and lynchings are paramount in this story, as are the state's anti-gallows and anti-lynching movements and the unique laws they spurred.

It is also the story of one of the twelve American states that no longer authorize capital punishment.

Just a few blocks away from Gilbert's statehouse, the large glass windows of St. Paul's Minnesota History Center majestically frame the state capitol's exterior. In the History Center's stacks and archives, aging county histories and boxes of yellowing documents tell the story of the state's executions and lynchings. Within the capitol itself are sculptures and paintings depicting many of the historical figures integral to this story. There is the towering, sword-wielding bronze statue of Civil War hero William Colvill, who led the charge of the First Minnesota Volunteers at Gettysburg. As a crippled veteran, Colvill pushed for the abolition of Minnesota's death penalty in 1865 and went on, as Minnesota's attorney general, to investigate a lynching in the southern part of the state. Also in the capitol are paintings of Governors Alexander Ramsey and William Merriam, who signed death warrants while in office, and Adolph Eberhart, who signed George MacKenzie's 1911 bill into law. Abraham Lincoln, immortalized as the colossal seated figure in the Daniel Chester French–designed memorial in Washington, D.C., is found here too, in a portrait that hangs in the house of representatives. Lincoln's handwritten order, approving the mass execution of thirty-eight Dakota Indians in Mankato, Minnesota, was donated to the Minnesota Historical Society in 1868 by Lincoln's secretary, a Minnesota native. An ambivalent Lincoln, caught in the cross fire of the Civil War and a deadly Indian uprising on the frontier, issued his 1862 order even as he spared the lives of over two hundred Dakota Indians also condemned to die by a military tribunal.[2]

What happened in Minnesota many decades ago caused a metamorphosis in the American political landscape. Minnesota was one of only a few states to require nighttime executions by statute in the late 1880s, and its "midnight assassination law" and the litigation it spawned accelerated a nationwide trend toward in-private, after-dark executions. Authored by Minneapolis legislator John Day Smith, a Civil War veteran who fought alongside William Colvill at Gettysburg, that 1889 law sought to eliminate the spectacle of public executions and helps explain why America's executions now take place in prisons and away from the public eye. Minnesota's 1921 anti-lynching law, considered model legislation when adopted, was not a first, but it did influence the national debate over lynching while ensuring lynchings became a relic of the state's past. That law was passed at Minnesota's capitol at the behest of NAACP leaders and was signed into law less than a year after the 1920 Duluth lynching of three African American circus workers suspected of gang-raping a white teenager.[3]

Although Minnesota's homicide rate is one of the nation's lowest, the state's past is pockmarked with acts of violence: premeditated murders, child rape, criminal assaults, and even—many years ago—lynchings and state-sanctioned executions. While infrequent, murders in the state have always been a fact of life, as they are today in Minneapolis and St. Paul, in suburban communities from Eden Prairie to White Bear Lake, and in smaller towns like Winona and Moose Lake. While no state death penalty law has been in place for over ninety years, Minnesota has managed to keep violent crime rates at very low levels. Minnesota's 1997 homicide rate, for example, was 2.6 per 100,000 people—a level far below those of active death penalty states like Texas, Florida, Virginia, and Louisiana, where rates ranged from 6.8 to 15.7 murders per 100,000 residents. Only a handful of states—mostly other non–death penalty states—have a lower murder rate than Minnesota.[4]

Executions and lynchings, of course, are not to be confused with one another. Whereas executions happen with the legal system's approval, lynchings are extrajudicial in nature and are carried out by a group of citizens acting under a pretext of authority. Executions and lynchings do share one central truth: at the end of the day, a human being is killed. Whether by the order of a judge in a black robe or by a group of Ku Klux Klan members in white hoods, the end result of executions and lynchings is the same: death. By weaving together the threads of Minnesota's past—a microcosm of the nation's history—and looking at crime and punishment in one state, *Legacy of Violence* aims to draw whatever lessons can be gleaned from the violent tapestry left behind by lynchings and a government's use of the death penalty.[5]

The intersection of race and the punishment of death cannot escape notice even in a northern state like Minnesota. Well over half of all persons lynched or executed in the State of Minnesota were of African- or Native-American descent, and Mankato's mass hanging and Duluth's triple lynching were both totally intertwined with issues of racial prejudice. The U.S.–Dakota War that broke out on the Minnesota frontier in the sweltering heat of August 1862 led to hundreds of deaths and, ultimately, to Abraham Lincoln's order sending thirty-eight Dakota Indians to their death. So many Indians were executed at one time that the mass execution had to be delayed for a week because of a lack of suitable rope in the small town where it took place. The Duluth lynching, which took place after John Robinson's Circus came to town by train, was plainly racially motivated: a hate crime, to use modern terminology. A June 1920 *Chicago Tribune* editorial openly said motives of "sex protection" and "race instinct" combined to cause the lynching and pointed to the alleged rape assailants' race as "negroes" as "an important factor in the psychology of the outbreak."[6]

While racial conflict dominates the chapters on these two historical events, the other chapters of *Legacy of Violence* trace the transition in Minnesota from public executions at midday to privately held, nighttime executions and what led to the death penalty's abolition. Nowhere in the country did this cultural and legal trend play out so dramatically as in Minnesota, where a bungled hanging outraged the public and a state law came under attack in the courts. These chapters also examine the media's role in the death penalty debate and track the back-and-forth struggle over lynching and the state's use of the gallows. One chapter— a case study of the media's powerful role in death penalty cases—is devoted exclusively to the trial of Ann Bilansky, the only woman ever executed in the state. Others are devoted to the passage and enforcement of John Day Smith's "midnight assassination law" and to the state's abolitionist or anti-lynching movements. In the nineteenth century, executions in Minnesota gradually moved out of the public commons and into jails or hastily built board enclosures. But Minnesota's anti–death penalty movement did not peak until after William Williams's botched hanging, exposed by Minnesota's newspapers in 1906 in blatant violation of Smith's law. Williams's horrific death led to statewide calls for capital punishment's abolition, and the *St. Paul Pioneer Press*'s unsuccessful First Amendment challenge to Smith's press-muzzling law had national ramifications for America's death penalty debate. That gag law, upheld by the courts as constitutional, was soon emulated in other states, and American executions moved into the night and out of public view and the public's consciousness.[7]

When people think of executions today, they often think of lethal injections, lengthy time-consuming appeals, or places like Texas where executions most frequently occur. While the method of killing used in Minnesota—hanging—has now gone out of favor, the same factors that led to executions and lynchings decades ago in Minnesota are the ones that drive America's death penalty today. Heartfelt reactions to violent crime and a desire for vengeance sparked calls for executions in the North Star State in the past two centuries just as they do in the twenty-first century in places like California, Georgia, and Louisiana. The questions this book explores are thus as relevant today to America's death penalty debate as they were a century ago in Minnesota: What is the role of law in society, and should the law permit the punishment of death to be inflicted? Is the death penalty an effective deterrent to violent crime, or does the death penalty merely brutalize society? What is the role of the press in America's death penalty debate, and what can and should that role be? And in an open, democratic society, what do laws requiring private, nighttime executions say about the state of America's democracy? These are questions of particular significance, because the issue of violence in American society is a real one and because over thirty-five hundred inmates now sit on death row in the United States.[8]

The Minnesota State Capitol, where lawmakers craft public policy and debate the weighty issues that affect people's everyday lives, is a proud symbol of Minnesota's heritage. Every year, thousands of school-children go there to watch their legislators at work. The beauty of the law—the work of those lawmakers—is that it can affect social change as society's values change. High atop the capitol's main entrance, at the base of the dome, sits a golden sculpture known as the Quadriga or *The Progress of the State*, a befitting symbol of that principle. Designed at Cass Gilbert's request by Daniel Chester French, the famed figure sculptor, the Quadriga depicts a chariot led by two youthful women and an elegant team of four horses abreast. The dazzling artistic effect of the Quadriga, with its horses, idealized figures, and Roman chariot covered in gold leaf, symbolizes Minnesota's hopes for the future and poses a challenge to all of us: What can we, as citizens, do to improve America's democracy and make America a better place to live?[9]

The death penalty is such a difficult issue for so many people because it comes into play only after the commission of a horrible crime. A murder—maybe of a child or teenager, or even a multiple murder—has occurred, and the public rightfully wants to see justice done. But the death penalty, as an issue, raises yet another troubling question that is worthy of consideration: Should society use violence—that is, state-sanctioned killing—to try to stop violence in our society? Or is there a better way, such as life-without-parole sentences, to reduce violent crime than the death penalty offers? A consensus came about in America over the past century—as reflected in anti-lynching laws passed around the country—that lynchings were wrong and unjust and had to be stopped. The practice of lynching, it is agreed today, constitutes an egregious and deplorable violation of a person's basic due process and human rights. The overarching question raised by *Legacy of Violence* is whether American executions should go the way of lynchings and be relegated to the past as they were in Minnesota many decades ago. This book seeks to inform that ongoing, highly contentious debate.

CHAPTER 1

Lynch Mobs and Public Hangings

Minnesota is, by far, mainly known for its blizzards and its below-zero temperatures, and as the Land of 10,000 Lakes—a message imprinted on the state's license plates. It is the home of attractions like the Boundary Waters Canoe Area Wilderness, the St. Paul Winter Carnival, and the Mall of America, and is the boyhood home of rock stars Bob Dylan and Prince. Laura Ingalls Wilder and F. Scott Fitzgerald both lived in the state, and in the Metrodome, in the shadow of Minneapolis's sky-scrapers, sports figures like outfielder Kirby Puckett hit World Series home runs and rounded the bases to thunderous applause. While famous Minnesota politicians like Hubert Humphrey and Walter Mondale once occupied the national stage as presidential candidates, one part of Min-nesota's past is hardly known at all: the history of lynchings and public executions within the state's borders.[1]

Public hangings and extrajudicial lynchings are, in truth, sprinkled throughout much of Minnesota's past, dotting the state's landscape like historical markers. The state's death penalty, at least formally, dates to 1849, when Congress created the Minnesota Territory. Under territorial law, all persons convicted of premeditated murder automatically received death sentences and were put in solitary confinement for lengthy periods of time prior to execution. The law in effect in 1851 mandated a full year of isolation before execution, while an 1853 amendment reduced that period to anywhere from one to six months at the judge's discretion. The governor could issue the warrant of execution only after the period of solitary confinement expired. Both before and after Minnesota became a territory, death was seen by many as an acceptable punishment for crime. Thus, when an Ojibwe man killed two whites in 1848, settlers did not hesitate to hang him. In Indian communities themselves, the murder victim's family had the customary right to kill the perpetrator; as late as 1893, the relatives of a murdered Chippewa chieftain lynched the murderer from a tree on the Cass Lake Indian reservation.[2]

The first man condemned to death by the government in the newly organized Minnesota Territory was a Dakota Indian, variously referred to as U-ha-zy or Yu-ha-zee. U-ha-zy was taken into custody by thirty soldiers from Fort Snelling in 1852 on suspicion of killing a German woman while she was traveling up the Minnesota River with her family. Records are sketchy, but district court minutes show that only three prosecution witnesses testified at U-ha-zy's trial, with the state's governor, Alexander Ramsey, listed as one of three defense witnesses. The jury found U-ha-zy guilty after his trial, and the court's minutes recount the reading of his death sentence: "The sentence of the court is, that you . . . be taken hence to the legal and proper place of confinement and there kept until under law, the Governor of this Territory shall by his warrant order your execution." "May God Almighty have mercy on your spirit," U-ha-zy was told.[3]

Because the territorial law at the time required that executions be delayed at least one year after the trial, U-ha-zy's sentence was not carried out right away. An unsuccessful appeal was filed by U-ha-zy's attorneys, and the long delay led to a pardon campaign, supported by several prominent St. Paul citizens. William Forbes, a successful Indian trader and interpreter, requested clemency on the grounds of U-ha-zy's intoxication, saying he "consequently knew not what he did." U-ha-zy's hanging, it was argued, would not promote morality. The founder of the St. Paul Presbyterian Church, Reverend J. G. Riheldaffer, even questioned whether a "savage" could comprehend "the importance we attach to human life; or appreciate our method of punishing the offender." Another clemency petition, signed by forty-five St. Paul women, called

U-ha-zy a "poor and unfortunate man" who was "without friends, money or influence." The women requested a commutation of his sentence to life in prison or at least a reprieve until the president of the United States could be informed of the case. Signers of the petition included Anna Ramsey, the wife of Minnesota's first territorial governor. When U-ha-zy's death sentence was carried out, however, Governor Ramsey was no longer in office, having relinquished his post to newly appointed Territorial Governor Willis Gorman, an Indiana Democrat.[4]

Just a day before U-ha-zy's hanging, Gorman denied a petition from several of the "most respectable ladies of St. Paul" to pardon U-ha-zy, removing the final obstacle to his execution. Invoking "duty to country," Gorman could find "no just reason" to commute U-ha-zy's sentence. The Dakota Indian, he concluded, killed a white woman "without a shadow of excuse." She had been "murdered by the side of a poor, but no doubt fond and devoted husband," Gorman indignantly proclaimed. Gorman's views coincided with those of a local newspaper editor, who said it would be a "disgrace to the name of justice in the Territory, if this scoundrel is allowed to go free." As a result of the refusal to grant clemency, the Minnesota Territory witnessed its first state-sanctioned execution on December 29, 1854, when U-ha-zy was hanged on the outskirts of St. Paul.[5]

A former officer in the Mexican War, Gorman approved of the whole affair, at least initially. However, he did not anticipate the public spectacle that would accompany the execution. One newspaper reported that "Total Depravity" was out early in the morning on execution day. The night before, in fact, the local population appeared not to have gone to bed at all. That night, guns and pistols were fired around the jail where U-ha-zy had been confined for two years, frequently disturbing sleeping residents. By 9:00 A.M., Ramsey County Sheriff Abram Fridley appeared a "strong friend of Total Depravity," for he started erecting the scaffold in one of St. Paul's most public places. The boisterous crowd applauded the sheriff's actions and cheered upon learning that the law, unlike in some states, did not prohibit public hangings. "Crucify him!" the mob cried out.[6]

Only through the determined efforts of Gorman and "many right-minded citizens" was the gallows taken down from the center of St. Paul. The execution, urged city authorities, simply could not take place within the public quarter. Eventually, Sheriff Fridley relented, and the noisy crowd marched with great pomp behind the sheriff and the prisoner to an uninhabited prairie. After the scaffold was reerected, U-ha-zy was hanged at around 3:00 P.M. According to one newspaper account, "Liquor was openly passed through the crowd, and the last moments of the poor Indian were disturbed by bacchanalian yells and cries." "A half drunken father," the account read, "could be seen holding in his arms a child, eager to see all; giddy, senseless girls and women chattered gaily with their attendants, and old women were seen competing with drunken ruffians for a place near the gallows." The crowd reportedly left the scene "satisfied and in high glee."[7]

Minnesota newspapers provided widely divergent coverage of U-ha-zy's hanging. While the *Daily Minnesotian* gave a complete report, other newspapers had "no inclination to witness the tragedy." The *Daily Minnesota Pioneer* did not even send a reporter to the hanging, leaving it "unable to give the lovers of the dreadful a detail of the poor fellow's suffering." "We are gratified to know that but few of our citizens were in attendance," that paper said. The *Minnesota Republican* also printed few execution details. It merely reported that the hanging represented a "disgusting scene," mirroring the view of historian Edward Neill, who called the execution a disgrace replete with "ribaldry and drunkenness." More than ten years after U-ha-zy's execution, the *St. Paul Pioneer* was still calling it a "beastly affair," reporting that "men, women and children thronged the gallows on St. Anthony Hill, and followed the victim with howls and cheers as though it was to be a delightful entertainment."[8]

Minnesota newspapers universally condemned the public spectacle created by U-ha-zy's execution. The *Daily Minnesotian*, a Whig newspaper with ties to Alexander Ramsey, declared that no future attempts should be made "to hang even a dog in the public streets of St. Paul." "The sooner the scenes connected with that transaction are forgotten," the editors wrote, "the better for the reputation of St. Paul and all

Minnesota." Even the previously uninterested *Daily Minnesota Pioneer* soon felt compelled to remark on the "barbarity" displayed by those in attendance. These "fiends incarnate," it said two days after the hanging, disturbed U-ha-zy's final moments with "laughs and jeers," and the "debauched in the crowd" acted "much more like savages" than the condemned man. The editors concluded that "every lover of decency in the community" should frown upon such conduct. Even so, in the wake of U-ha-zy's hanging, published articles frequently commented on the "Scriptural lawfulness" of capital punishment.[9]

Lynchings of Indians were hardly unknown in the surrounding area or in the years following U-ha-zy's execution. In 1848, for example, a mob in the Wisconsin Territory's St. Croix valley lynched Paunais, an Ojibwe Indian accused of killing a white trader. Morton Wilkinson, a prominent Stillwater citizen and at the time the St. Croix County Attorney, was among the lynch mob. Likewise, in the summer of 1857, three Indians were arrested for the murder of a pack peddler near Gull Lake. Because of the public outcry, Morrison County Sheriff Jonathan Pugh decided to take the prisoners—Charles Gebabish, "Jimmy," and Joe Shambeau—to St. Paul for "safe keeping." En route, a party of men in wagons and armed with revolvers overtook Sheriff Pugh and his deputy, seized the Indians, and forced them to confess. The Indians were hung by the roadside on the south edge of Little Falls, their bodies left hanging on the prairie until about ten o'clock the next morning. When, many years later, the first sheriff of Hennepin County recalled the lynching of Indians "for some deviltry" in Belle Prairie, he said they "did not excite any particular attention."[10]

Minnesota's first lynching of a white settler did not occur until after Minnesota was admitted to the Union in May 1858. On December 27, 1858, a mob of sixty men entered the town of Lexington to lynch saloonkeeper Charles Rinehart, suspected of murdering a thirty-six-year-old carpenter, John Bodell. Rinehart and Bodell had been seen going up the Mississippi River on a steamboat toward a piece of land Rinehart owned, and Bodell had told his wife that he was considering buying the 160-acre farm. After Rinehart borrowed a spade from a neighboring farmer, Bodell's body, with a bullet hole and stab wounds to the head, was later discovered and dug up. It was found just a half mile from where Bodell and Rinehart were last seen walking together. Le Sueur County's deputy sheriff refused to surrender the jail key to the mob, but he was wrestled to the ground and the key forcibly taken from him. During the struggle, the muscular Rinehart stripped off his handcuffs, taking some skin with them, and tore in two a half-inch iron staple securing his ankle. After breaking off a cast-iron stove leg to defend himself, Rinehart held off the lynch mob for over an hour before the mob subdued him by axing through the log structure. Rinehart was then dragged on a sled for three-quarters of a mile and hung from the limb of a tree. His body was buried, uncoffined, in a shallow grave. A St. Paul newspaper would later call the incident a "disgrace" that had stigmatized "the good name" of the state.[11]

The murder of twenty-five-year-old Henry Wallace in 1858 resulted in yet another Minnesota lynching, this time of Wright County resident Oscar Jackson, widely believed to have killed Wallace. Most damning of all was that Jackson had been seen with banknotes similar to some known to have belonged to Wallace. A grand jury indicted Jackson for Wallace's murder on October 6, 1858, and Jackson received several death threats while awaiting trial. Remarkably, after eighteen hours of deliberation, the jury found him not guilty on April 3, 1859—a stunning victory for his legal defense team, made up of three St. Paul lawyers, including former Territorial Governor Willis Gorman. The verdict was, not surprisingly, quite unpopular, and Jackson, concerned about his safety, quickly left Wright County, only narrowly avoiding being lynched by eluding fifteen men who followed him on the night of his acquittal.[12]

Foolishly, Jackson returned to Wright County on April 21, 1859, leading Wright County Sheriff George Bertram to issue an arrest warrant for Jackson on the charge of stealing items from Wallace's cabin. By the time Sheriff Bertram arrived at the house of Jackson's father-in-law to serve the warrant, a crowd had surrounded the house. The crowd built fires nearby, but Jackson, believed to be inside, refused to come out.

When Sheriff Bertram finally went to the door, he was admitted, and Jackson came downstairs to talk to him. Having hidden upstairs during the crowd's three-day siege, Jackson told Sheriff Bertram that he feared for his life. Only after the sheriff assured him that he would not be harmed did Jackson agree to surrender and did Sheriff Bertram disperse the crowd and usher his prisoner out of the dwelling.[13]

But less than a half mile from the house an armed mob overtook Sheriff Bertram's procession. The sheriff relinquished his prisoner without resistance and rode off with his deputies, failing even to report the incident. After taunting Jackson throughout the night, the lynch mob strung him up, even as his wife arrived to plead for mercy. Her pleas ignored, she was sent away distraught and empty-handed. The bloodthirsty mob hauled Jackson up and down two times, failing to get Jackson to confess but successfully mangling his neck. Only when Jackson was hoisted up for a third time, at around 2:00 P.M. on April 25, did his neck break. Jackson's body was left hanging from a beam that protruded from Wallace's cabin.[14]

On April 29, Minnesota Governor Henry Sibley called the lynching a "high-handed outrage" against "the peace and dignity of the State," and on May 2 offered a $500 reward for the apprehension and conviction of the perpetrators. "These deeds of violence must cease," he declared, "or there will be no safety for life or property in our midst." Despite Sibley's appeals, no one ever claimed the reward. On July 26, Jackson's widow made a complaint against Aymer Moore after Moore was recognized by one of her relatives at Minnehaha Falls. But when Moore was sent to Wright County, a party of thirty armed men freed Moore from the deputy sheriff's house where he was being detained. Sibley, having sent the state's attorney general to prosecute Moore, was notified at once, and ordered three armed volunteer militia companies to Wright County on August 5 "to subdue the spirit of ruffianism." After county officials promised to arrest three suspects if the troops were withdrawn, the troops went home and the bloodless "Wright County War" ended. Moore and two other lynch mob participants were arrested but were quickly released on bail. A Wright County grand jury later refused to indict any of them. The lynching of Oscar Jackson would go unpunished.[15]

Although gubernatorial pleas were made to curtail them, lynchings in Minnesota still took place after Jackson's violent death. One occurred on May 3, 1865, when John Campbell, labeled a "half breed" by the local press, was strung up in Mankato. The brother of Baptiste Campbell, one of the thirty-eight Indians hung in Mankato's 1862 mass hanging, John Campbell was lynched following the May 1, 1865, killing in Blue Earth County of settler Andrew Jewett, his wife, their aged parents, and a hired hand. Jewett was shot through the breast and struck with a tomahawk over his right eye, a bullet pierced his wife's heart, the seventy-three-year-old father was shot in the forehead, and the infirm mother was tomahawked in bed. The hired man, chopping wood in a nearby ravine, was killed "with a ball, a buckshot and an arrow." Only a baby, hit on the head and left for dead, was found unconscious in a garden and, miraculously, survived.[16]

After the slaughter, money, a horse, and some clothing were stolen from Jewett's homestead. Campbell was arrested as he walked on a road headed for Mankato, apparently on the way to visit his mother's home at nearby Traverse des Sioux. His "three-fourths Sioux blood" had aroused suspicion. At first, Campbell claimed that his name was Pelky and that he was a "half-breed Winnebago" who worked for a farmer. A man recognized him, however, and Campbell was soon forced to reveal his identity, though not before he was taken out of the county jail that night, tortured, and had a noose repeatedly put around his neck. Campbell, who steadfastly refused to confess to the Jewett murders, would only acknowledge that he was a deserter.[17]

The evidence against Campbell was incriminating but circumstantial. A search of his clothing found a lady's handkerchief, a wet towel with blood on it, and $5 in greenbacks. He also had on a broadcloth coat, a pair of new pants, women's white wool hose on his feet, and a pair of shoes that did not fit. These clothing items were taken to the Jewett family's relatives for inspection, and Eva Tyler, the sister of the murdered hired helper, identified the coat, pants, towel, shoes, and stockings as belonging to the Jewetts. While the clothing was being positively identified, a frontiersman, Peter Kelley, also arrived in Mankato. Kelley said that an old Indian trader and steamboat man, Louis Roberts, had told him that trapper Scott Campbell, "a halfbreed Sioux," had let it be known that his brother John Campbell was heading a band of Indians to steal horses and attack Mankato. Kelley, who knew Campbell, was the man who identified him at the jail. His true identity exposed, Campbell then claimed that he had been taken prisoner by a band of Indians but had managed to escape. Campbell still insisted that he knew nothing about the Jewett murders, claiming that he had misstated his name and tribe to conceal his identity and prevent his arrest for desertion.[18]

It was eventually reported that Marshall Fall, a second lieutenant in the army, had sent Andrew Jewett $500 to pay for a farm he had bid on at the sale of Winnebago lands. John Campbell, a scout who joined the Union army at Fort Snelling in September 1862, was in Fall's regiment and knew Fall well. The two had shared a tent together, and Campbell knew of the money being sent to Jewett, a politically active settler in the vicinity of Mankato, where the mass hanging of Dakota Indians had taken place less than three years earlier. Campbell had deserted from his unit, the Third Minnesota infantry regiment, and had come back to Minnesota to see his family and, perhaps, avenge his brother Baptiste's death. William Seeger, a fellow soldier and Campbell's boyhood friend, later described how a drunken Campbell had threatened to burn Mankato in retaliation for Baptiste's execution.[19]

After John Campbell's arrest, people poured into Mankato from surrounding towns like Garden City and South Bend until a crowd of eight hundred people had gathered in the vicinity of the jail. Speeches were made on the street corners advising against a lynching, while others in the crowd openly talked of hanging Campbell at once. Cries of "Hang the Villain" and "Get the Rope Ready" were heard everywhere. Those favoring a lynching feared that if military authorities took him into custody, he might escape the gallows. As a compromise, it was decided to try Campbell in the open air with an improvised court and a circle of spectators. A judge, a prosecutor, a defense lawyer, and a twelve-person jury were appointed on an ad hoc basis, tables and chairs were procured for the lawn, and the prisoner pled not guilty after dictating a letter to his mother professing his innocence. At the makeshift trial, Campbell admitted that he was an army deserter but swore that on his way home seven Indians had stopped him and made him wear the pair of pants, the coat, and the pair of shoes. The prosecution pointed out the conflicting statements Campbell had made and identified the clothes as belonging to the murdered family. The whole trial lasted four hours.[20]

The jury returned a guilty verdict in a half hour but recommended that Campbell be tried again at the court's regular term to be convened in about two weeks. The crowd, however, had other ideas. Though a respectable minority opposed a lynching, Mr. Jewett's personal friends shouted for vengeance. With chants of "hang him," a rush was made for the prisoner, and the mob began to drag him toward a leaning basswood tree on the corner of Hickory and Fifth Streets. The "friends of law and order" grabbed the prisoner to take him to the jail, but they were over-powered after a tense struggle in which revolvers and knives were drawn. The tug-of-war over Campbell finally ended when those opposing the lynching gave up for fear of rioting. A wagon belonging to a Garden City man was run under the tree, a rope tied to a nearby limb and tightened around Campbell's neck, and the wagon pulled away. But a failure to bind Campbell's hands resulted in Campbell grabbing the rope above his head as he called for a priest. After the wagon was reluctantly pulled back under him, Campbell prayed for five minutes with a Catholic priest, whom he told about a roll of money hidden in the bedding of his jail bunk. Campbell wanted the money to go to his mother, but after his hands were pinioned and the wagon pulled away again, Campbell's mother would get only her son's dead body. The concealed money went to Mr. Fall.[21]

On Christmas Day in 1866, two trappers from Mankato were also lynched in New Ulm after killing John Spenner in a barroom brawl. The trappers, Charles Campbell and George Liscom, were dressed in Indian garb and were imitating Dakota warriors taking scalps when the fatal saloon fight broke out. Campbell knifed Spenner, a local hero of the Dakota Conflict, after Spenner cut open Liscom's head with a hatchet.

Dressed in buckskins and moccasins and tanned from long outdoor exposure, Campbell and a barely conscious Liscom were hauled off to jail by the local sheriff. With Campbell mistakenly suspected of being the brother of John Campbell, lynched in Mankato the year before, the mob congregated at dusk. Its members dragged Campbell and Liscom out of the jail, stabbed them and beat them with sticks, and then hanged them from a ladder leaned against the jail. One of the ringleaders, John Gut, beat and kicked Campbell as he was being dragged outside and repeatedly stabbed Campbell's body as it swung from the ladder. That night, the bodies were cut down and unceremoniously stuffed under the ice on the Minnesota River. While Attorney General William Colvill went to Brown County to personally investigate, the local citizenry was so "tightlipped" that he proposed convening the grand jury in Redwood Falls so the wrongdoers would not escape punishment.[22]

After one grand jury returned no indictments, the astonished judge, Horace Austin, ordered that another one be convened in the fall, saying that he could continue calling grand juries "until the accused are tried, and if guilty, properly punished." At the next session, twelve men were indicted for first-degree murder, but only John Gut, an AWOL soldier, was held without bail and brought to trial. His lawyer, Charles Flandrau, emphasized that the state had put a bounty on Sioux scalps and that Gut mistook Campbell and Liscom for "half-breeds," but that defense failed, and Gut was convicted. Ignoring the jury's recommendation for mercy, Judge Austin sentenced Gut in February 1868, ordering that Gut be hanged between 10:00 A.M. and 2:00 P.M. In what can only be described as an ironic twist of fate, the very same Horace Austin, now as governor, commuted Gut's death sentence to life imprisonment two years later after a lengthy series of legal and court battles over Gut's life. Governor Austin commuted the death sentence based on the passage of an 1868 law, which gave jurors the power to decide if a death sentence could be imposed.[23]

Whenever a lynching or a state-sanctioned public execution did take place in Minnesota, hordes of spectators were sure to be there. On March 1, 1861, for instance, Henry Kriegler was hanged "on the

Commons in the Village of Albert Lea" before an estimated crowd of thirteen hundred to two thousand people. Kriegler rode to the gallows on a sleigh that carried his coffin and made no resistance as his death warrant was read. Kriegler's cries were "piercing and heartrending," a fact not soon forgotten by those in attendance. Despite clouds, fog, and melting snow, people traveled "some twenty, thirty, and some fifty miles to witness the execution." Kriegler, who had abused and mistreated his wife, had killed another man for protecting her. His last words, which he constantly repeated for ten minutes before dying, were "Me poor man, me poor man."[24]

Attempted lynchings also attracted public attention, as when a black man, Houston Osborn, only narrowly averted being lynched in 1895 after burglarizing and attempting to sexually assault a white woman. In another instance, in 1896, Frank Young, a waiter at Lake Minnetonka's Hotel St. Louis, was taken by some of his fellow waiters into the woods and twice strung up from a tree before being let go. Young was suspected of stealing $55 from a guest's hotel room. Likewise, "A Lynching Was Averted" was the newspaper headline in October 1920 when a Minnesota man was found to have raped a fourteen-year-old girl. Even in the 1930s, Wilbur Hardiman and James Johnson, described as "Negro workers who had just come up from the South," only avoided being lynched in Minneapolis through a gunshot fired in self-defense.[25]

Despite the lawless mobs and grave lapses of due process that pervaded this bygone era, the mid-1800s witnessed the nascent beginnings of Minnesota's anti–death penalty movement and a recognition of the necessity of the rule of law. Several prominent Minnesotans had publicly urged that U-ha-zy's death sentence be set aside, and at least some civic leaders had condemned lynchings and sought, if only halfheartedly, to bring lynch mob participants to justice. Governor Henry Sibley himself sought to try Oscar Jackson's killers in a court of law where they might be punished for their extrajudicial actions. While many public officials openly denounced lynchings, however, such spectacles continued to take place in the state. Otter Tail County residents, for instance, lynched fifteen-year-old John Trivett from a telegraph pole in 1882 on suspicion of robbing and murdering two land surveyors, Leo Thornbacker and Edward Washington, in Perham.[26]

A double lynching, in fact, took place in northern Minnesota in the early 1870s after fur trader John Cook, his wife Deantha, and their three children were murdered near Brainerd. A coroner's inquest found charred bones, children's teeth, and gold fillings at the site of the Cooks' burned-out homestead, and suspicion immediately fell upon a band of Chippewa Indians encamped nearby. "A continual vendetta is going on between the Indians, and whites of the border," David Day, a St. Paul doctor, noted after arriving to investigate. The tense aftermath of the killings only worsened when Helen McArthur, a schoolteacher, was found to be missing and feared dead. One Chippewa Indian, Bobolink, was arrested after selling items thought to belong to the Cook family, and two other Ojibwe Indians, Gegoonce and Tebekokechickwabe, were arrested too. Bobolink was whisked off to St. Paul's Ramsey County Jail after his apprehension to face an eventual death sentence, and the other two men were taken to Brainerd's jail on July 10 as a crowd of onlookers made threats against them. A hearing was set for July 25 for the Indians held in Brainerd, but the angry citizenry did not let the law take its course. On the evening of July 23, 1872, an organized group of fifty men took Gegoonce and his brother, Tebekokechickwabe, from the jail. As hundreds of Brainerd citizens looked on, the Indians were hanged from a pine tree in front of the Last Turn Saloon. The bodies were left twisting slowly in the evening breeze, and the lynching—done openly for all to see—brought more than a hundred angry Ojibwe Indians to town the next day in protest.[27]

With the lynchings occurring only ten years after the Dakota Conflict of 1862, many of Brainerd's citizens, located near bands of Chippewa Indians allowed to remain in Minnesota after the war, soon feared another Indian outbreak. This caused Crow Wing County Sheriff John Gurrell to telegraph Governor Horace Austin on the night of July 24 with a dire-sounding message: "Please send troops immediately. Town full of Indians and have been ordered to leave on your proclamation, but do not. Three white families have left today." Governor Austin received Gurrell's telegram at approximately 10:00 P.M., and by midnight an order had been issued to call out state militiamen armed with ball cartridges and muzzle loaders. In the tradition of America's minutemen, these soldiers, many of whom were Civil War veterans, boarded trains for Brainerd. On their arrival, however, they found railroad men and tough-looking characters who, in the words of one soldier, "appeared to be quite able to take care of themselves." Two of the National Guard units were ordered to return home after spending only one night in Brainerd, and the other soldiers returned to St. Paul on July 30 after admiring Indian women coming into town with blueberries. Thus ended the "Blueberry War," as it came to be known, without further incident.[28]

Another double lynching, this time of two brothers, took place in Todd County during the winter of 1879. The previous spring, a family by the name of Coldale had settled in the town of Ward near two bachelors, John and Michael Moede. "Black John" Moede later alienated the affections of Coldale's wife, and after Moede's house was burned, he blamed Coldale and openly made threats to shoot him. Just a few days later, Coldale and another man disappeared, and buckshot holes were found in Coldale's wall. A large pool of blood dripping into a bin of potatoes in the cellar, part of a finger, a bloody axe, patches of human hair, and brain tissue also were discovered. Suspicion immediately fell upon John Moede, who was arrested and taken to the county seat, Long Prairie, to be interrogated. After angry crowds gathered, the bearded, "villainous-looking" Moede—said to have a "thick bull neck" and "beadlike eyes"—became frightened and fully confessed. He claimed his brother, Michael, did the killing and admitted only to helping bury the dead. The victims' mutilated bodies were dug up, and on a Saturday night the prisoner was taken from the jail and hanged from a red oak tree by a two-hundred-man lynch mob, whose members wore blackened faces when they broke into the jail and Moede's cell with axes. His brother, Michael, was arrested on Sunday after leaving the county and was unwittingly taken back to Long Prairie, where he too was lynched by the awaiting mob.[29]

The city of Minneapolis would witness its own lynching less than three years later. At 4:00 P.M. on April 27, 1882, it was reported to a police officer that a tramp had lured a little girl away from her Fourth Avenue home. The policeman hailed a passing carriage and was soon in the vicinity of a group of women talking to a man. That man, upon seeing the approaching officer, wheeled and attempted to flee the scene. The officer gave chase and at Tenth Street and Sixth Avenue caught the man, whose clothing was covered with blood. After taking the suspect to the police station, the police began their investigation. They first visited the house of Mina Spear, the four-year-old girl who had been enticed away from her house with a nickel and a trip to the candy store. The girl, brutally raped and now bleeding badly, had been found nearby and brought back to her parents' home. There, physicians examined her and gave her needed medical attention. The suspect was soon identified as Frank McManus, a twenty-five-year-old drifter and ex-con from Boston. McManus first claimed to have gotten blood on his pants, underclothes, and hands in a fight the night before—a story at odds with the fresh blood on them—but later told a detective he committed the horrific crime.[30]

By 7:00 P.M., the rape of Mina Spear was the topic of conversation all over town, and by midnight, angry groups of men had gathered on the streets of Minneapolis intent on avenging the crime. At 1:00 A.M., the men gathered in front of the jail, demanding admission. On-duty Hennepin County Sheriff James Eustis said they could not enter, but he failed to deter the men, a half dozen of whom used their shoulders against the door and made their way inside. "We want that man," they demanded. Sheriff Eustis answered, "You can't have him," but was quickly subdued and shuttled off to a dark corner where he was held down. When Sheriff Eustis refused to hand over the jail keys or disclose where the prisoner was being held, a battering ram was secured, and the door leading to the jail's main corridor was broken down. The prisoners told the mob where McManus was confined, and for an hour and forty minutes, hammers fell upon the heavy iron door leading to McManus's cell. McManus insisted he was not the man they were looking for, but he was pulled from Cell No. 3 and taken to the Spear residence for a confirming identification. When Mrs. Spear saw him, she cried out, "That's the man; take him away, take him away. Oh! those eyes, I shall never forget them."[31]

After it was adjudged that they had the right man, the crowd left the Spear house and traveled up the avenue as mob members shouted things like "Now for a tree" and "Hang him." A large burr oak, situated opposite a high school and near a Baptist church, was found in an open lot on the corner of Grant Street and Fourth Avenue. A man ascended the tree, waiting anxiously for the end of the rope to be thrown to him, as McManus was interrogated about why he committed the crime. "I didn't," McManus replied, provoking cries of "You lie" and "We're going to make a terrible example of you." As the noose was about to be slipped over his neck, McManus asked to speak with one of the lynch mob leaders and confessed to being drunk when he committed the crime. As the rope went over the limb, strong hands grasped the rope, and a few pulls brought McManus's body into the air, where it whirled around. The end of the rope was fastened to the trunk of the tree, and by 4:00 A.M. the crowd's ugly business was done.[32]

McManus's lynching quickly turned into an even bigger public spectacle. In the morning, large crowds flocked to the site. By 7:00 A.M., there were one thousand people present. The surplus rope was cut up by souvenir hunters, and a photographer eerily snapped pictures of the dead man and the crowd. The coroner arrived at 7:40 A.M., and after the body was cut down, it was loaded in a wagon and driven to Warner's undertaking rooms. An inquest determined the obvious—McManus died by strangulation—and the public was then given a chance to view the body. Ultimately, the corpse was given to Minnesota College Hospital students as it was "considered best not to desecrate God's acre with its unholy presence." It was later determined that the tree from which McManus was strung up by the lynching bee was the very same tree that McManus had been seated under when he enticed the little girl to him.[33]

The local newspapers saw little wrong with the way McManus's life ended. The *Minneapolis Evening Journal* declared that every offender's right to trial is "sacred." Yet, the paper saw "exceptions to every rule" and stated that there are "occasions before which every law and every precedent must give way." The McManus case, it opined, was one of those because "human patience could not be expected to stand the strain." "There was a higher law that made his instant death necessary," the newspaper said, "and we thank God that there were men in Minneapolis brave and manly enough to execute it promptly." The *St. Paul Pioneer Press* also found no fault with the lynch mob's actions. "If their act was inspired by passion it was the generous passion that makes the groundwork of human justice," it concluded, adding that "[i]t is impossible to condemn the spirit that actuated the Minneapolis lynchers." The

The lynching of Frank McManus. Photograph by H. R. Farr; courtesy of the Minnesota Historical Society.

Minneapolis Tribune summed up many people's feelings: "The punishment provided by law, restraint of personal liberty during life, is one which utterly fails to even approach the measure of legal expiation demanded by the universal popular heart. The hanging of McManus with the omission of the usual legal formalities is not condemned by this community, nor, so far as known, by any person residing in this community."[34]

Over a decade later, one of the state's most notorious lynchings—surpassed only in notoriety by Duluth's 1920 lynching of three African American circus workers—took place in southern Minnesota. It was unexpectedly set in motion after two young men, Dorman Musgrove and Henry Cingmars, shot a farmer's dog in a dispute over a dogfight and then took a shot at the farmer, Ben Matthews, but missed. On the afternoon of June 24, 1896, Musgrove and Cingmars, armed with a Winchester rifle and a revolver, had provoked the altercation with Matthews three miles north of Glencoe and assaulted him. The badly beaten farmer had then followed the men and secured an arrest warrant, which was quickly put in the hands of the local sheriff, Joseph Rogers. A beloved public official, Sheriff Rogers and another man, wagonmaker Louis Link, took off in a buggy after the fugitives, who were headed south away from town. After catching up with them, Sheriff Rogers asked the men to come with him. "I want you fellows," he said. "I guess not," came the reply as one of the men shot toward Rogers's feet. As Sheriff Rogers reached for his revolver, the second man raised his rifle and fired at the sheriff's chest, killing him instantly. Link galloped away to get help as the desperados, eager to make their escape, stole Sheriff Rogers's revolver and headed for the woods.[35]

When the news reached Glencoe, townspeople were called together by the ringing of a fire bell, and armed citizens started a manhunt to track down Sheriff Rogers's killers. Surrounding communities were asked to join in the effort, and with upwards of three hundred men taking part, large search parties were formed in places like Hutchinson, Arlington, New Auburn, and Gaylord. When George MacKenzie, an area lawyer, came to his law office on June 25, he got a telegram from the McLeod

County Attorney informing him of Rogers's death. Like similar directives, it urged that a posse be organized to catch the culprits. MacKenzie set off with a team of horses, gathering men along the way to New Auburn. He soon met a farmer who told his posse that a woman oiling a windmill had seen two men crawling through a wheat field into a large marsh. They surrounded the marsh, and after some men began firing shotguns into it, the two fugitives jumped up and put their hands in the air. MacKenzie and another lawyer, Peter Cosgrove, talked the searchers out of hanging the prisoners on the spot, and the two captives were hustled off to Glencoe in a wagon.[36]

Threats of a lynching were quickly made, and fearful of more violence, the Glencoe mayor ordered that all saloons be closed immediately. At ten o'clock that night, with the townspeople growing more angry with each passing hour, the mayor and the county attorney sent a message to the state's governor. "Sheriff Rogers' murderers are in jail. We fear lynching." "Can you aid us with militia?" they asked. Twenty-five militiamen led by Captain Ed Bean were soon dispatched, boarding a train in St. Paul. After these men surrounded the Glencoe jail, the crowd gradually dispersed, though the next day Musgrove and Cingmars were moved to St. Paul for safekeeping pending trial. Dressed in blue overalls, Cingmars told Ramsey County sheriff's deputies that he was twenty-four years of age; Musgrove, wearing a worn, plain black suit, said he was twenty-seven. In jail, Cingmars told a reporter that he had shot at Sheriff Rogers's hand to "knock the gun out," and that Musgrove "didn't mean to shoot" but that his rifle "went off" and "struck the sheriff just above the nipple." Musgrove asked for a lawyer and would not talk, saying only that the shooting was the sheriff's fault. "We took a shot at that farmer's dog just to scare him," Musgrove recounted.[37]

The two prisoners retained nationally renowned criminal defense lawyer William Erwin, nicknamed the "Tall Pine Tree of the Northwest." They demanded separate trials and were eventually taken back to Glencoe. Musgrove's case was called first. After deliberating for nine hours, Erwin's "magnetic influence" became evident when the jury returned a guilty verdict not for first-degree murder, but for second-degree murder, a crime not punishable by death. Many townspeople wanted the death penalty meted out, but the jury was sharply divided, with its first ballot resulting in five votes for first-degree murder, five for second-degree murder, and two for manslaughter. The compromise verdict ultimately agreed upon—second-degree murder—angered many townsfolk. Though Erwin feared for his clients' safety, Judge Francis Cadwell assured him that talk of a lynching was unfounded. With Cingmars's upcoming trial slated for the following week, Glencoe citizens lost patience and decided to take the law into their own hands.[38]

At twenty minutes past midnight on September 6, 1896, a lynch mob leader knocked on the jailer's door and gained admission to the jail where Musgrove and Cingmars were sleeping. "All wore black masks and none but the leader spoke," the *Glencoe Enterprise* reported. The feet and hands of the jailer and his assistant were bound; then sledgehammers were used to break bolts that stood between the angry mob and the cell where Musgrove and Cingmars, now cowering and wide-awake, were crouched in a corner. Sheriff Rogers's murderers pled for their lives but to no avail; after Cingmars said, "Give my love to mother," the two men's mouths were gagged with handkerchiefs, and they were led out of the jail and a few blocks away to Buffalo Creek. A hundred-foot bridge ran over this stream, and after the rope was tied to an iron span, Cingmars's and Musgrove's bodies were unceremoniously pushed off the bridge. Ten feet below, the men's feet could be seen in the darkness dangling in the water. It was not until 1:00 A.M. that Sheriff Fred Sandman learned of the jail break-in and set out, along with the coroner, to find the dead men's bodies. When Cingmars's body was pulled up, one of his shoes was missing, showing that he died struggling to the end.[39]

Cingmars's mother, staying at a local hotel since before Musgrove's trial, was devastated by the news of her son's death. A Wisconsin native, she had made long and frequent visits to the jail to see her son, and when the coroner told her that her son was dead, she tore at her hair and exclaimed, "Oh, this is terrible. My darling boy, I wanted him to have a trial. I know he did not mean to kill the man." "God have mercy on us all, God have mercy," she shrieked, crying that she did not want to live anymore. "My darling boy, oh, my darling boy," she repeated dejectedly. After the undertaker came to make burial arrangements, Mrs. Cingmars regretted that a change of venue had not been secured. "Yesterday," she said, "as I went past a group on the street, someone said loud enough so that I could hear—'He should have been lynched before this trouble came.' But I never thought they would do what they have." The lawyer, Bill Erwin, was equally shocked. "My God, you must have been misinformed," he said on learning of the lynching. Striking his clenched fist on a table and calling it an outrage, Erwin angrily exclaimed, "Did the sheriff make no resistance to the mob?" "It is the duty of the state officials," Erwin railed, "to step in and apprehend and punish every man connected with the premeditated, heartless, inexcusable and cold-blooded double murder."[40]

Newspapers like the *Minneapolis Tribune* called the Glencoe lynching a "regrettable" act that had marred the state's "fair name" with "a lawless act of vengeance." The lesson the newspaper saw in the lynching, though, was not that lynch mob participants should be punished, but that the incident should be "a warning to courts and juries" that the "arts and eloquence of a noted criminal lawyer should not be permitted to blind our tribunals to the heinousness of crime." "Where an offense is clearly proven and there are absolutely no extenuating circumstances," the paper editorialized, "the acquittal of the accused or the lowering of the grade of the offense so as to secure a lighter punishment . . . is a mockery of justice." The newspaper said that lynching is "never justifiable under any circumstances," but that "it must be admitted that there was great ground for exasperation on the part of the murdered sheriff's friends and neighbors." The Minnesota attorney general and the local county attorney conducted a perfunctory two-day investigation, but the *Glencoe Enterprise* reported that "no clue to any of the participants in the crime was ascertained." An official finding was made that Musgrove and Cingmars "came to their death by hanging at the hands of parties unknown." "The midnight revel of Judge Lynch here on Saturday night," the local newspaper concluded, "has passed into history."[41]

The Glencoe lynching was hardly the only one that went unpunished. In 1918, Olli Kinkkonen, a Finnish man opposed to World War I, was tarred and feathered and then hung from a tree in Duluth's Lester Park. The local coroner ruled it a "suicide," but a $500 reward unsuccessfully offered by Minnesota Governor J. A. A. Burnquist seeking the arrest and conviction of anyone involved in Kinkkonen's death showed hardly anyone really believed Kinkkonen had taken his own life. And in the small mining town of Mountain Iron in 1893, a tramp from Quebec, Frank Belange, was taken from a little log jail, marched to the scene of his crime with a noose around him, and lynched from the limb of a birch tree. "That's a dead limb!" someone shouted in the crowd. "There'll be four dead limbs up there in a minute!" yelled someone else, in jest, in reply. Belange had brutally raped the four- and six-year-old daughters of a well-known clothier, Richard Giffin, and was led to his death "by as many hands as could find a hold" on him. Before being hanged, Belange confessed in French and English, telling the mob, "I am guilty and you are using me right." "I was drinking and must have been crazy," he said. The *Duluth Evening Herald* applauded "summary justice," and the local county attorney saw little wrong with the lynching either. "Of course such occurrences are to be deplored," he said, "but as to the advisability of putting the county to the large expense of bringing the participants to trial there is some question." "As near as I can learn," he told the press, the lynch mob participants were mostly businessmen, adding that "there is little use in indicting them." "I don't see as that there is anything to investigate," the prosecutor concluded, saying any trial "would be a farce, as you could not possibly convict."[42]

While lynchings and public hangings would eventually cease to occur in Minnesota, they would pass from the scene only after many decades, during which large crowds periodically gathered in public squares or beneath tree limbs to watch executioners at work or to take part in lynch mob activities. Eventually, at least some attempts were made by authorities to bring lynch mob participants to justice, and lynchings and public executions—once in vogue—gradually lost their allure. If multiple first-degree murder charges and the indictment of more than twenty men for rioting or instigating a riot following the 1920 lynching in Duluth of three circus workers represented the most coordinated attempt to hold lynch mob participants accountable for their actions, then the mass execution of thirty-eight Dakota Indians in Mankato, Minnesota, in 1862 exemplifies how very public American executions could be, as well as how profoundly such events could shape American history.[43]

CHAPTER 2

On Lincoln's Orders

Mankato's Mass Hanging

In March 1862, the first Episcopal bishop of Minnesota, Henry Whipple, wrote to President Abraham Lincoln asking that he "deal righteously with the Indian nations." "I ask only justice for a wronged and neglected race," Whipple pleaded. A man of considerable influence, Whipple had Revolutionary War officers and signers of the Declaration of Independence as ancestors, and his cousin Henry Halleck was Lincoln's general-in-chief for the Army of the Potomac. Arriving in Minnesota before Lincoln won the presidency in 1860, Whipple, through his missionary work, had gained the Indians' trust. He had converted many Indians to Christianity, performed baptisms and confirmations, and was even asked by a grief-stricken Ojibwe mother to bury her deceased child. Though Whipple saw the Indians as "heathens"—a scalp-dance in front of his Sioux Mission House did not impress him—he saw "civilization and Christianization" as promising the Indians a better future. Whipple urged Lincoln to replace the Indian bureaucracy's "dishonest servants" and "whiskey-sellers" with men of "purity, temperance, industry, and unquestioned integrity."[1]

In his letter, Whipple lambasted the U.S. government's "ill conceived" Indian policies and the treaty system that had divested Indian tribes of so much of their native lands. "We have broken up, in part, their tribal relations and they must have something in their place," Whipple wrote. "The sale of whiskey" and "the neglect and want are fast dooming this people to death," Whipple said matter-of-factly, noting how often Indians found themselves starving of hunger. "I would count every trial I have had as a way of roses if I could save this people," Whipple told Lincoln. When fall crop failure in 1861 turned into a harsh winter, the Dakota, or Sioux, people were on the verge of starvation, with the Mdewakanton band's Chief Little Crow even trading guns for food to feed his family. Bishop Whipple desperately urged Lincoln's administration to remedy the Indians' callous treatment by replacing annual annuity payments, which routinely flowed to white traders, with more schools, seeds, and farm equipment. A war-occupied Lincoln, however, had little time to seriously consider Whipple's pleas. Instead, Lincoln perfunctorily referred Whipple's letter to the secretary of the interior.[2]

During his presidency, Lincoln had hardly any time to devote to Indian affairs. The nation's Civil War consumed almost all of his waking hours, and by early 1862, that war had already taken a heavy toll on him. Lincoln accepted that in wartime "blood grows hot" and is spilt by men motivated by "[r]evenge and retaliation," but when one of his close friends, Colonel Elmer Ellsworth, was fatally shot in 1861 in the line of duty, the war hit close to home. An ex-clerk in Lincoln's Illinois law office, Ellsworth had been killed after cutting down a Confederate flag in Alexandria, Virginia, a flag Ellsworth knew bothered Lincoln as it was visible by spyglass from the White House. After Ellsworth's White House funeral service, Lincoln felt so moved that he penned a letter to the young man's parents, saying only rarely had such "bright hopes" been "so suddenly dashed, as in his fall." The prolonged Civil War only exacerbated Lincoln's bouts of melancholy and the insomnia he suffered throughout his life. Physically drained by the war, Lincoln lost over thirty pounds while president, leading one observer to say he looked like "a huge skeleton in clothes."[3]

The divestiture of Indian lands in Minnesota began long before Lincoln took up residence in the Executive Mansion. In 1851, Dakota chiefs of the Wahpeton, Sisseton, Mdewakanton, and Wahpekute bands signed the treaties of Mendota and Traverse des Sioux. These treaties ceded vast tracts of land in the Minnesota Territory and elsewhere to the

United States for less than ten cents an acre, leaving seven thousand Dakota Indians with two small reservations bordering the upper Minnesota River. A pair of additional treaties, signed in 1858, relinquished to land-thirsty settlers nearly a million more acres of land for a price to be fixed by the U.S. Senate, determined two years later to be a paltry thirty cents an acre. Lincoln's approval of the Federal Homestead Law in May 1862 also radically changed the Indians' way of life. As the government gave 160 acres of publicly owned land to anyone occupying the land for five years, thousands of settlers flocked westward. The white population, even before the 1862 law took effect, literally exploded over the course of a few years. In 1850, only six thousand whites lived in the Minnesota Territory; that number rose to two hundred thousand by 1856, with newly built railways soon bringing even more. The Upper Sioux reservation, centered at the Yellow Medicine Agency, at least included the sites of old Indian villages, but the Lower Sioux reservation, headquartered at the Redwood Agency, was situated on prairie land far away from favored woodlands and hunting grounds.[4]

Designed to turn the nomadic Dakota into farmers, these 1850s treaties deeply fractured Indian communities. As Indians grew dependent on government annuity payments, corrupt bureaucrats showed favoritism to those adopting white ways. In no time at all, once cohesive villages were split into hunting-and-fishing "blanket" Indians and converts to Christianity who took up farming and dressed like whites. The farmer Indians, seen as traitors for abandoning Dakota customs, were harassed by their more traditional tribesmen and derisively called "cut-hairs" for cutting their long hair. The harassment campaign eventually escalated to cattle killing, burning of haystacks, and open threats against those who farmed. Sioux resentment and mistrust only swelled as fraudulent traders' claims regularly robbed Indians of their annuity payments— money Whipple told Lincoln the Indians did not know how to spend. After a series of broken promises and treaty violations, a crisis erupted when, in the summer of 1862, a tardy congressional appropriation delayed a $71,000 shipment of gold coins bound for the hungry Dakota. The Indians asked Whipple how much money they would receive that year, and Whipple answered, "Twenty dollars per head, the same that you have always received." But Whipple felt mounting anxiety as he learned that the Indians, aware of the government's financial strain during the Civil War, were hearing rumors that no annuity payments would be sent at all.[5]

By mid-1862, U.S.–Dakota relations were appalling. Five thousand gaunt Dakota Indians, far from the buffalo ranges, gathered at the Upper Sioux reservation in mid-July and demanded to be fed from a warehouse full of provisions. Lincoln's newly appointed Indian agent, Thomas Galbraith, part of the corrupt patronage system Whipple so deplored, only distributed food to the famished Indians as a last resort to avoid violence. At one point, five hundred Dakota Indians had surrounded a hundred U.S. Army soldiers in early August, breaking into the warehouse with axes to gain access to sacks of flour. A tense standoff had ensued in which a loaded howitzer was aimed at the warehouse door to stop the pillaging. Just fifteen months earlier, Whipple had written Galbraith to ask that he help the Indians. "[W]e have dispossessed them," Whipple said, noting how dishonest agents had taken the Indians' money and "blasted his home by the accursed fire water."[6]

To the southeast, the Dakota Indians at the Redwood Agency, many of whom had planted corn and other vegetables, had received some provisions of their own in early June. However, they too were still awaiting their annual annuity payment and were at the point of starvation. Cutworms had infested the fall harvest of 1861, and the Indians were subsisting on half-grown potatoes, a little flour, and a few wild ducks and pigeons. One highly influential Indian leader waiting with disgust was Taoyateduta, meaning "His Red Nation." Also known as Little Crow, Taoyateduta, in his early fifties, was part of a dynasty of Mdewakanton leaders. Feeling a loss of identity, a downtrodden Taoyateduta had long seen the unstoppable wave of white immigration. In 1851, he had been the first chief to sign the U.S.–Mdewakanton treaty with a quill pen, at which time the Indians had been duped into signing a traders' paper—thought to be a duplicate copy of the treaty—that gave white creditors the right to deduct often bogus debts from annuity payments. It was a pattern of deceit that stretched from one presidential administration to the next. In 1837, Little Crow's father, Big Thunder, had signed a treaty for tribal lands east of the Mississippi River, forcing Big Thunder to relocate his village. When a few barrels of foodstuff and useless beads, ribbons, and silk cloth arrived in lieu of cash after the

Chief Little Crow. Photograph courtesy of the National Anthropological Archives, Smithsonian Institution (3505-B).

signing, Big Thunder felt cheated. Now that the 1862 annuity payment was late, Taoyateduta felt equally betrayed by the whites.[7]

As he awaited the annuity payment's arrival, Taoyateduta felt torn between two cultures. In the spring of 1862, Little Crow had been humiliated when he unexpectedly lost his bid to be, once more, the Mdewakanton's tribal speaker. That honor went instead to Traveling Hail, a farmer Indian, representing a shift in power within the Dakota Nation. Trying to reclaim his standing within the tribe, Little Crow began by late June to adopt white customs. He started attending the Episcopal mission, cut his hair, and even wore white man's clothing, something he had done in the past only rarely—donning a suit, for example, for an 1861 photograph at the request of Alexander Ramsey, Minnesota's second elected governor. As tensions grew in 1862, Little Crow demanded that the traders extend more credit to the Indians for needed food and blankets. He warned the traders, "When men are hungry they help themselves." But Andrew Myrick, one of the store-keepers, callously told Little Crow and other Indians, "So far as I am concerned, if they are hungry, let them eat grass." When Myrick's insult was translated, the infuriated Indians jumped up and yelled a series of war-whoops. Their anger only intensified when the following day signs appeared in the traders' stores reading "NO CREDIT FOR INDIANS." Although a distribution of food briefly appeased the enraged Indians, Whipple's worst fear, an Indian uprising, would soon be at hand.[8]

On August 17, 1862, just one day after the undistributed gold annuity shipment arrived in St. Paul and just three days after Lincoln held a historic White House meeting with the country's black leaders, the Indians' frustrations gave way to violence. That Sunday morning, Chief Little Crow—whose half-brother, White Spider, worked at one of the trader's stores—attended church at the Redwood Agency's Episcopal chapel. He listened attentively to the sermon and shook hands with congregation members, but the violent acts of four Dakota men that same day forced Little Crow to choose between his newly adopted white ways and the angry cries of his own people. At around noon, the four Dakota men, returning home from a failed hunting trip in Minnesota's

Big Woods, killed five settlers in Acton after one of the Indians called one of his traveling companions a coward for refusing to take some eggs belonging to a white man. The murders, carried out when many of Minnesota's male settlers were fighting on southern battlefields, sparked the tinderbox that turned into the Sioux Uprising, or, as it is known today, the Dakota Conflict or U.S.–Dakota War. A letter Whipple wrote in April 1862 to Minnesota Senator Henry Rice presciently warned of the perilous situation, a crisis Lincoln might have averted if only he had had the time to reform the corrupt Indian system. "I believe he is not afraid to do his duty," Whipple wrote of Lincoln as he pressed Rice to meet with the president about the Indians' predicament. "If he could hear the cries which ring in my ears, if he could see what I have seen," Whipple wrote, "he would act."⁹

After the four Indians responsible for the Acton killings made their way home on stolen horses, the village elders immediately feared indiscriminate reprisals. Chief Shakopee's men were eager to preemptively drive the whites out of their homelands, but Shakopee was reluctant to start a war without the backing of other Indian chiefs. Only Little Crow, a tested warrior, it was concluded, could lead the Dakota to victory in an all-out war. Little Crow had organized war parties against the Chippewa, or Ojibwe, the Dakota's bitter enemy, and he had risen to power by fighting for his father's chieftainship after his father accidentally shot himself in the chest with a gun. His rivals, two half-brothers, were summarily executed in the aftermath of his successful bid to succeed his father, although a gunshot that broke both of Taoyateduta's forearms left his wrists deformed for life. Though Little Crow feared the whites' military power, he was not afraid to speak his mind, at one point angrily accusing government officials of lying and talking to the Indians like children and forcing them to "live like white people."¹⁰

At a hastily organized war council, a gathering of Indian chiefs, including Shakopee, Traveling Hail, and Little Crow, listened to the story of the Acton murders. One village leader told the chiefs at Little Crow's bedside, where they gathered late at night, that they would drive out the Americans and get back their land. Traveling Hail strongly opposed any bloodshed, bluntly saying, "We should not talk about war with the Americans." "Dakotas are brave and proud," he said, "they are not fools." Taoyateduta himself told those favoring war that they were "full of the whiteman's devil water" and that gun-toting whites, if provoked, would "come faster than you can count." In leading Indian delegations to Washington, D.C., in 1854 and 1858, Little Crow had seen the whites' armed forces and their latest weaponry. "The whitemen are like the locusts, when they fly so thick that the whole sky is a snow-storm," Little Crow warned. "You may kill one, two, ten, yes, as many as the leaves in the forest yonder, and their brothers will not miss them. Kill one, two, ten, and ten times ten will come to kill you." Even so, Little Crow reluctantly agreed to lead the Indians on the warpath after being called a coward. "Is Taoyateduta without scalps? Look at his war feathers! Behold the scalp locks of your enemies hanging there on his lodgepoles!" Little Crow angrily answered those who blamed him for selling their lands to the whites. "Braves, you are little children—you are fools. You will die like the rabbits when the hungry wolves hunt them in the Hard Moon. Ta-o-ya-te-du-ta is not a coward: he will die with you," Little Crow relented.[11]

When the sun rose that morning on the small collection of traders' stores at the Redwood Agency, Dakota warriors, dressed in breechcloths and painted for war, attacked it over the objections of Indian chiefs like Wabasha and Traveling Hail. The uprising's first victim was James Lynd, a clerk in Nathan and Andrew Myrick's newly built store. "Now I will kill the dog who wouldn't give me credit," a warrior taunted Lynd before killing him. In retaliation for his earlier insult, Andrew Myrick's head was decapitated, his body filled with arrows and a scythe, and his mouth stuffed with grass. All told, thirteen people lost their lives in the initial raid, and others were killed while fleeing, with refugees flocking to Fort Ridgely, southwestern Minnesota's only military outpost. Three whites were shot on Little Crow's own orders, and when the fort's commander tried to quash the uprising, he and many of his men lost their lives in an ambush at Redwood Ferry. Just six weeks earlier, Whipple had visited the Lower Sioux reservation for the laying of a church cornerstone and had been told by Wabasha, "We think our Great Father may have forgotten his red children and our hearts are very heavy."[12]

By midday on August 18, almost fifty German farmers had been killed in Brown County, and indiscriminate bloodshed soon displaced other settlers' panic-stricken disbelief. Wielding knives and tomahawks, warring Indians, like Cut Nose, killed settlers in hand-to-hand combat and took as captives women and children, including the Dakota wife of ex–Indian agent Joseph Brown. After physician John Wakefield sent his wife, Sarah, and their two children toward Fort Ridgely with George Gleason, a clerk at the Redwood Agency's warehouse, Gleason was shot by Hapa, a drunken and belligerent combatant. Mrs. Wakefield and her children's lives were saved only by Chaska, Hapa's more level-headed companion. A farmer Indian, Chaska took Mrs. Wakefield and her children to Shakopee's camp and safeguarded them until they were freed six weeks later. Christian Indian John Other Day, married to a white saloon waitress, himself led Dr. Wakefield and over sixty refugees out of harm's way. Overnight, Little Crow's small village, consisting of his house and a few tepees, was transformed into a chaotic encampment of two hundred lodges, with Little Crow intimidating captives even as he urged his warriors not to kill women and children but to "make war after the manner of white men."[13]

As the conflict spread like wildfire, twenty-three counties were depopulated of white settlers. Whole families were killed, cabins looted, barns and haystacks set aflame, and horses and cattle stolen. As casualties mounted, refugees poured into Fort Ridgely and made their way toward larger cities like Minneapolis, St. Cloud, and St. Paul. The Indians' attacks soon became widely reported atrocities as local newspapers tried to stay abreast of what was happening. Near New Ulm, Dakota warriors killed the driver of a horse-drawn wagon, raped and took hostage Mattie Williams, and mortally wounded a girl. More than a dozen whites were slaughtered in the Scandinavian settlement of West Lake, and near the state's western border, traders' clerks and government employees were killed in the vicinity of a trading post. Around Murray County's Lake Shetek, the Indians viciously attacked a small group of settlers in a swamp, killing fifteen and leaving only a handful of survivors, like William Duley, to tell about what had happened. President Lincoln's private secretary, John Nicolay, was in Minnesota at Lincoln's request to monitor treaty negotiations with the Chippewa Indians, and when talks broke down, Nicolay told the White House he feared "open hostility" with the Chippewa in a day or two. On August 27, Nicolay wrote Secretary of War Edwin Stanton to inform the administration that "the settlers of the whole border are in panic and flight, leaving their harvest to waste in the field," and that howitzers, cavalry, guns, and 500,000 cartridges were needed.[14]

After the stagecoach finally rode into Fort Ridgely carrying kegs of gold—the now too-late Dakota annuity money—that army post and nearby towns came under siege. With Little Crow mounted on a white horse, the Indians took some of the fort's outbuildings in their first assault but were repulsed by artillery fire and howitzer shells. Two days later, after heavy rains, war-painted Indians on ponies used guns and blazing arrows against the fort, but the fort's wet shingles would not catch fire, and the fort's occupants persevered. Although an army sergeant said, "[t]he balls fell as thick as hail," heavy cannon fire kept attackers like Cut Nose and Little Crow at bay. The bustling German settlement of New Ulm, with a population of close to nine hundred people, beat back two Indian attacks as well. Under the command of ex–Indian agent Charles Flandrau, a state court jurist, a badly outnumbered, poorly armed group of militiamen repelled the Indians while paying a heavy price. Over two dozen defenders lost their lives, and Little Crow's totem, a crow's skin, was found atop one victim's body. In all, 190 New Ulm buildings were destroyed by fire. Ultimately, the town's inhabitants were forced to evacuate to Mankato in a caravan of 153 wagons.[15]

As soon as Governor Alexander Ramsey got wind of the Indian uprising, he went to Fort Snelling to assess troop readiness. He then drove to the stone house of Minnesota's first governor, Henry Sibley, at Mendota. Sibley had staked out land claims and invested heavily in property along the Minnesota River, and Sibley and Ramsey were close friends. Though without military training, Sibley understood the Dakota language, was politically astute, and had slept in Indian lodges and hunted elk with Little Crow. Representing John Jacob Astor's American Fur Company, Sibley had traded with the Indians for twenty-eight years and had represented traders at the 1851 treaty negotiations, where Ramsey told the Indians, "Your Great Father has proposed this treaty we are about to complete, because he is your friend. Those who participate in it will be sustained by him." Sibley and Ramsey had both worked closely on treaty negotiations to make enormous sums of money at the Indians' expense. In one instance, Sibley had secured for himself $145,000 for claimed fur overpayments, and in another, Ramsey had deducted a 15-percent commission for the handling of Indian money. The morning after Ramsey's visit to Mendota, Sibley, newly commissioned as a colonel, was on a steamboat with four companies of men to fight the warring Indians. "This outbreak must be suppressed, and in such manner as will forever prevent its repetition," Ramsey said later in a proclamation.[16]

Bishop Whipple was in St. Paul when news of the Indian uprising reached him. At Sibley's request, Whipple rode through the night to Faribault to help organize its citizenry. After arriving at sunrise and sending a boy with a clanging bell through the streets to ask men to meet at the town's hotel, Whipple told everyone about the massacre. He then took down names of volunteers and gun and horse owners, telling them to join Sibley in St. Peter. Though Whipple's missionary work among the Indians was his life's passion, his allegiances ran deep to Minnesota's white settlers. Only in May 1861 had Whipple preached to the Civil War–bound First Minnesota Volunteers at Fort Snelling. Though elected regiment chaplain, Whipple declined due to his local duties, and the chaplaincy went instead to clergyman Edward Neill, later one of Lincoln's secretaries. Whipple felt sickened by the Indian uprising, but he, more than anyone, understood its causes. In a letter to President James Buchanan, Whipple had long before raised the specter of an Indian uprising, presciently warning Lincoln's predecessor that "a nation which sowed robbery would reap a harvest of blood." After arriving in St. Peter, where stoves and tents lined the streets, Whipple now

Bishop Henry Whipple. Photograph courtesy of the Minnesota Historical Society.

had to bandage refugees' bloody injuries brought on by white indifference to the Indians' suffering. Dutifully, Whipple organized a makeshift hospital at St. Peter's courthouse and sewed up wounds after a local doctor set fractured limbs and performed amputations.[17]

When President Lincoln heard about Minnesota's Indian uprising, he was immersed in Robert E. Lee's invasion of Maryland and had little time to deal with the new crisis. Billed as "the Rail Splitter" in his bid for high office, Lincoln was no stranger to frontier living and felt considerable kinship with the Minnesota settlers' plight. His namesake, his grandfather Abraham, had been killed by Indians in Kentucky while planting corn, and his father's life was spared only by an adept rifle shot. Lincoln's orphaned father told this story so much that his impressionable son—the future commander in chief—would later say that it became "the legend more strongly than all others imprinted upon my mind and memory." Although southern battlefields weighed most heavily on him, Lincoln could no more ignore Minnesota's Indian outbreak than he could the one that happened thirty years earlier in his home state. In 1832, two thousand Sauk and Fox Indians led by Black Hawk sought to reclaim Illinois lands that had been ceded away by treaty. Lincoln enlisted to fight the Indians, and while seeing no combat, was elected a militia captain. Lincoln later poked fun at his military record, saying he had "a good many bloody struggles" with mosquitoes but "never fainted from loss of blood." Now, three decades later, living in the Executive Mansion, Lincoln found himself inundated with mail and telegraph messages demanding federal aid to quash Minnesota's Indian rebellion.[18]

On August 25, 1862, Governor Ramsey, who had supported Lincoln's 1860 presidential nomination, telegraphed Lincoln asking for a one-month extension of the Civil War's draft deadline. Ramsey told Lincoln he had already requested an extension from the War Department but had been turned down. "The Indian outbreak has come upon us suddenly," Ramsey's telegram pled, desperately seeking to delay filling Minnesota's quota of 5,362 men. "Half the population of the State are fugitives," it said. "I appeal to you, and ask for an immediate answer. No one not here can conceive the panic in the State." Lincoln's own secretary,

German immigrant John Nicolay, supported Ramsey's request for over five thousand guns and joined Indian Commissioner William Dole and Mankato resident Senator Morton Wilkinson, Lincoln's friend, in sending another telegram: "We are in the midst of a most terrible and exciting Indian war. Thus far the massacre of innocent white settlers has been fearful. A wild panic prevails in nearly one-half of the State." Lincoln, regularly monitoring telegrams at the War Department's telegraph office, sent a short reply on August 27 to Ramsey's telegram. It read: "Yours received. Attend to the Indians. If the draft can not proceed, of course it will not proceed. Necessity knows no law. The government can not extend the time." The Civil War required men to fight it, and Lincoln was unwilling to set the dangerous precedent of making an exception to the draft deadline.[19]

In late August, Colonel Sibley's small contingent of men advanced to St. Peter and eventually relieved Fort Ridgely. But Sibley's fourteen hundred men, facing violent rainstorms and a lack of ammunition, did not move right away against the Indians; instead, Sibley cautiously waited for supplies and reinforcements. Calling the Indians "red devils" in a letter home, Sibley told his wife that he would pursue the Indians "with fire and sword." "My heart is steeled against them," Sibley told Ramsey, "and if I have the means, and can catch them, I will sweep them with the besom of death." Only after scouts assured him no Dakota combatants lurked nearby was Sibley finally pressured into sending out a 170-man party to bury corpses that had lain for days in the hot August sun. That burial detail dug graves for dozens of decomposing bodies but then chose to camp near Birch Coulee, an ill-selected ravine where under cover of darkness over two hundred Indians encircled the soldiers' camp and then attacked it, leading to a pitched battle. When Sibley finally rode into the besieged camp with reinforcements on September 3, he found thirteen dead soldiers, forty-seven wounded men, and ninety dead horses. One of the soldiers' tents was riddled with 104 bullet holes. Indian attacks also befell settlements on the edge of Minnesota's Big Woods even as seventy-five of Little Crow's warriors broke ranks from him, finding fault with his war tactics. Skirmishes occurred near Acton, on Hope Lake's shoreline, and at Hutchinson and Forest City, though hastily erected timber stockades foiled the marauding Indians' plans.[20]

By September 1862, Lincoln was feeling the immense strain of presiding over a languishing war effort. General Robert E. Lee had out-foxed Lincoln's army in Virginia, and after the Union's defeat at the second battle of Bull Run in late August, it looked as if the war might never be won. Washington, D.C., itself was a pathetic sight. Its streets were unpaved, and its residences were mostly old wooden structures. Bad storms cut Pennsylvania Avenue into ruts as heavily loaded army wagons rolled down the nearly impassable street, and cows, chickens, and goats meandered amid broken whiskey bottles, rotting garbage, and dead cats. In mid-September, Lincoln himself sprained his wrist—an injury re-quiring medical attention two weeks later—while checking his runaway horse. When it happened, Lincoln had been on his morning ride to the White House from his summer retreat, a cottage three miles away where Lincoln read poetry and drafted portions of the Emancipation Procla-mation. In the ever chaotic Washington, D.C., area, troops and army hospitals—thirty-five by 1862 holding thirteen thousand wounded sol-diers—were literally everywhere. As a boyish-looking corporal from Maine, John Day Smith, described the nation's capitol, "Disorder and gloom reigned supreme." The U.S. Capitol dome, which Lincoln wanted capped to symbolize the nation's will "to go on," was unfinished and covered with black scaffolding. As Smith observed, "the Union cause at this time was dark."[21]

Though the outlook was bleak, Lincoln carefully monitored troop movements with maps and colored pushpins in his dark green-wallpapered office. He also insisted on seeing all Executive Mansion vis-itors who mobbed the corridor and stairs outside of his office, deluging the sleep-deprived Lincoln with an endless stream of generals and ad-mirals, senators and congressmen, and widows and office seekers. One of his September 1862 visitors was Bishop Whipple. Accompanied by his cousin, General Henry Halleck, Whipple told Lincoln that corrupt Indian agents and traders had caused the bloodshed. Lincoln was sym-pathetic, and Whipple reported later that the president appeared "deeply moved." But with three hundred letters a day flooding the White House, whether from autograph or pardon seekers, Lincoln had very little time to fully consider the U.S. government's Indian policies. Embroiled in a crisis outside of Minnesota over Indian loyalty to the Union cause, Lincoln wrote a letter in September 1862 saying that a "multitude of cares" had kept him from examining U.S.–Cherokee relations. Lincoln only had time to tell Whipple a homespun story: "Bishop, a man thought that monkeys could pick cotton better than negroes could because they were quicker and their fingers smaller. He turned a lot of them into his cotton field, but he found that it took two overseers to watch one monkey. It needs more than one honest man to watch one Indian agent." Despite his busy schedule, Lincoln did tell a friend about his meeting with Whipple and, if only conditionally, pledged, "If we get through this war, and I live, this Indian system shall be reformed."[22]

A personal tragedy added only more strain to the overworked president's life. As pressure grew to rein in the Confederacy, Lincoln was still coping with his son's death, most likely from typhoid fever. The Lincolns' son Willie fell ill before a large party at the newly renovated White House, and as his condition worsened, Lincoln spent many hours by his bedside, stroking his son's hair. "The President is nearly worn out," one cabinet member noticed. Willie died in February 1862, and a grief-stricken Lincoln sobbed into his hands, confiding to his private secretary, "Well, Nicolay, my boy is gone—he is actually gone!" Long after Willie's funeral, Lincoln, an avid reader of Shakespeare, would shut himself in a room and cry alone, reciting passages from *Macbeth*, *King Lear*, and *Hamlet*. The Lincolns had already lost three-year-old Edward and were now heartbroken again by Willie's death. Wearing black veils, Mary Lincoln lay in bed crying for weeks, unable even to attend the funeral. A devoted father who had taken his sons to his Springfield law office and pulled them around in a wagon, the president turned to God for solace, twice returning alone to his son's crypt to lift the coffin lid. It was in this depressed state of mind that Lincoln had to issue war orders and deal with Minnesota's Sioux outbreak.[23]

Minnesota politicians had their own problems to face. Frustrated at the lack of help from Washington, D.C., an increasingly blunt Governor Ramsey telegraphed President Lincoln on September 5 at five o'clock in the morning. "Those Indian outrages continue," his telegram read. "I asked Secretary Stanton to authorize the United States Quartermaster to purchase, say, 500 horses. He refuses. . . . This is not our war; it is a national war. . . . Answer me at once." Ramsey's pestering paid off. By the end of the day, the War Department had named Major General John Pope as the commander of the newly established Military Department of the Northwest, headquartered in St. Paul. An Illinois acquaintance and once Lincoln's favorite, Pope had served under Henry Halleck in the West and had worked side by side with Lincoln at the War Department's telegraph office. Falling out of favor with Lincoln after losing the second battle of Bull Run, an angry and bitter General Pope was reassigned to Minnesota, where he ordered Sibley to "exterminate the Sioux." Ramsey himself wanted the Sioux "driven forever beyond the borders of the State," and on September 11, fifty thousand cartridges arrived on General Halleck's orders for that purpose. Additional manpower came to the state in early September, arriving at Fort Snelling on a steamer. Lincoln had ordered over 250 infantrymen from Minnesota's Third Regiment, just paroled from Confederate captivity after a humiliating surrender in Tennessee, back to their home state "just as fast as the Railroads will carry them" to "the seat of the Indian difficulties."[24]

The loss of men and horses at Birch Coulee was a major setback to Colonel Sibley, who lacked sufficient cavalry to pursue the Indians. Speculating that Little Crow might want a truce, Sibley left a stake on the Birch Coulee battlefield with a simple message posted to it: "If Little Crow has any proposition to make to me, let him send a half-breed to me, and he shall be protected in and out of camp." In his initial reply, Little Crow cited as the war's causes Myrick's insult and that "our children are dying with hunger." Taoyateduta hinted that a truce-for-hostage deal might be possible, but Sibley responded pointedly, "You have murdered many of our people without sufficient cause." "Return me the prisoners, under a flag of truce," Sibley demanded, "and I will talk with you then like a man." Little Crow's next communiqué asked "what way" peace could be made for his people, but Sibley curtly replied, "You have allowed your young men to commit some murders since you wrote your first letter. *This is not the way to make peace.*" When Chiefs Wabasha and Taopi sent Sibley a letter seeking peace behind Little Crow's back and offered to release the captives, Sibley told the Indians to gather on the prairie in full sight of his troops with a white flag. Saying no innocent person would be harmed, Sibley told the Indians he would be "glad to receive all true friends of the whites" but warned he was "powerful enough to crush" all who opposed him.[25]

At a tribal council near the mouth of the Chippewa River, the Dakota Indians hotly debated whether to keep fighting. Standing atop a barrel, one tribal leader shouted that he opposed "continuing this war" and "further outrages," calling those "who will cut women's and children's throats . . . squaws and cowards." Wabasha's son-in-law, Rdainyanka, disagreed, imploring his fellow tribesmen, "I am for continuing the war, and am opposed to the delivery of the prisoners." "I have no confidence that the whites will stand by any agreement they make if we give them up," Rdainyanka warned. "Ever since we treated with them their agents and traders have robbed and cheated us. Some of our people have been shot, some hung; others placed upon floating ice and drowned; and many have been starved in their prisons." "We may regret what has happened, but the matter has gone too far to be remedied," Rdainyanka argued. "Let us, then, kill as many of the whites as possible, and let the prisoners die with us," he resolved. Little Crow agreed. "Did we ever do the most trifling thing, and the whites not hang us?" he asked. "As for me, I will kill as many of them as I can, and fight them till I die." "Disgrace not yourselves by a surrender to those who will hang you up like dogs," Little Crow said, "but die, if die you must, with arms in your hands, like warriors and braves of the Dakota."[26]

The ever cautious Sibley finally led his troops upriver from Fort Ridgely on September 19 in pursuit of the Indians. On foot and horseback, they traveled through the Minnesota River valley, and after four days of marching, encamped on the shore of Lone Tree Lake. Having left their camp near the Chippewa River, the Indians found Sibley's encampment, and Little Crow immediately favored a night attack. But Solomon Two Stars, a Little Crow relative, dismissed that idea as cowardly, and an ambush at daybreak was planned instead. A few men from Minnesota's Third Regiment, though, foiled the plan when they set out in wagons to go foraging for potatoes and melons at the Upper Agency three miles away. The soldiers came so close to the Indians spread out in the tall grass along the road that the Indians had to rise up and fire their weapons. Swinging his blanket over his head, Little Crow let out a loud war-whoop even as the attack on the small wagon train gave Sibley's larger force time to organize a full-scale counterattack. And the soldiers quickly took the upper hand. By battle's end, a cannon ball had killed Chief Mankato, and more than a dozen Indians lay dead. To avenge their own losses, soldiers scalped dead Indians, angering Sibley. "The bodies of the dead, even of a savage enemy," Sibley chided, "shall not be subjected to indignities by civilized and Christian men."[27]

The debacle at Lone Tree Lake demoralized the warring Indians, and a dejected Little Crow returned to his camp to find that the Indians desiring peace had seized the captives and dug rifle pits to protect them. To avoid a tribal civil war, Little Crow ordered the release of captives who remained within his control, and he and other tribal leaders, including Shakopee and Medicine Bottle, then hastily gathered their families so they could set out on the open prairie. A messenger returning from Sibley's camp suggested that Little Crow surrender, but Taoyeduta only laughed derisively, saying, "Sibley would like to put the rope around my neck, but he won't get the chance." "Now we had better all run away and scatter out over the plains like buffalo and wolves," Little Crow declared before leaving. Other Indians put their fate in Sibley's hands, having gotten a message from Sibley on September 24 that "[s]uch of the Indians as have not had anything to do with the murders of the whites will not be injured by my troops; but, on the contrary, they will be protected by me when I arrive, which will be very soon." "I have not come to make war upon those who are innocent but upon the guilty," Sibley had communicated reassuringly.[28]

Still fearful of a trap, Sibley's troops warily left Lone Tree Lake on

September 25. But the next day, Sibley's men marched into the Indian camp without incident with colors flying. "White flags were fastened to the tips of tepee poles" and "every conceivable object," one observer recalled later. "The Indians and half-breeds assembled in considerable numbers," Sibley would report to Pope, saying, "I proceeded to give them very briefly my views of the late proceedings; my determination that the guilty parties should be pursued and overtaken, if possible." In all, 91 whites and roughly 150 mixed-blood prisoners were liberated, and over the next few days, the total number of captives freed rose to 269. Among the rescued women and children were Mrs. Wakefield and rape victim Mattie Williams. Those freed were quickly taken to Sibley's encampment, dubbed Camp Release, and about twelve hundred Indians were taken into custody. That number climbed to almost two thousand as Sibley led Indians to believe that they would be treated fairly, perhaps as prisoners of war, if they surrendered. "It is probable I shall not order any execution of the guilty until I can get those understood to be coming down to surrender themselves in my power," Sibley told Pope, explaining his strategy.[29]

Within days of the Indians' wholesale surrender, President Lincoln rewarded Sibley by promoting him to the rank of brigadier general. The president's life had, by this time, grown even more hectic. Just days earlier, following the human carnage at the Battle of Antietam, Lincoln had kept a promise to his "Maker" by issuing the Emancipation Proclamation. In it, Lincoln admonished southern states that he would sign an order freeing all slaves in Confederate states if the rebellion was not ended by the first of the year. "I must do the best I can, and bear the responsibility of taking the course which I feel I ought to take," a determined Lincoln told his cabinet. Like the president, Sibley was charting his own course of action: not to free slaves, but to punish the captive Indians. While Lincoln suspended the writ of habeas corpus, calling for the arrest of all persons guilty of any disloyal practices and telling White House visitors, "I am environed with difficulties" and "can only trust in God I have made no mistake," Sibley set up a five-man military commission. The commission's purpose would be to summarily try "the mulatto, mixed bloods, and Indians engaged in the Sioux raids and massacres." The Indians would not be treated as prisoners of war. Instead, they would be charged with crimes like murder, rape, and robbery.[30]

The military commission first convened at Camp Release, where several of the freed captives remained to testify and where the disarmed Indians were shackled together in twos with leg irons, fed principally corn and potatoes. Later, the trials relocated to trader François La Bathe's small, partially damaged log house at the Redwood Agency in what quickly became known as Camp Sibley. La Bathe himself had been killed in the initial raid on the agency. Rev. Stephen Riggs, who knew the Dakota language, gathered incriminating evidence—in effect, serving as "the Grand Jury of the court," as one man put it—and by October 4, twenty-nine trials were finished, with the pace of the trials accelerating as time went by. Many prisoners were sentenced to die on the testimony of a few witnesses, with mixed-blood David Faribault, Little Crow's wartime buggy driver, testifying in over sixty-five trials. Joseph Godfrey, a mulatto man with a French Canadian father, a black mother, and a Dakota wife, testified in fifty-five cases, turning state's evidence after being sentenced to death. Only after many Indians were sentenced to death was Godfrey's death sentence reduced by Lincoln to ten years in prison, only three of which he actually served. Lieutenant Rollin Olin, a twenty-two-year-old with no legal training, oversaw the proceedings as the judge advocate, aided by Ramsey County prosecutor Isaac Heard, the military commission's trial recorder. Often convicted on unreliable hearsay evidence, none of the accused were afforded lawyers or other customary criminal trial rights. A two-thirds vote was sufficient to impose a death sentence, and over a hundred of those condemned to die were convicted solely on the basis of their own, sometimes perfunctory statements.[31]

Only a few brave religious leaders publicly urged restraint. In an article penned in September 1862, Bishop Whipple called the "late fearful massacre" an appalling "calamity" that brought "sorrow to all our hearts." Citing broken-up homes and an "entire border stained with blood," Whipple said it was no wonder "that our people cry vengeance." But Whipple, whom the state's Indians called Straight Tongue, wanted the causes of the bloodshed to be examined. The U.S. government had encouraged "savage life," he said, "by payment of money, by purchases of scalping-knives and trinkets," and by the "sale of fire-water," making "devils of red men." Whipple lamented that "the Indian Department is the most corrupt in the Government," and said that the "nation cannot afford to be unjust." Although Whipple had no desire to "shield the really guilty" from punishment, he worried about the execution of the innocent and the fate of those who did not murder anyone themselves. Referring to deeds of violence against the settlers, Whipple bluntly asked, "At whose door is the blood of these innocent victims?" "I believe that God will hold the nation guilty," Whipple said, saying the war's settlement should "call down the blessing of God." The Indians' fate should be decided by "calm thought" and God-fearing judges, Minnesota's Episcopal bishop proclaimed.[32]

The pace of the military proceedings, however, was extraordinary. Some cases were heard in less than five minutes, and by mid-October, more than one hundred trials were finished. Believing that an example was necessary, Sibley told Pope that he planned to execute the guilty immediately. With Pope favoring swift executions too, the military commission cast aside legal niceties and adjudicated up to forty-two cases in a single day. The commission's recorder, Isaac Heard, wrote later that the trials became "very monotonous" and that if testimony showed a prisoner had been a battle participant, that was sufficient for the death penalty's imposition. It was only necessary, Heard concluded, for each case to occupy a few moments. "I don't know how you can discriminate now between Indians who say they are and have been friendly, and those who have not," Pope told Sibley, resolving the issue by saying that "I distrust them all" and that the guilty, "whatever the number," should be hanged. Sibley's views were much the same. "It is probable there are some innocent men among the prisoners," he wrote on October 14, "but it is impossible to winnow them out now." When Sibley questioned his own authority to execute the Indians, Pope pressed his superior, General Halleck, on October 13, "Do I need further authority to execute Indians condemned by military commission?"[33]

When the commission wrapped up its work in early November, 392 prisoners had been tried, and 303 sentenced to die. In a letter to his wife, Sibley was circumspect: "I have to review all the proceedings, and decide the fate of each individual. This power of life, and death, is an awful thing to exercise, and when I think of more than three hundred human beings are subject to that power, lodged in my hands, it makes me shudder." Even those acquitted of crimes remained imprisoned as Sibley rubber-stamped the commission's findings except for the death sentence of John Other Day's brother, which he remitted for lack of evidence. "I see the press is very much concerned, lest I should prove too tender-hearted," Sibley confided to his wife. The only charge often specified by the tribunal was the generic allegation that an Indian prisoner "did, between the 19th of August and the 28th day of September, join and participate in various murders and outrages committed by the Sioux Indians on the Minnesota Frontier," and Sibley told Pope that he intended to hang the Indians even if the commission proceedings were not "exactly in form." Bishop Whipple and Commissioner of Indian Affairs William Dole found the number of death sentences excessive. Whipple urged clemency for those involved only in battles as opposed to murdering defenseless women and children, and Dole thought a mass execution would be "a stain upon our national character." Whipple went one step further, writing to Senator Rice to have him deliver a letter to President Lincoln. "We cannot hang men by the hundreds," he wrote, saying "we have no right to do so," and that as "an independent nation," they are "prisoners of war." "The leaders must be punished," he said, "but we cannot afford by . . . wanton cruelty to purchase a long Indian war—nor by injustice in other matters purchase the anger of God."[34]

After Pope doubted his own authority to execute the condemned prisoners, the issue came up when Pope's report on the ongoing trials was read aloud at President Lincoln's October 14 cabinet meeting. A still grief-ridden Lincoln, his second-floor White House office just down the hall from where his son Willie had died, quickly moved to delay any hangings. Having toured Harper's Ferry and the Antietam battlefield only a week earlier, Lincoln was in no mood to order a mass execution.

On October 17, Pope told Sibley that "[t]he President directs that no executions be made without his sanction," although Pope felt certain that Lincoln would ultimately approve of the commission's work. Pope was so confident that executions would go forward quickly that he telegraphed the condemned men's names to Lincoln at the staggering cost of $400. On November 10, a cost-conscious Lincoln, wanting more time, wired back, asking for "the full and complete record of these convictions" and "a careful statement" indicating "the more guilty and influential" of the "culprits." "Send all by mail," Lincoln admonished. An accomplished trial lawyer, Lincoln felt uncomfortable making life-and-death decisions without reviewing the evidence more closely. Too busy to do it himself, Lincoln assigned two aides, George Whiting and Francis Ruggles, to comb through the trial transcripts and make recommendations regarding which prisoners should be executed.[35]

Worried about the president's intentions, Governor Ramsey quickly telegraphed Lincoln. "I hope the execution of every Sioux Indian condemned by the military court will be at once ordered," Ramsey urged. Referring to the Sioux Indians as "assassins" and "ravishers" of "wives and sisters and daughters," Ramsey felt strongly that even Indians who were not executed should be exiled and told Lincoln "[p]rivate revenge" would take the place of "official judgment" if he did not act. A preoccupied Lincoln endorsed Ramsey's telegram on November 11: "Respectfully referred to Secretary of War." Only a week earlier, northern midterm elections had dealt a crippling blow to Lincoln's Republican Party, with five states Lincoln won in 1860—including his home state of Illinois—sending Democratic majorities to Congress. When candidly told by a Pennsylvania congressman that some Republicans, concerned about tardy troop movements, "would be glad to hear some morning that you had been found hanging from the post of a lamp at the door of the White House," a depressed Lincoln, who often had for breakfast nothing more than an egg and a cup of coffee, replied in a subdued voice, "You need not be surprised to find that that suggestion has been executed any morning." Angered by accusations he was personally responsible for the war's failure, Lincoln would lash out at a general who questioned

Lincoln's tactics, saying, "I think I could not do better; therefore I blame you for blaming me."[36]

General Pope sent the trial transcripts to Lincoln on November 15 but replied right away to Lincoln's letter on November 11, contending that "the only distinction between the culprits is as to which of them murdered most people or violated most young girls." Pope warned Lincoln that the people of Minnesota would take matters into their own hands and kill all of the Indians—"old men, women, and children" alike—if Lincoln did not allow the executions "without exception." Alluding to frequent funerals and "terrible outrages" committed upon "poor women and young girls," Pope told Lincoln that dead bodies were being found daily. "These things influence the public mind to a fearful degree," Pope lectured Lincoln, brazenly telling the commander in chief that "your action has been awaited with repressed impatience." Already out of patience, Governor Ramsey wanted to try the Indians in state court if Lincoln failed to act, with Pope advocating that approach too. Fears of mob violence were real. As the wagon train of shackled Indians moved through New Ulm on its way to the Mankato area's newly dubbed and fortified Camp Lincoln, an angry mob hurled bricks at the Indians. Two Indians were killed in the attack, and a bayonet charge and over a dozen arrests were needed to stop it.[37]

When word got out that Lincoln might not carry out all of the military commission's sentences, a public outcry arose from Minnesota's newspapers and its white citizens and elected officials. A Stillwater newspaper, stating, "We ask you, Abraham Lincoln, has crime become a virtue?" said that "DEATH TO THE BARBARIANS! is the sentiment of our people." Three hundred St. Paul residents signed a petition demanding the Indians' execution, and a Mankato paper boldly declared that the condemned Indians would be executed "either by the order of the President, or by *the will of the people*, who make Presidents." U.S. Senator Morton Wilkinson and Congressmen Cyrus Aldrich and William Windom also joined in, writing a personal letter to Lincoln. "We protest against the pardon of these Indians," it read. Calling attention to stories of rapes and mutilation "well known to our people," these politicians told Lincoln that if the executions did not go forward, "the outraged people of Minnesota would dispose of these wretches without law." Their letter admonished Lincoln: "We do not wish to see mob law inaugurated in Minnesota, as it certainly will be, if you force the people to it." Pope wired Lincoln at midday on November 24 with an equally blunt message: "I trust that your decision and orders in the case will be transmitted as soon as practicable, as humanity to both the troops and Indians requires an immediate disposition of the case."[38]

The Civil War, demanding so much of Lincoln's time already, now had a new front in the West: the soldiers' fight against Minnesota's non-surrendering Indians. While the state's politicians lobbied for speedy executions, many easterners and religious leaders sought mercy for the captive Dakota people. Lincoln put his faith in God's will. At a White House prayer meeting Lincoln told a Quaker woman that God had permitted the Civil War "for some wise purpose of his own, mysterious and unknown to us." As Lincoln contemplated what fate would befall the Indians, Bishop Whipple traveled to Washington, D.C., to lobby the president, and telegrams arrived in late November from Pope and Ramsey seeking speedy executions. Whipple's personal appeal swayed Lincoln a great deal. After their meeting, Lincoln said Whipple "talked with me about the rascality of this Indian business until I felt it down to my boots." In a November 28 conference with Senator Wilkinson and Representative Aldrich, Lincoln bought some time by promising to make a final determination on the Indians' fate after he completed his annual message. That same day, Governor Ramsey wired Lincoln, "Nothing but the speedy execution of the tried and convicted Sioux Indians will save us from scenes of outrage."[39]

During the Civil War, Lincoln felt extreme ambivalence about army executions, and deciding the Dakota Indians' fate was no easier. In 1861, when his commander of the Department of the West sought to end guerrilla warfare in Missouri by ordering that arms-bearing civilians be shot, Lincoln directed him to withdraw the order. "Should you shoot a man, according to the proclamation," Lincoln warned, "the Confederates would very certainly shoot our best men in their hands in retaliation, and so, man for man, indefinitely." Perceived by many as too soft on the rebels, Lincoln's decision was roundly criticized, even by some of Lincoln's closest friends. His old law partner, William Herndon, lambasted Lincoln: "Does he suppose he can crush—squelch out this huge rebellion by pop guns filled with rose water. He ought to hang somebody and get up a name for will or decision—for character. Let him hang some Child or woman, if he has not Courage to hang a *man*." Only as the Civil War's casualties climbed higher did Lincoln's approach become more draconian. After the Confederacy announced that captured black Union soldiers would be put to death, an infuriated Lincoln issued an "Order of Retaliation" in July 1863 proclaiming that "for every soldier of the United States killed in violation of the laws of war, a rebel soldier shall be executed."[40]

On December 1, 1862—the same day Lincoln sacked all the officers who voted to surrender Minnesota's Third Regiment in Tennessee—President Lincoln gave his annual message to Congress. "[W]hile it has not pleased the Almighty to bless us with a return of peace," he said, "we can but press on, guided by the best light He gives us, trusting that in His own good time, and wise way, all will yet be well." Saying "[t]he Indian tribes upon our frontiers have, during the past year, manifested a spirit of insubordination," Lincoln specifically referred to Minnesota's Sioux Indians. These Indians, he said, had "indiscriminately" killed "not less than eight hundred persons" with "extreme ferocity." "How this outbreak was induced is not definitely known, and suspicions, which may be unjust, need not be stated," Lincoln concluded, noting only that "Minnesota has suffered greatly from this Indian war." Yet, Lincoln acknowledged the failure of the U.S. government's Indian policies. "I submit for your especial consideration whether our Indian system shall not be remodelled," Lincoln told the nation. "Many wise and good men have impressed me with the belief that this can be profitably done."[41]

Though Lincoln wanted reform, his view of Indians differed little from those held by other midwesterners. At a meeting with Indian chiefs at the outset of his presidency, Lincoln had spoken condescendingly to the Indian delegation, saying things like, "Where live now?" and "When go back Iowa?" In a visit with Indians in March 1863, Lincoln no longer used broken English, but his translated words revealed Lincoln's stereotyped view of Indians as violent simpletons. "We pale-faced people think that this world is a great, round ball," Lincoln said, "and we have people here of the pale-faced family who have come almost from the other side of it to represent their nations here and conduct their friendly intercourse with us, as you now come from your part of the round ball." Whites are "numerous and prosperous," Lincoln added, "because they cultivate the earth, produce bread, and depend upon the products of the earth rather than wild game for a subsistence." Lincoln viewed Indians as uncivilized wards of government, and while telling the Indian delegation why farming accounted for the whites' prosperity, he added another reason, without irony. "Although we are now engaged in a great war between one another," Lincoln said, "we are not, as a race, so much disposed to fight and kill one another as our red brethren."[42]

Lincoln, who still remained undecided on December 1 about what to do, angered many Minnesotans by failing to reveal his intentions in his annual message. In a letter sent that very day to newly appointed Judge Advocate General Joseph Holt, Lincoln sought Holt's guidance: "Three hundred Indians have been sentenced to death in Minnesota by a Military Commission, and execution only awaits my action. I wish your legal opinion whether if I should conclude to execute only a part of them, I must myself designate which, or could I leave the designation to some officer on the ground?" Holt quickly replied, "I am quite sure that the power cannot be delegated, and that the designation of the individuals, which its exercise involves, must necessarily be made by yourself." Holt advised, "I am not aware of any instance in which the delegation of this delicate and responsible trust, has been attempted." Holt then suggested that Lincoln consult with the attorney general to determine the "regularity" of the military proceedings. In the end, however, Lincoln would look to what his two aides, George Whiting and Francis Ruggles, had to say about what should be done.[43]

Tensions in Minnesota and the nation's capital escalated as Lincoln mulled over what to do. The letter from Minnesota's federal representatives, Morton Wilkinson, Cyrus Aldrich, and William Windom, sent on the eve of Lincoln's final decision expressed fear and contempt for what Lincoln might decide. "We have learned, indirectly, that you intend to pardon or reprieve a large majority of the Indians in Minnesota," the letter began. "If this be your purpose," it pleaded, "we beg leave most respectfully to protest against it." "Mr. President, let us relate to you some facts with which we fear you have not heretofore been made acquainted," the three congressmen wrote. They emphasized that "[t]hose Indians whom (as we understand) you propose to pardon and set free," murdered "one thousand of our people," took into captivity "more than one hundred women and girls, and, in nearly every instance, treated them with the most fiendish brutality." One eighteen-year-old girl, the letter recounted, had her arms bound and was "ravished by some eight or ten of these convicts before the cords were unloosed from her limbs." "Without being more specific," the letter added, "we will state that all or nearly all the women who were captured were violated in this way."[44]

Saying that Agent Galbraith had "faithfully and efficiently" performed his duties "for the welfare of these Indians," Wilkinson, Aldrich, and Windom communicated a simple message: "Mr. President, there was no justification or pretext even for these brutalities." Belittling a delegation of Pennsylvanians who called upon Lincoln to ask that mercy be shown to the Indians, these Minnesota politicians clamored for a mass execution. "These Indians are called by some, prisoners of war. There was no war about it," they said. "It was a wholesale robbery, rape and murder." These three members of Minnesota's congressional delegation then appealed to Lincoln's political instincts, not so subtly hinting that he would lose support in the Midwest if he failed to heed their advice. "The people of Minnesota, Mr. President, have stood firm by you, and by your Administration," they said, telling Lincoln that "our people have not risen up to slaughter" the Indians "because they believed that their President would deal with them justly." Senator Henry Rice did not sign this letter but felt compelled to write his own letter to the press just two days later. "Every guilty Indian should perish—not one should be spared that he might boast to the Indians of the Plains of his brutal feats."[45]

The situation was incredibly tense, with the Dakota Indians held in an open field at the mouth of the Blue Earth River, dubbed Camp Lincoln, in what one soldier, hardened by Minnesota's winter, called "cold and dreary camping." As midnight approached on the stormy, snowy day of December 4, 1862, nearly two hundred angry civilians armed with clubs, hatchets, and knives moved to attack that encampment. The soldiers on guard acted quickly, arresting and disarming the angry citizenry, but the attack forced Colonel Stephen Miller, charged with protecting the condemned prisoners, to abandon the camp. In acknowledging the soldiers' own desire for the "universal execution of the guilty savages," Miller thanked his men for doing their duty "so long as the avenues of government point to the final and certain vindication of right and justice." As the prisoners were moved to a more secure log jail in Mankato and Governor Ramsey complained of the tardiness of executive action, the U.S. Senate adopted a Senator Wilkinson–sponsored resolution demanding that Lincoln explain everything he knew "touching the late Indian barbarities." On December 6, an increasingly tense Sibley telegraphed his commanding officer to report the aborted lynching attempt at Camp Lincoln: "Please telegraph the facts to the president, and ask instructions." Just two days later, Sibley telegraphed another military officer: "Ask the President to keep secret his decision, whatever it may be, until I have prepared myself as best I can. God knows how much the excitement is increasing and extending."[46]

A mob mentality existed in Minnesota, but Lincoln would not be swayed by the mob's demands—at least not all of them. Just as he had forcefully decried the lynchings of blacks in Mississippi over two decades earlier, Lincoln still despised mob rule and felt that courts of justice were where the fate of people's lives should be decided. Lincoln was leaning toward executing some of the condemned Indians, something he saw as necessary to maintain order in Minnesota, but he still had not decided how many of the Indians would be put to death. On December 4, Whipple wrote Lincoln again, outlining the causes of the uprising, and also wrote Sibley. If Sibley had "any doubt" about the fairness of the trials, Whipple wrote him, "I know your heart would agree with mine for a searching examination." When Sibley wrote back, he defended the military commission's work, saying a "great crime against our common humanity demands an equally great atonement."[47]

Lincoln's track record on military executions gave Minnesotans few clues as to what he might do with the Dakota Indians. The military code allowed execution for a variety of offenses like mutiny, giving aid to the enemy, or sleeping on duty. As president, Lincoln approved many military death sentences for murderers, rapists, and deserters. Yet, he had a well-deserved reputation for commuting military death sentences, often dishing out lesser punishments like one-year's hard labor or a loss of pay for six months. Indeed, throughout his time in office, Lincoln never let a sleeping sentry be executed for neglecting his nighttime duties and often handed out pardons or commutations in pell-mell fashion with his rationale, if any, scribbled out by him in a sentence or two. Of thirteen courts-martial for desertion that he reviewed in 1862, Lincoln approved death sentences for just two of the men and pardoned or remitted the others. On October 25, 1862, shortly before he decided the Indians' fate, Lincoln commuted the death sentences of a spy and a drunken private who hit his superiors. Aware of Lincoln's unpredictable proclivities with respect to military pardons, Minnesotans anxiously awaited his judgment on the Indians' fate as Governor Ramsey urged calm, issuing a proclamation asking the state's "good citizens" to "await the decision of the overburdened president."[48]

Setting aside a morning almost every week to review court-martial sentences, Lincoln dreaded making life-and-death decisions. "Doesn't it strike you as queer," he told an Indiana politician, "that I, who couldn't cut the head off of a chicken, and who was sick at the sight of blood, should be cast into the middle of a great war, with blood flowing all about me?" Lincoln had such disdain for killing that after shooting a turkey at age seven, he vowed never to kill wild game again. On one day in office, Lincoln agonized over court-martial cases for six hours, and on another, he reviewed seventy-two cases. When Judge Advocate General

Joseph Holt urged more military executions, Lincoln protested, "I don't think I can do it," even though he often reluctantly followed his advisers' death penalty recommendations to curtail desertions with brief notes like "Sentence approved. A. Lincoln." "They say," Lincoln once remarked, "that I destroy discipline and am cruel to the Army when I will not let them shoot a soldier now and then. But I cannot see it. If God wanted me to see it, he would let me know it, and until he does, I shall go on pardoning and being cruel to the end." "I don't believe it will make a man any better to shoot him," Lincoln famously observed. As Friday, the traditional day for executions, drew near, the Bible-reading Lincoln would dismiss even close friends so he could pour over clemency papers before what he called "Black Friday." "Get out of the way," he told one friend, "tomorrow is butcher day and I must go through these papers and see if I cannot find some excuse to let these poor men off."[49]

On December 6, the overworked president, making almost daily visits to the nearby War Department, finally made his decision. It came just a day after his advisers, George Whiting and Francis Ruggles, recommended which Indians they thought should be put to death; it also came just one day after John Kessler, a thirty-six-year-old German farmer in the 103rd New York Infantry, was hanged in Washington, D.C., for bayoneting an officer. Lincoln had reviewed Kessler's file and approved the death sentence. Following Lincoln's protocol, Whiting and Ruggles gave Lincoln their report, pulling the military commission's files for the cases under review so the president could see them. In his order, laboriously written out by Lincoln on Executive Mansion stationery, he ordered Brigadier General Sibley to execute thirty-nine of "the Indians and Half-breeds" on Friday, December 19, directing that Sibley hold the other condemned prisoners "subject to further orders." The men to be executed were listed by their names—"Rda-in-yan-kan," "Ha-pan," "Shoon-ka-ska," and so on—and by numbers—"No. 19," "No. 24," "No. 35"—in Lincoln's own hand. A copy of Lincoln's order, scrivened by John Nicolay, was dispatched to Sibley by special messenger on December 8 but not actually put in Sibley's hands until December 15. The reaction in Minnesota was swift. An angry Sibley, wanting every condemned Indian hanged, predicted Lincoln's decision would cause a drawn-out "war of races" and "an incalculable loss of human life." But Lincoln's decision was final; he would not approve more executions.[50]

On December 11, Lincoln complied with the Wilkinson-authored Senate resolution by transmitting to the Senate the information that body had formally requested, including the original execution order that Lincoln had written out in longhand. Lincoln emphasized that he had "received, through telegraphic dispatches and otherwise, appeals in behalf of the condemned, appeals for their execution, and expressions of opinion as to proper policy in regard to them." He then gave the rationale for his order. "Anxious to not act with so much clemency as to encourage another outbreak on the one hand, nor with so much severity as to be real cruelty on the other," Lincoln explained, "I caused a careful examination of the records of trials to be made, in view of first ordering the execution of such as had been proved guilty of violating females." Contrary to his expectations, Lincoln wrote, only two such cases were found by his aides. Feeling that two executions would not satisfy Minnesotans, Lincoln then "directed a further examination, and a classification of all who were proved to have participated in *massacres*, as distinguished from participation in *battles*." This enlarged group numbered forty, but since Joseph Godfrey, the mulatto, had been recommended for a ten-year prison term, Lincoln ordered only thirty-nine executions. The distinction between "massacres" and "battles" was suggested by Bishop Whipple, who saw a clear difference between "fiendish violence" and the guilt of "timid men" who, under death threats, "engaged in some one battle where hundreds were engaged."[51]

On December 15, Sibley replied to Lincoln's order for execution delivered to him that day by special messenger. Sibley told Lincoln that the date fixed for the execution, December 19, was too short for preparation to protect the other Indians and preserve the peace. Asking for authority to postpone the execution by one week, Sibley advised Lincoln that the execution had to be managed with "great discretion" and "as much secrecy as possible" to prevent citizen unrest. Colonel Miller had sent a telegram to Sibley asking for a delay for another reason. "There was no rope in Mankato except bed-cords," Miller explained later, noting that if the execution date had not been postponed he would have had to "rig a single gallows, splice the bed-cords, and hang the Indians one at a time." Lincoln sent a telegram to Sibley, moving the execution date to December 26, and not wanting any miscommunication to occur, asked the telegraph operator to "please send this very carefully and accurately." Sibley's reply to another Lincoln directive, relative to Chaskaydon, shows Lincoln paying close attention to events in Mankato. A mixed-blood prisoner, Chaskaydon, also known as Robert Hopkins, had been sentenced to die by the military commission, but Lincoln had not listed him on his handwritten, December 6 death warrant. Because Hopkins, Case No. 163, had an identical name with another Chaskaydon, Case No. 121, Lincoln told his secretary, John Nicolay, to send Sibley a message so he would pay "special attention to the case of Robert Hopkins, alias Chaskaydon." Lincoln feared that Hopkins would be sent to the gallows in error because of the confusion caused by the names. "The President desires to guard against his being executed by mistake before his case shall be finally determined," Nicolay told Sibley.[52]

Colonel Miller, a Lincoln supporter in 1860 and the man elected Minnesota's governor in 1863, brought the bad news to the condemned Indians whose sentences Lincoln had approved. Through an interpreter, Miller told them that "[t]heir Great Father at Washington, after carefully reading what the witnesses testified to in their several trials, has come to the conclusion that they have each been guilty of wantonly and wickedly murdering his white children." Several Indians stoically smoked pipes while Colonel Miller's statement was delivered, with one Indian knocking ashes from his pipe and filling it anew with his favorite kinnikinnick. The process of identifying those on Lincoln's list was no small task, as many of the Indians had similar names, like Chaska, the Dakota word for first-born males, and the thirty-nine condemned Indians had to be separated from the rest of the prisoners. The commission's findings were all by number, but as Stephen Riggs noted later, "no one could remember which number attached to which person." In the week leading up to the execution, the condemned men were moved to a stone building, and missionaries fluent in Dakota prayed with the Indians and baptized many of them. Bishop Whipple agreed with Sibley that the truly "wretched Indians" had to be punished as they had "forfeited their lives" by sinning and breaking "the laws of God and man." Whipple simply believed that the commission acted "with such haste as to forbid all justice."[53]

Fearing riots, Colonel Miller imposed martial law as execution day approached. Miller shut down local saloons as a preventive measure, and his posted order banned all liquor consumption within a ten-mile radius of the meticulously engineered scaffold, constructed of heavy white oak timbers. While hundreds of people flocked to Mankato to watch the execution, in Washington, D.C., Mrs. Lincoln was preparing to serve Christmas dinner to wounded Union soldiers at area hospitals that she and the president would visit on Christmas afternoon. The condemned Dakota Indians, chained to the floor, slept or smoked to pass the time, and in their final days, said good-byes to a few relatives and friends who were allowed to visit them. Wabasha's son-in-law, Rda-in-yan-ka, or Rattling Runner, dictated a letter to Wabasha that began, "You have deceived me. You told me that if we followed the advice of General Sibley, and gave ourselves up to the whites, all would be well; no innocent man would be injured." "I have not killed, wounded, or injured a white man, or any white persons," his letter continued, "yet to-day I am set apart for execution, and must die in a few days."[54]

On a mild, wet winter day, December 26, 1862, the largest mass hanging in U.S. history took place in Mankato. "There was scarcely any snow," as one historian writes, "and the day was so warm that people went about in their shirt sleeves." Ironically, just six days before, President Lincoln—in his most acclaimed executive act—signed his final Emancipation Proclamation, declaring that all slaves in Confederate states "are, and henceforward shall be free." While the Emancipation Proclamation drew praise from anti-slavery abolitionists, Lincoln's execution order sending Dakota Indians to their death only drew an early morning crowd of men, women, and small children who arrived on lumber wagons pulled by oxen.[55]

At 7:30 A.M., the Indians' iron shackles were removed and their hands tied with cords. As they were bound, the Indians—with their faces painted vermilion and ultramarine and adorned with eagle plumes and owl feathers—talked, smoked, and sang a plaintive death song. A French-born Catholic priest, Father Augustin Ravoux, who had kept a nearly all-night vigil with the Indians, then knelt and read from a Dakota prayer book. After saying a 5:00 A.M. mass at Mankato's Catholic parish, the priest had awoken the Indians who were still asleep. "Come, my little flock," he told them, "we have to pray and prepare for death." Outside, people occupied roofs and windows of buildings and even the opposite bank of the nearby Minnesota River. At exactly 10:00 A.M., the condemned were led in twos into the street and past lines of soldiers. As they ascended the diamond-shaped scaffold, they chanted a death song—"Hi-yi-yi, Hy-yi-yi"—and did a death dance to keep up their courage. One man smoked a pipe, while another, on the gallows itself, puffed a cigar he had gotten from a reporter. Among the condemned were Tazoo, convicted of raping Mattie Williams; Cut Nose, a leader of the soldiers' lodge; and White Dog, who was at the battle of Redwood Ferry. One of

The mass execution of thirty-eight Dakota Indians. Sketch by W. H. Childs from *Frank Leslie's Illustrated Newspaper*; courtesy of the Minnesota Historical Society.

the three mixed-bloods condemned to die was Baptiste Campbell, who said Little Crow had threatened to kill him if he didn't "kill all the white men I met." Tatemima, or Round Wind, convicted on the suspect testimony of two young boys, got a last-minute presidential reprieve, lowering the final death toll to thirty-eight men.[56]

As up to four thousand people crowded the streets, white muslin caps were drawn over the men's heads and nooses adjusted around their necks. The signal officer, Major Joseph Brown, had been instructed to "beat three distinct taps upon the drum," and as the slow, measured beats sounded, the Indians' singing grew louder. The soldiers now off the platform, the Indians called out their names to each other and repeatedly chanted, in Dakota, "This is me." On the third drumbeat, Dakota Conflict survivor William Duley cut the scaffold's triggering rope with an axe. All at once, thirty-seven bodies were, as Isaac Heard put it, "left dangling between heaven and earth." Duley had lost three children in the fighting at Lake Shetek, and his wife and two remaining children were captives. When the scaffold's platform dropped at 10:15 A.M., there was "one, not loud, but prolonged cheer" from citizens and soldiers alike before the spectators fell silent. As the Indians' bodies swayed back and forth, some of the condemned men managed to clasp hands with one another in a final show of solidarity. One of the ropes broke in the drop as Rattling Runner's body fell to the ground, and his lifeless body had to be quickly strung up again. The anguished wails of Indian women confined close by could be heard, and all thirty-eight men were pronounced dead twenty minutes later, their bodies then cut down and loaded into four army wagons. The Indians were buried in a four-foot-deep mass grave on the adjacent riverfront sandbar, where later that night, men like Dr. William Mayo, seeking cadavers for medical research, dug up the dead bodies.[57]

The day after the execution, Sibley telegraphed President Lincoln: "I have the honor to inform you that the 38 Indians and half-breeds ordered by you for execution were hung yesterday at Mankato, at 10 A.M." "Everything went off quietly, and the other prisoners are well secured," Sibley proudly reported. It was not long, though, before the realization sunk in that mistakes had been made. The marshal of the prison told Bishop Whipple that a man was hanged by mistake. "The day after the execution," the marshal said, "I went to the prison to release a man who had been acquitted for saving a woman's life, but when I asked for him, the answer was, 'He is not here; you hung him yesterday.'" Chaska, Sarah Wakefield's savior, was confused with Chaskaydon, who killed a pregnant woman and cut a fetus out of her womb. Before the military commission, which found Chaska to be an accomplice in George Gleason's murder, Mrs. Wakefield had called Chaska her "protector." Demonized for supposedly having an adulterous affair with Chaska during her captivity—a charge she vehemently denied—Wakefield felt relieved when she saw Lincoln's order, which did not have Chaska's number, Case No. 3, on it. Chaskaydon, Case No. 121, was on Lincoln's list, but only after the mass execution did Mrs. Wakefield learn of Chaska's death by reading a newspaper. The prison marshal, acknowledging the error, told Bishop Whipple, "I could not bring back the redskin." Another Indian, who had boasted of killing a trader with an arrow when, in actuality, a bullet had killed him, was hung for lying. Because of the lie, an officer told Whipple, "we hung the rascal."[58]

The dying declarations of the condemned Indians ranged from incredulous to defiant to remorseful to penitent. Chaska's statement, summarized by a missionary under the name "Chas-kay-dan," reflected his disbelief that he should be slated for execution: "He saved Mrs. Wakefield and the children; and now he dies while she lives." White Dog complained of not having a chance "to tell the things as they were" and rebut the "false testimony brought against him." "He says that his position and conduct at the ferry was misunderstood and misrepresented" and that "he wanted peace and did not command the Indians to fire" on the soldiers at Redwood Ferry. Baptiste Campbell thought he deserved a new trial, saying he "did not speak advisedly when before the military commission" and that he had fired over a settler's head, not at the settler, and only because he felt compelled to do so by Little Crow. In shaking hands with opponents of the war, Tazoo said two days before his execution that he regretted not following their advice. "You were right when you said the whites could not be exterminated, and the attempt indicated folly," he told them.[59]

Just as more settlers and U.S. soldiers would die in the years to come in a protracted series of U.S.–Indian wars on the plains, Mankato's mass execution was just part of the Dakota Indians' suffering. Annuity payments were cut off, and in 1863 Congress voided the Indians' treaties altogether, taking their reservations from them. And many more Indians would die. As over sixteen hundred uncharged Indians were taken to Fort Snelling, a drunken white woman in Henderson snatched a baby from its Indian mother's arms and tossed the newborn to the ground, killing the child. Once interned inside Fort Snelling's stockade, scores of Indians died of sickness and disease, many of measles. The Indians were later loaded on overcrowded river transports, pelted with stones as they stood on deck, and unceremoniously dumped at the Dakota Territory's desolate and uninhabitable Crow Creek reservation. Hundreds of Indians had died by 1866 when the survivors were finally sent to a new reservation in the Nebraska Territory. The condemned Indians Lincoln saved from the gallows were transported to Davenport, Iowa, where more than a third of them died in prison before being reunited three years later with their families. Over one million acres of prime Indian land would be sold to all-too-eager white immigrants, and white-Indian relations would never be the same.[60]

In the wake of the mass execution, the Indians' primary advocate, Bishop Whipple, and the nation's commander in chief, President Lincoln, tried to make amends with the Dakota people, if only through small, individual acts of mercy. Lincoln used his pardoning power. In 1863, he pardoned mixed-blood prisoner David Faribault "on evidence that he acted with the Indians under duress"; in 1864, he also pardoned over two dozen Indians, ordering that they "be liberated and sent to their families." One Indian, who fired only one shot at a fort and three shots at New Ulm in the fighting, was pardoned by the president with the stroke of a pen: "Sentence disapproved. A. Lincoln." The mixed-blood, professed Christian Robert Hopkins was pardoned too for helping save white settlers; thus, Hopkins, Case No. 163 on the roster, was permanently saved from the gallows. Whipple ministered to Indians at Fort Snelling and also convinced white authorities to allow a few Indians like Taopi, a witness in the Dakota war trials, to remain in Minnesota. Fearing for his life, Taopi had urgently told Whipple: "Taopi cannot go to his people. You hung men at Mankato whose friends will require their blood at my hands. If I go I shall die. I shall never have a home until I sleep in the grave."[61]

Lincoln, like Whipple, ultimately rejected an eye-for-an-eye mentality. "'*Lex talionis*,' is the law of barbaric life," Whipple wrote long after Lincoln's assassination, explaining the doctrine: "A man is killed,—another must die in his place." "This goes on year after year," Whipple lamented, "and is the first cause of war between Indian tribes. A willingness to forgive injuries is the first sign of the power of the religion of Jesus Christ." Toward the end of his own life, Lincoln told Secretary of War Edwin Stanton, "[B]lood can not restore blood, and government should not act for revenge." The president's words and deeds showed his weariness of bloodshed. In January 1864, Lincoln commuted one Ohio soldier's death sentence to "hard labor" for the war's duration "not on any merit in the case," which Lincoln described as a "really bad one," but simply "to evade the butchering business." In February 1864, Lincoln ordered that all deserters sentenced to death be imprisoned instead until war's end at the Dry Tortugas, a desolate, fortified island off the coast of Florida. Lincoln's second inaugural address, calling for "malice toward none," sought reconciliation, and just days before Robert E. Lee's surrender at Appomattox, Lincoln met with a Confederate leader and pledged to "save any repentant sinners from hanging." As Lincoln pardoned a deserter only a few days later on April 14, 1865—the same day Lincoln was shot—Lincoln observed, "Well, I think this boy can do more good above ground than under ground." Indeed, when Lincoln's Republican Party lost strength in the 1864 election and Lincoln carried Minnesota by only seven thousand votes, the state's newly elected senator, Alexander Ramsey, told Lincoln that if he had hung more Indians, he would have carried his "old majority." "I could not afford to hang men for votes," Lincoln bluntly replied. Though Sibley and Ramsey pressed for more executions in early 1863, Lincoln, calling it "a disagreeable subject," refused to order them.[62]

In the end, Little Crow, the beleaguered Dakota leader, and Lincoln, who ordered Mankato's mass hanging, would themselves die untimely deaths. After seeking refuge in Canada, Little Crow returned to Minnesota in 1863, only to be shot on July 3 by Nathan Lamson while picking raspberries along Scattered Lake with his son Wowinape. The townspeople of Hutchinson celebrated Taoyateduta's death by desecrating his body, with boys spending the Fourth of July on main street, putting firecrackers in the corpse's ears and nostrils. After Little Crow's body was thrown in a garbage pit, a cavalry officer severed the head from the torso, and Lamson collected a $500 reward offered by General Pope. Little Crow's scalp and parts of his body were later exhibited and then shelved at the Minnesota Historical Society. Not until 1971 was Little Crow's grandson allowed to bury his grandfather's bones in South Dakota. Two other Sioux chiefs involved in the uprising, Medicine Bottle and Shakopee, would also be executed at Fort Snelling in November 1865.[63]

Lincoln's fateful decision to go see the Ford's Theatre's production of *Our American Cousin* would end Lincoln's own life. On April 14, 1865, Shakespearean actor John Wilkes Booth, the pro-slavery southern sympathizer who watched abolitionist John Brown's execution, shot Lincoln in the head with a derringer. Earlier in the day an upbeat Lincoln had met with his cabinet and seemed intent on charting a new course for the nation. "There are men in Congress . . . who possess feelings of hate and vindictiveness in which I have no sympathy and could not participate," Lincoln told his cabinet, saying, "I hope there will be no persecution, no bloody work, after the war is over. No one need expect me to take part in hanging or killing those men, even the worst of them." "Enough lives have been sacrificed," he said. Ironically, after Lincoln's body was transported by train back to his home state, the walls and rotunda floor of Lincoln's tomb in Springfield, Illinois, his final resting spot, were partially constructed of stone quarried near Mankato, Minnesota.[64]

The Dakota Conflict, which claimed hundreds of lives, left a painful legacy in Minnesota and elsewhere, breeding bloodshed between U.S. Army troops and Indians for decades to come. The last major Indian offensive of the Dakota Conflict was a six-week siege of Fort Abercrombie, a Dakota Territory army post. However, smaller Indian raids took place in the summer of 1863, and full-fledged U.S.–Dakota battles were fought at places including Dead Buffalo Lake, Whitestone Hill, and Killdeer Mountain. At the battle of Big Mound, one of Sibley's men was struck and killed by a lightning bolt in the heat of combat. Much to Lincoln's and Halleck's chagrin, Minnesota soldiers would fight the Indians for a long time to come instead of fighting on southern battlefields to end the scourge of slavery. The bitterly fought series of Indian wars on the plains finally ended at South Dakota's Wounded Knee in December 1890, when on a snow-covered field, nearly three hundred, mostly unarmed Indians were slaughtered by American troops. "[T]hey shot us like we were a buffalo," one Sioux survivor recalled of the grisly massacre of men, women, and children. Only in 1987 did Minnesota Governor Rudy Perpich declare the 125th anniversary of the Dakota Conflict to be a "Year of Reconciliation," and only in 1998 were the remains of Marpiya Okinajin, also known as He Who Stands in the Midst of Clouds, or Cut Nose, reburied after being found in a Mayo Clinic doctor's office.[65]

CHAPTER 3

The Execution of Ann Bilansky

The execution of women in the United States is—and always has been—a rare phenomenon. Women are still executed, but only sporadically, as was the case in 1998 when the State of Texas executed convicted killer Karla Faye Tucker—the first woman executed in that state since the Civil War. Last-ditch pleas for mercy, joined by conservative televangelist Pat Robertson, set off a media-driven, worldwide movement to save Tucker's life. However, Texas Governor George W. Bush and the Texas Board of Pardons refused to stop her execution. Freely admitting to murdering her ex-lover with a pickaxe, the thirty-eight-year-old Tucker, a born-again Christian, died by lethal injection for a crime she committed while drunk and on drugs. In all, only a handful of women, condemned to die for crimes like smothering children or poisoning a husband or a fiancé with arsenic, have been executed in America in recent times.[1]

Like Tucker's high-profile case, the drama-filled execution of a woman once happened within Minnesota's borders. Her name was Ann Bilansky, a tall, childless woman who had come in April 1858 from Pleasant Hill, Illinois, to St. Paul, Minnesota, at the behest of John Walker, her ill nephew. After arriving in the state's bustling capital of ten thousand people, she first lived in a small shanty with Walker. Soon, however, she married Stanislaus Bilansky, an early pioneer. Her new husband, on his third marriage, was a short, heavyset bar owner in his early fifties. He lived in a three-room house on St. Paul's Stillwater Road and drank heavily. And Stanislaus was abusive. His second wife had left him after nine years of marriage, leaving three small children, ages ten, eight, and six, in Stanislaus's custody after their divorce. Ann Bilansky dutifully took care of these children and the aging, frequently ill Stanislaus, who often said he was near death. A poor man, Stanislaus owned little more than a small cabin, doubling as his bar and a small grocery store, and a two-room shanty behind it. At Stanislaus's urging, John Walker built and then lived in that shanty. Because of the allegations of premeditated murder, Ann Bilansky's case, as well as her execution in 1860, would generate enormous public debate over capital punishment.[2]

The death of Stanislaus Bilansky came about, whether by natural causes, suicide, or murderous intent, in early March 1859 after his condition worsened, with Stanislaus vomiting and complaining of a stomach ailment. Dr. Alfred Berthier was called to Stanislaus's bedside on March 6, and he prescribed a tonic of absinthe and water to be taken before each meal, feeling his patient merely had indigestion. Stanislaus supplemented this treatment with Graffenburg pills, his favorite medicine, but though he remained in bed, his illness took a dramatic turn for the worse. On March 10, Stanislaus told a visiting neighbor, Lucinda Kilpatrick, that he "had as leave die as live," and while he was gravely ill, his wife, Ann, was seen tearfully asking Stanislaus what she should do with the children if he should die. At 3:30 A.M. on March 11, Stanislaus summoned his son Benjamin to ask for a tumbler of liquor, and a half-hour later Stanislaus was dead. Later that morning, his boarder, John Walker, helped with funeral arrangements. The funeral was scheduled for March 12, and a bland death notice ran in the newspaper. "[A] Polander who came to this city in 1847," it read, "died in this city yesterday morning after a sickness of two weeks." Because Ann Bilansky had no money, Walker paid for the coffin and the burial plot. It was only as the funeral procession was preparing to leave for the cemetery that officials of the Ramsey County coroner's office arrived at the Bilansky house to conduct an inquest.[3]

After a doctor examined the body, a hastily assembled coroner's jury heard testimony from, among others, Walker, Kilpatrick, and Rosa

Scharf, a housekeeper hired during Stanislaus's illness. The coroner's jury concluded that Stanislaus died of natural causes but was very critical of Ann Bilansky for failing to summon the doctor in her husband's final hours—something soon reported in the newspaper. Although Stanislaus's body was buried on Saturday, March 12, at 5:00 P.M., that evening Kilpatrick decided to change her testimony. At her husband's urging, Kilpatrick told the St. Paul police chief that on February 28 she had been out shopping with Ann and saw her purchase arsenic from a drugstore. Ann Bilansky told Kilpatrick at the time that her husband had asked her to purchase arsenic to poison rats in the cellar. In light of Kilpatrick's new testimony, Stanislaus's body was exhumed for a postmortem examination, and John Walker and Ann Bilansky were arrested on Sunday afternoon. Ann Bilansky was about to be vilified by the press as her husband's murderer, with the March 15 morning edition of St. Paul's leading newspaper saying suspicion had it that Mr. Bilansky was poisoned by his wife. It reported that Mrs. Bilansky bought arsenic ten days earlier and that she and Walker, "a man said to be her nephew," were taken into custody and were "on very intimate terms" prior to her marriage.[4]

At the second coroner's jury that convened at 3:00 P.M. on March 15, Kilpatrick and Scharf gave new testimony, and druggist W. H. Wolff testified that a postmortem chemical test had revealed a single crystal that "under the microscope, resembled arsenic." A doctor, J. D. Goodrich, also testified before the panel but was more equivocal as to the presence of poison. "The medical testimony was as guarded and non-committal as modesty and professional abstruseness could make it," the *St. Paul Pioneer and Democrat* reported. Although the paper found the evidence "unsatisfactory," the second coroner's jury wasted no time in finding that Stanislaus died of arsenic poisoning. A grand jury indicted Mrs. Bilansky for the murder of her late husband, and the district judge, Edward Palmer, set a May 23rd trial date. The case would be tried by New Yorkers. Ann's attorney, New York–born and Yale-educated John Brisbin, entered a plea of not guilty; another New York native, Isaac Heard, who became Ramsey County Attorney in 1857, would try the case on the state's behalf.[5]

The trial was conducted at the Ramsey County courthouse, an elegant, four-pillared building just three blocks from the Mississippi River. In his opening statement to the jury, Heard argued that Mrs. Bilansky had purchased arsenic and had "lived on improper terms" with Walker. Saying Mrs. Bilansky and Walker had "occupied the same room," Heard suggested that Walker was not Ann's nephew but was, instead, her illicit lover. In other words, an adulterous affair and a desire "to get rid of a disagreeable husband," to use Heard's words, were the motive for first-degree murder. As part of the prosecution's circumstantial case against Ann Bilansky, Heard made Lucinda Kilpatrick the state's principal witness, charging that Ann's own statements proved an intent to kill. Heard, trying to prove Mrs. Bilansky's guilt beyond a reasonable doubt to the all-male jury, also called housekeeper Rosa Scharf and local doctors, among other witnesses.[6]

On the witness stand, Kilpatrick testified that after purchasing fabric on February 28, she and Ann Bilansky went to Wolff's drugstore. Because the druggist did not offer arsenic powder for sale, the two women walked to the Day and Jenks pharmacy. There, Ann bought ten cents worth of white arsenic powder in a small jar and then asked Kilpatrick for bacon rinds to put it on. According to Kilpatrick, Mrs. Bilansky said her husband wanted the arsenic to kill rats from a neighboring mill, but then said she would not mind "giving him a pill." If her husband "should drop away sudden," Mrs. Bilansky supposedly worried, however, people "would suspect her." Kilpatrick testified that she never saw Ann and Stanislaus Bilansky quarreling, but that she had heard that Ann was planning to go to North Carolina to settle up some business. Ann had been widowed before her marriage to Stanislaus, and her first husband had lived there before dying in a railroad accident. Kilpatrick also testified that Stanislaus had complained of a loss of appetite and a burning sensation in his stomach, and that after his death, Ann Bilansky did not cry and tried to conceal her arsenic purchase. "She asked me to swear I bought the arsenic," Kilpatrick testified, to which Kilpatrick purportedly told Ann: "[I]f they do not find arsenic in the stomach they can do nothing with you." Kilpatrick swore that Mrs. Bilansky's reply to that comment was, "suppose he took it himself." Kilpatrick also testified that Stanislaus told her that he disliked the relationship between Walker and his wife.[7]

Brisbin's cross-examination of Kilpatrick called the veracity of her testimony into question. With Mrs. Bilansky reportedly "smiling behind her handkerchief," her lawyer grilled Kilpatrick, trying to prove that it was Kilpatrick, not Mrs. Bilansky, who had had an amorous relationship with Walker. Mrs. Kilpatrick admitted knowing Walker prior to Stanislaus's final marriage. However, when Brisbin asked Kilpatrick whether she had had "illicit intercourse with a great number of persons," including Walker, prior to her own marriage, Kilpatrick refused to answer. From the bench, Judge Palmer sustained Heard's objections to this whole line of questioning, including a question about whether she had a child from a prior marriage. "Our friendly terms were broken up over a month ago," was all Kilpatrick would say about Walker, adding, "I can't tell the time when the coldness commenced." Brisbin then pointed to several anonymous love letters to show Kilpatrick's relationship with Walker. "I offer to show that during the months of January and February 1859 she sent presents and letters of affection to Walker," Brisbin told Judge Palmer. But when Kilpatrick was shown these letters and asked whether she had written them, she refused to say, and Judge Palmer did not compel an answer. When Brisbin confronted Kilpatrick with a ring and asked Kilpatrick whether she had given it to Walker, she again refused to answer Brisbin's question.[8]

Rosa Scharf's testimony also was put before the jury by the prosecution. Scharf, who boarded with Kilpatrick during the trial, lived with the Bilansky family from March 2, 1859, until shortly after her new employer's death. Scharf testified that she sometimes made soup for Stanislaus, but that only two or three days after she started working for him he became bedridden. She said Stanislaus died in great pain and that Walker—who, she testified, exchanged "glances" with Ann Bilansky—visited Stanislaus's house twice during his illness and early in the morning after he died. Although Scharf said Stanislaus generally ate with his family, she testified that on one occasion, he left the table for "want of appetite" and "got some beer and set it on the stove." Scharf said Ann Bilansky prepared Stanislaus's meals when he was sick, that Stanislaus vomited eight to ten times a day, and that while she never observed any quarreling, Mrs. Bilansky did not treat Stanislaus "as I think a husband should be treated." Scharf testified that Mrs. Bilansky asked her to wash some of Stanislaus's dishes separately, and that while she and Ann were returning from the funeral in a carriage, Ann told her that her husband "must have taken poison." Scharf added that Walker and Mrs. Bilansky whispered to one another and "did not look natural."[9]

The housekeeper also made the scandalous statement that on the night after the funeral Mrs. Bilansky had undressed in front of Walker. According to Scharf, Ann put on her nightclothes in the sleeping room as Walker got ready for bed in the adjoining barroom. The door between the rooms was open, and despite the fact that Scharf and the children were present and that Walker and Mrs. Bilansky slept apart from one another, Scharf was appalled and found something in their "faces and eyes" that looked unnatural. "I asked her the next morning how she could do so before Walker," Scharf testified about the undressing incident. "She said she was so used to him that she didn't mind him," Scharf reported Ann's response. The *Pioneer and Democrat* published this testimony, which convinced the newspaper reporter that Walker and Mrs. Bilansky were having an adulterous affair. Scharf's testimony quickly became the talk of the town and painted Ann Bilansky in the worst possible light.[10]

Before the jury, Scharf also testified that Mrs. Bilansky was planning a trip to the South, that Stanislaus feared she would never return, and that Stanislaus suspected that Walker was not really Ann's nephew. The newlyweds, it seems, were experiencing severe marital problems. Scharf testified that Stanislaus asked her what she thought of his marriage, and that the Bilanskys did not sleep together while she was there. She testified that she overheard Mrs. Bilansky—who, she conceded, treated the children very kindly—say her husband was jealous of Walker. Scharf further testified that when she saw an elderly man walking one day, Ann had pointed him out as being rich. Scharf said she "didn't care for old gentlemen," but that Mrs. Bilansky had said, "if I didn't love him I might give him something to make him sleep himself to death." When Scharf asked what that might be, Ann supposedly said "a good many things," one of which was arsenic, but that one must know "how much to give" so he "wouldn't wake up again." Scharf's testimony laid the foundation for the rest of Heard's case.[11]

The prosecution called several other witnesses at trial in quick succession. The druggist, W. H. Wolff, confirmed that he refused to sell arsenic to Mrs. Bilansky, not out of any suspicion of her but just as a general policy. Stanislaus's son, Benjamin, testified that he went to get Dr. Alfred Berthier but revealed on cross-examination that his father had demanded the tumbler of liquor from him a half-hour before dying. The boy further testified that he had once seen his father's cat catch a five-inch mouse, and that his father had gotten sick after hunting and had threatened to whip him if he ever went to see his own mother. William Prutt, a tailor, said Stanislaus was afraid of dying and complained of headaches, and that Mrs. Bilansky once offered to give away their cat, telling him that she had seen neither a rat nor a mouse. On cross-examination, Prutt admitted drinking ale and smoking at Stanislaus's bar but said he did not make it a "habit" to "get drunk" there. His drinking, he insisted, did not affect his memory, though he acknowledged being "tipsy" and "under the influence of liquor" from time to time. Prutt also recalled that Ann Bilansky had told him that Stanislaus had "abused his constitution by laying out nights" hunting and drinking whiskey.[12]

Stanislaus's treating physician for nine years, Dr. Berthier, also testified at trial, saying that his patient's health was good, though noting that Stanislaus had fallen from his wagon three years earlier. His patient, he said, was not injured by liquor even though he "drank pretty well." Stanislaus, a stout, excitable, and nervous man, the doctor remembered, complained of headaches and frequently came to get medicine to "clear his stomach." When Dr. Berthier saw him in bed before he died, Stanislaus told him he had been taking Graffenburg pills "to keep his bowels open." The doctor advised him to stay on them if they helped. Dr.

Berthier further testified that Mrs. Bilansky told him that before her husband vomited for the first time, he was very angry with her because she would not sleep with him because he had a fever. The doctor said he saw no symptoms of poisoning while initially attending his patient, but thought he had simply eaten too much meat and gotten his feet wet prior to becoming ill. "His face was redder than usual," the doctor recalled on the witness stand.[13]

The defense did its best to call the state's case into doubt and got Dr. Berthier to admit that Stanislaus had a "gloomy disposition," often complained of troubles, and came to see him fifteen to twenty times a year. The doctor said Stanislaus suffered from "hypochondria" and had complained about his lungs and taken several boxes of pills for his bowels. He recalled that Stanislaus told him his wife was going on a trip in March to North Carolina, and that he thought she might not return. Stanislaus "was disposed to be jealous," he said, noting that his patient feared that Walker might accompany his wife. The doctor also testified that Stanislaus had sworn off drinking hard liquor five weeks before dying but had not given up beer and had been fined for selling liquor without a license. At trial, Dr. Berthier confidently stated that sudden abstinence after a long use of liquor makes for a weak, more sensitive stomach. Scoring a point for the defense, Dr. Berthier conceded that it was possible that the liquor drunk by Stanislaus shortly before he died "might have produced death." On redirect, the prosecution got Dr. Berthier to emphasize that Stanislaus had once told his wife that she should not go out with Walker. It is a "free country," Ann Bilansky had supposedly replied, in hearsay testimony based solely on a conversation Berthier had had with his ailing patient.[14]

Since nobody had actually seen Ann Bilansky poison her husband, the next witnesses at trial were sworn to help build the state's circumstantial case against her. William Branch, a neighbor, testified that Stanislaus complained of a "burning heat" in his stomach and that his vomit had food and blood in it. Robert Gibbons, the administrator of Stanislaus's estate, testified that he inventoried the contents of the house but had seen no arsenic or rats in it. The cross-examination of these witnesses, however, was fairly effective. Branch, while testifying that he saw nothing about Stanislaus that showed suicidal tendencies, admitted on cross-examination that Stanislaus was eccentric, moody, and jealous, and "had the blues." "I told him if he didn't stop drinking it would kill him," Branch testified. Likewise, Gibbons admitted on cross-examination that he was present at the inquest and saw nothing odd about Ann Bilansky's conduct. Gibbons also said he made no special examination for rats in the cellar, which he noted had decaying boards.[15]

Two other neighbors also testified for the state. Orrin Branch noticed that Stanislaus's vomit had blood in it, and J. R. Winter testified that on a visit prior to Stanislaus's death he saw no rats. On cross-examination, though, Branch admitted that Stanislaus was trouble-prone, often complained of debts and his inability to pay them, had gotten wet while hunting, and spoke of "sick spells" and "taking pills." Stanislaus even showed him his wooden pill box. Branch also testified that Stanislaus told him that he had heard that Walker had slept with his wife while he was away. Branch testified that he told Stanislaus that he had "no such wife" and was "a jealous hearted man," and that Stanislaus later told him that the man who had said his wife was having an affair had come back and apologized for what he had said. When Stanislaus had been away for awhile, Branch himself admitted wondering aloud whether Stanislaus "hadn't hung himself." He noted only that Stanislaus later reappeared with two packs of cards and a box of cigars in his hands. If Heard was relying on these witnesses to prove his case, he must have been sorely disappointed. J. R. Winter admitted seeing rat-infested potatoes and beets at Stanislaus's house and said that Ann Bilansky never tried to hasten the funeral. Winter also testified that he advised Stanislaus to send for Dr. J. H. Stewart, a prominent local physician, but that Stanislaus had refused. Dr. Stewart's fee—"$15 or so"—was too much for Stanislaus's liking. Portraying Stanislaus in a less than favorable light, Winter called Stanislaus a "singular man" who "used to regret a good deal about other people getting rich at his expense."[16]

When it came time for Heard to lay out the prosecution's medical evidence, he chose not to call Dr. Goodrich to testify at all. Instead,

Dr. Thomas Potts and Dr. William Morton took the stand. A University of Pennsylvania graduate, Dr. Potts testified that he, Dr. Morton, and Dr. Goodrich had done a two-hour postmortem examination in Wolff's store and placed the yellowish brown fluids from Stanislaus's stomach into a glass jar for testing. He said they found a healthy liver and no indications of disease except an "old adhesion" in Stanislaus's right lung. But Stanislaus's stomach and intestines, he noted, had inflammation of recent origin and were consistent with arsenic poisoning. Dr. Morton testified that the adhesion would only have been a mere inconvenience, asserting that the half-dollar-size patches of inflammation on the stomach were caused by poison. Testifying about a battery of chemical tests done in St. Paul and Chicago on the stomach fluid—conducted with substances like nitric acid, lime water, and charcoal and with copper foil, an evaporating dish, and heated glass tubes—Dr. Morton said the tests showed arsenic in quantities sufficient "to destroy life." He also testified that he noticed a garlic smell when heat was applied to the tested fluid as part of what he called the "experiment" and that a microscopic examination revealed the presence of arsenic in the form of "an eight-sided crystal." Saying only two to five grains of arsenic would be lethal, Dr. Morton produced several vials said to contain small quantities of arsenic. If nothing else, it was dramatic medical testimony and very damaging to Ann Bilansky's defense.[17]

The defense, however, was able to take a little steam out of the prosecution's case. Dr. Potts admitted on cross-examination that he had little experience in postmortem examinations and had never performed one on a victim of arsenic poisoning. He also conceded that chronic alcohol abuse or an overdose of pills could have caused the inflammation. In his own testimony, Dr. Morton admitted that of the six known chemical tests used to check for arsenic, two were unreliable, two had failed to produce evidence of arsenic poisoning, and one had not been used at all. Only a "reduction test," using heat, yielded a ring in a test tube that was said to be consistent with the presence of arsenic. After being questioned about hypochondria—described as "a mental depression about some fancied disease"—Dr. Morton also testified that he messed up at least one of the tests by using nitric acid instead of sulfuric acid. He admitted that he did not consider the liquid tests "infallible in a criminal case," and that he had not "applied himself particularly to chemistry." He had never tested for arsenic before, he conceded, and had sold Stanislaus two boxes of Graffenburg pills just a few weeks before his death. These pills, if taken all at once, he said, could have been lethal.[18]

The prosecution rested its case on May 28 after calling a Polish immigrant, Frank Churneck, who Lucinda Kilpatrick encouraged to testify. Through an interpreter, Churneck said he worked for Stanislaus for six weeks, observed quarreling in English that he did not understand, and saw Ann Bilansky go into John Walker's shanty between 3:00 A.M. and 5:00 A.M. while Stanislaus was away. At this critical juncture, Brisbin, the lead defense lawyer, was ill, but Judge Palmer ordered the case to proceed anyway. Thus, it fell to Brisbin's associate, A. L. Williams, to lay out the defense's case. "I can't believe, it is not possible, after having heard this testimony to come to the conclusion that this defendant is guilty," Williams argued in his opening statement. "Now what is the proof, where has there been any evidence to establish that?" Williams asked, alluding to the prosecution's suggestion of a romantic link between his client and Walker. "[N]one whatever," he concluded. The defense, Williams said, would prove that the Bilansky house was near a flour mill and had been plagued by rats after a house cat had been given away. The defense also promised to raise questions about Stanislaus's business dealings and his health, suggesting that he may have committed suicide. Twenty-six-year-old John Walker would take the stand himself to deny having had any improper relationship with his forty-year-old aunt.[19]

The defense's first witness, Stanislaus's second wife, Ellen Truett, testified that she had lived with Stanislaus for a decade, that he was a depressive, violent drunk, and that he had been obsessed about dying in the month of March. She said that he was sedentary around the house, that she had left him three years earlier, and that she had not seen him for over a year until he unexpectedly came to her house two weeks before he died. He had "no business at my house," she testified, describing how he had knocked on the door and "walked in and helped himself to a chair." She recounted how he had come to beg forgiveness for every-thing he had said or done and repeatedly asked her to see his new wife. But Truett, who by the time of Ann Bilansky's trial had taken custody of the three children, refused to do so. She told Stanislaus only that she forgave him, that he should treat his new wife "better than he had me," and that he "ought to die a better man." "He was a very strange man," she testified at trial, telling jurors how she had seen Ann Bilansky cry on the way home from the funeral.[20]

Other witnesses were also called to buttress the defense case. Ten-year-old Benjamin Bilansky testified that he never saw John Walker and Ann Bilansky go to bed together, never told his father that as had once been suggested, and that the family home was infested with rats. A neighbor, G. B. Galinska, spoke in detail of Stanislaus's money concerns, saying Stanislaus often said he "had as soon die as live," and that Stanis-laus owed $200 for which he was paying 36 percent interest. Defense witnesses also further corroborated Stanislaus's financial problems, tes-tified that Stanislaus had a solitary nature and was a heavy drinker, and said that they had seen evidence of rats in his home, gnawed vegetables, for example. "He was subject to the blues," Galinska said, adding that Stanislaus had once asked him if he had any traps to loan him to catch rats. The new owner of Stanislaus's house, Stephen Tuttle, testified that he saw no trouble between Stanislaus and Ann Bilansky, and that he saw Walker frequently and had never seen anything improper between him and Mrs. Bilansky. One of Ann's acquaintances, Nora Davis, also testi-fied that she never saw anything improper, and that after the arrest of John Walker and Ann Bilansky, Lucinda Kilpatrick had said that she hoped Walker would never get out and that both he and Mrs. Bilansky would "swing."[21]

Because Ann Bilansky never took the stand, John Walker was the crucial defense witness. On the stand, he testified that after Ann came to Minnesota, she first stayed at the Merchant's Hotel. He testified that his aunt came to St. Paul only after he wrote her several times when he was sick, but when she did come, eventually moved in with him until she got married at Stanislaus's house. "I was in the habit of visiting once a week, usually on Sunday afternoon," Walker testified at trial about his contacts with Ann. Walker vehemently denied having any "improper intercourse" or "improper intimacy" with the woman he matter-of-factly called his aunt. He recounted how Stanislaus had come home wet and shivering after hunting, and how he had given Stanislaus a half tumbler of liquor and some arrowroot in a tin cup to make him feel better. "He complained of sickness until he died," Walker testified. Walker said Stanislaus told him he would not see Dr. Stewart, who had treated Walker for typhoid fever, out of a concern for being overcharged. Walker said he paid for the burial plot because Ann Bilansky had no money, that she was perfectly composed at the inquest and grieved by Stanislaus's death, and that Lucinda Kilpatrick fed Stanislaus a plate of food and a bowl of soup on the Monday before he died. Walker added that he and Kilpatrick "fell out a short time" ago, and that Stanislaus had told him that he gave the family's cat away because he was going to poison the rats instead.[22]

The defense also put on its own scientific evidence through St. Paul's city physician, Canadian-born Joseph Vervais, who had studied chemistry while in the British army. Dr. Vervais testified that the post-mortem examination of Stanislaus Bilansky's body was defective, particularly in a criminal case, as it failed to examine and analyze Stanislaus's brain, spinal marrow, rectum, bladder, and genital organs, and the blood of his liver. "I should not think it sufficient to find the cause of death," Vervais concluded. The test that allegedly detected the presence of arsenic in a ring might have been flawed, Vervais testified, saying additional tests were warranted but not done. "These rings might have formed by overheating the glass. The first rings amount to nothing," Vervais said, testifying that he was not satisfied any arsenic was present. Vervais also suggested that Stanislaus's death might have been caused by cholera, a disease, he said, that resembles arsenic poisoning.[23]

After the defense rested its case, Judge Palmer instructed the jury. "This is a serious and solemn duty—a duty more serious and more solemn than I have ever before, and hope we may ever again be called upon to perform," he began. "The issue in this case involves the life of a human being," he said, emphasizing that Ann Bilansky was charged with an awful crime for "the purpose of illicit intercourse with another" and with having carried out the crime "coolly, deliberately, and with the most subtle instrument—poison." The jury deliberations began mid-day on June 3, just a day after the nearby flooding Mississippi River had risen nineteen inches in a few hours. Sitting on the twelve-man jury, which took less than six hours to reach its verdict, was Justus Ramsey, the brother of Minnesota's soon-to-be governor Alexander Ramsey. As Ann Bilansky sat silently in the tense courtroom, the jury entered, and its foreman read the verdict on the charge of first-degree murder: "Guilty." After the jurors were polled one by one, the word "guilty" was called out again in quick succession. At that point, the defense, left with no other option, moved to arrest the judgment and for a new trial. The new trial motion was based principally on the objections Judge Palmer had sustained to the defense's questions of Lucinda Kilpatrick and Rosa Scharf on cross-examination.[24]

Judge Palmer heard these motions on June 16 but denied them less than a week later. Ann Bilansky had already been convicted in the judge's courtroom, and Palmer saw no reason to order a new trial. He, after all, had just ruled on the very legal issues that the defense now raised on Mrs. Bilansky's behalf. The motion for a new trial then went up to the Minnesota Supreme Court, where Justice Charles Flandrau sat in judgment. Before the state's highest court, Brisbin argued that his client should not be subjected to the death penalty under a customary doctrine of English law called benefit of clergy, which was intended to spare literate persons from death sentences. Brisbin also argued that Judge Palmer committed reversible error by failing to require Kilpatrick to answer questions about her relationship with Walker. The Minnesota Supreme Court, however, refused to overturn the trial court's rulings. It too saw no errors warranting a new trial.[25]

In an opinion authored by Justice Flandrau, the state's highest court affirmed Ann Bilansky's first-degree murder conviction on July 23, 1859. "She was indicted for murder, and the evidence discloses that the murdered party was her husband," Flandrau wrote at the outset of his opinion. The court ruled that the benefit of clergy doctrine was unavailable to Mrs. Bilansky, and that the trial court "was right in holding that the crime was murder in the first degree." The Minnesota Supreme Court also ruled that because "[f]ornication and adultery are made crimes by our statutes," Lucinda Kilpatrick could refuse to answer questions that might lead to self-incrimination. "[I]t may well be questioned whether the interrogations" that were put to Kilpatrick, Flandrau ruled, "did not tend to show an illicit intercourse between Walker and herself." "This case does not disclose any abuse of the court's discretion in excluding the testimony," Flandrau stated. "In this case, the sentence can be but one penalty," the court ruled, yet added that "as we are wholly unacquainted with the facts of the case, and the condition, physically or morally, of the prisoner, we prefer remanding the case to the district court for sentence."[26]

With hopes of a new trial dashed, Ann Bilansky acted out of desperation. On the evening of July 25, 1859, an inattentive jailor left her alone in a hallway after dinner. While the jailor was procuring some keys from an adjoining office, she escaped through a basement window. After fleeing to the Lake Como area and hiding in some tall grass, she eventually made contact with Walker, her alleged paramour. He gave her some men's clothes to wear, but a plan to transport her out of state was foiled by police after handbills offering a $500 reward for her capture were distributed by the county sheriff. They called attention to the escape of a "murderess" who was "tall in stature," "very talkative" with a "masculine" voice, and who had "lapped" teeth, "grey eyes, light hair," and a "Roman nose." Authorities arrested Walker and Mrs. Bilansky just a week after her escape as the two of them were walking to St. Anthony. Walker was jailed for over a month, but a Ramsey County grand jury refused to indict him on September 13. With Willis Gorman now acting as her attorney, Ann Bilansky reappeared before the trial judge on December 2, 1859, for sentencing. "If I die in this case, I die an innocent woman. I don't think I have had a fair and just trial," she told the court. Amid her sobs, Judge Edward Palmer announced that she would be "hung by the neck" until death and ordered that she be put in solitary confinement for one month. "May God, in His infinite compassion, have mercy upon your soul," he intoned. Judge Palmer directed the sheriff to select the execution site, and he forwarded the certified record of the case to Governor Henry Sibley, who had the legal responsibility of fixing the execution date.[27]

In the wake of the sentencing, tremendous pressure was put on Sibley to commute the death sentence. On the very day that Ann Bilansky's conviction was affirmed by the Minnesota Supreme Court, Justice Flandrau penned a personal letter to Sibley asking for clemency for her. "I cannot leave town without saying a word to you," his letter began, explaining that "the sentence of the law will necessarily be death." "It is my firm conviction that a strict adherence to the penal code will have a salutary influence in checking crime in the State," Flandrau wrote, "but it rather shocks my private sense of humanity to commence by inflicting the extreme penalty on a woman." Flandrau was convinced of Ann Bilansky's guilt, but wanted Sibley to be merciful. "I believe she was guilty," Flandrau wrote, "but nevertheless hope that if you can consistently with your view of Justice and duty, you will commute the sentence which will be pronounced, to imprisonment." Unwilling to set an execution date, Sibley, a Democrat, let his term expire on December 31, 1859, leaving the political problem to his Republican successor, Alexander Ramsey. A popular politician, Ramsey had served as Minnesota's first territorial governor from 1849 to 1853, and was elected mayor of St. Paul in 1855. Though they remained close friends, Sibley had beaten Ramsey in the hotly contested 1857 gubernatorial election by a mere 240 votes.[28]

Following the imposition of Ann Bilansky's death sentence, strenuous efforts were made at the Minnesota Legislature to abolish capital punishment. On December 13, 1859, less than a week after the legislative session convened, the Minnesota House of Representatives asked its Judiciary Committee to "inquire into the propriety of abolishing capital punishment." This resolution was introduced by Representative Henry Acker. The Judiciary Committee produced its report later that month, and its members unanimously recommended that capital punishment should be retained, citing six reasons. First, premeditated killing "ought to be distinguished from every other crime by a distinctive punishment." Second, "the universal feeling of mankind, in all ages and all places, has been that he who had willfully shed the blood of his fellow, had thereby forfeited his own." Third, "the death of the murderer is sanctioned by divine authority." Fourth, abolishing capital punishment would only "increase the crime of murder." Fifth, the penal code "almost precludes the possibility of an innocent person suffering the death penalty," especially because of the governor's pardoning or commuting power. And finally, "the abolition of capital punishment would lead to what is termed 'Lynch law.'"[29]

In spite of those legislators' views, a bill was introduced in the house of representatives on January 18, 1860, by Representative G. W. Sweet, to prohibit the execution of females. It provided, "No woman or girl convicted of murder in the first degree, shall suffer the penalty of death, but that punishment in such cases shall be imprisonment in the State prison for life." On the same day, a bill to abolish capital punishment altogether was also introduced in the Minnesota Senate while another house bill sought to require executions to be conducted in private in jails. The bill to outlaw the death penalty, authored by Senator J. H. Stevens, would not be debated in the senate until early March, as the legislative session drew to a close. The bill to abolish public executions was vigorously resisted by death penalty opponents and was tabled by the house less than a month after its introduction.[30]

When Governor Ramsey took office on January 1, 1860, he did not make an immediate decision about Ann Bilansky's fate. While she languished in solitary confinement, though, one of the prosecution's key witnesses, Rosa Scharf, killed herself. Found in a comatose state in early January 1860 by a new family that she was working for, Scharf died of an overdose of laudanum. She had purchased the laudanum from Dr. Morton's drugstore a few days before, and an empty vial of it was found in her room. At the coroner's inquest, one doctor testified that Scharf's symptoms were similar to those produced by arsenic. The very night of Scharf's death, she had visited the Kilpatricks. Andrew Kilpatrick testified that Scharf had asked him what would happen to Ann Bilansky. These events, however, had no sway on Ramsey's decision regarding appeals to spare Ann's life.[31]

Ramsey was lobbied intensely, of course, by those seeking to save Mrs. Bilansky from the gallows. The editor of a St. Cloud newspaper, Jane Grey Swisshelm, urged Ramsey to commute the death sentence in no uncertain terms. A vocal opponent of slavery and one of the few female newspaper editors of her day, Swisshelm wrote: "How long shall our Statute Books be disgraced by this code of vengeance and blood; and the most ferocious passions of the human breast fed and fattened in the name of Justice? One execution begets a dozen murders; and the code of 'blood for blood' works around in a circle." Citing the "savage instincts of savage humanity" that led "the Chippewa to follow his Sioux foe to avenge the death of his murdered relatives," Swisshelm decried the death penalty, calling it a "code of blood." "No civilized society holds that the individual has a right to avenge murder, and as the powers of organized society are simply those delegated to it by the individual members, whence comes this right to society?" Swisshelm asked rhetorically. "The stream cannot rise above its fountain; and if the individual has no right to take life, no collection or combination of individuals can have such right," Swisshelm wrote.[32]

Although the fifth commandment says, "Thou shalt not kill," the Old Testament contains many passages that were invoked in the nineteenth century by the defenders of capital punishment. Exodus contains the oft-quoted law of *lex talionis*—"life for life, eye for eye, tooth for tooth"—and passages like, "Anyone who strikes a man and so causes his death, must die." Swisshelm attacked death penalty proponents' reliance on such religious passages. "It will not do to go back to the Old Testament law given to Noah and Moses," Swisshelm wrote. "The government to which these laws applied were theocracies—the executives acted simply as the agents of the Divine Will; and the Giver of life has right to take it by any agency He sees fit to employ. But this Government is based upon the will of the people." Swisshelm explained that the modern state, which "denies the Higher Law as supreme authority," lacks the authority to kill its citizens because the government has "no more right to execute a murder than the murderer had to execute his victim." "If Mrs. Bilansky is hung," Swisshelm railed, "Judge Palmer, Governor Ramsey, the Sheriff, and all aiders and abettors are as much murderers as she can possibly be, and as much deserving of the gallows."[33]

In spite of these pleas for clemency and attacks upon his character, Ramsey issued Ann Bilansky's death warrant at the end of January. He instructed Ramsey County's sheriff to carry out the sentence between the hours of 10:00 A.M. and 2:00 P.M. on Friday, March 23, 1860. In those days, by custom or superstition, executions were usually conducted at midday on Fridays, and Mrs. Bilansky's would be no exception. St. Paul's *Pioneer and Democrat* commended Ramsey's decision, which was heavily influenced by his brother Justus's belief in Ann's guilt. "There is no doubt of her guilt," the newspaper said, "and we can conceive of no sufficient reason why the law should not be allowed to take its course, or why anyone should desire for a commutation of the sentence." Ironically, Swisshelm, the divorced, single mother who wrote anti–death penalty essays in the 1840s, felt much differently about capital punishment after the Dakota Conflict when it came to punishing the Indians. "Exterminate the wild beasts," she demanded then in full agreement with Ramsey's views, saying "Uncle Samuel" could spare more than thirty-eight Indians to "atone" for the murdered settlers.[34]

Despite Governor Ramsey's views of Ann Bilansky's guilt, the Minnesota Legislature acted quickly to try to save her. On January 31, 1860, the house of representatives debated Representative Sweet's bill providing that no "woman or girl" be executed, with Representative Henry Acker calling for the total abolition of capital punishment. Acker moved that the word "person" be substituted for the words "woman or girl," but Sweet objected to the amendment as being designed "to kill the bill." After the amendment passed on a close vote, Acker moved that the amended bill be reported to the house with the recommendation that it pass. This motion carried by a tally of twenty-eight to twenty-five, although the amended version of Sweet's bill was defeated by a vote of twenty-two to thirty-three on the afternoon of January 31.[35]

The next day, February 1, 1860, Acker introduced a new abolitionist bill to commute Ann Bilansky's sentence to life imprisonment at the state prison. It was a seesaw battle. On February 3, the house of representatives voted down Acker's bill, but five days later, Sweet, believing the hanging of a woman would be a disgrace, successfully moved to take up Acker's bill again. Although some legislators opposed the bill because it attempted to usurp judicial authority and the governor's pardoning power, Acker's bill finally passed the house by a vote of forty-one to thirty-two. But the battle did not end there. Abolitionists did not gain a clear victory until after a motion to reconsider that vote failed by a vote of thirty-three to forty-one. After Acker's bill passed the house, the *Pioneer and Democrat* reported that capital punishment opponents "chuckled, and not very quietly either," because one provision in the bill prevented capital punishment altogether.[36]

On February 9, Acker's bill was referred to the senate, where one senator pledged to use all of his "energies and power" to secure the bill's passage. Soon thereafter, though, the senate struck out the section of Acker's bill abolishing capital punishment in its entirety. On the senate floor, some legislators, including Senators William McKusick and Thomas Cowan, emphasized that they opposed the execution of women. Cowan, for example, argued that "it was an outrage on public sentiment to make a poor, friendless woman the first victim in the State, to the death penalty." Other legislators, like Senator J. H. Stewart, opposed efforts to commute Ann Bilansky's sentence. Arguing that she "had a full, fair and impartial trial," Stewart wanted the law to take its course because Mrs. Bilansky was "a devil incarnate." Ultimately, the senate passed Acker's bill, as amended, by a vote of nineteen to thirteen. After much legislative wrangling over the house's subsequent refusal to concur in the senate amendment, both the house and the senate eventually approved the bill to commute Ann Bilansky's sentence to life imprisonment.[37]

Before Governor Ramsey announced whether he would veto Acker's bill, state senators debated a bill to abolish capital punishment, sometimes in a highly caustic fashion. Senator D. C. Evans of Blue Earth County, for instance, proposed that those who favored capital punishment "might have a waiver inserted for their personal benefit." Not surprisingly, this tongue-in-cheek suggestion was rejected, and on a fairly evenly divided vote the abolitionist bill failed to pass and was tabled, leaving only Acker's bill, which itself had come under fire, to be considered by Ramsey. Senator J. S. Winn from Winona actually wanted Acker's bill retitled "A bill for the encouragement of prostitution and murder." "The object she had in view of getting rid of her husband," Winn contended, "was that she might live with her paramour, with whom she had for a long time been associated on terms of disgraceful intimacy, during the time her husband was living." This acerbic amendment, though, went down in flames by a vote of thirty to two. The debate over Ann Bilansky's life was too serious for such antics.[38]

On March 8, Ramsey vetoed Acker's bill. The proposed commutation was contrary to sound public policy, he said, citing Mrs. Bilansky's "full, fair and impartial trial." Pointing to a "fearful" rise in crime and his dislike of lynch mobs, Ramsey recalled the horrible nature of what the jury had found she had done: "She sat by the bedside of her husband," Ramsey said, "not to foster, but to slay." "She watched without emotion the tortures she caused," he lectured, "and, by and by, administered no healing medicine, no cooling draught, but ever under guise of love and tender care, renewed her cup of death." A husband, he added, "will not suspect that she who has sworn to love and cherish will betray and destroy; and it shocks the moral sense of the whole community to believe it." Ramsey found the convicted killer's motive particularly egregious. "The reckless woman," he wrote, "having violated her marriage vows, and betrayed her husband's bed, hesitated not to sacrifice her husband's life." The *Pioneer and Democrat* congratulated Ramsey on his "good sense" and "sound statesmanship" in vetoing the measure, and Acker's last-ditch effort to override the governor's veto failed to garner the requisite two-thirds vote of house members.[39]

By then, Governor Ramsey had little sympathy for Ann Bilansky, particularly in light of his brother's views. "The approaching execution of Mrs. Bilansky," he recorded in his diary in March, "subjects me to much annoyance on the part of persons asking her commutation."

Clemency petitions had poured into Ramsey's office. One request asked for mercy for "a friendless, helpless woman" whose guilt was "doubted by many good people," while another beseeched Ramsey "not to uphold the gallows." John Brisbin's petition said he could now prove that Stanislaus Bilansky once tried to poison himself, and Willis Gorman's petition called attention to the "undue prejudice" against Ann Bilansky in the press and the dispute between doctors as to the presence of arsenic. "I firmly believe her to be innocent," Gorman ended his petition. Just six days before her execution, Ann Bilansky herself even wrote a four-page letter to Ramsey, saying she had "patiently waited" to prove her innocence after being "imperfectly and unfairly tried." Her husband suffered from "melancholy," she pled, charging that the chief witnesses against her were influenced by "evil motives." On the day before her execution, Ramsey County's district attorney—the man who prosecuted her—even wrote that he had "grave and serious doubts as to whether the defendant has had a fair trial." These pleas, however, had no effect on Ramsey's outlook on the case. The execution, he determined, would go forward.[40]

The *Pioneer and Democrat* also wanted Ann Bilansky hanged but called upon Ramsey "to make the execution as private as executions usually are in States where public executions are prohibited." The authorities obliged or—more accurately, perhaps—tried as best they could to make Bilansky's hanging as private as they thought they could under the circumstances. In preparation for the execution, a large fence was erected around the gallows in St. Paul's courthouse square. That decision, made by Ramsey County Sheriff Aaron Tullis in light of changing mores, was widely praised. The *St. Paul Pioneer Press* applauded Tullis for "rendering the execution as private as the means at his command permitted." Efforts to exclude the public from watching the hanging, however, were largely ineffectual. The building of the fence drew many curious onlookers who discussed the approaching execution, and when the structure was finished, the gallows posts were still visible to people on the street. Spectators only a few feet above street level had a fair view inside the enclosure.[41]

By the time Ann Bilansky was slated for execution, the privatization of American executions was well under way. By 1835, five northeastern states had enacted laws forbidding public executions out of a growing sense that public executions were brutalizing and demoralizing to society and in response to America's anti-gallows movement, which had gained strength in the mid-1800s. By 1860, nineteen states, including the midwestern states of Illinois, Indiana, Iowa, Kansas, Michigan, and Ohio, had outlawed public executions. Bilansky's execution would be semiprivate, not because any Minnesota law required it, but because Sheriff Tullis decided to exclude the general public. Ramsey himself got a petition in mid-March signed by thirteen public schoolteachers, all begging that if Mrs. Bilansky's execution must take place, it should be carried out in private. "[T]he spectacle of a public execution," the petition urged, "would exercise a highly injurious effect on the sensitive and impressionable minds of children and youth."[42]

On Ann Bilansky's execution day, March 23, 1860, the crowd started assembling early in the morning. Its members stood on stone piles, roofs, and any elevated spot in proximity to the scaffold so that they could see within the enclosure. Carriages and hay wagons clogged up streets, and St. Paul's leading newspaper reported it was "a curious crowd" made up mostly "of persons of German and Irish birth." At ten o'clock that morning, the Pioneer Guard, wearing heavy overcoats and fatigue caps, marched into the square, which was by then thronged with people. They carried ball cartridges in readiness for an emergency, and only after much trouble were they able to clear the crowd from the vicinity of the fence. The line of sentinels then formed, whose duty it was to keep all spectators at least twenty feet from the enclosure.[43]

At 10:15 A.M., Sheriff Tullis led Ann Bilansky out of the jail amid high winds. She wore a black robe and a veil over her head. "Don't let a crowd see me," she pleaded with her escort before leaving the jail. "I am willing to meet my God, but I don't want to have a crowd see me die." But it was too late for that. The crowd outside had already swelled to between fifteen hundred and two thousand people. The short procession from the jail to the enclosure, located just across the public square, was anything but private. Once within the enclosure, the procession ascended the steps of the gallows. The heads of those on the platform were then visible to anyone at street level. Others, who had perched themselves atop roofs, carriages, and hay wagons, enjoyed a virtually un-obstructed view of the entire proceedings. In all, about one hundred persons entered the enclosure, including some twenty-five to thirty women. These women, some carrying crying infants, had gained admittance before the gate could be shut.[44]

Additional crowd members, not gaining admittance, "ran the guard" to obtain positions at the fence. Through numerous small openings, these spectators were able to get as good a view of the execution as those inside. After five minutes of prayer, Ann Bilansky made her dying declaration, "I die without having had any mercy shown me, or justice. I die for the good of my soul, and not for murder. . . . Your courts of justice are not courts of justice—but I will yet get justice in Heaven." "I am a guilty woman," she added, "but not of this murder." Then, after forgiving everyone who "did me wrong" and uttering her last words, "Lord Jesus Christ receive my soul," a black cloth bag was drawn over her head and the rope fixed around her neck. By and large, the spectators were solemn when the execution was carried out and quietly dispersed after the drop fell. Only a few onlookers took pieces of the rope for mementos or as "a remedy for diseases." Ann Bilansky had become the first—and to date, the only—woman executed in Minnesota.[45]

Mrs. Bilansky's execution stirred great controversy at the time. Right after it, the *Daily Minnesotian* came out "furiously and strong" for capital punishment, labeling death penalty opponents "very weak persons, who allow their nerves alike to control their judgments and their tears." The *Pioneer and Democrat* expressed its general support for capital punishment but registered a dissent to the *Daily Minnesotian*'s pointed attack. "[M]uch of the best talent in our land has been and is arrayed against the infliction of death for crime," the editors said, describing the "most disgusting feature" of the hanging as "the eagerness and persistency with which females sought to obtain eligible places to view the dying agonies of one of their own sex." The *Pioneer and Democrat* further opined the day after the execution that Stanislaus's "reputation for wealth" had been the "inducement" for Ann Bilansky's marriage and that while intoxicated at times, Stanislaus was "a harmless, inoffensive man." Just a few months earlier, that very newspaper had recoiled at what it called a "cold blooded" and "cunning" murder "apparently without any adequate motive." "It could not have been for money for the man was poor; nor to get rid of matrimonial chains which were no restraint on the inclinations of the murderess," it had previously concluded.[46]

Even in the twenty-first century, the events surrounding Ann Bilansky's execution—and unanswered questions about her guilt or innocence—continue to spark debate. St. Paul's Great American History Theatre recently produced a play called "A Piece of the Rope" about Bilansky's hanging. "What was fascinating about the story," Excelsior playwright Jeffrey Hatcher noted, pointing out that Bilansky had been called a "harlot" by the press before her death, "was that it was a murder mystery that seemed to touch on a number of aspects of society at the time." "It touched on law; it touched on science, politics, journalism," Hatcher said. A new article titled "Justice in Heaven," authored by Matthew Cecil and published in *Minnesota History* magazine, says that "[i]t is impossible from a vantage point more than 130 years distant to determine with certainty whether justice was served by the conviction of Ann Bilansky." After closely examining the evidence, all Cecil can say is that Ann Bilansky's trial was "clearly flawed" and that reasonable doubt exists as to the murder charge against her because "[w]itnesses with questionable motives and shaky scientific evidence made up the majority of the prosecution case." The truth, in all likelihood, will never be known: Stanislaus Bilansky went to his grave, whether by illness, suicide, or premeditated poisoning, and his wife, Ann Bilansky, went to her death, all the while professing her innocence.[47]

Ann Bilansky's execution, like Karla Faye Tucker's death by lethal injection, represented a rare American phenomenon: the state-sanctioned killing of a woman. From colonial times to the present, only a very small percentage—about 3 percent of all American executions—have been of women. In fact, of the over 3,500 people now on death row, only a few dozen are women. The only thing that seems clear about the Bilansky case is that Ann Bilansky's execution left an indelible impression on those who watched it. Nicholas Pottgeiser, a spectator, recalled the event vividly even four decades later. "I was determined to see that hanging, and when I failed to get on the inside, I pushed a large knot out of one of the boards in the fence and seated on a barrel I took it all in; but I don't know as I would care to see another," he recounted. "I can see that woman yet," he said, "as she looked when brought from the jail and marched to the gallows."[48]

CHAPTER 4

The Gallows Reconsidered

Executions versus Life Sentences

The death penalty was imported to the American colonies from England, where executions took place at locales like Tyburn and the Tower of London. Many English executions were of lower-class thieves or murderers, but others, like the beheading of King Henry VIII's second wife, Anne Boleyn, showed that even royalty and women were not exempt from death sentences. Boleyn, who failed to bear the king a male heir, was charged with adultery and treason and executed in 1536, with Henry VIII marrying eleven days later. The death penalty, in fact, has been inflicted throughout history on women and men alike for a wide array of offenses. In the American colonies, public hangings were used to punish murder and rape, rebellion and witchcraft, and blasphemy and sodomy. Although Minnesota's constitution is silent on the death penalty issue and no capital punishment statute currently exists in the state, what motivated lawmakers to allow executions in years past can only be ascertained through historical records. What can be said definitively of executions like those of Anne Boleyn and Ann Bilansky is that they sparked enormous public controversy. In the case of Ann Bilansky, her hanging triggered an anti–death penalty crusade in the heartland, in Minnesota—a state that authorized capital punishment from its inception.[1]

The abolitionist movement, globally, dates to 1763, when a young Italian jurist, Cesare Beccaria, published a short treatise called *On Crimes and Punishments*. Beccaria advocated penal confinement as a substitute for the death penalty, and his book drew widespread attention in both Europe and the United States. Thirty years later, in 1793, Pennsylvania became the first state to divide criminal homicide into two categories, with the imposition of the death penalty restricted to persons convicted of first-degree murder. This law and others like it gradually narrowed the categories of death-eligible offenses and served as the precursor to the abolitionist movement's first victory: the repeal of the death penalty in Michigan in 1847. That triumph in Michigan was followed by the death penalty's abolition in Rhode Island in 1852, and in Wisconsin a year later. The Minnesota Territory, when formed in 1849, had adopted "the laws in force in the Territory of Wisconsin at the date of the admission of the State of Wisconsin." Because Wisconsin law at that time provided that murderers "shall suffer the punishment of death," the imposition of the death penalty was permitted by law in Minnesota from the very start.[2]

After Ann Bilansky's execution in 1860, many prominent Minnesotans continued to push for the death penalty's abolition, no doubt spurred on by successes in other states and by St. Paul's well-publicized hanging. On January 15, 1861, Representative J. D. Hoskins led the way by introducing a legislative resolution, asking that the House Judiciary Committee "bring in a bill abolishing capital punishment." His resolution, however, was voted down with ten "ayes" versus twenty "nays." The same year, the Minnesota Legislature also debated whether executions should be done publicly or privately. Because no new law was passed, though, local county sheriffs retained control over executions. The most memorable push came four legislative sessions later when Representative William Colvill, who led the First Minnesota Regiment's famous charge at Gettysburg, introduced his own bill to abolish capital punishment. An imposing, six-foot-five-inch war hero, Colvill survived the deadly battle in which his regiment suffered one of the highest casualty rates of any military unit in the entire war. Even Colvill's war hero status, however, could not carry the day. The execution of the thirty-eight Dakota Indians in Mankato was still in recent memory, and Minnesotans were not ready to do away with death as a punishment. Colvill's 1865 bill never even reached a house vote.[3]

After these decisive legislative failures, still-hopeful death penalty foes renewed their efforts in 1868, a year that would bring more success. On February 3, Representative N. H. Miner of Stearns County introduced a bill to abolish the death penalty in all cases unless jurors specifically prescribed the punishment of death. Convicted murderers not sentenced to death would receive life imprisonment at "hard labor," be isolated in solitary confinement for twelve days each year, and during that time, be forced to subsist on a "bread and water diet." Miner's bill was given little chance of success, but just five days after being proposed, it passed the house of representatives by a vote of twenty-eight to eight. Several newspapers quickly criticized the house's action, with one newspaper calling Miner's bill "an encouragement to lynch law."[4]

However, Miner would not give up. On February 17, 1868, it was announced that national abolitionist leader Marvin Bovee, a lifelong Democrat, would come to Minnesota to speak out against capital punishment. A former Wisconsin state senator, Bovee had successfully led the movement to abolish Wisconsin's death penalty in 1853 and was much in demand as a speaker. He spent months at a time on the road crusading against American death penalty laws, traveling to nearly half the states of the Union and giving over twelve hundred public speeches. These trips cost Bovee thousands of dollars, but he freely expended his own money in support of what he called a "grand cause." In 1867, Bovee had succeeded in getting the Illinois Legislature to pass a bill he drafted that gave juries the right to punish first-degree murderers with the death penalty, a sentence of not less than fourteen years, or life imprisonment. It was not an outright victory, but Bovee believed that if jurors were allowed to sentence convicted murderers, they would impose punishments less than death.[5]

Because of his success in Illinois, Bovee was sought after by Minnesota's governor, William Marshall, and other state officials to promote a similar law in Minnesota. Invited to speak to both houses of the Minnesota Legislature in mid-January 1868, Bovee accepted. A New York collaborator, anti-gallows activist Gerrit Smith, even sent Bovee $50 toward the "Minnesota campaign." Bovee's opposition to capital

Marvin Bovee. Photograph courtesy of the State Historical Society of Wisconsin (X3) 7874.

punishment was resolute. Once calling the death penalty "a dark spot resting on us Christians," Bovee expressed concern that "[a] life once taken can never be restored." He would now lecture in the hall of the Minnesota House of Representatives. The *St. Paul Daily Pioneer* did not favor his views but recommended that its readers listen to what he had to say. "The discussion of the subject," proclaimed the paper, "can do no harm."[6]

On the evening of February 19, Representative Miner called the meeting to order, and Governor Marshall introduced Bovee, the Waukesha County, Wisconsin, farmer turned anti-gallows crusader. In addressing his audience, Bovee said that "men are apt to nourish prejudices imbibed in childhood." "They don't like to change their views without good reasons," he said, "but when they have those reasons, they should not fear to change." The government, Bovee argued, should not have the power to take human life, and Bovee said that neither Michigan, Rhode Island, nor Wisconsin had seen crime increase since abolishing the gallows. "Abolish it," he asserted, speaking of capital punishment, "and it would bring better men to the jury box." The following day, the *St. Paul Daily Pioneer* conceded that Bovee had made an "eloquent" appeal for abolition. The *St. Paul Dispatch*, a self-styled "radical Republican" newspaper, was not as impressed. It described Bovee as "an interminable old bore."[7]

On March 4, the state senate passed Miner's bill by a vote of thirteen to three. An amendment was offered to the bill a day later, however, that sought to make the bill inapplicable to offenses already committed. After the amendment was accepted by unanimous consent, the bill passed again. The house of representatives quickly concurred with the amendment, and Governor Marshall signed the bill into law on March 5, 1868. The law, requiring jurors to affirmatively vote for death sentences, made life sentences the norm. The *St. Paul Dispatch*, displeased at the passage of the new law, mocked Bovee even as it refused to give him any credit for the law's passage. "The 'man in the moon' had fully as much influence on the Minnesota Legislature as Mr. Bovee," it said. The paper, referring to Bovee, harshly reported: "He appeared here after the bill had been introduced, reported upon, discussed and the members committed for and against it. Eight members of the legislature, by actual count listened to his speech, and the only effect it had was to disgust them with the subject." "If he had arrived here two weeks earlier the bill would have been defeated," it said sarcastically.[8]

Ironically, Minnesota's next hanging, of farmer Andreas Roesch, took place just one day after Miner's 1868 law took effect. To Roesch's great misfortune, the new law did not apply to "any act done, nor offense committed" prior to its passage. Consequently, the law did not invalidate his death sentence. Because Governor Marshall failed to intervene, Roesch, a convicted killer from Lafayette, was hanged in St. Peter, Minnesota, on March 6, 1868. Although those wishing to never see another execution in Minnesota were unable to save Roesch's life, the abolitionist movement had achieved its first significant victory: the presumptive punishment in murder cases would now be a life sentence, not death. In fact, after the enactment of the 1868 law, no other state resident except Roesch would be executed under the auspices of state authority for the next sixteen years. On January 18, 1873, a Becker County jury found an Indian named Bobolink guilty of first-degree murder and recommended death, in one of the few cases where a death penalty was recommended by jurors under the 1868 law. However, Bobolink later suspiciously died in jail of what was termed "the quick consumption," making an official state-sanctioned execution unnecessary.[9]

The heinous nature of Roesch's crime most likely accounts for the Minnesota Legislature's unwillingness to make the 1868 law retroactive for crimes committed before its passage. Roesch, a Swiss immigrant, was fond of killing his neighbor's animals. At a trial for one of these killings, a sixteen-year-old boy, Joseph Sauer, testified against Roesch, creating bad blood between them. After the trial, Roesch threatened the boy's life, and authorities later discovered Sauer's dead body when he failed to return home from hunting. Roesch was convicted of murdering the boy with a shotgun, largely on the strength of Roesch's own son's testimony. Unbeknownst to Roesch, his son had witnessed the murder and, to Roesch's chagrin, turned state's evidence. Roesch's unsuccessful defense at trial was that his son had committed the crime. Roesch was sentenced to death in November 1867, with the judge ordering that he be hanged between 10:00 A.M. and 2:00 P.M. A petition was circulated to spare Roesch's life, but that attempt failed. Although Governor Marshall temporarily postponed Roesch's execution to consider the petition, he ultimately decided to let it go forward.[10]

Minnesota's last execution under pre-1868 law, that of Roesch, was less of a public spectacle than Ann Bilansky's hanging. At Governor Marshall's request, preparations were made to conduct the execution in private. Accordingly, a sixteen-foot-high board fence was constructed next to the jail, and the gallows was built within the resulting enclosure. Nicollet County Sheriff Azra Stone invited only law enforcement officials, clergy, and newspaper reporters to attend the hanging, and to ensure the execution would be as private as possible, he came for the prisoner earlier than anticipated by the public. Despite his early arrival, some people were already there to see it and insisted on watching the proceedings. No less than a dozen people, including five newspaper reporters, were anxiously waiting in the jail by the time Roesch was brought out at around 10:30 A.M. Outside, approximately one hundred to three hundred people had gathered around the jail, some on housetops, though it was later reported that "the utmost good order prevailed." A totally private execution in 1868 was simply not in the cards, no matter how much effort was taken to make it so.[11]

After the execution, many newspapers went to great lengths to quickly disseminate the news of Roesch's death. The *St. Paul Dispatch* reported: "Our special correspondent was present at the execution, and by rapid driving reached Le Sueur with his report in time to telegraph it in full to this evening's *Dispatch*. This is but a moderate sample of the enterprise the *Dispatch* will display in gathering news for its readers." The execution did not take long. After a white cap was drawn over Roesch's head, the trap was swung open. The prisoner immediately fell some six feet, but "bounced back" when he reached the end of the rope. When this happened, some boys outside, who were looking through the cracks in the fence, shouted, "he's twitched up, he's gone, and that's all of him." Because the hanging was carried out earlier than local farmers expected, it was not as well attended as it might have been otherwise. According to one newspaper, only forty people were admitted into the enclosure to witness the execution. While many heavily loaded teams of horse-drawn wagons were seen coming into town after the execution was over, the *St. Peter Tribune* reported that it was a "compliment to the character" of St. Peter citizens that very few of them were present.[12]

The controversial 1868 anti–death penalty law, however, soon produced a legislative backlash from those who saw it as soft on crime. Over the next several years, multiple attempts were made to nullify the law, with the first repealer bill introduced on February 23, 1869, less than a year after the 1868 legislation went into effect. The bill's author, state senator William Lochren, was a well-known lawyer from St. Anthony who had fought with the Civil War's heroic First Minnesota Volunteers. He would later become the trial judge who sentenced the notorious Barrett boys, Timothy and Peter, to death in the late 1880s for killing a streetcar driver. Just three days after the introduction of Senator Lochren's bill, though, it was tabled. Despite Lochren's backing of it, the bill languished and failed to pass after a referral to the Senate Judiciary Committee.[13]

In 1875, Republican Governor Cushman Davis also urged the repeal of the 1868 law, saying it had "subversively changed" the punishment for murder. In his annual legislative message, Davis decreed that the death penalty must not be "left to the caprice, to the mistaken sympathy, or to the fear of responsibility of the jurors." He condemned the 1868 law, expressing outrage that it let "red-handed" murderers escape death sentences. It was at that time a widely accepted rule that a guilty plea procedurally foreclosed the impaneling of a jury. Because only juries could impose death sentences under the 1868 law, defendants who pled guilty could be sentenced only to life imprisonment by the sitting judge. One newspaper complained about the "peculiarity" of Minnesota's law, "by which a jury may find a verdict upon which the judge must sentence the prisoner to be hung, but if the prisoner should plead guilty, the judge has only the power to sentence him to imprisonment for life." But efforts to repeal the 1868 law went unanswered by the Minnesota Legislature in both 1875 and 1876. The 1875 repealer bill cleared the house of representatives by a vote of sixty-seven to nineteen but was voted down in the senate. The 1876 bill to restore the death penalty met a similar fate. It passed the house by a slimmer margin, fifty-five to forty-four, but never came up for a senate vote.[14]

Heinous crimes frequently spark calls for the death penalty's infliction, and it was no different in Minnesota when the 1877 repealer bill came up for debate in the wake of a deadly and infamous bank robbery. On September 7, 1876, the notorious James-Younger gang, dressed in dusters and armed to the hilt, robbed the First National Bank of Northfield, Minnesota. In the horseback raid, two of the bandits, Clell Miller and Bill Chadwell, lost their lives, and in the robbery and deadly shoot-out that followed, other gang members were wounded. Nicholaus Gustavson, a Swedish immigrant, was shot on the dusty streets of Northfield amid shouts of terror and breaking glass, and one of the bank's bookkeepers, Joseph Heywood, was murdered. Heywood had refused to open the bank vault's safe holding $15,000. Three of the robbers, Cole, Jim, and Bob Younger, were later cornered and captured near Madelia, Minnesota, after a manhunt led by Civil War general John Pope, then residing in Mankato. Another outlaw, Charlie Pitts, was killed in the fierce gun battle that ensued near Madelia. Two unidentified men, believed to be bank and train robbers Frank and Jesse James, narrowly escaped. In July 1876, the James-Younger gang had robbed a train in Missouri, making its members some of the country's most wanted outlaws.[15]

The deadly Northfield bank robbery netted only $280, but it quickly aroused a bloodthirsty urge for vengeance. Among the rewards offered in the aftermath of the robbery were a $700 reward put up by the Winona and St. Peter Railroad, a $1,500 reward offered by Minnesota's governor, John Pillsbury, and a $500 reward per outlaw offered by the First National Bank. After the three Younger brothers were forced to surrender near Madelia two weeks after the raid, rumors ran wild that a lynching party from Northfield was on its way to end their lives. Sheriff James Glispin and Captain W. W. Murphy, two of the men who captured the Younger brothers, forcefully stated that they would not allow the prisoners to be lynched. "These men are all badly wounded and have surrendered; no one is going to harm them while I live," Murphy said. When told of the lynching rumor, a badly hurt Cole Younger, weakened from loss of blood, told the authorities: "You fellows just roll me over with my face to the door and give me back my gun and I can take care of myself for a while." "I do not want any of you to give up your lives for me," he said. Eight days after their capture, a local newspaper reported on the Younger brothers' stay in Madelia: "The captured robbers all speak in praise of the good treatment they have received since their capture. They expected to be lynched when caught and are quite cheerful over the prospect of a civilized hanging bee."[16]

While the Minnesota Legislature prepared for its 1877 session, the Younger brothers awaited their court appearances in the Faribault jail. In mid-October 1876, the outlaws were arraigned on charges of robbing the First National Bank and attacking one of the bank tellers with deadly weapons. They were also brought up on murder charges for the deaths of Joseph Heywood and Nicholaus Gustavson. Defense attorney Thomas Rutledge of Madelia advised the men to plead guilty to the charge of murder so they would not be hanged. When the men were brought into the crowded courtroom in irons, they accepted that advice, pleading guilty to the charges on November 18. Judge Samuel Lord sentenced each of them to life imprisonment at the Stillwater state prison. The prosecutor asked that a jury be impaneled in a "forlorn hope" that the death penalty might be meted out, but Judge Lord quickly denied that motion. A local newspaper commented that by pleading guilty the men "saved the county the expense of a long and tedious trial" and, at the same time, "saved themselves from the gallows."[17]

In his 1877 inaugural message, delivered in early January, Governor Davis's successor, John Pillsbury, renewed the demand for repeal of the 1868 law. A New Hampshire native, Pillsbury had come to Minnesota from the East to make a fortune, which he did, first as a merchant and then in sawmilling and flour milling. Like his predecessor, Pillsbury abhorred that murderers could avoid death by preventing a case from reaching the jury, who alone could inflict it. His objection to the law was amplified by the guilty pleas of the three Younger brothers in November 1876 before Judge Lord, who refused to impanel a jury. These outlaws, Pillsbury believed, had eluded the punishment that "the popular verdict would have demanded." The Northfield raid and what was, at the time at least, the largest manhunt in U.S. history had taken lives and affected many others, including Pillsbury's. Just the summer after the Northfield bank robbery, the governor himself had bought a pair of horses that had almost been stolen by the gang of desperadoes outside of Northfield following the raid. What should be done with the Younger brothers was on everyone's minds, and it was a topic that no politician could ignore.[18]

Despite the public outcry over the Northfield robbery, a slew of bills introduced in 1877 to repeal the 1868 law all failed to gain legislative approval. Representative H. H. Gilman's house bill, introduced on January 12, wanted death sentences for first-degree murderers unless a judge or jury believed life imprisonment was sufficient punishment. It passed the house by a vote of sixty-two to thirty-six but failed to gain senate passage. A senate bill, put forward on January 22, sought to prescribe the death penalty for murder unless the jury fixed the penalty at life imprisonment. That bill, intended to stop "the Younger dodge of pleading guilty in order to save the neck," passed the senate by a vote of twenty-two to ten but never came up for a full house vote despite a favorable House Judiciary Committee recommendation. Representative G. R. Hall's bill, introduced on February 9, proposed making first-degree murder punishable by death or life imprisonment in the judge's discretion but was tabled just ten days after its introduction. Yet another bill to repeal the 1868 law and make premeditated murder punishable by death was introduced in the senate on February 10 but was also tabled shortly thereafter.[19]

But detractors of the 1868 law would not give up. During the next legislative session, Representative Peter McCracken, a Fillmore County farmer, introduced a bill on January 27, 1879, to restore the death penalty. The House Judiciary Committee recommended that the bill be tabled—the fate of so many bills—but McCracken rescued it and got it referred to the Committee of the Whole. A man with a reputation for having "something to say on almost everything," McCracken told fellow legislators that he "had been impressed when on a late visit to Still-water," where the Younger brothers were confined, that a prisoner might make "a strike for freedom and kill a half dozen guards, but could only be punished by imprisonment for life." Although the House Judiciary Committee agreed to forward McCracken's bill to the full house, that body voted down the bill on a close vote. Efforts by Pillsbury and McCracken to repeal the 1868 law in the 1881 legislative session also failed to bear fruit.[20]

Just when it looked as if the 1868 law might stand forever, the May 1882 lynching in Minneapolis of Frank McManus, for molesting a four-year-old girl, boosted the odds that the law might be repealed. That lynching raised the stakes in Minnesota's ongoing death penalty debate, and during the 1883 legislative session, Senator James O'Brien authored the bill that would at last repeal the 1868 law. His bill sought to make death the punishment for first-degree murderers unless "exceptional circumstances" warranted a life sentence, and proposed that trial judges—as opposed to jurors—determine whether such circumstances were present. O'Brien explained that his bill would prevent a guilty plea from allowing a murderer to escape death. With the McManus lynching in recent memory, O'Brien's bill easily passed the state senate by a vote of twenty-six to two and sailed through the house by an equally safe margin, fifty-six to twelve. After gaining the signature of Governor Lucius Hubbard, an ex–Civil War general and newspaper editor, the law took effect in early March 1883.[21]

An act establishing Minnesota's official penal code, enacted in 1885 and effective on January 1, 1886, later recodified the 1883 law, making no substantive changes to it. The new code resolutely proclaimed, "Murder in the first degree is punishable by death." The harshness of this statutory clause was mitigated only by the language that followed it: "if in any such case the court shall certify of record its opinion that by reason of exceptional circumstances the case is not one in which the penalty of death shall be imposed, the punishment shall be imprisonment for life in the state prison." Whatever hopes death penalty opponents held out that Minnesota's trial judges might routinely find "exceptional circumstances," those hopes were quickly dispelled in the years to come. The passage of the 1883 law and the new penal code signaled the end of a more than fifteen-year de facto moratorium on executions in Minnesota.[22]

The first man to swing from the gallows after the passage of the 1883 law was convicted murderer John Waisenen, a Finnish immigrant. Waisenen and another man, John Norland, were arrested for the robbery and murder of Waisenen's employer, Joseph Farley. Norland committed suicide in the Duluth jail before he could be put on trial, but Waisenen, a laborer in his early twenties who spoke only broken English, was found guilty of murder and sentenced to die. The execution, like so many before it, was semiprivate. Less than a hundred people were issued tickets to attend the August 1885 hanging in Duluth, and those in attendance were restricted to twenty-five prominent Duluth citizens and sheriffs, clergy, physicians, and members of the press. Although St. Louis County Sheriff S. C. McQuade refused many requests for tickets, nearly one thousand persons gathered outside the eighteen-foot-high enclosure for the event. "The crowd was made up, not of the better class of citizens," one newspaper reported, "but of loafers and idlers, who had nothing better to do than to watch with morbid curiosity for some sign of the approaching execution." One boy even climbed to the top of a nearby telephone pole to catch a glimpse of the top of the gallows.[23]

As at all prior executions, there was a certain amount of ceremony involved, and as at many others, some disorder. At 2:45 P.M., Sheriff McQuade began slowly reading Waisenen's death warrant to him, pausing every three or four words to allow a Finnish interpreter to confer with the condemned man. Then, shortly before 3:00 P.M., Waisenen was led out of the St. Louis County jail. As he walked the fifty yards to the enclosure, the crowd surged forward, and the police had great difficulty preventing the mob from entering the enclosure or climbing the fence. Once Waisenen was finally inside and order was restored, approximately

The lynching of John Kelliher. Photograph courtesy of the Minnesota Historical Society.

seventy spectators looked on as the condemned man was led up the stairs to the scaffold's platform. While Waisenen stood on the trap door, clergymen recited two short prayers, one in English and one in Swedish. The clergymen then left the platform. The trap was swung open at 3:02 P.M., and Waisenen was pronounced dead twelve minutes later. The death warrant, requiring the execution to take place between 9:00 A.M. and 5:00 P.M., had been faithfully carried out by Sheriff McQuade. The spectators' "appetite for the spectacle," though, was "somewhat reduced after they saw the hands turn purple." Waisenen left behind his wife, a hotel laundress, and a two-year-old child.[24]

Less than a year after that execution, Minnesota witnessed another lynching, that of John "Big Red" Kelliher. Having murdered John Convay, a well-liked and soon-to-be-wed village marshal, Kelliher was taken from the local county jail and hanged from an oak tree by an angry mob. The 10:00 P.M. lynching, which took place on June 23, 1886, in Becker County, happened after Convay was killed while trying to stop a fight between Kelliher and a rival pimp and gambler. The lynch mob numbered five hundred, and after Kelliher was suspended in the air, his body was riddled with bullets. The *Minneapolis Tribune* called the lynching "a barbarous and disgraceful act" and noted that news of it had been published throughout the East and would "confirm the impression that Minnesota is a lawless frontier state." Saying one crime does not justify another, the newspaper stated that even the vilest criminal is entitled to a trial. The paper proclaimed that every jail should be equipped with "a Gatling gun, intended for business" and blasted the local county sheriff for his cowardice in not stopping the mob. The lynch mob itself also incurred the paper's wrath. "Those who have engaged in such deeds," it lectured, "can never cleanse themselves from the stain of blood."[25]

The next state-sanctioned execution occurred in Minnesota shortly thereafter, on April 13, 1888, when Nels Olson Holong was hanged. A contemporary of Jack the Ripper, Holong had been convicted of killing fifteen-year-old Lilly Field in the town of St. Olaf, mutilating the girl's body, and throwing the pieces of it into a hog pen. When her brother found her naked, dismembered body the next day, it had been partially eaten by hogs. A hired farmhand from Iowa, Holong had been kicked in the head by a horse when he was a teenager and had never been the same. An insanity defense was offered at trial, but the jury took less than fifteen minutes to find Holong guilty of first-degree murder. While over two thousand signatures were obtained in hope of commuting his sentence, Republican Governor Andrew McGill refused to intercede. Instead, McGill promptly forwarded the death warrant to Otter Tail County Sheriff Alonzo Brandenburg, requiring the execution to take place between 9:00 A.M. and 5:00 P.M. at such place as the sheriff might select. Upon receiving the death warrant, Brandenburg sent invitations to sheriffs all over the state, informing them that the execution would take place in Fergus Falls. He also announced that representatives of the press would be allowed to attend the execution—a fairly common practice.[26]

At the hour appointed by Sheriff Brandenburg, 2:00 P.M., the condemned man was led to the scaffold. After entering the board enclosure, a pastor offered a short prayer in Norwegian. "We beseech Thee to have mercy on this man and his sinful soul," Pastor Wold prayed. "Be with him through the valley of death and bring him to Thy kingdom." He concluded with the Lord's Prayer. Around five hundred people surrounded the enclosure as the execution took place. "Be a man Nels," the sheriff told Holong as he pulled the lever. A few people succeeded in mounting a high building nearby in order to see the scaffold, and one person shouted down to the crowd with each successive step of the hanging. Only fifty spectators, limited to sheriffs, doctors, newspapermen, Holong's jury, and several ministers, watched from within the enclosure. Several policemen kept the crowd away from the enclosure and were "quite zealous till the last." The same Italian hemp rope used to hang John Waisenen was used to kill Holong.[27]

On January 8, 1889, the twenty-sixth session of the Minnesota Legislature officially convened. The start of the session, however, was quickly overshadowed by the looming prospect of two double hangings. By late January, convicted murderers John Lee and Martin Moe were scheduled to hang in Alexandria in mid-February for a crime that very much held the public's attention. Lee had quarreled with and killed Charles Chalin over a girl Lee planned to marry, and Moe had counseled Lee to commit the murder. And by late February, Timothy and Peter Barrett were scheduled to hang in Minneapolis on March 22, 1889, for the murder of Thomas Tollefson, a streetcar driver. The deadly robbery, which netted the trouble-making Barrett brothers a paltry $20, took place near the cemetery at the corner of Lake Street and Cedar Avenue in Minneapolis. Their murder trials attracted added notoriety because they were represented by Bill Erwin, the skilled criminal defense lawyer, and because their own brother, "Reddy" Barrett, took the witness stand to implicate them in Tollefson's murder.[28]

In preparation for the double hanging of John Lee and Martin Moe in Alexandria, Douglas County Sheriff A. W. DeFrate built a jail yard enclosure and invited other county sheriffs to attend the execution. Letters poured in seeking permission to attend, but Sheriff DeFrate, as was customary, invited only law enforcement officers, physicians, ministers, and newspaper reporters to attend the execution. When DeFrate announced that only ticket holders would be admitted, the local newspaper, the *Alexandria Post*, objected to the hanging's private nature: "Why is it that executions are not generally public in this country? The prime object of hanging is the warning it is intended to convey; but when such occasions are conducted with so much privacy, they lose half the terror they are intended to create."[29]

On execution day, a snowstorm forced Sheriff DeFrate to construct a board roof over the scaffold. Despite the bad weather, by 7:00 A.M. a "stream of people" could be seen wading through snowdrifts to the jail. Some were visiting sheriffs seeking passes, and others were farmers. "Of the people from surrounding towns who were eager to witness the execution," one newspaper reported, "nine-tenths were saloonkeepers." All wanted passes, but few got them. At around 10:00 A.M., John Lee was hanged as planned; however, in the final hours, Martin Moe's sentence was unexpectedly commuted to life imprisonment by Republican Governor William Merriam, who also commuted to life imprisonment the death sentence of another criminal, William Lenz, not long thereafter.

The trial judge had called on the governor, and eleven of the jurors had signed a petition asking that Moe's sentence be commuted; Merriam had concluded that Moe's drunken state when the crime was committed warranted a lesser punishment. After Lee's body was taken away, fifteen hundred people were permitted to enter the enclosure to inspect the scaffold. Only then did the crowd disperse.[30]

Hennepin County Sheriff James Ege took execution-day preparations a step further for the Barrett boys' upcoming hanging by sending out invitations to it. They tersely read: "The execution of Timothy and Peter Barrett will take place in Hennepin County Jail in Minneapolis on Friday, March 22, 1889, at 11 A.M. This will admit you." A great deal of drama ensued as pleas were made by "ministers, several ladies and a number of Scandinavians" up until the last minute to save the two boys from the gallows. Addie Boyd, a young girl infatuated with Pete Barrett, made a desperate attempt by pleading with the governor's private secretary to use his influence to spare Pete's life. And Mrs. Barrett, the boys' mother, got a private meeting with the governor himself. With many citizens requesting admission, Sheriff Ege felt compelled to tell the local press that "there will be no need of people applying to him, for he cannot accommodate another person." He wanted "men holding invitations to understand that they cannot bring friends with them." The execution site would hold only 150 people, and the sheriff wanted an orderly execution if Governor Merriam refused to intervene, as turned out to be the case.[31]

On March 22, the Barrett boys were hanged as planned in the Hennepin County Jail. With an estimated five thousand people waiting outside it, the trap was sprung open at 11:14 A.M. after priests conducted a short ceremony on the scaffold. County sheriffs and newspaper reporters with telegraphic instruments packed the spectators' platform inside. "Every inch of space was utilized by the lookers-on," but a photographer, John Bodley, was notably missing. Having expressed his desire to record the Barretts' last scene on the gallows, he had been imprisoned the day before for selling "obscene pictures" that depicted the condemned men in jail. The murder victim's widow, Mrs. Thomas

On The Scaffold

The execution of the Barrett brothers. Courtesy of the Minnesota Historical Society.

Tollefson, who remarried while the Barrett brothers were "under the surveillance of the death watch," was also unable to attend. When Mrs. Tollefson and her new husband, Morris Lonsberry, requested passes, policemen told her "no ladies would be present at the execution."[32]

After the double hanging, Sheriff Ege was paid $1,000 for "the terrible work he performed so artistically." At the funeral, the grief-stricken mother, Mrs. Barrett, threw herself on the rosewood caskets. "If I was dead and lying alongside the remains of my sons," she sobbed, "I would be happy." In examining the Barretts' bodies at the morgue, skull-measuring phrenologists tried to ascertain the Barretts' criminal dispositions from their cranial development. Other curiosity seekers also appeared. Over two thousand people, in fact, were permitted to view the gallows that took the Barrett boys' lives. When rumors swirled about that the Dime Museum would display the gallows in the near future, Sheriff Ege quickly dispelled them. "There is no truth in this whatsoever," he said. The sensational hanging of the Barrett boys soon became the talk of the town and the subject of local sermons. The *St. Paul Pioneer Press* even suggested that the hanging would make "a good, live topic for Sunday school consideration."[33]

CHAPTER 5

The "Midnight Assassination Law"

The United States witnessed a resurgence of anti–death penalty activity and reform in the 1880s as politicians came to see executions as unseemly spectacles, even when privately done. More American states chose to outlaw public executions, a few states passed laws mandating nighttime executions to discourage execution-day crowds, and civic leaders, having watched the spectacle of hangings for many years, sought out what they saw as less gruesome ways to kill people. Much of this legislative activity, though not all, was centered in the Northeast and the Midwest, and it often involved attempts to sanitize the news surrounding executions. One of the states that saw legislative activity was Minnesota, and another was New York, where a legislative commission was formed to inquire into "the most humane and practical method known to modern science" of putting people to death. The commission issued its report in 1888, finding that death by electricity could be done in a "strictly private" manner and would be more humane than the gallows.[1]

Although New York, New Jersey, and Massachusetts all outlawed public executions in 1835, the New York legislative commission believed much more needed to be done to stop the brutalizing effect of executions. Commission members worried especially about the demoralizing tendencies of executions and saw detailed press reports of them as merely stimulating others to commit crimes. The result of the commission's work was the passage by New York's legislature of the Electrical

Execution Act of 1888, whereby condemned criminals would be electrocuted behind prison walls. The new law provided that no previous announcement of the day or hour of the execution was to be made, except to official witnesses, and it became a misdemeanor for any newspaper to print any details of an execution beyond the fact that the prisoner was executed. The law's controversial press-muzzling provision was not repealed until 1892 after it led to the indictment of New York newspapers that violated the law's anti-publicity provision.[2]

Like the Northeast, the Midwest witnessed a flurry of activity of its own in the 1880s. In 1885, Ohio passed legislation requiring executions "before the hour of sunrise," and Indiana passed a similar law on March 6, 1889. The Indiana law required executions to take place inside the state prison, and Ohio's law required them to take place "within the walls" of the penitentiary. Colorado also got into the act by passing a law in 1889 requiring executions to be held at the state penitentiary and "enclosed from public view." The warden was responsible for setting the execution date, and the time fixed by him was to be "kept secret and in no manner divulged, except privately" to the persons invited to attend the event. The law further provided that "[n]o account of the details" of any execution could be published "in any manner." Any person who violated the statute could be fined up to $500 or imprisoned for thirty days to six months. Minnesota was quick to follow suit, with the death penalty becoming a particularly hot topic of debate during the state's 1889 legislative session.[3]

In the wake of John Lee's execution in Alexandria, a bill sponsored by attorney Charles R. Davis came before the Minnesota House of Representatives to abolish capital punishment. A St. Peter legislator, Davis argued that the death penalty lacked a "moral, religious or civil" foundation. Objecting to the death penalty's "irremediable" nature, he openly challenged capital punishment supporters to show that "where it has been abolished crime has been increased." Other legislators, like St. Cloud lawyer Frank Searle, stepped forward to oppose the bill, fearing a repeal of the death penalty would only prompt people "to take the law in their own hands." Death penalty proponents carried the day. On

March 12, 1889, Representative Davis's bill was tabled on a vote of thirty-seven to twenty.[4]

On March 18, Senator Frank Day, a "progressive" legislator from Fairmont, took a different approach. He introduced a bill to make electricity the mode of inflicting capital punishment. New York had become the nation's first state to substitute electrocution for hanging, and Day wanted Minnesota to follow suit. To further reduce the carnival atmosphere that often prevailed at executions, Day also proposed that the state penitentiary warden execute death sentences instead of county sheriffs. The governor would name the week in which the execution would occur, but the warden would pick the precise date. Only one jurist, the sheriff and county attorney, two physicians, seven guards, and a clergyman would be permitted to attend the execution, and the bill further provided that no account of the execution could be printed in the newspapers.[5]

Standing alone, Senator Day's proposal to ban newspapers from covering executions was, given its author, a bit odd. The publisher of the *Martin County Sentinel* in Fairmont, Day was a newspaperman in a family of distinguished newsmen. But for Day, the abolition of capital punishment—his ultimate objective—took precedence over any First Amendment concerns he might have had at the time. He had undoubtedly been following the 1888 legislative developments in New York, as had many other Minnesotans. In the February 7, 1889, edition of the *St. Paul Pioneer Press*, Hennepin County District Judge John Rea vocally expressed his own views: "I believe that the details of an execution as published in the newspapers are demoralizing, and I would like to see executions so privately done that the only announcement in the papers would be, Blank was executed at such an hour." An editorial in the *Martin County Sentinel* expressed Day's hope: "We believe the new plan will take the place of the brutal and barbarous rope and scaffold, and when that is done the next thing in the way of progress and reform is to abolish the death penalty altogether."[6]

Day's bid to substitute electricity for hanging, the first of many such calls for change in the state, picked up a major newspaper endorsement from the *Minneapolis Tribune* but failed to pass. The Senate Committee on Retrenchment and Reform recommended that the bill be tabled, and the senate adopted that recommendation, killing the bill. A State Medical Society meeting, where a doctor lectured on electricity as a means of inflicting death, almost surely contributed to the bill's demise. When the doctor attempted to illustrate his theory with a dog and an "excellent apparatus," the electrical charge only produced a prolonged howl from the animal. The dog continued howling even after the battery "poles" were switched, and in desperation the doctor asked his assistants to shave off the dog's hair. This made a restless society member quip that the doctor should "remove" some of the dog's "bark" instead. Although the electric chair was called "less revolting," the Minnesota Legislature never approved of that then-novel execution method.[7]

As with many American law reform movements, it was a dramatic event that spurred on Minnesota's anti–death penalty activists in 1889. The hanging of the Barrett boys in March 1889 served as a powerful catalyst and "set the tongues of reformers wagging" about the need to abolish capital punishment. Just ten days after the double hanging, Representative Davis's bill to outlaw capital punishment was resurrected. Although Davis, the bill's sponsor, was absent, Representative John Day Smith, a Civil War veteran and leading attorney, "championed the bill." The first speaker to argue in the bill's favor, he invoked Scripture and said innocent men had been executed to "satisfy the law." Representative Searle, who previously favored capital punishment, also spoke in support of the legislation. The Barrett brothers' execution had dominated the news, and many legislators were troubled by all of the notoriety heaped upon the murderers. The *Pioneer Press* sarcastically remarked that the Tollefson murder had resulted in "8,718,613 inches of free advertising for the Barrett family." The "sickening details" of the Barrett hanging "broadcast over the land" had convinced Searle of the need to abolish the death penalty.[8]

Other legislators, incensed at the idea, opposed the bill. For example, Representative Ferdinand Husher, a Norwegian immigrant, vehemently argued against the abolitionist measure. "This talk about the sacredness of human life is nonsense," he said. "[H]ave we not a right to kill a man who assaults us?" Quoting scriptural passages, Husher stressed that "he who takes the sword shall perish by the sword." After a short debate over the proper interpretation of this biblical passage, John Day Smith made a motion to report the bill favorably. This motion narrowly lost, and consideration of the bill was then indefinitely postponed. A newspaper report later described the close vote on Smith's motion as "surprising" because "hardly a single vote was recorded against the re-establishment" of capital punishment only four years earlier.[9]

Smith, a Lincoln Republican, introduced his own bill on March 29, 1889, to abolish public executions—a practice Smith found particularly repugnant. Born in 1845 in Litchfield, Maine, Smith was no stranger to violence. He had enlisted at age seventeen and fought in the Civil War for a Maine infantry regiment that suffered heavy casualties during the war. Smith's unit frequently fought alongside Minnesota soldiers, including at Gettysburg with the heroic First Minnesota Volunteers. After the war Smith went to Brown University, obtained his law degree in Washington, D.C., and practiced law there before moving to Minneapolis. Smith was a family man and a well-respected legislator. Described as having a "gruff exterior" yet a "tender heart," Smith had three children of his own, frequently helped neglected kids in the community, and went on to be a state senator, a Hennepin County judge, and a law teacher.[10]

In the army, Smith's regiment marched across the skeleton-littered Bull Run and Chancellorsville battlefields, and at Gettysburg the Confederates relentlessly shelled his regiment. Two hundred sixteen men in Smith's infantry regiment were killed or wounded at Gettysburg, and Smith himself suffered a leg wound on the third day of the fighting. Also wounded at the battle of Jerusalem Plank Road, Smith grew a beard and mustache to cover the scars of a nearly life-ending facial wound he received in 1864 when a bullet tore out some of his teeth and part of his jawbone. Smith's unit also witnessed multiple public executions of deserters, a practice Smith called "sickening" and a "relic of barbarism" that served no deterrent purpose. Smith's unit once saw the body of a Confederate spy hanging from the limb of a tree, and Smith called it "a ghastly sight."[11]

Such spectacles were certainly on Smith's mind when he proposed his bill to outlaw public executions. The *Minneapolis Tribune*, liking Smith's proposal, quickly endorsed the idea of prohibiting the "disgusting and sickening sensationalism" surrounding executions. The "extreme penalty of the law," the paper editorialized, "should no longer be a source of fun for coarse crowds." After the Judiciary Committee recommended the bill's passage, the house of representatives passed it by a vote of sixty-four to zero on April 15, 1889. The senate vote was nearly unanimous too. On April 22, in the final hours of the legislative session, the senate passed Smith's bill by a tally of twenty-eight to one. The governor signed the bill, and the new law took effect on April 24, 1889.[12]

The final version of Smith's bill required that executions occur "before the hour of sunrise" and "within the walls of the jail" or "within an enclosure which shall be higher than the gallows." Upon issuance of a warrant of execution, prisoners would be kept in solitary confinement. Only the sheriff and his deputies, the prisoner's attorney, a priest or clergyman, and the prisoner's immediate family members could visit the condemned inmate. The new law also severely restricted attendance at executions themselves. The only persons who could attend executions were the sheriff and his assistants, a clergyman or priest, a physician, three persons designated by the prisoner, and no more than six other persons designated by the sheriff. In this regard, the Smith law resembled other state laws around the country that strictly limited public attendance at executions to only six to twelve "reputable" or "respectable citizens." The Smith law also forbade newspaper reporters from attending executions and stated that "[n]o account of the details" of an execution, except that "such convict was on the day in question duly executed," could be published in any newspaper. Any violation of the law was punishable as a misdemeanor.[13]

Smith, a popular Memorial Day speaker, was reportedly "happy" and "pleased" over the passage of his "pet measure," stating his intention to proceed against any newspaper that violated the law. "The law is intended to promote morality," he said. "It is degrading to humanity to witness executions the way they are sometimes conducted in the

John Day Smith. Photograph by Lee Brothers; courtesy of the Minnesota Historical Society.

country. The sheriff strings his man up out in an open field and invites the whole country to see him do it. The law will prevent all that." St. Paul's *Daily Pioneer Press* expressed similar sentiments, stating that the Smith law was designed "to rob an execution of much of its horror by strictly limiting the number of witnesses and excluding the representatives of the press." However, the *Minneapolis Journal* called into question the law's constitutionality, saying the law's most unique feature, the prohibition on the publication of execution details, had yet to be tested. "A number of lawyers have expressed the opinion that the newspaper feature of the law won't hold water," the paper reported. The *Minneapolis Tribune* later said the law's mandate of before-sunrise executions "is principally based upon the hope that an execution in the early morning hours will prevent the appearance of details in the morning papers."[14]

The passage of Minnesota's "midnight assassination law," so dubbed by local newspaper reporters, was quickly followed by the July 19, 1889, hanging of Albert Bulow in Little Falls. A horse thief, Bulow had murdered a man after a quarrel in a wagon and then left the man's body on the roadside. Morrison County Sheriff Henry Rasicot reportedly "performed his duties faithfully, obeyed the law literally, and won the commendation of everyone by his wise and prudent course." Not a single newspaper reporter was allowed to enter the place of execution, and no one got "tickets of admission" except those allowed by law. The execution warrant demanded that the hanging occur between 1:00 A.M. and 4:00 A.M., and Sheriff Rasicot complied with that directive, springing the trap at 1:47 A.M. within a high board enclosure adjoining the jail. One newspaper reported that it was "so dark in the shadows of the enclosure that the features of those who were there could hardly be distinguished." The "morbidly curious" were forced to bore holes in the board fence to see what was happening inside. The hundreds excluded from the enclosure had to call at the Harting and Son's morgue later that day to see Bulow's face.[15]

In the wake of Bulow's hanging, newspapers severely criticized the Smith law. The *Brainerd Journal* called the provision requiring nighttime executions "a relic of barbarism that ought to be repealed at the first opportunity," and described Smith as "undoubtedly insane" and "a madman." The *Little Falls Transcript* was only slightly more charitable: "While there are perhaps some good features of the Smith hanging law, we have failed to learn of anybody who endorses it as it now is. The barbarity of killing a criminal in the night is disgusting to people who are not savages." "The John Day Smith execution law," wrote the paper, "was so indefinite that many papers have been unable to learn just what should be done in order to please that narrow minded gentleman." The *Alexandria Post* complained that the Smith law confined newspaper descriptions of executions to "four columns" and editorial comment, saying it was not proper to limit the media's free speech rights.[16]

Many newspapers, in fact, blatantly violated Smith's law by printing detailed accounts of Bulow's execution. The *Daily Pioneer Press* reported numerous details, including such minutiae as the size of the hangman's rope, and the *St. Paul Dispatch* graphically described the execution, which was illuminated only by three lanterns suspended from the beams of the scaffold. The *Dispatch*'s front-page story said that "[t]he crowd was orderly, but the general sentiment was unanimous that the execution ought to be public." At 1:48 A.M., Sheriff Rasicot "pulled the lever" and the "murderer dropped five feet and ten inches to the space below." After the straps and noose were adjusted and the trap sprung open, the paper reported, the guards outside, in whispers, asked crowd members to stand back while Sheriff Rasicot left the enclosure. "[T]here were tears in the eyes of both he and his son as they passed into their private apartments in the jail building," another journalist reported.[17]

A separate article in the *St. Paul Dispatch* editorialized that newspaper readers were now "in possession of every essential detail" of Bulow's execution and "of many details that are not essential," making the *Dispatch* and all of its counterparts "misdemeanants." It called the Smith law "unique as a piece of paternal, sumptuary law-making," sarcastically musing about why Smith did not appoint a press censor, and criticized lawmakers for dictating to the public "what they shall and shall not do." The paper lamented the reading public's "morbid" propensity but concluded, "If the people of this state desire to know the particulars of the execution of criminals they have an unquestionable right to be informed. It is their business." "They pay for its transaction," the paper said, "and they should not be deprived of the right to decide for themselves whether that business is properly or improperly transacted and to know, on unexceptionable authority, whether it has been transacted at all."[18]

The newspaper saw a slippery slope. "If such legislation as this of Mr. Smith is legitimate and proper, where is the line to be drawn?" the paper asked in the first of a series of questions. "Why, if a newspaper is to be prevented from reporting the particulars of criminal executions, should they not also be prohibited from reporting the proceedings of criminal trials, of any murder or suicide, or street brawl, or railroad accident, or political gathering?" The paper feared that the Smith law signaled the erosion of press freedoms. "Why not, on the principle of this law, have it determined on some scientific basis what sort of reading is and what is not of the 'morbid' variety; tell us what novels we shall read and shall not read; and whether it is possible for a given mind to grow 'morbid,' for instance, in the perusal of religious books?" The newspaper believed that the public's right to know trumped any possible motive behind the law's passage. "It is, after all," the paper argued, "of some moral importance for the public to be informed, as they have been informed in spite of Mr. Smith and his law, that the braggart, swaggering murderer, Bulow, lost control of his wonderful 'nerve' when confronted with the certainty of expiating his crime, in the form of the scaffold."[19]

John Day Smith, the law's author, was out of town during the Bulow hanging. The *Minneapolis Journal* described his reaction upon his return: "He is not at all pleased with the way the newspapers have treated him and his new law. He says that allusions made to him were unmannerly. He is even bitter in his abuse of the newspapers for what he terms the slush and filth that they print." When asked whether the newspapers that printed reports of the Bulow hanging would be prosecuted, Smith replied that he had "nothing to say." In reality, there was little Smith could say as he was a member of the legislative branch, which had the responsibility for making laws, not the executive branch, which enforced them. When interviewed, Smith recognized this fact of life by stating with a smile, "I am not the prosecuting attorney, you know."[20]

Despite the onslaught of criticism, Smith was quick to point out the effect his law had on the Bulow hanging. "Before the law was passed," Smith said, "Sheriff Rasicot said if the people wanted to see the hanging he would put a rope around the scaffold and hang him in the open air." "Was it not better," Smith asked rhetorically, "that that man should be slid off in the night away from the sight and view of the crowd than that the execution of the law should be made the occasion of a gala day and a circus?" Trumpeting the legality and wisdom of his law, Smith urged that newspapers be "controlled" for the "health and morals of the community" and said that "the best sentiment of the community favors the law." When a reporter remarked, "the papers all over the country are opposed to it," Smith replied, "No, they are not. The best papers in the state have expressed themselves in favor of it. I don't mean the daily papers in St. Paul and Minneapolis."[21]

Some newspapers did, in fact, defend Smith's law. The *Martin County Sentinel*, published by Smith's legislative colleague Senator Frank A. Day, ran an editorial titled "Disreputable Journalism" in the wake of Bulow's hanging. It said that the St. Paul and Minneapolis daily newspapers, by reporting minute details of the execution, had "disgraced themselves" and "the profession of journalism." "To every refined and sensitive nature these accounts were revolting," the *Sentinel* lambasted its higher-circulation contemporaries. "They cultivated in the young a taste for sensational blood-and-thunder literature which could but result in their moral debasement." The small-town newspaper then lectured the dailies. "The press of the country," it said, "should at all times be the staunch and unyielding defender of law, the active promoter of all reforms tending to the social, moral and intellectual welfare and culture of the people." "Instead of adhering to these principles," it charged, Twin Cities' newspapers "entered into a rivalry with each other" with respect to the Bulow hanging "to see which could commit the most flagrant and wanton violation of law."[22]

If the Twin Cities' dailies were the evil culprits, the *Martin County Sentinel* had only praise for the new legislation and its author. The newspaper claimed that the Smith law had popular support and was a valid and reasonable regulation of the press. "The law was admitted by all to be a good one and passed both houses of the Legislature by a practically unanimous vote," the paper said. It added: "The attorney general decided that there was no constitutional objections to it and the desire of all good people was for its strict enforcement. The hanging of the Barretts in Minneapolis had ripened public sentiment for this reform." The paper's editorial emphasized that the sheriff overseeing the Barrett boys' execution had "issued printed invitations to hundreds, the same as would be issued to a wedding, a reception or a banquet." Although the *Sentinel* wanted the offending newspapers to be "unsparingly prosecuted" for violating the Smith law, no editors or publishers were prosecuted at that time. Ironically, just before the passage of the Smith law, the *Sentinel* had itself printed a detailed account of the Barrett boys' hanging.[23]

The next test of the Smith law came just two months later. On September 20, 1889, Thomas Brown, in his midtwenties, became the second person to hang under the law's auspices. Clay County Sheriff Jorgen Jensen hanged Brown in Moorhead, Minnesota, at 4:30 A.M., for the murder of a policeman, Peter Poull. Jensen, who chose the execution time, faithfully complied with the law, and the local newspaper itself took extra care to publish very few execution details. The paper stated only that "no mishap or hitch of any kind" occurred and that "Brown's neck was broken and he died without a struggle." While the *Moorhead Daily News* knew many details of the execution, it refrained from publishing them. Instead, the paper published a history of Brown's crime and a summary of the events leading up to the execution. The paper proclaimed that Smith's law did not prohibit the publication of these kinds of particulars. Meanwhile, other newspapers, like the *St. Paul Dispatch*, continued to describe the smallest execution details.[24]

In the next two years, three more hangings, all of convicted murderers, occurred in Minnesota under Smith's law. Sheriff James McLaughlin hung William Brooker in Pine City on June 27, 1890.

William Rose was "swung into eternity" in Redwood Falls on October 16, 1891. And twenty-two-year-old Adelbert Goheen was hanged on October 23, 1891. The death warrants for these men all had the embossed seal of the State of Minnesota affixed to them—a standard practice—along with a blue ribbon. The warrants, as did subsequent ones signed by Minnesota governors, also specifically referenced the Smith law. For example, Rose's death warrant, signed by Governor William Merriam in September 1891, stated that the hanging had to be conducted "before the hour of sunrise" in accordance with that law.[25]

The first of the three men, William Brooker, was hanged in the Washington County jail for killing William and Lillian Coombs. The couple had sheltered Brooker's wife from him, and Brooker gunned them down for "coaxing and driving" his wife away. "I desire to state to the world that what I did was the result of protecting the sanctity of my home," Brooker told the press before his execution. "[M]y wife would go to the Coombs house, leaving my children with no food to eat," Brooker complained, saying that he had to prepare food for his four children and that it made his "heart ache to see the neglect they had suffered on account of this Coombs family." A dull thud at 3:30 A.M. informed the crowd outside the jail that Brooker was "in the throes of death." When asked if he had anything to say before going to his death, Brooker stated, "No, I only hope that my neck will be broken. I want a good job done, and hope that everything will go off all right." The execution, however, did not go as planned. An autopsy showed that Brooker's neck did not break, and Brooker swung from the scaffold for half an hour before physicians pronounced him dead from strangulation.[26]

William Rose, the next man to hang, was convicted after three trials of killing a neighboring farmer, Moses Lufkin. The murder occurred at 8:15 P.M. at the house of Eli Slover when a shot was fired through an open window. "I am shot through the body, killed deader than hay," Lufkin moaned as he fell to the floor. Rose and Lufkin had quarreled over Rose's courting of Lufkin's twenty-year-old daughter, who had fallen in love with Rose but then stopped seeing him. A feud between the Lufkin and Rose families only fueled speculation that twenty-seven-year-old

Rose was the killer. To add to the intrigue, Lufkin was actually awaiting the outcome of a slander suit against Rose's parents at the time of the murder. At the first trial, Slover did not positively identify Rose as the killer, and other witnesses said only that they saw a man built like Rose riding a horse in the direction of Slover's farm. Footprints beneath the window fit Rose's shoe print, but the horse prints of the suspected murderer showed unshod hoofs while Rose's horse was shod in front. The first jury deliberated for over two days without reaching a verdict, and the second jury, which heard evidence that Rose had threatened Lufkin's life, was hopelessly split after Slover once again failed to positively identify Rose as the murderer. Only after a third trial, at which Slover fingered Rose as the killer, did the jury unanimously convict him over the protestations of Rose's defense lawyer, William Erwin.[27]

Many state residents, in fact, harbored serious doubts about the veracity of Slover's testimony at the third trial and questioned the propriety of the death sentence that Rose received upon his conviction. Rose's third trial had begun in November 1889, and before his October 1891 execution date, Grace Lufkin, the object of Rose's affection, had slashed her throat with a razor. Her suicide, in May 1890, only created more questions about Rose's guilt, though it did not stop the execution. A large crowd with several drunken men in it gathered for Rose's hanging, at which Sheriff C. W. Mead allowed only his friends, cronies, and a local newspaper editor into the enclosure. One newspaper described the small, unpainted shanty as more resembling a "slaughter house, where the lives of cattle are taken," than as a place where a human being should be hanged. Only when musket-carrying guards deserted their posts to watch the execution through available crevices were reporters able to look through knotholes to obtain a complete account of what occurred inside.[28]

When the trap swung open at the Redwood County jail at 4:56 A.M., Rose's one-hundred-ninety-pound body broke the rope. Sheriff Mead whispered "pick him up," and officials quickly carried Rose's unconscious body back up the scaffold. A second noose was placed around his neck, and the trap was sprung again at exactly 5:00 A.M. This time the rope held. In bidding goodbye on the gallows, Rose proclaimed his innocence and called Slover the guilty man. Rose's final statement blamed the governor for his fate. "I consider Governor Merriam one of the most unfair men on earth," he said. "We met when he was not governor. It was on the banks of Lake Kampeska, South Dakota. He was with a party of hunters and requested me to do a petty service for him. I refused and he insulted me. He probably remembered that incident when he refused to pardon me, an innocent man." In a farewell letter, Rose said he had been wrongfully accused, and dejectedly told his parents, "Oh God, if I could only prove to the world my innocence what would I give."[29]

Public opinion was sharply split on the issue of Rose's guilt or innocence, and doubts about the evidence against him lingered long after his death. "The fact that Slover's memory was better on the third trial than on the other two has always been pointed to with suspicion," the *Redwood Gazette* wrote in 1900. Newspaper coverage of Rose's execution created a stir too. The *Minneapolis Tribune* saw the execution as "more like a hog killing than a judicial execution," a Redwood Falls paper accused reporters of describing it "in the most horrible manner," and the *Redwood Gazette* accused newsmen of breaking the Smith law "into smithereens" by writing up "sensational details for their papers." Indeed, the *St. Paul Globe*, which ran a story titled "Dropped to Death" on the morning of the execution, soon became the execution's second victim. The story said Rose was hung "in the early dawn," but failed to publish the hour and minute of death, as was often done; instead, it confidently proclaimed that there were "no sensational features, no terrible details" to Rose's hanging. This statement was obviously false and did not go unnoticed by the *Globe*'s competitors.[30]

The other major newspapers in Minneapolis and St. Paul quickly accused the *St. Paul Globe* of committing the "very cheap trick" of making up facts to scoop the other papers. The *St. Paul Pioneer Press* said those who ran the *Globe* used "journalistic enterprise" to "evolve facts out of their inner consciousness." An editorial in the *Minneapolis Tribune* was even more sarcastic: "It costs a little more and requires time and trouble to secure the news, but it pays better in the long run. Newspapers, like politicians, may fool part of the people part of the time, but they cannot fool all of the people all of the time." The *Globe's* only defense was that its reporter dashed to the telegraph office right after "the sounds of the falling weights told him that the deed was done." It emphasized that news coverage of executions was particularly difficult because the law forbade reporters from attending executions. Reporters, it said, have to depend on information obtained from others, who attend hangings "not to tell, but to act."[31]

The Smith law did make writing news stories about executions much more difficult even if the law was ineffective in stopping newspapers from printing such stories. Although one local newspaper editor managed to witness Rose's hanging, no newspaper reporters at all watched Adelbert Goheen's execution in 1891 in the Fergus Falls jail. Goheen, convicted of murdering Rosa Bray, a woman he led to believe he would marry, had committed the murder near an insane asylum, and his victim's frozen body was found on a railroad crossing. Otter Tail County Sheriff John Billings did not like the Smith law but reluctantly agreed to comply with it. Even so, newspapers were soon reporting what took place at the hanging anyway. After the condemned man had his last meal, a bowl of oyster soup, and spoke his final words, "Let her go, Jack," Sheriff Billings let the trap drop at 12:15 A.M. Only official witnesses and spectators allowed by law were present, but it was quickly reported that the hangman's noose was later divided up "among numerous applicants."[32]

The executions of Brooker, Rose, and Goheen all led to pervasive and severe press criticism of the Smith law. The *Pine County Pioneer* called the law "the aimless product of a crank's mind," saying that a law requiring executions "at the dark hour of midnight" was shameful and should be repealed. The *St. Paul Pioneer Press* decried the "injustice" and "absurdity" of Smith's law, as well as the "partiality" shown local newspapermen in terms of execution attendance. While a reporter for the *Sleepy Eye Herald* gained access to "the slaughter pen" for Rose's execution, the Twin Cities dailies' reporters were "steadfastly refused admission."

The *Minneapolis Tribune* also declared the well-intentioned Smith law, intended to "squelch if possible that unhealthful and morbid interest" surrounding executions, a total failure. It pointed out that "[m]ore sentimental twaddle has been written about the last days of William Rose than ever appeared in print" in any prior case, and that felon Adelbert Goheen "is more talked about today than any ten living and virtuous people in the state." At least one trustworthy representative of the press, it concluded, should be present to give "a brief and unsensational account" of executions. The *St. Paul Pioneer Press* joined the reform chorus, asking for the repeal of the Smith law's provision relative to publication of execution details.[33]

The debate over the Smith law eventually spilled over into the legislature. In 1897, Representative A. F. Ferris introduced a bill in the Minnesota House of Representatives to allow press access to executions. Calling for executions at the Stillwater state prison before sunrise, Ferris's bill, which passed the house by a wide margin but died in a senate committee, would have taken away control of executions from local officials and allowed up to four press representatives to attend hangings. In house debate, Representative Sylvanus A. Stockwell called the bill "a silent yet eloquent argument" to abolish capital punishment, asking a series of questions of his colleagues: "What has Stillwater done that this disgrace should be put upon her?" "Why should the warden of the penitentiary be made into the state's hangman?" "If capital punishment is a deterrent from crime, why should it not be executed in the places where crime occurs?" "It will be a dangerous policy," Stockwell argued, "to introduce this punishment into the penitentiary among men susceptible to influences of this character."[34]

Newspapers and legislators were not alone in considering the propriety of the Smith law. Prior to William Rose's execution, the U.S. Supreme Court also weighed in on its constitutionality in considering the fate of convicted killer Clifton Holden. The case of *Holden v. Minnesota*, decided in 1890, pitted the State of Minnesota against Holden, a man convicted of first-degree murder in Redwood County in May 1889. A jury had found that Holden had shot a man in the head with a pistol in November 1888, and Holden had been sentenced to death in February 1890 after the Minnesota Supreme Court refused to grant him a new trial. The legal controversy arose when in May 1890 Governor William Merriam issued Holden's death warrant, which mandated compliance with the Smith law. The warrant directed that Holden be "confined" in the county jail until his execution date, and that he be executed "before the hour of sunrise" in accordance with that law.[35]

The issuance of Holden's death warrant prompted Holden to file a habeas corpus petition in federal court against the State of Minnesota. Death without solitary confinement, the petition said, was the prescribed punishment for first-degree murder under the law in effect when Holden committed his crime. It then contended that the Smith law, which required solitary confinement before execution, was an unconstitutional ex post facto law because it impermissibly increased his punishment. Holden also claimed Smith's law contained a provision that repealed all prior inconsistent laws, arguing that this repealing clause granted him complete amnesty for his crime. These arguments, aimed at freeing a convicted murderer, could not be taken lightly by the prosecution, for in March 1890, the U.S. Supreme Court had found Colorado's new, 1889 death penalty law to be an impermissible ex post facto law as applied to two convicted murderers. The Court found Colorado's law problematic because it added solitary confinement—a punishment of "the most important and painful character"—to the punishment for murder. As a result, two killers had walked out of prison free men because their crimes were committed prior to the Colorado law's passage. An outraged dissenting justice lamented that the two men were being "turned loose on society."[36]

In response to Holden's petition, Minnesota Attorney General Moses Clapp asserted that the Minnesota law under which Holden was convicted "has never been repealed." And Clapp specifically denied that Holden was being kept in solitary confinement, saying that Holden could receive visitors and had been permitted to mingle with other prisoners during the day. Ultimately, the federal circuit court held that Holden's death warrant "is not contrary to law or in violation of the Constitution of the United States, and that Clifton Holden is not entitled to his liberty." That decision forced Holden to take his case to the nation's highest tribunal, the U.S. Supreme Court, which agreed to hear it.[37]

In his appellate brief, Holden acknowledged that one issue of fact was whether law enforcement officials "disobeyed" Smith's law by giving him "the liberties of the jail." Holden rejected the state's attempt to frame the issue in this way, however, saying it was unimportant whether or not he had actually been kept in solitary confinement. The Smith law has "full force and operation," Holden argued, taking the position that "the actual manner of his imprisonment is irrelevant to the question in debate." Holden viewed the Smith law as not unconstitutional in and of itself, but asserted that the law, by adding solitary confinement to his punishment, became an unconstitutional ex post facto law as to his case. He found it inconceivable that a jailor could by the manner of confinement cause his release or his execution, and argued again that Smith's law contained no "saving clause" and that he was entitled to amnesty.[38]

In its responsive brief, the State of Minnesota countered that the Smith law was not an unlawful ex post facto law because it "in no wise affects the pre-existing law as to the imposition of the sentence" but pertained only to the manner of the penalty's infliction. The state's brief emphasized that the "text" and "spirit" of the Smith law were "in harmony with the greater light and broader humanity of the age." The law, it argued, "is tenderly regardful of the abject condition of the accused" by allowing spiritual advisers and "the ministration of friends," yet sought to "forestall the gathering of the thoughtless disorderly mob" at executions. By excluding reporters from them, it contended, the law "strives to minimize the evils of too much publicity of such awful scenes."[39]

After hearing oral argument, the U.S. Supreme Court decided against Holden. In its December 1890 decision, the nation's highest court held that the Smith law did not invalidate Holden's death sentence and that Holden failed to prove that he was actually being held in solitary confinement. One sentence of the Court's opinion, though not necessary to resolving Holden's ex post facto and amnesty claims, fully sanctioned private, nighttime executions. Whether a convict "shall be executed before or after sunrise, or within or without the walls of the jail," the Court ruled, "are regulations that do not affect his substantial rights." The "same observation," it said, could be made as to "the number and character of those who may witness the execution" and "the exclusion altogether of reporters." "These are regulations which the Legislature, in its wisdom, and for the public good, could legally prescribe," it declared. Ironically, after the court of last resort rejected Holden's appeal, his death sentence was set aside by the state's governor, who commuted Holden's punishment to life imprisonment.[40]

In spite of the Supreme Court's ruling in the *Holden* case, the provisions of the Smith law restricting execution attendance were frequently ignored. On October 19, 1894, for example, teenagers Charles Ermisch and Otto Wonigkeit were hanged on a double gallows in St. Paul for murdering a bartender. Wonigkeit said he and Ermisch, a carpet layer, only intended to rob Kahlmann's saloon, but that a deadly shoot-out

The execution of Charles Ermisch and Otto Wonigkeit. Courtesy of the Minnesota Historical Society.

ensued after the German bartender, William Lindhoff, reached for a pistol. Governor Knute Nelson's signature sent Ermisch and Wonigkeit to their death even though citizens like Fremont McManigal, a real estate and insurance broker, urged the governor to show mercy because of the boys' youth and their unfortunate upbringing. Fifty men, among them newspaper reporters and the sheriff's friends, packed the enclosure for the 5:05 A.M. hanging, with a parade of fifteen thousand people viewing the gallows beforehand. Flasks of whiskey were passed among the spectators inside the enclosure, and newspapers later accused attendees of coming "to get a few minutes of doubtful entertainment" and of "making an orgy of a solemn act of justice."[41]

After the double hanging, the *Minneapolis Tribune* reported that there had been "quite a wide-spread popular protest against the hangings of the two boy murderers." Ermisch and Wonigkeit were both only nineteen years old, and the clemency petitions that tried to save them pointed out, for example, that Wonigkeit's stepfather had treated his stepson in a "harsh, cruel and inhumane" manner, forcing the boy to work in a saloon, where he became addicted to alcohol. The newspaper wrote: "[T]hey have hardly had a fair chance in life, their surroundings from their earliest years having been vicious, and it is felt that the state owed them something better than death on the gallows." Ramsey County Sheriff Charles Chapel expressed similar sentiments. "The youth of the men and other features of the case," he said, "will have much to do with bringing about the feeling that will surely result in the repeal of the laws providing for capital punishment." Noting growing anti-gallows sentiment, the *Minneapolis Tribune* even suggested establishing a penal colony in the Aleutian Islands instead of inflicting the death penalty. The Minnesota Legislature, though, neither abolished executions nor switched from hangings to electrocutions, as others urged.[42]

The death penalty was now being used more frequently than ever, and many more murderers would die on the gallows in the years to come. In 1894, in fact, one of Minnesota's most notorious crimes occurred, which newspapers found impossible not to report about in the most melodramatic way. That crime and the resulting press coverage of it vaulted John Day Smith, in his role as an attorney, back into the capital punishment limelight, if only for a short time. The crime had all the elements of a sensational murder case. On the night of December 3, 1894, Claus Blixt, a janitor and off-hour elevator operator, murdered Catherine Ging, an unmarried, twenty-nine-year-old dressmaker, near Lake Calhoun. Blixt lived in an apartment complex owned and managed by William Hayward, and Hayward's two sons, Harry and Adry, lived there too and occasionally helped their father in the office. These familial relationships, however, would soon be strained to the breaking point as one of the Hayward sons had become involved in a plot to kill the young dressmaker. Smith entered an appearance for one of the men, Harry Hayward, who was quickly implicated in the murder-for-hire scheme.[43]

A professional gambler, Harry Hayward was most likely deeply in debt when he hatched his foolhardy scheme to kill Ging, his would-be bride. He first lent her large sums of counterfeit money and then took out a $10,000 insurance policy, naming himself as the beneficiary, on her life. The policy was purportedly security for her indebtedness to him. Next, Harry took Ging to a restaurant and got her to publicly display a big roll of cash, building her image as a person who recklessly carried money and—at the same time—as a potential robbery target. The deadly life-insurance scheme was destined for failure. When Harry could not get his brother, Adry, to kill Ging, he turned to Blixt, a man of low intelligence. Blixt made the perfect fall guy. He had been fired once as a dishonest bartender, twice as a dishonest streetcar conductor, and Harry, who had earlier convinced Blixt to torch a barn, could now blackmail his accomplice. But still, Blixt agreed to commit the murder only after Harry offered him $2,000 of the insurance money, threatened his life, and forced him to drink a full bottle of whiskey. "Drink it all, damn you. You haven't nerve enough for this job without it," Harry threatened Blixt. Full of liquor, Blixt finally relented. He shot Ging in the head on a secluded buggy ride. Creating an alibi, Harry rushed off to the Grand Opera House with a date for a theater performance while Blixt carried out the crime.[44]

In just four days, Harry's plot unraveled. Before the murder, Harry's brother, Adry, told a man named Levi Stewart that Harry planned to kill Ging. While Stewart refused at first to believe Adry, Ging's murder convinced him to contact the county attorney. Authorities immediately arrested Blixt and the Hayward brothers. The bond between brothers was strong, and, initially, Adry would not incriminate Harry, even though Harry had already told him the details of his crime. When confronted by Stewart, however, Adry broke down and revealed Harry's plot. While no charges were brought against Adry, both Harry and his accomplice, Blixt, were indicted for first-degree murder. The murder charges would soon turn into a much publicized legal affair the likes of which Minnesota had never seen.[45]

Harry Hayward's lead trial attorney was the highly regarded criminal defense lawyer Bill Erwin, the renowned "Tall Pine Tree of the Northwest." Harry's defense team included John Day Smith, an accomplished trial lawyer and, from 1891 to 1895, a state senator. The trial lasted forty-six days, and a total of 136 witnesses testified, but the jury returned a guilty verdict against Harry in less than three hours. Harry's strategy of trying to pin the crime on his brother, Adry, did not work, with the jury flatly rejecting the suggestion that Adry might have killed Ging for money. As John Day Smith looked on, Judge Seagrave Smith sentenced Harry to die in March 1895. The Minnesota Supreme Court affirmed that sentence in November of that year, leaving scant hope for the condemned man. Blixt, who was tried separately, received only a life sentence and died at the state prison in August 1925.[46]

Hayward's death sentence sparked cheers from many quarters, but anguish and renewed opposition to the death penalty from others. After his client's conviction, John Day Smith mounted a strenuous effort to get Hayward's sentence commuted. A group of physicians joined in, filing a petition questioning Hayward's sanity, and a second petition, containing 156 names, was dropped off at the governor's mansion by Smith himself. Smith later penned a personal letter to Governor David Clough, emphasizing a simple message: "[T]he state cannot afford to hang a lunatic." Smith urged Clough to acquaint himself with Hayward's mental condition and asked that the governor's decision be "a righteous one," noting that "[t]he execution of a madman would be a miserable spectacle." But Clough refused to commute Hayward's sentence, and the execution date was set for December 11, 1895. The execution warrant, which referenced Smith's law and had a gold, embossed seal of the State of Minnesota on it, was delivered to the county sheriff by the state capitol's "colored janitor," the same man who had delivered the Barrett boys' death warrants. "Well, we have to do all kinds of work in getting through this life," the janitor told the newspaper. The warrant specifically commanded that Hayward's hanging occur "before sunrise." By fixing the execution date for a Wednesday, Clough broke the superstitious tradition of conducting executions on Fridays.[47]

The scheduling of Hayward's hanging for midweek was not the only thing unusual about the execution. Prior to execution day, Hayward oddly requested that the gallows be painted red. This request was honored. With clemency denied, Hennepin County Sheriff John Holmberg was deluged with requests from people wanting to see Hayward hang. Some even offered to pay for the privilege of attending, and Hayward himself wanted a public execution, suggesting it be held outdoors. Although the law only allowed a limited number of people to attend executions, curiosity seekers came to Minneapolis from all over Minnesota, Iowa, and Wisconsin, seeking passes. Sheriff Holmberg turned them away with as much grace as possible, but many people were angered that they were not being allowed to see the execution. No one, it seemed, wanted to miss the big event.[48]

By December 10, the Minneapolis jail office was becoming so packed with visitors that the jail's outer door had to be locked. Curiosity seekers gathered outside the jail all day long, making crowd control a major issue, and large numbers arrived at around 6:00 P.M. Inside the jail, Hayward had been amusing himself by making hangman's nooses from short lengths of hemp for souvenirs and was dictating the exploits of his life, replete with tales of gambling, murder, and womanizing in places like San Francisco and Pasadena, California. Hayward told a deputy sheriff that his first killing was of a horse in St. Louis and that he had also shot a "nigger" in San Antonio, Texas, and been involved in another shooting in Denver. Earlier, Hayward had fabricated a story about having a wife, and in the streets newsboys had hawked papers with cries of "All about Harry Hayward to hang on Wednesday!" The noisy herd of people became so dense at one point that deputies refused to open the jail door, even to those with passes.[49]

Around midnight, John Day Smith, who made Hayward promise to declare his trust in Christ on the scaffold, visited Hayward. Smith was active in church affairs—a deacon at Minneapolis's First Baptist Church and later a member of Calvary Church—and his Christian faith guided him throughout his life. After Smith's visit, deputies clothed Hayward in a black robe and cap, and Sheriff Holmberg led him to the gallows. When asked for a final statement, Hayward rambled on for quite some time. Eventually, out of respect for his attorney, Hayward kept his promise to Smith. "[H]e is a religious man," he said of Smith, "and I told

The execution of Harry Hayward. Courtesy of the Minnesota Historical Society.

him I would pledge him what he asked of me to say. I pledged it to him, although if I honestly believed it, I would say it, and satisfy myself, and it was this: 'Oh, God, for Christ's sake, forgive me for my sins.'" It was not Smith's first time ministering to a dying man. At Gettysburg, Smith had prayed with a dying seventeen-year-old Confederate soldier from Georgia who had been shot through one of his lungs.[50]

On the gallows, Hayward had words of reconciliation for his brother, Adry, who had visited him at the jail. "[H]e has done me no wrong," Harry Hayward said. "I have done him a great injustice and wrong, and I have asked for his forgiveness and received it," he concluded. After he uttered his last words, the trap was swung open at 2:05 A.M., and Hayward, in front of dozens of witnesses, died just a few minutes later. "A half dozen women, evidently from Sheriff Holmberg's household, attempted to get in," said the *Minneapolis Tribune*, "but the sheriff ordered them back." All kinds of medical tests were then conducted, and a doctor's postmortem examination concluded that Hayward was insane. After Hayward's body was cut down, cranial measurements were taken, and the autopsy determined that he had an "abnormal" brain and an "unusually thick" skull. The red gallows was later sold to the Palace Museum, which had already obtained a phonographic recording of Hayward's voice, and Sheriff Holmberg was paid $250 for his services. Hayward's grief-ridden mother, torn up over the execution, strewed white carnations over her son's coffin.[51]

Following Hayward's hanging, the *St. Paul Pioneer Press* expressed its high regard for private executions. "It is a wise provision of our modern laws," it said, "that these horrible spectacles are no longer ghastly public shows for the entertainment of crowds of brutal men and women, but are secluded as far as possible from the public gaze." The *Minneapolis Tribune*, however, believed that even further reform was needed. "Out in Colorado," the paper wrote, "the law governing executions requires that the condemned man shall be taken to the penitentiary as soon as sentence is pronounced, instead of being kept in the county jail." "This tends to do away with much of the local morbid interest and excitement that grows up about a condemned murderer," the *Minneapolis Tribune* confidently proclaimed. The paper asked the next legislature to adopt "an act modeled on the Colorado law."[52]

When the Smith law was in effect, newspaper reporters went to great lengths and used their ingenuity—dressing as a priest, for example—so they could gain access to and watch executions. From 1896 to 1905, ten more men swung from the gallows in Minnesota, and though reporters usually found ways to get in, sometimes they did not, as was the case with C. D. Crawford's execution. Dubbed the "Box Car Murderer" after shooting a harvest hand on a freight train, Crawford was hanged at 1:48 A.M. on December 5, 1905. Sherburne County Sheriff E. L. Ward obeyed the Smith law by refusing to admit reporters, and only thirty-five to forty men, most of them visiting sheriffs, witnessed the hanging in an Elk River enclosure. Sheriff Ward's compliance was most likely the result of a personal letter from newly elected Governor John A. Johnson, a popular Democratic politician. A former newspaper editor, Johnson called Sheriff Ward's attention to the Smith law and suggested in a polite, yet firm tone that Ward had a duty to enforce the law. After Crawford's execution, one newspaper accused Sheriff Ward of refusing to admit Crawford's three invited friends because Ward suspected they were newspapermen—a charge Ward denied—even as calls for executions to take place at the state penitentiary in Stillwater fell on deaf ears.[53]

In accordance with Smith's law, all Minnesota hangings from 1896 onward—and they took place with some frequency—occurred before sunrise under local supervision. In 1896, confessed killer John Pryde, a twenty-one-year-old cook who shot a man in the head, was hanged at 1:05 A.M. in Brainerd. In 1897, a man known as George Kelly (he never revealed his true identity) was hanged in a shed in Center City adjoining the local courthouse at 12:56 A.M. He requested that he be hanged "as soon as the law allows," and his body was later interred in a potter's field in the town of Sunshine. A year later, convicted murderer John Moshik, sentenced to die for shooting a man in the back and stealing a watch and $14, was hanged in the Hennepin County Jail at 3:35 A.M., while a noisy, partly drunken mob of one thousand people waited outside. Moshik, who claimed to have a dual personality, had been housed in the jail's "insane ward," and Sheriff Alonzo Phillips pulled the lever himself, not wanting his deputies to have to perform that grim task themselves. And the list goes on. Ole Olson, who killed his eighteen-year-old, soon-to-be-married daughter Josephine, was hanged in 1903 in Aitkin at 1:50 A.M. Charles Henderson, the only black man legally executed in Minnesota, was hanged in Duluth at 1:40 A.M. in 1903 for stabbing his mistress seventeen times with a large knife. And in 1904 in Walker, wife-murderer William Chounard was dispatched at 1:07 A.M.[54]

County sheriffs—one served drinks and refreshments after an execution while an underling cut the hangman's rope to distribute to guests—often violated the spirit of the Smith law. This was done by inviting more than six witnesses, invariably men only, and then deputizing them as execution "assistants." Thus, at an execution closely monitored by newly elected Sibley County Attorney George MacKenzie, Sheriff August Gaffke deputized 125 men at the local courthouse before Theodore Wallert's 1:00 A.M. hanging in Henderson. Before Wallert was hung on March 29, 1901, MacKenzie met with Gaffke and reportedly "laid down" the law. The sheriff promised to obey the Smith law, much to the consternation of newspapermen, but the practice of deputizing dozens of men went unchallenged. Before the 12:45 A.M. hanging of Andrew Tapper in Chaska on February 18, 1902, 150 people were sworn in as deputies. Tapper murdered Rosa Mixa, a hotel waitress and co-worker with whom he was infatuated. He ate nothing, read the Bible, and tried to commit suicide three times before his execution, once trying to hang himself with his own suspenders. When wife-murderer Joseph Ott was hanged in drizzling rain at 1:27 A.M. in Granite Falls in 1898, over four hundred spectators crowded the enclosure. Ott killed his spouse with a billy club after a quarrel in which he refused to attend a wedding with her. These executions, and the way in which reporters covered them, and county sheriffs disregarded the Smith law at them, set the stage for a legal showdown over the Smith law.[55]

CHAPTER 6

The Botched Hanging of
William Williams

The press-muzzling provision of Minnesota's "midnight assassination law" had been ignored for so long by county sheriffs and newspapers that the law's author, John Day Smith, must have wondered if his law would ever be fully obeyed. While Minnesota executions after the law's passage were universally conducted at night, county sheriffs had, by and large, laxly enforced the other provisions of the law, often admitting, for example, far more witnesses than the law allowed. The state's newspapers had taken colossal liberties with the Smith law too, regularly describing executions in great detail in print, much to the pleasure—or, depending on one's viewpoint, the chagrin—of their readers. By century's end, Smith must have felt what every legislator comes to know at some point in time: it is one thing to pass a law, it is quite another to have the executive branch squarely behind it and have law enforcement authorities enforce it. If Smith was still praying in 1905 that his aging law would be resolutely enforced, his prayers were about to be answered, if only in a way that, by then, Smith could not have predicted. Well over a dozen years after its passage, the "midnight assassination law" was about to take center stage in what would become one of the state's most hard-fought legal battles.

The controversy over the Smith law—and the renewed interest in it—began when Edward Gottschalk, a condemned prisoner, committed suicide. A tinsmith and fisherman in his early thirties, Gottschalk had mutilated and nearly decapitated a butcher named Christian Schindel-decker with a meat cleaver and killed another man, tossing his weighted-down body into the Mississippi River. Already under a sentence of death, Gottschalk hanged himself in July 1905 when a member of his deathwatch went home for dinner. In the guard's absence, the depressed Gottschalk took his own life rather than wait for the scaffold to do its grisly work. Gottschalk's suicide note accused Ramsey County Sheriff Anton Miesen of treating him "like a dog," and Gottschalk's death alle-viated the need for Miesen's executioner duties. Indeed, the *St. Paul Pioneer Press* later reported that Gottschalk committed suicide not only to hasten death but to prevent the sheriff from getting a $500 fee for the hanging. Whether that was true or not, everyone remained convinced of one thing: Gottschalk's depraved disposition. A medical examination of Gottschalk's brain revealed an "abnormally thick skull," leading a physician to conclude that Gottschalk had "peculiar, if not criminal traits."[1]

The state's governor, John A. Johnson, opposed capital punish-ment. Prior to Gottschalk's suicide, though, a gubernatorial spokesman had told the press that the governor "will, of course, execute the law." Johnson had set Gottschalk's execution for August 8, 1905, a date corre-sponding with a meeting in St. Paul—Miesen's home turf—of the Inter-state Sheriffs' Association, made up of lawmen who frequently were execution invitees. For the execution, Sheriff Miesen had selected a room in the jail's basement that could hold up to two hundred people, and he had sent out enough invitation cards to make it economical to print them. The cards declared: "You have been appointed Deputy Sheriff to assist me at the Execution of Edward Gottschalk. You will report at County Jail at 1 o'clock a.m. sharp, August 8, 1905."[2]

The existence of these cards was not discovered until after Gottschalk's suicide. When they were unearthed, however, the *St. Paul Pioneer Press* quickly charged Sheriff Miesen with intending to violate the spirit, if not the letter, of the Smith law. The newspaper opined that the cards make "the hollow pretense of appointing deputies as if there were not already more than enough deputies to afford all possible assistance in the execution." The paper concluded that it was "high time" that "abuses of this kind, with their purely brutalizing effects, should be brought to an end." Curiously, this charge came from the *Pioneer Press*, which had itself in recent years blatantly violated the Smith law by publishing highly detailed accounts of executions. Little did that newspaper know that it would soon find itself on the receiving end of a similar charge of lawbreaking and embroiled in a legal dispute over the Smith law.[3]

The discovery of the invitation cards immediately led to calls for moving executions to the state prison. After Gottschalk killed himself, the *Pioneer Press* declared that a "stop should be put to all possibility of turning an execution into a public orgy and spectacle." "[T]he only effectual way to put a stop to this sort of thing, as long as sheriffs ignore the plain intent of the law, is to impose the duty of carrying out death sentences on state prison authorities," the paper proclaimed. Sheriff J. W. Dreger of Minneapolis, president of the Interstate Sheriffs' Association, agreed, but the proposal met with resistance from the very man Dreger proposed assume the responsibility for overseeing executions.

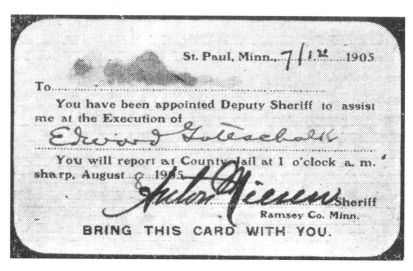

An invitation to Edward Gottschalk's execution. Courtesy of the Minnesota Historical Society.

The state prison warden opposed the plan, saying it would negatively affect other prisoners. In the end, the proposal to centralize executions at the state prison went nowhere. Executions would remain subject to local control.[4]

Shortly before Gottschalk's suicide, another development was afoot in the courts: the conviction of William Williams for first-degree murder. In a much publicized crime, Williams had killed a teenage boy, Johnny Keller, and his mother. An English laborer, Williams had worked as a miner and a steamfitter before befriending the teenager two years earlier while they were both hospitalized for diphtheria. Keller had roomed with Williams in different places in St. Paul, and in the summer of 1904 had gone to Winnipeg with him on two occasions. After Keller's mother sent her son a ticket to return home, he did so, but in between Keller's two separate stays in Canada, Williams and Keller's father had quarreled over his son's relationship with Williams. The father told Williams that he would rather put his son in a reform school than let the boy go with Williams again. Although Johnny Keller had gone the second time anyway, once he returned to St. Paul, it would be his last trip to Winnipeg or anyplace else.[5]

In a fit of rage Williams shot Johnny Keller and his mother in April 1905 when the boy refused to go back to Winnipeg with him—a trip the boy's mother did not support either. Williams's out-of-town letters to Keller had contained professions of love intermixed with threats but had gone unanswered. "I want you to believe that I love you now as much as I ever did," read one letter, saying "it won't be long before we will be together." Another read: "Keep your promise to me this time, old boy, as it is your last chance. You understand what I mean, and should have sense enough to keep your promise." When Williams came back to St. Paul intent on seeing Johnny Keller, the boy's father was away, and at the Keller home, Williams shot Johnny Keller at close range while he lay in bed. A bullet pierced the back of Keller's skull, leaving powder marks and singed hair, and another bullet wound was found in the back of the boy's neck. With Keller's death, their relationship—of whatever nature, homosexual or not—came to an abrupt end.[6]

William Williams. Photograph courtesy of the Minnesota Historical Society.

The murder trial of William Williams began in May 1905. A police officer testified that Williams appeared at the station on the night of the shooting and said that he had shot someone at a flat at No. 1 Reid Court. A doctor also took the stand for the state, testifying that Williams told him he did not know why he shot Johnny Keller, only that he wanted the boy to come with him. Williams himself testified that he had not slept for three nights prior to the shooting, had been drinking that day, and that Mrs. Keller scolded him when he showed up at the Keller residence. After saying she would not let her son go with him, Williams testified, he and the boy had gone to bed until the mother rushed in and seized the boy, exclaiming, "You can't go out of here now." At that point, Williams said, he lost all consciousness. He claimed that the next thing he knew he was in her room with a revolver in his hands and the room full of smoke. Williams's unsuccessful defense at trial, as articulated by his lawyer, was "emotional insanity."[7]

Williams's case would put Sheriff Miesen and three Minnesota newspapers on a collision course with the Smith law. On May 19, 1905, Williams was found guilty of intentionally killing Johnny Keller, whom Williams, in the Minnesota Supreme Court's words, had "a strong and strange attachment to." "There is no evidence to support this defense of complete lapse of memory and consciousness," the court would rule later, "except the defendant's improbable testimony to the effect that up to the moment the fatal shots were fired he remembered everything in detail and everything that occurred after they were fired, but has no recollection of firing them." The deck was stacked against Williams from the start. Williams made incriminating statements prior to trial, his suspected sexual orientation likely aroused bias, and to make matters worse, death penalty opponents were not allowed to sit as jurors. During jury selection, Ramsey County Attorney Thomas Kane had successfully excluded otherwise acceptable jurors because of their scruples against the death penalty's infliction.[8]

The early twentieth century's judicial system moved with considerable speed. Right after Williams's verdict was read, the trial judge told him that he would be "hanged by the neck until dead." The appeal process was relatively quick too. On December 8, 1905, the Minnesota Supreme Court affirmed Williams's conviction and death sentence, saying Williams had shot Keller with "premeditated design to effect his death." One justice dissented, however, believing that Williams should get a new trial because of irregularities in the proceedings. After considerable deliberations, the jury had returned to the courtroom and asked the judge to answer the following question: "If John Keller was shot by defendant in the sudden heat of passion, on the spur of the moment, immediately following a scuffle with Mrs. Keller, with intent to kill, but without previous intention, would that be murder in the first degree?" The trial judge had responded by simply rereading its instructions—the same instructions that had already confused the jurors. This troubled the dissenting justice, especially in light of other things that happened at Williams's trial.[9]

Most unsettling, during the trial the jurors read and accepted as true a newspaper article not admitted as evidence. Headlined "TWO MURDERERS PLOT TO ESCAPE" and subtitled "GOTTSCHALK AND WILLIAMS BLUDGEON READY FOR USE," it said Williams had confessed to plotting to escape by unscrewing a piece of gas pipe to use against a jailor. The accusation against Williams was false, the dissent said, lamenting that this was not known by jurors until the trial was over. The dissenting judge also interpreted Williams's letters to Keller differently. The letters "show a relation of great friendship, trust, and confidence" and "an unusually deep attachment and unselfish interest in the boy," but "when all the letters are considered as a whole," the dissenting judge wrote, "they are inconsistent with the theory of a deliberate and premeditated murder." Williams had seen "dark days" but had committed the crime "in the heat of passion, or at least without deliberation," the dissenter wrote, finding that the record did not show that Williams had "any base relations with the boy."[10]

The appeal resolved, Governor Johnson wasted no time in setting Williams's execution date for February 13, 1906, a date the federal courts let stand. Because Sheriff Miesen had previously invited a large number of his friends to watch Gottschalk's execution, Johnson sent

Miesen a sternly worded letter accompanying Williams's death warrant. His letter asked Miesen to "observe" that the Smith law "is very specific as to who may witness executions of this state." His letter then commanded Miesen, in no uncertain terms, to rigorously adhere to the provisions of the Smith law:

> In view of violations of this law in the past I deem it necessary to charge you with a strict observance of the law. It has been customary in some cases for the sheriff to designate many people as deputy sheriffs for the sole purpose of permitting them to be present and witness the execution.
>
> Persons permitted by you, except those specifically named in the statute, must not exceed six in number. I trust that the custom that has hitherto obtained will not obtain in this instance.
>
> It is the duty of this office to hold all officers of the law to a strict accountability in the performance of their duties in upholding the majesty of the law and it would become my duty in case this law is violated to take proper action in the premises.
>
> Believing you will do your full duty in this matter and be governed strictly by the letter and spirit of the law, I am, sir, yours with great respect.[11]

Sheriff Miesen pledged to follow the provisions of the Smith law, and his actions, at least initially, appeared aimed at making good on that promise. When asked for execution-day invitations, Miesen told people that he did not make the law, and that his duty was to strictly enforce it. Although the law had never been interpreted by a Minnesota court, Miesen took the word "assistants" in the statute to mean only those on his staff, not such persons as the sheriff might deputize for the night. When one invitation seeker was shown the statute, the response was angry: "To hell with the law, I want to see the execution." Miesen did not like refusing such requests, but he was under intense political pressure to restrict the number of invitations and found himself wedged between a rock and a hard place. According to one report, "[T]he sheriff, who stands accountable to the governor for obedience to the requirements of his office, knows that he has the alternative of facing two potent factors in his future career—the authority of the governor of the state to remove him for disobedience, and the political power wielded by persons who become enemies through his refusal."[12]

On February 13, 1906, Sheriff Miesen hanged Williams on schedule in the Ramsey County Jail's subbasement. But the much publicized execution did not go as planned. For one thing, Williams did not act penitent on the gallows. He was, instead, defiant till the end. "Gentlemen, you are witnessing an illegal hanging," he said. "This is a legal murder." Williams's last words were these: "I am accused of killing Johnny Keller. He was the best friend I ever had, and I hope I meet him in the other world. I never had improper relations with him. I am resigned to my fate. Goodbye." Worse yet, when the trap door was swung open at 12:31 A.M., Williams's body immediately hit the floor. "He's on the floor!" shouted the spectators. Miesen, who had attended a dinner party earlier that evening, had miscalculated the length of the rope. Three deputies, standing on the scaffold, instantly seized the rope and forcibly pulled it up. They held up Williams's body for fourteen and a half minutes until the coroner pronounced him dead from strangulation. Williams's attorney, James Cormican, called the execution "a disgrace to civilization" as his client, dangling at the end of the rope, died.[13]

After the hanging, several newspapers printed detailed accounts of it in blatant violation of the Smith law's gag provision. The *St. Paul Pioneer Press* reported that "the death trap was swung in the basement of the county jail, and fourteen and a half minutes later William Williams was pronounced dead." Some execution details were described, but remarkably, the paper did not report that the hanging was botched. The paper blandly reported that "the trap was dropped, and with a snap the body hung suspended." Other newspaper stories were more graphic. For example, the *St. Paul Daily News* reported that Williams's "feet touched the ground by reason of the fact that his neck stretched four and one-half inches and the rope nearly eight inches." It added that the three sheriff's deputies, identified by name, took turns holding up the body by pulling on the rope so Williams's strangulation would take place.[14]

Likewise, the *St. Paul Dispatch* described in great detail the nearly fifteen minutes that the spectators were forced to endure. The paper reported:

> Slowly the minutes dragged.
>
> The surgeon, watch in hand, held his fingers on Williams' pulse as he scanned the dial of his watch.
>
> Five minutes passed.
>
> There was a slight rustle, low murmurs among the spectators and then silence.
>
> Another five minutes dragged by.
>
> Would this man never die?
>
> Fainter and fainter grew the pulsations of the doomed heart as it labored to maintain its function.
>
> The dead man's suspended body moved with a gentle swaying.
>
> The deputies wiped their perspiring brows with their handkerchiefs.
>
> Members of the crowd shifted from one foot to another.
>
> There were few murmurs, which died at once.
>
> Eleven, twelve, thirteen minutes.
>
> The heart was beating now with spasmodic movement, fainter and fainter.
>
> Fourteen minutes—only a surgeon's fingers could detect the flow of blood now.
>
> Fourteen and a half minutes.
>
> "He is dead," said Surgeon Moore.
>
> The end has come.[15]

In the aftermath of the hanging, the *St. Paul Dispatch* reported that Sheriff Miesen, despite his pledges, had violated the Smith law by inviting more persons than allowed by statute. That newspaper also reported that Governor Johnson's office was "going to probe the sheriff's office" but expressed the view—perhaps in light of the paper's own violation of the law—that Miesen had not committed "any offense that calls for gubernatorial review." The *Minneapolis Journal*, by contrast, wanted Governor Johnson to punish anyone who flagrantly violated the Smith law. "Perhaps the deposition of one sheriff would do as much to enlarge respect for the Smith law as anything that could be done," the newspaper editorialized, saying that politicians "like to oblige their friends" but not "at the risk of losing their jobs." The newspaper praised Smith's creation as "a good law," blaming lax enforcement on "political sheriffs" and recalling Harry Hayward's hanging where "upward of a hundred persons" were present. "There is no sense nor civilization in making the execution of a criminal a public spectacle," the paper argued, "and the world has come a great ways since condemned men were hanged in the public square for the edification of men and women and children."[16]

After Williams's execution, many of the state's newspapers once again urged that executions be conducted at Stillwater's state penitentiary rather than in local jails. The *St. Paul Dispatch* wrote that county-controlled executions perpetuated a "local morbid element that exists in human nature." "Just as long as a hanging is made in a local jail," the paper opined, "will newspapers that give all the news feel it necessary to give 'the bare details' of the affair." Only if convicts were executed at the remote Stillwater prison would newspapers "give no more value to it as news than could be put in the space of a 'stick' or two of type." The *St. Paul Pioneer Press* also argued for Stillwater as the place for executions because the state prison warden "is directly responsible to the board of control, and not to the public," and "would not dare to ignore the law in respect to witnesses even if he wanted to." It feared that leaving executions in the hands of local officials "subject to local influences and desirous, for political reasons, to cater to friends and local newspapers" was bound to result in more execution attendees than allowed by law. The newspaper believed that by moving executions to the state prison they would be out of sight and out of mind and therefore less newsworthy. "So long as executions are made local affairs," the paper said, "they will be local spectacles, local scandals, and ought in the interests of decency to be fully reported." But such calls for moving executions to Stillwater failed to go anywhere, as they had failed in the past.[17]

Meanwhile, a gubernatorial investigation of Sheriff Miesen's conduct was getting under way. On the evening of February 13, 1906, Governor Johnson, a former publisher of the *St. Peter Herald*, announced that an investigation of Williams's hanging would be conducted. "I shall examine into the execution," he proclaimed, "and if there has been the slightest violation of the law, even a technical violation, Sheriff Miesen will have to answer for it." "I meant just exactly what I said," Johnson remarked, "when I sent the letter cautioning Miesen and if he has violated the law I shall go after him." Johnson understood from "official circles" that only ten persons attended the hanging, but a St. Paul newspaper article titled "The Only Newspaper Man Who Witnessed the Hanging" freely said that thirty-two people watched it. "I have laid aside all the accounts in the newspapers and shall examine them carefully tomorrow," Johnson concluded, warning that the sheriff's office would be held accountable if it could be proved that reporters were present with the cognizance of the sheriff or his deputies.[18]

The next day, Governor Johnson questioned Sheriff Miesen in his private office. Official reports said the governor went after the sheriff "real fierce," but every explanation Miesen offered, however lame, was accepted. Johnson credited Miesen's feeble explanations that a newspaper reporter slipped in through an oversight when a door was left unlocked, and that twenty of the people who watched the hanging were deputies. While Johnson found Miesen obeyed "the letter of the law," the details of Williams's death nonetheless "grated on the governor's nerves." The death penalty is a "survival of the relic of the past," Johnson said, saying he would seek the death penalty's abolition and that "the sooner it is done away with the better." "If I as governor personally had to aid in the execution of a condemned man," he told a friend, "I would resign my office in preference to carrying out such a duty." Johnson's exoneration of Miesen quickly led to a charge of political favoritism. In its article, "Won't Do a Thing to the Sheriff," the *St. Paul Pioneer Press* wrote that "a search of the political calendar suggests that this is the closed season on Democratic sheriffs." Both Johnson and Miesen were Democrats.[19]

Meanwhile, the activities of the state's newspapers in relation to the Smith law had themselves come under scrutiny. On February 15, representatives of the Law and Order League formally protested the newspaper accounts of Williams's botched hanging. They first complained to Municipal Court Judge John Finehout, who referred them to the county attorney's office, where Ramsey County Attorney Thomas Kane courteously heard their complaint but directed them to the prosecuting city attorney, Emil Helmes. Although Helmes was busy, he met them late that afternoon. Finally, after lodging numerous complaints, the Law and Order League successfully alerted Ramsey County District Judge George Bunn to the newspapers' legal violations.[20]

Citizen complaints soon turned into a full-blown criminal investigation. On February 19, a Ramsey County grand jury convened before Judge Bunn, who singled out the newspapers' violations of the Smith law. "There is but one thing I desire to call your attention to at this time," Bunn told the grand jurors, "and that is this: I call your attention to the fact that it is the law of this state relating to executions that the newspapers shall publish only a bare statement of the fact that the convict has been executed." "I call your attention," he continued, to "the apparent gross violation of that law by all the newspapers of this city, with reference to the execution of Williams lately." Although Bunn made his own views clear, he left what to do about the newspapers' flagrant violations in the grand jury's hands. After pointing out the newspapers' misconduct, Bunn stated, "Now, there is a matter that in your discretion you may take up and consider." This was the first time that a Minnesota court had ever taken notice of the gag provision of the Smith law.[21]

On March 2, after a "lively discussion" following Judge Bunn's highly suggestive comments, the twenty-one-member grand jury indicted three St. Paul newspapers: the *St. Paul Pioneer Press*, the *St. Paul Dispatch*, and the *St. Paul Daily News*. The three newspapers were indicted on "the crime of publishing a detailed account of the recent Williams hanging." One faction of the all-male grand jury, opposing the indictments, felt that the portion of Smith's law relating to newspapers had been "carried out in the breach rather than in the observance." The other faction "took the view that that law was on the books and if it was a bad law the best way to defeat it would be to obey it to the letter." After several sessions, where County Attorney Kane's advice was frequently sought, a slight majority voted in favor of the indictments. The "true bills" were drawn up against the newspapers in their corporate capacities and not against the managers, editors, or reporters. A violation of Smith's law was a misdemeanor, punishable by up to a $100 fine or ninety days imprisonment, but since grand jurors did not want to see any newspapermen go to jail, Kane announced that the newspapers, if found guilty, would only be fined. Although Sheriff Miesen was widely believed to have flagrantly violated the law, the grand jury did not indict him.[22]

Rumors existed that the three St. Paul newspapers, wishing to test the constitutionality of the Smith law, actually helped to procure the indictments by bringing evidence before the grand jury. A headline in the *Minneapolis Journal*, in fact, was titled "St. Paul Newspapers Procure Indictments." An editorial in the *St. Paul Pioneer Press* certainly did not dispel these rumors, perhaps even lending credence to them. The newspaper noted that it had "demurred and will carry the case to the supreme court for a ruling on the validity of the law." Even though "its own ox" had been "gored," the paper could find no fault with the attempt to enforce the law, saying, "If it is an improper provision either it should be declared so by the courts or it should be repealed by the legislature." Alluding to the notion that the rule of law must be upheld, the *St. Paul Pioneer Press* wrote: "[T]he way to secure repeal by court or legislature is to force the issue. So long as it is on the statute books, it, like other laws, should be enforced."[23]

Although indicted, the *St. Paul Pioneer Press* sympathized with the "spirit and purposes" of the Smith law. The paper editorialized: "There has been altogether too much sickening pandering to morbid tastes and too much cultivation of those tastes by hyperbolical accounts of the doings of murderers before executions and of the executions themselves." The paper noted that in its news coverage it "tried to treat the Williams hanging as it treats all other news matters." The paper tried "to give a decent and uncolored story" and "to give essential details, omitting ghastly particulars, without pandering to the demand of the morbid." In short, it had attempted "to avoid the methods of 'yellow journalism,' in which some of the other newspapers delight to revel." The *Pioneer Press* wrote that had all stories of hangings been of the type it published, "there would have been no occasion for the John Day Smith law."[24]

While the *Pioneer Press* happily attacked the journalistic integrity of its competitors, that newspaper was indignant about having been indicted under the Smith law for printing news. "[W]e do not believe it is a safe or a proper law, so far as it attempts to regulate newspaper accounts," the paper wrote. The *Pioneer Press* pointed out that newspapers themselves had exposed violations of law by reporting about Sheriff Miesen's mishandling of Williams's hanging. "Here was a case," the paper said, "of atrocious bungling in the execution itself and of flat violation of the law and the direct orders of the governor." Calling the Smith law "palpably unsafe," the *Pioneer Press* criticized the law's intended effect. Under the Smith law, it said, "newspapers could make no reference to either the execution or to the presence of witnesses prohibited by the same law or any of the other circumstances which it was of importance that the public should know." The *Pioneer Press* feared the worst if newspapers were silenced. "Under the press muzzling provisions of this law," it said, "the worst orgies could be held and even the cruelest barbarities could be practiced, and those responsible for them would be protected from criticism and exposure."[25]

The *Pioneer Press* emphasized that it had, ironically, first drawn attention to the lack of enforcement of Smith's law. In printing a facsimile of one of Sheriff Miesen's invitations to the Gottschalk hanging, it had exposed Miesen's plan to violate the law. It was this article that had prompted Governor Johnson to pen his letter to the sheriff to remind him of the law. Only after pointing out the law's lack of enforcement had the paper been indicted. The paper quipped, "The alleged publication of the alleged facts regarding the recent alleged hanging of a reputed convicted murderer seems to be producing more alleged effect than the alleged exposure of alleged irregularities at the time of the alleged hanging."[26]

St. Paul's newspapers were soon defending their own actions in court. On March 3, the three indicted newspapers were formally arraigned and pled not guilty, and later filed demurrers to the indictments on the ground that publishing execution details did not constitute "a public offense." In appearing before Judge Bunn on March 10, all three newspapers alleged that Smith's now infamous law contravened a clause of the state constitution that said "[t]he liberty of the press shall forever remain inviolate and all persons may freely speak, write and publish their sentiments on all subjects, being responsible for the abuse of such right." The newspapers' lawyers, raising the specter of a parade of horrors, argued that a county sheriff could carry out an execution "in a brutal manner without the public ever knowing anything about it." "While it might be proper to prohibit gruesome details of the execution, which appeal to the morbid tastes of a part of the community," it was argued, "a plain uncolored statement of the manner of the carrying out of the mandate of the law is not against the morals of the community." Indeed, it was noted that the Smith law did not prohibit the publication of pamphlets or books containing the same subject matter as that which newspapers were prohibited from publishing.[27]

The newspapers believed that executions were newsworthy events and that the public had a right to know what was done and said at them. The Smith law, the papers' lawyers contended, should not be allowed to prevent the publication of a condemned convict's dying words or an execution-day admission of guilt. The State of Minnesota's representative, charged with enforcing the state's laws, took a decidedly different view. Ramsey County Attorney Thomas Kane asserted that the Minnesota Legislature possessed the power to enact the Smith law. He said the object of the law was to prevent the publication of execution details that appealed to morbid tastes and lowered public morals. Judge Bunn, at hearing's end, took the matter under advisement. That same day, March 10, the law's author, now Judge John Day Smith, was in the news for an unrelated reason, having held a newsboy in contempt of court for creating a disturbance in his courtroom.[28]

Just over a month later, on April 16, 1906, Judge Bunn upheld the constitutionality of the "midnight assassination law" in open court. His written order stated in plain language that the "object and chief purpose of the act was to avoid general publicity." "It is quite clear that forbidding the publication of the details," Bunn ruled, "tends strongly to accomplish the purpose of the act." Bunn, skeptical of the value of news reportage about executions, found: "The purpose of the act is in a large measure defeated if the morbidly curious public, who are forbidden to see the hanging, may satisfy their curiosity by reading the ghastly details in a newspaper, and feasting their eyes on pictures of the scene."[29]

Judge Bunn had no doubt that the Minnesota Legislature had the right to pass the Smith law. He wrote: "The legislature has said that the publication of the details of an execution is bad for public morals. Its decision should be upheld unless the court can see plainly that it is wrong. I think the decision is right, and the law wise and wholesome." He specifically cited the U.S. Supreme Court's 1890 decision in *Holden v. Minnesota* in support of his ruling, but because of the issue's importance, he agreed to certify the question of the statute's constitutionality to the Minnesota Supreme Court. Thus, on May 8, 1906, Bunn formally certified the case for appeal at the request of the *Pioneer Press's* attorneys, Frederick Ingersoll and Charles Hart. The *St. Paul Dispatch* and the *St. Paul Daily News* agreed to be bound by the result of the *Pioneer Press's* case.[30]

On appeal, the *St. Paul Pioneer Press* did not contest that the Minnesota Legislature had "the power to restrict the publication of matters which tend to demoralize or degrade the public morals." The newspaper vehemently contended, though, that the Smith law went too far. "While conceding that the gruesome details of an execution of a criminal are not necessary subjects of public information," the newspaper's appellate brief argued, "we assert that there are many things surrounding the manner of an execution which the public are entitled to know and upon which the public are entitled to pass criticism." For example, the newspaper asserted that the public should know the condemned man's dying declarations and how the sheriff performs his duties. Arguing the Smith law was overbroad, the *Pioneer Press* said, "The statute in question prohibits not only those things that are detrimental to the public, and we concede that ghastly accounts of gruesome details might be harmful in effect, *but prohibits everything* save the legal conclusion, that the execution took place."[31]

The *Pioneer Press*, believing, perhaps, that it would be too radical to argue that newspapers had the right to print anything whatsoever about executions, took the more centrist position that "sensational" articles should be the subject of "proper censorship," but that its own article did not cross the line. Its brief declared that "it is true that cartoons illustrating such affairs are objectionable and that the publication of all degrading or demoralizing particulars should be forbidden," but then argued that its own article about Williams's death was not sensational and fell outside its own vaguely defined category of objectionable material. The *Pioneer Press* article, the newspaper's lawyers said, was "remarkably brief, well timed and carefully written." There were no cartoons in its edition, the paper pointed out, and there was no attempt to give the news story about Williams's execution "more than ordinary prominence in the paper."[32]

The State of Minnesota disagreed, arguing in its responsive brief that Smith's law was intended "to make all future executions secret except so far as certain specified witnesses may be present." "The obvious purpose of the act," the state said, "is the suppression of details which are nauseating and horrible and whose dissemination arouses morbidness." Publication of execution details, it contended, "tends only to gratify a debased morbid curiosity or sensualism which is demoralizing to the public good." The state surmised that the publication of such details might even "tend directly to promote crime, while subserving no useful purpose." It argued that the press was not deprived of its right to print news because the law authorizes the publication of the fact that criminals are executed. Thus, the state argued that the Smith law did not prevent newspapers from editorializing on "the advisability of capital punishment."[33]

On February 21, 1907, the Minnesota Supreme Court upheld the constitutionality of the Smith law, ruling that the "evident purpose of the act was to surround the execution of criminals with as much secrecy as possible, in order to avoid exciting an unwholesome effect on the public mind." To accomplish this objective, the court believed that executions "must take place before dawn, while the masses are at rest, and within an inclosure, so as to debar the morbidly curious." The court specifically upheld the statutory provisions barring newspaper reporters from attending executions and prohibiting the publication of execution details. This was necessary "to give further effect" to the law's "purpose of avoiding publicity." "Publication of the facts in a newspaper would tend to offset all the benefits of secrecy provided for," the court ruled. The court noted that the *Pioneer Press* article was "moderate" and did not "resort to any unusual language, or exhibit cartoons for the purpose of emphasizing the horrors of executing the death penalty." This fact, however, did not save the *Pioneer Press* from running afoul of the Smith law. The court stressed that "if, in the opinion of the Legislature, it is detrimental to public morals to publish anything more than the mere fact that the execution has taken place, then, under the authorities and upon principle, the appellant was not deprived of any constitutional right in being so limited."[34]

The *St. Paul Pioneer Press* denounced the ruling, even though it was "in full sympathy" with any law suppressing "purely unimportant and unwholesome details of an execution." It declared that the Smith law "is not so entirely wise as its intent is worthy." The hanging of Williams "showed that except for publication in newspapers of something more than a bare mention there was no way in which to inform the public whether a hanging was properly or even legally conducted." The newspaper emphasized its own role—as part of the Fourth Estate—in serving as a check and balance on governmental abuses of power. The Smith law's prohibition on reportage of accounts of executions, it claimed, "goes a little too far" because it "throws the door wide open to unmolested violation of the other clauses of that law." Under the Smith law, the paper contended, a sheriff, "secure in the knowledge that no newspaper can describe what occurred, can make a hanging a gala occasion." "The pressure upon a sheriff to admit to an execution more than the prescribed witnesses is so great," the paper noted, "that few of them withstand it." Also, the *Pioneer Press* asserted that the law's exclusion of newspaper reporters from executions left newspapers dependent on hearsay accounts in their newsgathering activities.[35]

As a result of the Minnesota Supreme Court's ruling, the case against the *St. Paul Pioneer Press* was remanded back to the district court to be tried on the merits. After a series of continuances, a twelve-person jury was finally impaneled on March 17, 1908, though the *Pioneer Press* refused to enter a plea. This forced the court to enter a not guilty plea for it. Justice—at least once it got under way—was swift. The next day, the jury returned a guilty verdict, and after that, it was not long before the legal challenge to the Smith law was at an end. On March 19, the district court imposed a $25 fine against the *Pioneer Press*, marking the end of the dispute between that paper and the State of Minnesota. The *St. Paul Dispatch* and the *St. Paul Daily News*, the two other interested parties, were each fined $25 as well.[36]

These fines and the criminal case against the *Pioneer Press* and its St. Paul counterparts put Minnesota newspapers on notice that authorities would no longer turn a blind eye to violations of the Smith law. Given the importance of the state's death penalty debate, some of the state's newspapers almost certainly entertained thoughts of violating the Smith law again. However, any contemplated acts of civil disobedience by such hard-to-intimidate journalists were never given the chance to come to fruition. No more state-sanctioned executions would occur in Minnesota, and the abolition of the state's death penalty was just over the horizon.

CHAPTER 7

The Abolition of Capital Punishment

The bungled hanging of William Williams cost Sheriff Anton Miesen his job in the next November election. It also fueled Minnesota's abolitionist movement, part of a larger national effort begun in earnest in 1845 with the founding in Philadelphia of the American Society for the Abolition of Capital Punishment. The national anti-gallows campaign achieved only limited success in its early years, with only one state, Michigan, abolishing the death penalty in the 1840s, and just two states, Rhode Island and Wisconsin, doing so in the 1850s. No state abolished the death penalty during the Civil War, and only Iowa, Maine, and Colorado outlawed executions after the end of that war and before the turn of the century. Not until the twentieth century's first two decades, the Progressive Era, did America's anti–death penalty movement hit full stride, with nine states abolishing capital punishment between 1907 and 1917.[1]

The death penalty's abolition in Minnesota came in 1911, but the story of how it happened goes back much further as earlier legislative debates laid the foundation for what was to come. Two decades before, bills to abolish executions were introduced in the Minnesota Legislature in both 1891 and 1893 by Representative Hans Bjorge, an Otter Tail County farmer and merchant. Wanting to substitute life imprisonment as the punishment for murder, Bjorge argued that innocent people had been executed and criminals "turned loose" because juries were reluctant to impose the death penalty. Although some Hennepin County residents signed a petition in 1891 urging the death penalty's abolition, a motion to table Bjorge's legislative proposal that year easily passed. His bill in 1893 passed the house of representatives by a vote of sixty-seven to twenty-six but then never reached a vote on the senate floor despite a six-to-five Senate Judiciary Committee vote reporting Bjorge's bill out of committee. Senator John Day Smith—an expert parliamentarian also promoting bills that year against animal cruelty—was the chairman of the badly divided committee that at least gave Bjorge's bill a fighting chance.[2]

The 1895 legislative session saw debate over the death penalty's morality intensify. In that year, two more anti–death penalty bills were introduced in the Minnesota House of Representatives. The first of these, seeking to substitute life imprisonment for death, was introduced by Representative John Knuteson, a Polk County farmer. On the same day that jurors convicted Harry Hayward of first-degree murder, the House Committee on Crimes and Punishment recommended the passage of Knuteson's bill. The full house and senate bodies, however, were not impressed. When the President of the Senate, Frank Day, announced in March 1895 that Hayward had been found guilty of murder, applause erupted in the senate chamber. Later that month, with the passage of new legislation unlikely, the house voted to table Knuteson's bill.[3]

The 1895 bill of Representative Edward Zier, a Minneapolis physician, also failed to pass. That bill sought to substitute life sentences for executions, but after being recommended by a house committee, it was tabled by the full house after lively debate. Some legislators, including Henry Johns and Jens Grondahl, spoke in favor of the bill, finding capital punishment to be a "relic of barbarism," while others spoke out against Zier's bill. "The blood of Catherine Ging," Representative Patrick Kelly implored, "is crying for vengeance, and by all means retain the present law on the statute books until her murderers have been hanged, as they deserve to be." Representative J. D. Jones was equally virulent. "I believe the skeleton hands of the murdered victims are stretching up from their graves through their thin covering of earth

beckoning to us for vengeance," he said. Another death penalty pro-
ponent, Representative Henry Feig, called the abolitionist movement
part of "the wave of sentimentality which sweeps over the country every
little while."[4]

A new bill to abolish capital punishment was introduced in the
house of representatives in 1897 by Representative Sylvanus A. Stockwell, a pacifist and flamboyant life insurance agent who served off and on
in the legislature for many years. Stockwell won a victory when the
House Committee on Crimes and Punishment recommended the passage of his bill, but that committee's feisty chairman, Representative
Samuel Littleton, vowed to defeat the bill in the full house. On the
house floor, the Republican lawyer was true to his word. "This is called
a barbaric relic," Littleton said, "but if it is, it is the only barbaric relic
that has found its way onto the statute books of every civilized nation."
Littleton sarcastically called the state penitentiary "almost a palace,"
saying, "it struck me as a very nice place for a summer resort where
one might take his family and spend a few days." Although Stockwell
asked for "the breaking of one more link in the chain that binds us to
our savage ancestry," the house voted down his bill seventy-three to
twenty-three.[5]

After the turn of the century, legislative efforts to abolish Minnesota's death penalty resumed. In 1901, Representative Peder Hendricks,
an Otter Tail County farmer, introduced an abolitionist bill, which the
house of representatives later voted to "indefinitely postpone." Two
more proposals introduced in 1905 also failed to pass despite the infre-
quency with which death sentences were being handed out around that
time. The first bill, introduced by Senator John Alley, a Wright County
lawyer, would have made life imprisonment the punishment for first-
degree murder unless jurors voted for death. A second bill, introduced
by Representative John Lund of Minneapolis, would have simply substituted life imprisonment as the punishment for first-degree murder. In
1904 and 1905, Minnesota had thirty-nine prosecutions for first-degree
murder, of which only three death sentences were imposed. Although
Lund's bill never made it out of committee, Alley's bill, amended to make

death the punishment for first-degree murder unless the judge or jury determined otherwise, passed the senate by a vote of forty-four to four but went no further.[6]

During the 1907 legislative session, abolitionist sentiment grew as multiple bills were debated in St. Paul's newly built, domed state capitol building. Representative Frederick Phillips, a White Bear lawyer concerned about the "evil effect" of hangings at county jails, first proposed that executions take place before sunrise at the Stillwater state prison. He cited as an example the hanging of William Williams, where "men, women and children came in groups" to get "a glimpse of the prisoner." Phillips believed that if executions were moved to the state prison, these "hanging parties" would end. Phillips's bill retained the provisions of the Smith law that precluded newspapers from printing execution details and reporters from attending hangings. Although one newspaper called Phillips's bill "a sensible, wholesome measure" because of the "cruel" and "unwholesome" practice of "local executions," saying they are frequently bungled by "inexperienced hands," the full house voted to table Phillips's bill despite the newspaper endorsement of it. Local hangings, the *St. Paul Pioneer Press* had argued to no avail, aroused such interest that "all newspapers, whether justifiable or not," felt compelled to cover them, with the paper predicting that only executions at the state prison would "half the interest" in these spectacles.[7]

A second bill was introduced in 1907 by Representative Fred Wright, a Minneapolis lawyer. His bill sought to move executions to the Stillwater state prison and to substitute the electric chair for hanging as the method of execution. "Electrocution was the coming process," he said. The state prison warden, Henry Wolfer, agreed that "the present method is not what it ought to be and that there should be a central place where executions could be performed methodically and uniformly and away from the usual notoriety." However, Wolfer did not want to oversee executions at the state prison. "I feel that placing this duty on the head of that institution," he said, "is hardly in keeping with the spirit of the general purpose of the institution, not because of the effect on the warden but because of the effect upon the inmates." He emphasized that "[t]he state has a duty to those inmates and the duty of reforming them is hardly compatible with the duty of performing executions." Wolfer suggested that, instead, the state execute people in a building on an island "away from where people congregate." After Wright's bill was referred to a house committee, it was reported back without recommendation, and no further action on the bill was taken.[8]

Phillips and Wright, the authors of the two prior death penalty bills, later introduced a third bill in the 1907 legislative session. The Phillips-Wright bill sought to make life imprisonment the punishment for first-degree murder and to prohibit the pardoning of convicted murderers absent indisputable evidence of innocence. A house committee recommended the passage of a slightly modified version of the Phillips-Wright bill, but when the bill came before the full house, Phillips offered an amendment providing for death as the punishment when a person already sentenced to life imprisonment commits murder. This proposed amendment was voted down, however, with Representative Frank White of Elk River arguing "that if capital punishment is to be abolished, it should be abolished entirely." In the end, the house voted forty-seven to thirty-four to table the Phillips-Wright bill, finding unpersuasive the arguments of Representative Clarence Miller from Duluth, who believed abolition would facilitate better verdicts because juries hesitate to send someone to the gallows.[9]

In 1909, the abolitionists redoubled their efforts, again renewing their legislative fight. The hanging of William Rose in Redwood Falls in 1891 had left a bad taste in Representative C. M. Bendixen's county, leading Bendixen, a farmer, to introduce his own bill to abolish capital punishment. Bendixen also introduced a companion bill that sought to take away the Board of Pardons' right to grant reprieves and to commute the sentences of convicted first-degree murderers. In house debate, Representative George MacKenzie, a Gaylord lawyer, spoke in support of the measure, urging that the state abandon its "barbaric power of taking human life." "The law is inconsistent," MacKenzie argued, in that "it makes it unlawful for a man to take his own life, yet lets the state take life." The death penalty's infliction, he added, only nourishes revenge, demoralizes the community, and hinders the prosecution and punishment of crime. "If the death penalty deters others from murder," he asked rhetorically, "why not have executions public?" But the house voted down Bendixen's bill by a vote of thirty-five to thirty-one, with opponents of the bill invoking the case of the Younger brothers, who avoided execution through their guilty pleas. Bendixen's bill to change the powers of the Board of Pardons also failed to pass, with a house committee recommending that the bill "be returned to its author."[10]

The Minnesota Legislature, which normally met every other year, did not convene in 1910. However, in December of that year, Ramsey County Attorney Richard O'Brien publicly called for the death penalty's abolition. Just a year earlier, a Ramsey County jury had acquitted the wife of Louis Arbogast, a prosperous St. Paul butcher, of first-degree murder, and O'Brien worried about the ability of his office to obtain murder convictions with a death penalty law in place. Louis Arbogast lived with his wife, Mina, and several daughters, and on May 13, 1909, at 4:00 A.M., after screams from the Arbogast household awoke neighbors, Louis's naked body was found on a gasoline- and blood-drenched burning bed. The back of Louis's skull had been smashed in, and both Mina and their attractive daughter Louise were eventually indicted for first-degree murder. Only after Mina's acquittal was the case against Louise—who invoked her Fifth Amendment rights at her mother's trial—dismissed. O'Brien explained his anti–death penalty stance: "There are many men, otherwise competent to serve as jurymen, who honestly have conscientious scruples against taking a life into their hands." At one point during its deliberations, the jurors in the Arbogast case had asked the judge if Mina could be found guilty of some crime other than first-degree murder. Through a newspaper, O'Brien pleaded with the public a year after the Arbogast case was over, "I wish somebody would start agitation for the abolition of capital punishment in this state." O'Brien's wish would soon be granted.[11]

The thirty-seventh session of the Minnesota Legislature convened on January 3, 1911, and a day later, in his inaugural message, Governor

Adolph O. Eberhart
Minnesota's Progressive
Governor

Campaign poster for Adolph O. Eberhart. Courtesy of the Minnesota Historical Society.

Adolph Eberhart called for the death penalty's abolition. Eberhart had been just thirty-nine years old when the death of Minnesota's beloved governor John A. Johnson, once considered a serious presidential contender, elevated Eberhart to the governor's post. A Swedish Republican, Eberhart had served in the legislature and practiced law in Mankato before being elected lieutenant governor. Although Eberhart had a reputation for evading controversial issues, he stepped forward on the issue of the death penalty in his legislative message. "I am firmly convinced," he said, that more first-degree murder convictions would result "if either capital punishment were abolished, or imposed only in extreme cases, and then only upon the order of the court or the unanimous recommendation of the jury." "The old argument against its abolition on the ground that the board of pardons would frequently reduce the life sentence," he noted, had been refuted by the actions of the current Board of Pardons. "I believe the interests of justice and humanity demand the repeal of the law," Eberhart concluded, predicting crime would be reduced by the abolition of "this antiquated practice in criminal procedure."[12]

A powerful legislative ally of Governor Eberhart was longtime death penalty opponent George MacKenzie, elected to the Minnesota Legislature in 1905. A Civil War veteran's son, Representative MacKenzie's influential ancestors included a famous Scottish lawyer and the first Liberal premier of Canada. MacKenzie's maternal grandfather, who owned the Illinois country home where MacKenzie was born in 1857, was a big-game hunter who kept a cabinet full of rifles and whose walls were adorned with the heads and antlers of Scottish stags as well as tiger hides and lion skins. These hunting trophies from India and Africa were much admired by George MacKenzie as a boy, and MacKenzie would take up his grandfather's passion for the outdoors, becoming one of Minnesota's first conservationists. Amid a varied career as a schoolteacher, farmer, bricklayer, and pioneer lawyer, MacKenzie enjoyed fishing and hunting geese, buffalo, elk, antelope, and even mountain lions. His far-flung travels put him in dangerous situations where he witnessed gunfights and murders, and on one of his many hunting trips, he befriended Teddy Roosevelt, future president of the United States.[13]

On January 5, 1911, MacKenzie introduced his own bill in the house of representatives to outlaw capital punishment. State-sanctioned violence, he concluded, was simply not the answer to fighting crime. One of the bill's early supporters was Henry Wolfer, the Stillwater state prison warden. "I never have favored capital punishment," Wolfer said, "and the more I study methods of dealing with the criminal classes the more convinced I am that the death penalty should not be invoked." Wolfer emphasized that the death penalty did not deter crime. "Experience shows and penologists are quite agreed that as a deterring influence this form of punishment is without effect." As state prison warden, Wolfer believed that criminals deserved a second chance. Along with Archbishop John Ireland and Civil War hero William Colvill, Wolfer had in pardon hearings even supported the release of the Younger brothers, whom MacKenzie had visited at the Faribault jail where they were held pending trial.[14]

By mid-January 1911, the morality of Minnesota's death penalty was very much on the minds of Minnesota legislators, and the contentious debate over this irrevocable sanction would soon reach fever pitch. Another abolitionist bill was introduced in the state senate on January 9 by Senator Edward Peterson, a Litchfield lawyer, and it was reported on January 11 that legislators were "beginning to discuss capital punishment." Although Peterson's bill was never reported out of the Senate Judiciary Committee, where it was referred, the *Minneapolis Journal* noted that Representative MacKenzie "is getting ready to make a hard fight in the house for his bill." That newspaper aptly framed the issue: "The question is put up to the legislators harder than ever this year, in view of the fact that two condemned men are waiting for the governor to fix the date of execution, and the governor is delaying his action in hope that the legislature will relieve him."[15]

On February 23, before MacKenzie's bill came to a vote in the Minnesota House of Representatives, a Le Sueur County grand jury requested that the legislature inquire into why Governor Eberhart "refuses and neglects" to set an execution date for convicted killer Martin O'Malley. The grand jury's resolution criticizing Eberhart, coming only four months after O'Malley was sentenced to death for poisoning his two

George MacKenzie. Photograph courtesy of Malcolm MacKenzie.

stepchildren, was presented on February 24 to both houses of the legislature. "I have always been opposed to capital punishment," Eberhart told the press, explaining his refusal to set an execution date while he anxiously waited to see whether MacKenzie's bill would pass. "I have been told that the MacKenzie bill will pass and until its consideration nothing will be done," he said, though he expressed his willingness to carry out O'Malley's execution if it did not. "I do not have to fix the date of hanging until I am ready, and for the reasons given I am going to take all the time necessary," he said. "You can say, though, that I will not shirk my duty if I find the abolishment of capital punishment impossible." Eberhart soon got the news he wanted. The same day that the grand jury's resolution was presented to the legislature, the house chamber's Committee of the Whole recommended passage of MacKenzie's bill by a vote of fifty-seven to twelve.[16]

Though his prior legislative efforts had met with opposition, MacKenzie felt his bill now had momentum. In the legislative debate, he gave an eloquent anti–death penalty speech, imploring his fellow legislators:

> Mr. Speaker. Six years ago in the first Legislature which convened in this beautiful building, I had the honor of lifting my voice in support of a bill similar to the one now under consideration . . . and as the years have gone by, my earnest conviction that Capital Punishment is wholly wrong has become deepened and settled. . . .
>
> If punishment is what you want to inflict, would it not be much more of a punishment to incarcerate the criminal within prison walls, where conscience might bring remorse to torture him through the slow lapse of years, cut off from the job and sunshine of freedom, not hearing the songs of the wild birds, sense the breath and perfume of the flowers, where no rustle of the autumn leaves could reach him? . . .
>
> Did Domitian stamp out Christianity by putting to death 40,000 Christians? . . . Did the English retrieve their fallen fortunes in France by burning Joan of Arc or crush Erin's love and hope of liberty by the execution of Robert Emmet? Have women ever been unfaithful since Henry

VIII made an example of Anne Boleyn? Have army spies been unknown since Nathan Hale gave up his life for his country? . . . If the death penalty is meant to deter others from committing murder, why are not our executions public?

Why does the law provide that an execution must be private and be carried into effect between darkness and dawn? Why do we throw the mantle of night over this "legal" crime? If it is to deter others, why not have full newspaper accounts with illustrations of the gruesome means? Why not hold the execution on the public square in the full glare of the noon-day sun, where every one could look and see the black-capped figure on the gallows, standing in the center of the trap, feet and hands tied?

The fear that if life imprisonment be substituted as the penalty for murder the pardon board may turn dangerous individuals loose after short confinement may be readily removed by the passage of a bill recently introduced which takes from the Board of Pardons the power to pardon for murder in the first degree.

With that argument against abolition disposed of, I know of none other that should deter us a moment from removing this awful responsibility from our Executive Department and from heeding the wishes of our State Association of Sheriffs which recently adopted a resolution in favor of the abolition of Capital Punishment. I ask you gentlemen to vote for this bill in the name of humanity, in the name of progress, reason, expediency, public policy, and in the name of advancement for mankind, and in the name of a grander, a higher and nobler civilization.

Let us bar this thing of Vengeance and the Furies from the confines of our great State; Let not this harlot of judicial murder smear the pages of our history with her bloody fingers, or trail her crimson robes through our Halls of Justice, and let never again the Great Seal of the Great State of Minnesota be affixed upon a warrant to take a human life. . . .

It was a rousing speech, and when MacKenzie concluded, the house members gathered in Cass Gilbert's new capitol building warmly applauded it.[17]

By 1911, MacKenzie was hardly alone in vocally opposing the

death penalty. St. Paul attorney Charles Orr, for example, believed that "if the matter had been left in the hands of attorneys of the state, hanging would have been abolished long ago." Even prior death penalty proponents like newspapermen George Mattson and W. D. Washburn spoke in favor of MacKenzie's bill. Representatives Mattson and Washburn, who had both opposed abolition only two years earlier, were now convinced that the death penalty only brutalized society and served no useful purpose. The idea of moving to life sentences was something most legislators found appealing, and only a few voices were raised in defense of executions. Representative Knute Knutson, for instance, said his "sympathies went out to the friends of the victim of the murderer rather than to the criminal," while others simply feared that convicted murderers might be paroled. This latter concern was alleviated, however, by the passage in the house of representatives of Joseph Keefe's bill on the same day the MacKenzie bill cleared the house. Keefe's bill took away the Board of Pardons' right to pardon convicted first-degree murderers unless their innocence could be established beyond a reasonable doubt. Although it never made it through the senate, Keefe's bill passed the house by an overwhelming vote of ninety-five to four.[18]

On February 28, widespread support for MacKenzie's bill expressed itself as the full house passed his bill by an overwhelming vote of ninety-five to nineteen. This represented a personal triumph for MacKenzie, who had worked tirelessly for the bill's passage for six years. A religious man, MacKenzie had come to see capital punishment as an antiquated form of violence at odds with his vision for the state. MacKenzie's opposition was, at its core, rooted in experience. As Sibley County Attorney from 1901 to 1905, MacKenzie had come into office on the heels of the first-ever death sentence handed out in Sibley County. The convicted murderer, Theodore Wallert, was prosecuted by MacKenzie's predecessor, and county attorney–elect MacKenzie was sitting in the courtroom when the prisoner was sentenced to die by the tearful judge, Francis Cadwell. After chants of "hang him, hang him" were heard in the courtroom as Wallert was led into it on the fateful day, the judge had rejected an insanity defense. The packed courtroom exploded with applause when

Judge Cadwell rendered judgment after hearing conflicting medical testimony from local doctors. It was after watching Wallert hang in 1901 and seeing vigilante hangings in the West and a hanging in Redwood County that MacKenzie came to oppose the death penalty.[19]

As a state legislator, MacKenzie wanted to abolish the gallows—and worked hard to do it—even as he deplored acts of criminality. Wallert's crime in MacKenzie's own county, arising out of a bitter domestic dispute, had, in fact, shocked and outraged the entire state. The oldest son of a German wagonmaker, Wallert had come to America in 1889 and married a widow who had a farm but insufficient means to support her children. The marriage lasted nine years, but Wallert moved out after severe marital difficulties arose. After his wife filed divorce papers, Wallert returned to his former home a few months later and set fire to the family's barn in the middle of the night while his wife and stepchildren were sleeping inside the house. Wallert then crawled through a house window, hollered "fire," and stabbed his wife and four children to death with a carving knife as they came down from upstairs. A fifth stepson, Otto Steinburn, was badly wounded in the bloodbath. Although cries of "Lynch him" were heard following his capture, Wallert was sent to the gallows only after confessing his guilt in open court and making four suicide attempts. Estranged from his family prior to the murders, Wallert was upset that his wife had never deeded the farm to him and refused to sleep with him. Wallert also said she and her children had made a "slave" of him and called him "an ox, bull, fool, and all sorts of names." "I had no intention of killing any of the children," Wallert said, adding he did not know why he did it.[20]

MacKenzie fervently felt capital punishment was barbaric and unnecessary, as it did not stop crime. Seeing the death penalty as vengeful, uncivilized, and even dangerous because of its irrevocable nature, MacKenzie worried a great deal about the execution of the innocent. Having read writers like Italian jurist Cesare Beccaria, who had proposed doing away with the death penalty almost 150 years earlier, MacKenzie was of the belief that the death penalty only "lessens the sacredness of human life." In studying the issue, MacKenzie had looked to many sources, including God, for guidance. "If one individual, or a dozen individuals, or a score of them, have no right to take a human life," MacKenzie believed, it would not make a death sentence "any less a murder in the sight of that Supreme Power" just because "a printed excuse, known as a statute," was "enacted by many people who call themselves a State." The death penalty's infliction, MacKenzie thought, only "demoralizes the community," a fact highlighted, he noted, by "the almost universal custom of private executions."[21]

After the MacKenzie bill passed the Minnesota House of Representatives, its advocates knew it would have a harder time in the senate. The *Minneapolis Journal* even speculated that the bill in its present form might need revision as some lawyers were worried it could offer complete freedom for condemned murderers Martin O'Malley and Michelangelo Rossi and interfere with pending cases. Governor Eberhart had refused to fix execution dates for O'Malley or Rossi, and the *St. Paul Pioneer Press* went out of its way to report that "Martin O'Malley is a problem." It told its readers that "the law books are being searched with the greatest care" in an attempt to resolve O'Malley's case, and that court cases from eastern states were being reviewed by Attorney General George Simpson to determine what to do. The newspaper noted that the state's chief legal officer had asked that the MacKenzie bill be held in abeyance until it could be decided just what changes, if any, were needed to see that O'Malley did not go free instead of being hung.[22]

Despite the bill's remaining hurdles, MacKenzie's wife was fully convinced after the house vote that her husband's bill was destined to become law. Martha MacKenzie had always been a strong advocate for the bill, and the legislative vote meant as much to her as it did to her husband. George had first met "Mattie," a minister's daughter, on a fishing trip, and like her husband, she was a religious person as well as an expert rifle shot. They had been married in 1879 on Mattie's seventeenth birthday, lived to celebrate a sixty-fifth wedding anniversary, and enjoyed the outdoors and hunting and fishing together into old age. "My wife did not care for any kind of games, such as cards, dancing," MacKenzie would write later. When the couple went back to their hotel after Minnesota's historic anti–death penalty vote, Mattie threw her arms around George and kissed him, saying, "You have now accomplished what I have always prayed for." An energetic and dynamic woman, Martha had always played a big role in George's political career, entertaining governors, magistrates, and other civic leaders at their home. And Mattie had always taken a keen interest in law and politics. It was one of his wife's lifelong friends, Emma Buttman Brown, who had lent George the law books he needed prior to his 1886 admission to the bar. Indeed, George once shared a law practice with Mattie's brother.[23]

Martha MacKenzie's faith in her husband's bill was tested in the legislative process but proved well-founded. After the bill was transmitted to the senate on March 1, it was immediately referred to the Senate Judiciary Committee. The bill slumbered there for a week but was then reported back to the full senate without recommendation. The long wait, however, was soon over. After resolving itself into the Committee of the Whole, the senate recommended passage of MacKenzie's bill on March 30. While George and Martha MacKenzie were extremely pleased by that vote, a final senate vote on the bill would not take place until April 18, the last day of the legislative session. The legislative showdown over the death penalty would go down to the wire, with two lives, those of Martin O'Malley and Michelangelo Rossi, at stake.[24]

At the state capitol, it was an incredibly hectic time, and the last-minute crush of legislative business posed the risk that any bill might get lost in the shuffle, die in committee, or be set aside for a collateral reason. In 1911, it was the cases of O'Malley and Rossi that posed the greatest threat to MacKenzie's bill because so many people favored their execution. To complicate matters, the Minnesota Board of Pardons held a special session on March 25 to consider O'Malley's and Rossi's applications for commutation of their death sentences to life imprisonment. The pardon board took the cases under advisement but then decided that nothing would be done unless the legislature passed MacKenzie's bill. By putting the fate of O'Malley and Rossi back into legislators' hands, the Board of Pardons only increased the pressure on lawmakers. After the board announced its wait-and-see intentions, in fact, threats were made on the streets of Le Sueur to lynch O'Malley, the seventy-six-year-old man still being held in the local county jail. The county sheriff, Patrick Keogh, had already stationed armed guards around the jail to protect O'Malley, and Governor Eberhart had promised help from the militia if necessary. Because of the strong sentiment in Le Sueur County favoring O'Malley's execution, he was eventually taken to the Carver County jail for safekeeping. For O'Malley and Rossi, MacKenzie's bill was most likely their last, best hope.[25]

If the state capitol's corridors had become a pressure cooker by late March, the heat was turned up a notch further by mid-April because of a provision of the state constitution requiring the Minnesota Legislature to adjourn at midnight on April 18. It would, in the end, be a race against the clock. Indeed, it was only in the closing hours of the legislative session on April 18 that the senate finally passed MacKenzie's bill before adjourning for the year. No debate on MacKenzie's bill actually occurred on the senate floor because of the lack of time and because polling showed that at least thirty-five senators favored it. MacKenzie had done his homework; the senate passed his bill by a vote of thirty-five to nineteen. Governor Eberhart signed the bill into law on April 22, marking the death penalty's end in the state, a momentous achievement. Eberhart proudly proclaimed that the abolition of capital punishment entitled legislators "to a large measure of credit."[26]

In the aftermath of the bill's passage, local newspapers described why Minnesota's abolitionist movement had succeeded. The first reason related to the "barbarity" of capital punishment and the unwillingness of jurors to convict guilty persons out of fear that the gallows would be used. The *St. Paul Pioneer Press* wrote that abolitionists had maintained that hanging was so repulsive to most people that many criminal defendants escaped punishment even though convictions were warranted by the evidence. "Jurors are loath to vote death even when they are not in doubt about the guilt of the accused," the paper stated, concluding that capital punishment had come to be viewed as "a detriment rather than an aid in the suppression of crime." "It should be much easier to secure convictions under the new law," the paper predicted, noting that jurors

IT SEEMS NO LONGER TO BE AN EFFECTIVE WEAPON AGAINST THE FIEND.

Cartoon from the *St. Paul Pioneer Press*, 1905. Courtesy of the Minnesota Historical Society.

are "more willing to return verdicts when they know the punishment to be meted out will not be irrevocable." The *Minneapolis Journal* agreed: "The abolition of capital punishment will have the effect of making conviction easier in many murder cases. Juries hesitate to condemn a man to death, even when the evidence is plain. But imprisonment for life leaves room for the liberation of the condemned man, if new evidence is discovered that clears him."[27]

Another reason for the success of Minnesota's abolitionist movement was the Board of Pardons' willingness to curtail the use of its pardoning power. After the state senate voted to abolish hanging, the *St. Paul Pioneer Press* remarked that one objection that had been urged against life imprisonment was "the claim that too many life-term prisoners are pardoned after serving a few years." The eventual parole of the Younger brothers was certainly one decision that in the past had sparked enormous controversy. The *Minneapolis Journal* likewise emphasized that the main objection to life imprisonment was that "by reason of unwise use of the pardoning power such sentences are rarely carried out." The newspaper pointed out that this objection had been taken care of by the Board of Pardons. "This body acts with great caution and wisdom on all applications for pardons," the paper declared.[28]

Before Governor Eberhart signed the MacKenzie bill into law, the Board of Pardons commuted the death sentences of Michelangelo Rossi and Martin O'Malley to life imprisonment. The board was worried that unless this action was taken, the two men might wholly escape punishment on a legal technicality. Their commutations were not the result of clemency appeals but came about because of the legislature's anti–death penalty legislation. Eberhart signed MacKenzie's bill before the appropriate local officials received the two men's notices of commutation. MacKenzie himself was glad that "[t]he horror of seeing men strangled to death"—as at the hanging of Theodore Wallert in his own county—would be "wiped out."[29]

The botched hanging of William Williams in 1906 also contributed to the death penalty's demise. The press coverage of that gruesome spectacle caused Minnesota's governor to call for the abolition of capital punishment, and the high-profile press challenge of Minnesota's "midnight assassination law" brought attention to the abolitionist cause. After Williams's grisly death, all death sentences were set aside until the death penalty was abolished in 1911, and the newspapers' blow-by-blow recital of the botched hanging made it Minnesota's last state-sponsored execution. Although John Day Smith had fought for the death penalty's abolition, it was the violation of his own law that played a key role in fueling Minnesota's anti-gallows movement. Indeed, Smith was not even present for much of the 1911 legislative session. Badly overworked as a juvenile court judge, Smith suffered a nervous breakdown in February 1911, and on the advice of his family physician, left for Berkeley, California, where he spent two months with his daughter. Smith resigned from the bench in 1913 when it became clear his disabling illness would prevent him from performing his judicial duties, and his final years were spent in a state of "semi-invalidism" until he died in 1933.[30]

After many hard-fought legislative battles, the abolitionists, led by Representative MacKenzie, had triumphed; no longer would people be put to death in Minnesota. The very next year, in 1912, the Minnesota Supreme Court captured the essence of the sweeping penal reform that had taken place through the new legislation. "No longer is proportionate punishment to be meted out to the criminal, measure for measure," the justices wrote, "under the barbarous doctrine of an eye for an eye and a tooth for a tooth." Instead, "the unfortunate offender is to be committed to the charge of the officers of the state, as a sort of penitential ward, to be restrained so far as necessary to protect the public from recurrent manifestations of his criminal tendencies." The people of Minnesota would witness more acts of violence in the years to come, but state-sanctioned violence had, at long last, come to an end.[31]

Minnesota's 1911 abolition of capital punishment—sustained to this day—represents a unique chapter in the history of America's anti–death penalty movement. The outbreak of war had often been the death knell for America's anti-gallows movement, yet in Minnesota the death penalty was not reinstated even though other states brought back executions with the onslaught of World War I. In fact, of the nine states

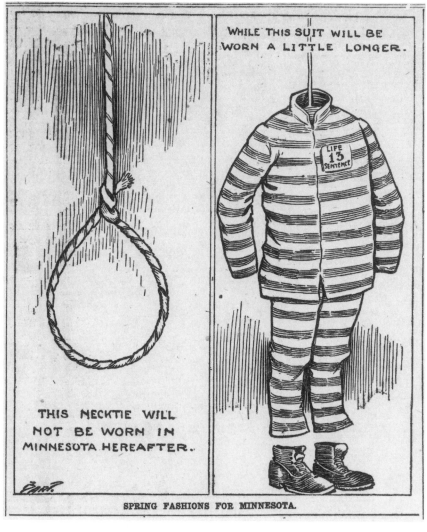

Cartoon from the *Minneapolis Journal*, 1911. Courtesy of the Minnesota Historical Society.

that abolished capital punishment in the Progressive Era, only two, Minnesota and North Dakota, refused to reinstate it by the 1930s. Even the tragic 1920 lynching of three African American circus workers in Duluth—triggered, some claimed, by the absence of a state death penalty law—did not lead to the death penalty's reinstatement in the North Star State. Minnesota's anti-gallows movement, with all of its fits and starts, thus remains a shining example of how a group of determined citizens can change even a centuries-old form of punishment.[32]

CHAPTER 8

A Travesty of Justice

The Duluth Lynchings

Efforts to reinstate Minnesota's death penalty followed swiftly on the heels of Representative George MacKenzie's 1911 legislative victory. In the next election, Ernest Pless, a young Republican miller from Gibbon, ran against MacKenzie, defeating him by a substantial vote. Pro–death penalty sentiment in MacKenzie's legislative district almost surely contributed to the loss. A local newspaper, in fact, had expressed the view in 1911 that life sentences were an inadequate punishment for crimes like the James-Younger gang's notorious bank raid. "The old-timers will remember that many years ago Minnesota did away with capital punishment in response to a demand of mawkish sentimentalists," the paper said. "This was followed by an epidemic of homicide and lynchings," it added, "winding up with the well remembered Northfield bank robbery and murder." While Pless won the election, he was unable to pass a new death penalty law. MacKenzie still knew many influential legislators, and Pless's 1913 bill to reinstate capital punishment floundered. Other pro–death penalty bills introduced in 1913, 1915, and 1919 also failed to garner enough support to become law.[1]

Though efforts to reinstate capital punishment always failed at the state legislature, the people of Duluth, living along the rocky shore of Lake Superior, decided to take the law into their own hands in the 1920s. It all started when a traveling circus from Peru, Indiana, the John Robinson's Circus, came to town in yellow and red train cars. An arch near Duluth's Grand Avenue marked the circus entrance, and after a morning street parade of clowns, camels, hundreds of horses, and the most exotic of caged wild animals, the grounds themselves had been lit up with electric and gas lights. A ticket wagon, popcorn wagons, a sideshow tent, an army of performers, and, of course, the big top, were all there to entertain circus-goers of all ages at two shows, one at 2:00 P.M. and one at 8:00 P.M. The sideshow tent was called Madam X or the pit tent because it held a lady in a pit with snakes. A suspected black-on-white gang rape, brought to public light by the most unreliable of accusers, sparked the lynching bee of three black circus hands.[2]

On June 14, 1920, despite threatening storm clouds, hundreds of Duluthians had enjoyed the circus and the evening's big top show. The roughly fifteen hundred circus employees had then started packing for their trip to the show's next stop: Virginia, Minnesota. It was a hectic time with little opportunity for loafing, and the circus hands, many of whom were black, were ridden by "bosses" so the circus would move speedily from town to town. As the railroad cars were being loaded

Advertisement for John Robinson's Circus in Duluth. Courtesy of the Minnesota Historical Society.

up, eighteen-year-old stenographer Irene Tusken and James Sullivan, her teenage boyfriend, lingered at the circus grounds. They had met earlier that night and chatted with a group of teenagers before wandering around to watch the takedown drill in operation. It is unclear what happened a few minutes after the city's curfew whistle sounded at 9:00 P.M., but whatever it was—an aborted robbery or sexual escapade, a prostitution or whiskey seller's transaction run amok, or perhaps nothing more than a petty slight—it soon put Duluth in the national spotlight. After the encounter, the teenage couple rode a streetcar to the girl's home and—at that point, at least to the outside world—nothing at all seemed to be the matter. The girl nonchalantly said goodnight to her father, and the girl's escort, a boat spotter, went home after dropping her off so he could change clothes for his midnight to 8:00 A.M. shift at the Duluth Missabe and Northern Ore docks. Not until after 1:00 A.M. did the boy, a recent high school graduate, tell his father that a gun had been put to his head and that his girlfriend had been gang-raped. Patrick Sullivan, the boy's father and a night superintendent at the ore docks, wasted no time in notifying the authorities. His son's life and the girl's reputation, he thought, would not be threatened and tarnished so easily, at least not without severe consequences.[3]

At around 2:00 A.M., the irate father telephoned Duluth's police chief, John Murphy, awakening him at home. The call got Murphy out of bed, and he immediately sped down to the West Duluth docks, where he met Patrick Sullivan and his agitated son. There, Mr. Sullivan and the boy told Murphy that "some niggers" had raped Irene Tusken. At around ten o'clock, "Jimmie" Sullivan claimed, six blacks confronted him and Irene as they were leaving the circus grounds. One man grabbed his arm, he said, and another, he claimed, placed a pistol to his head and said, "Be quiet or I'll blow your brains out." The boy told Murphy that while he was held hostage, the men dragged his girlfriend to a clump of bushes and "ravished" her. This caused Murphy to telephone a railroad yardmaster, so that the circus train could be held up. After assembling a group of Duluth police officers, a determined Murphy led his men to the train depot to investigate. The officers, convinced of the truth of the boy's story, angrily boarded the train at the Canadian Northern railroad yard and pulled all the blacks out of their sleeping cars. "Get out of here, you black son-of-a-bitch, you," an officer barked at Max Mason, a twenty-one-year-old, five-foot-four-inch laborer from Alabama. The police chief was equally blunt. "I want to talk to every nigger that was idle between about nine and ten o'clock last night," he commanded.[4]

In the police raid, over a hundred black circus hands like Max Mason were forced to line up in the rain. "Get on over there in line," a police officer yelled at Mason. Once outside, the circus foremen helped separate the big top workers and the waiters—believed by the police chief to have been "idle" at the time in question—and then had the foremen check them off to see that every man was there. A blue-uniformed policeman barked out a threat: "There was six of you niggers raped a white girl on the circus grounds last night. We'll have everyone of you in jail in ten minutes if we don't find those six. So you boys that know something better start talking." When young Jimmie Sullivan, whose scurrilous charges started the whole affair, was brought out to identify the assailants, however, he became hesitant, telling Murphy, "They look pretty much alike to me. I don't know for sure." A police officer urged the boy to try again, saying, "it would be terrible to arrest the wrong people." But still, the boy failed to specifically finger anyone. When Irene Tusken and her father, a mail carrier, arrived at the depot, the girl said the men's faces were not that familiar to her either. When Mason came up, the police asked him his name and his whereabouts between 9:00 and 10:00 P.M. the prior evening. "I was working," he said, at which point officer A. G. Fiskett asked the girl, "Is he the one?" She shook her head, indicating no, and Mason was told to get back on the train. Unable to pick out anyone by face, the girl picked out five men anyway based on their size and physique, with interrogation and suspected false answers to police questioning resulting in eight more arrests. The thirteen detainees were then driven to Duluth's downtown jail, where they were further interrogated as the circus train continued on to Virginia. Only when no incriminating statements were forthcoming were seven of the men set free.[5]

The six men who remained in custody were Elias Clayton, Elmer Jackson, Nate Green, Isaac McGhie, Loney Williams, and John Thomas. All of them were between the ages of nineteen and twenty-two, and many of them could not read or write. Police Chief Murphy suspected five of the six men of participating in the alleged rape, while Isaac McGhie, locked up in a cell on the second floor of the station house, was held only as a material witness. After the five suspected rapists were thrown behind bars, Murphy—arrested himself on federal liquor-smuggling charges just a few weeks later—decided to make more arrests in Virginia. There, local sheriff's deputies, anxious to get confessions, arrested ten more blacks. Max Mason was arrested as he was serving oatmeal to a crew of circus workers. "I want you," an officer told him, refusing to say why Mason was under arrest. One officer even pointed a pistol at Mason, saying, "Talk! Let's have the whole story." When Mason said he knew nothing, the officer replied, "You know plenty, all right. If you don't talk, I'll kill you!" Only after cocking the pistol and momentarily holding it to Mason's ear did the sheriff's deputy finally holster his weapon.[6]

In the meantime, Dr. David Graham, the Tuskens' family physician, was summoned to Irene Tusken's home on the morning of June 15. The whole family was agitated and upset, but Dr. Graham's gynecological exam revealed nothing abnormal. "I am unable to say what occurred from what the examination disclosed," the doctor concluded. "I think she suffered most from nervous shock." A private detective interviewed the girl later. She told the detective that "four negroes" had grabbed her arms and shoulders, but she had fainted and that the blacks were walking away when she regained consciousness. Asked, "Did you feel any ill effects after the assault?" the girl answered, "Yes, my arms were a little sore." The skeptical detective probed further, asking why she did not immediately report the alleged attack. The girl answered only, "I do not know, but I thought it best to keep it quiet." When the detective started asking tougher questions, the girl's mother abruptly terminated the interview. "My daughter is not well," she said. Afterward, the same detective called on Dr. Graham, asking what signs of a sexual assault were present. "I don't think she was raped," the doctor told him.[7]

The alleged assault was not reported in the June 15th morning edition of the *Duluth News Tribune*, but gossip traveled fast among working-class Duluthians. By late afternoon, angry blue-collar crowds, already bitter that the city's U.S. Steel plant had begun importing low-wage black laborers from the South, had gathered on Duluth's streets and openly talked of a lynching. At a pool hall, William Lashells, an engineer at a local steel plant, overheard a plot to lynch the jailed blacks. This frightened him. Seeing enraged men gathering on the street, he called the police upon returning home. "There's a mob from West Duluth coming down to the station tonight to take the niggers out and kill them," Lashells warned. An hour and a half later, a mortified Lashells saw men on Central Avenue talking of blowing up the jail with dynamite, and by 5:00 P.M. young men had begun congregating across the street from Duluth's police station. When a businessman stopped by the station at 5:40 P.M. to say a lynching attempt might be made that night, Sergeant Oscar Olson told him he had already heard those rumors and that the police were ready.[8]

But Sergeant Olson was wrong; the Duluth police were not ready for what was to come. As growing numbers of enraged men gathered in front of the police station, Louis Dondino's truck slowly wound its way through West Duluth's streets. Men on board shouted things like, "Come on! Show what kind of men you are! The niggers raped that girl, and she might be dead!" and "What if the girl had been your wife or daughter?" Men of all ages, cheered on by the crowd, fell in behind the truck, and by 6:00 P.M., the hot-headed parade had reached Fourth Avenue West and Superior Street, just six blocks from the jail. By that time, one group of young men had already taken yards of rope from Siegel's Hardware Store across the street from the station. "This is on the house, boys," the retail clerk, referring to the rope, had said, adding: "You're doing a good thing." The front-page headline in the early edition of the city's evening paper, the *Duluth Herald*, only fueled the mob's rage. "West Duluth Girl Victim of Six Negroes," the headline proclaimed, with the article saying that three men under arrest had already confessed after being "sweated" for some time.[9]

Sergeant Olson, at six-foot-two and weighing an imposing 285 pounds, did not instruct the switchboard operator to call in off-duty policemen until 7:00 P.M. "We'll be alright," a nervous Olson assured the other officers. "Let's not lose our heads. That's the main thing." But Olson was far from certain that he had the manpower to stop a lynching. The green truck loaded with men was moving up and down Superior Street, and Olson knew he might need help. He called the St. Louis County Jail to try to reach Sheriff Frank Magie, but Magie was not there. Olson also telephoned the fire department for backup and fire hoses to repulse the gathered mob if that proved necessary. The men on the truck were now yelling, "Let's hang the black niggers" and "Join the necktie party." Sergeant Olson had earlier suggested to the jailer, Fred Harling, that the prisoners should be taken elsewhere for safekeeping, but they concluded that it would be too dangerous to do so. If something happened to the prisoners, they decided, it might look like the police had turned them over to the mob. As the tense situation worsened, a worried local attorney, Hugh McClearn, set off to find two district court judges who might intervene to stop a full-blown riot.[10]

McClearn and the two judges arrived at the police station just as bricks were being hurled at it, smashing most of the police department's front windows. As one of the judges, Bert Fesler, tried to convince crowd members to disperse, District Judge William Cant moved to the front of the station to address the angry mob. "Men, I can understand your anger tonight," he pleaded, silencing the crowd by holding up his hands. Someone shouted back, "Damn right!" but Judge Cant tried to shame the audience into letting the law take its course. "This is wrong," he said. "Look at what happened in Omaha. The riot there disgraced that city. The honor of Duluth is at stake. Most of you are all law-abiding citizens, and if you do this terrible thing, you will never live it down, and neither will Duluth." But the mob was not to be dissuaded. "Hell, judge," one man shot back, "You'd only have to hang 'em yourself anyways. We'll save you the bother." Realizing his words alone were doing little good, Judge Cant tried to quiet the crowd, then left to place an urgent call to Duluth's police chief, John Murphy, in Virginia. The situation soon went from bad to worse, however, as Public Safety Commissioner William Murnian arrived at police headquarters at 7:45 P.M. "Watch yourself, Murnian," he was heckled. "The only thing worse than a nigger is a nigger-lover."[11]

Located to the rear of the police station, Duluth's city jail was under siege, and no one knew when the police chief would be back from Virginia. "How does it look, Oscar? How many men do you have?" a distressed Murnian asked Sergeant Olson. "Just eleven right now," the sergeant answered, "But more are on the way." Before heading upstairs to his office, Commissioner Murnian simply told Sergeant Olson to handle the situation as best he could. Olson, intent on preserving order, gathered his men together. "Boys," he said, "it looks like we might get trouble here." "But we can handle it," he told them. "Let's not have anybody chewing the rag or getting into arguments with those folks on the street. It's best not to talk to anybody. That'll make things worse. Avoid shooting as long as you can. We have almost no ammunition." "I don't feel like starting to shoot and lose out on top of it all," Olson explained. "But if things get hot, shoot if you have to." As the mob lurched outside and rocks broke through the station's windows, Olson telephoned to try to get more bullets and stationed six of his men in front of the station, with five others assigned to guard the rear.[12]

That evening, a group of Duluthians had gone by the Tuskens' house. They called out to Mrs. Tusken, who was standing on the porch, and asked how young Irene was doing. "She's in bed," the mother replied in a weak voice, rubbing her eyes. The mother's remark, however, was mistook for "she's dead"—a pivotal event in the night that followed. As false rumors of Irene's death circulated among the mob, the crowd's anger swelled to new heights. By shortly after 8:30 P.M., about two dozen men were so mad that they tried to gain entry to the jail through its garage. Using clubs, Sergeant Olson and his men repulsed this effort, but the five to ten thousand crowd members assembled outside the jail soon went into a frenzy. A man climbed onto the hood of taxicab and yelled, "The girl assaulted is in critical condition. She's in the hospital if she's not already dead. What would you do if it were your sister? In the South, those niggers would have been dead ten minutes ago!" Cheers rose from the crowd, and anyone touting restraint was booed and hissed. "Let's stop yakking!" "Let's get 'em!" yelled others.[13]

Elected to office by the predominately working-class crowd loitering outside the jail and violently disturbing the peace, Public Safety Commissioner William Murnian decided it would be best to issue an order that no guns or clubs be used against the mob. Murnian told a reporter, "I do not want to see the blood of one white person spilled for six blacks." When Murnian was spotted looking out a window, someone shouted, "We're going to get those niggers, Mr. Murnian! Give us one of them to start with anyway!" Murnian did not answer, leaving a police lieutenant, Edward Barber, to call back, "The prisoners are in my custody. I am responsible for them. They are guaranteed protection under the law." "We'll take them from you, Lieutenant," a member of the mob yelled back. "We'll wreck this damn jail and everyone in it." The risk of a lynching—however unthinkable—was now painfully clear.[14]

Hurled rocks forced Lieutenant Barber to take cover as the mob bore down on the jail's front door. A fistfight ensued, and to beat back the crowd, five men led by Sergeant Olson rushed to a nearby fire hose already connected to a hydrant. When the water burst out, Olson sprayed the mob with its forceful stream, gradually working his way back to the front of the station. But six members of the mob rammed the station's rear wooden doors with a railroad iron. This forced Olson to lumber to the back, hollering, "Hold 'em boys!" When he finally realized he had lost control, Olson appealed to the crowd: "This is against the law! We need the help of every law-abiding man here!" But Olson's cries for help were futile. Angry crowd members shouted back, "The law's no damn good!" "We're the law now, mister," and "What's the matter with you policemen? We're paying you fellows and now you go protecting these niggers!" It was not long before the makeshift battering ram smashed down the jail's back door, and water hoses—one of which was cut to stop its water flow—were unable to hold back the mob. After scuffling with firefighters, mob members had actually gained control of a water hose themselves and turned it on police, forcing them back into the station and flooding the station house. Inside, a Duluth newspaper-man anxiously confronted Lieutenant Barber: "What about using your guns?" "No, we can't," Barber replied, "We'll start real trouble if we do." Though Olson fought back and, for a time, manned a fire hose by himself, the mob eventually kinked it, forcing him to retreat inside too.[15]

The tide had now turned decidedly against police officers, some of whom fled down fire escapes and onto surrounding sidewalks as five hundred mob members poured into the jail. As the jail's hallways and staircases became clogged, a dejected Sergeant Olson muttered to his men, "Boys, what're we gonna do?" All too soon, men were hammering on the cell room door and would eventually bash a large hole in a sixteen-inch-thick brick-and-mortar wall in their efforts to get to the prisoners faster. As this was going on, attorney Hugh McClearn climbed a stepladder in the hallway and pleaded with the men to stop. "Give the courts a chance to administer justice according to the law," he yelled as the hammering continued in the ninety-degree heat. "Sgt. Olson says there are six niggers here. Three of the men the police have no dope on at all. They may be absolutely innocent." "We don't care if they are guilty or innocent!" one man retorted. "Kill the black snakes!" After hollering "Wait!" and identifying himself as an attorney, McClearn was asked, "We don't have no electric chair or hanging in Minnesota, ain't that right?" "No," McClearn shook his head. "Then what happens to the niggers, lawyer?" someone asked him. McClearn told the sweaty men, "If they're convicted, they'll get five to thirty years," to which many men yelled back, "To hell with the law!" before pulling McClearn off the ladder. Mounting the ladder himself, Olson made one last plea for calm, saying, "We don't even know if we got the right Negroes. That circus had nearly two hundred of them, and we arrested thirteen. And the girl and her young man couldn't identify a single one." "Let's wait ten minutes and check it out," Olson implored, trying to buy time. "No!" the response came.[16]

His own life now at risk, Sergeant Olson splashed through the ankle-deep water on the jail floor and went to the basement, where a few of his men were huddled together tending their wounds. "Jeez, Oscar," one fellow officer told him, "you done the best you could." But Olson urged his men to rally. "Come on, boys," he cajoled. "We will run out the back way and up the avenue and run into the crowd and take the hose away from them." Finding no takers, Olson returned upstairs to see what if anything could be done, while Lieutenant Barber worked the crowd, asking the women in it to take their husbands and boyfriends home. Only after a jet of water from the mob's hose hit him in the face did an exhausted and bruised Barber push his way back into the jail, only to be pinned against a wall and immobilized. By then, the circus workers were terrified, with Isaac McGhie, on his knees, sobbing. "Help me, Jesus . . . help me, Jesus. Lord Jesus, please help me," he prayed. Relentlessly, the mob took turns ramming a railroad iron against the cell room's grilled door, with one man, Henry Stephenson, swinging a sledgehammer over his head. "We are going to lynch those niggers!" he shouted. Eventually, the steel door, tearing noisily, gave way.[17]

Now in the darkened cell room—a power failure having left it pitch-black—the mob frantically searched for the black men trapped inside. One man lit up a flare but then tripped, dousing the red flame in the inch-deep water on the cell block floor. As the angry men boxed out the few police officers still trying to stop them, Lieutenant Barber refused to give up hope. "Stop this before you murder innocent men!" he pled. "We don't care if they are innocent or not!" someone shot back, in what was becoming the mob's mantra. One man, peering into a dark cell, then spotted nineteen-year-old Loney Williams huddled in a ball beneath a cot next to the wall. "There's one!" the man cried, prompting the cursing mob to try to saw through the bars. Moving onto his cot, a petrified Williams vomited. "You are going to be sorry for this night's work! These men would be punished by the law! You are doing wrong! Stop, before it's too late," a teary-eyed Barber shouted at the mob. "Get 'em! Kill the black sons of bitches!" a man shouted in reply, ignoring Barber's pleas.[18]

Upstairs, Isaac McGhie was found in the boys' division of the jail. He was taken from his cell and savagely beaten. Shoved downstairs and hit in the face, McGhie lost a tooth and suffered a broken nose before urinating in his pants. "Oh, God, oh, God—oh God," he begged. "I am only twenty years old. I have never done anything wrong. I swear I didn't. Oh, God, my God, help me." While prisoner John Thomas told the angry mob, "Nobody here done nothin'," the cell of nineteen-year-old Elias Clayton was broken into, and Clayton was punched into submission. With three whites pushing others away, McGhie was dragged into Clayton's cell as a half dozen whites grilled their black captives. "We're going to find out which nigger's guilty! The rest of you stay back. We want to be fair," one man gesticulated. Gathered together in the sweltering, cramped cell, the black men were violently interrogated. Punches were thrown and a prisoner's head slammed against the cell bars. "Now, which one of you did it? Out with it—," one man commanded. "Come on, talk—damn you!" ordered another. "Who was the man who had the gun?" demanded one man. "Never mind the questions—let's just kill these niggers!" someone else shouted. "The militia will be here before we can hang 'em."[19]

The black prisoners professed their innocence. "So help me, God, I did nothing and I know nothing," Isaac McGhie sobbed. "The miserable black savages are lying," the response came. John Burr, one of the whites in the cell, only then began to sense the scope of the tragedy that was unfolding before his eyes. A twenty-four-year-old shipyard employee, Burr worked part-time in a West Duluth pool hall to earn extra money. He needed it to help cover expenses for his newborn baby and had, at first, told people in the pool hall that he would not participate in storming the jail—a jail that was now scattered with broken glass, strewn office records, and smashed furniture. After being swept up by the mob atmosphere, Burr found himself standing uncomfortably in front of the black prisoners, realizing there was no way to tell who might be guilty or innocent. When the mob tried to seize Loney Williams, Burr jumped in front of him saying, "No, leave him be. This boy has a good story." After the mob shouted to be given someone, McGhie, closest to the cell door, was grabbed by the hair and pulled out of the cell, with Elmer Jackson shoved out next.[20]

Beaten and kicked out onto Superior Street, McGhie and Jackson were thrown from man to man until their shirts were ripped off their bodies. Realizing resistance was futile, neither man fought back as they were violently hauled up Second Avenue East. While men and women in the crowd jostled to kick McGhie, all he could do was beg for his life. The procession stopped abruptly at a light pole on the corner of Second Avenue East and First Street, just one block from the jail. There, Elmer Johnson, a nineteen-year-old accountant for the Duluth Street Railway Company, had climbed the pole so he could witness the lynching. He thought it would take place on a tree but now shuddered as he found himself an integral instrument of the mob's work. Seeing Johnson positioned at the top of the pole and gripping a metal arm that extended over the street, someone hollered to him, "Toss this rope over the top, kid!" As the mob screamed in anticipation of what was to come, Johnson, surveying the mob, did as he was told. A Catholic priest rushed to the pole to try to save McGhie. "Men, you don't know this man is guilty," Father William Powers pleaded. But after invoking God and asking the mob to stop, he was pushed back into the crowd. "To hell with the law!" crowd members yelled. "Remember the girl!"[21]

As a noose was pulled around McGhie's neck, he futilely cried out, "God be with me. I'm not the right man." His body was drawn up then fell as the rope loosened, only to be hoisted up again a few feet off the pavement. "String him up so we can see," the mob called out. As a new rope was brought forward, Elmer Jackson was dragged to the pole too. The young man from Topeka, Kansas, who had served overseas in the army, resignedly took some dice from his pocket and threw them to the pavement as he was led to the pole. "I won't need these any more in this world," he said. A youth offered the dice back to him, saying, "Well, you might want to roll them in the next," but it was an empty gesture; Jackson, whose mother had died just the year before, knew his luck, such as it had been in life, had run out. "Let the sailor tie the knot," a man near the pole motioned to another man in a U.S. Navy uniform. The sailor put the noose around Jackson's neck, and without a struggle, Jackson was strung up next to McGhie's lifeless body. When Police Chief Murphy finally arrived at the station around 11:30 P.M., he tried to get in and ordered the mob to disperse, but he was pushed away, unable to do anything on his own. As Murphy left to call up the militia, nineteen-year-old Elias Clayton was brought to the light pole. Clayton pleaded for his life: "Please, Oh God, don't kill me! I am innocent." But the crowd's hate-filled cries, "Lynch the third one! Lynch the third one!" sealed Clayton's fate.[22]

After being punched in the face, a noose was drawn over Clayton's head and his body yanked high up the pole. As with McGhie and Jackson, Clayton's clothing would be stripped off him down to his waist. Convulsing as he choked, Clayton was brutally kicked in the face by a man on the pole, who, in descending, fastened the rope to a spike, suspending Clayton's body in the air. Car lights were shone on the victim's bloody body, and only when a photographer came to snap photos was Clayton's corpse cut down so it would be in the pictures. The camera's shutter clicked as photographer Ralph Greenfield eerily snapped shots of a large group of white men in hats standing in a posed semicircle, all joking

The lynching of Isaac McGhie, Elmer Jackson, and Elias Clayton. Photograph courtesy of the Minnesota Historical Society.

around the dead bodies. "Send them pictures to Alabama," one person said. "Tell 'em to keep their niggers." Murphy's men, issued rifles with fixed bayonets, finally succeeded in dispersing the crowd and evicting the rioters from the badly damaged police station. Murphy then loaded the three remaining black prisoners into his dented police car and sped to Superior, Wisconsin, where the men would spend the night at the local jail. The dead bodies of the lynched men would be put on public exhibition at the morgue until the NAACP protested, and the photographer would later be fined for selling and displaying "obscene pictures."[23]

Minnesota Governor J. A. A. Burnquist had, upon learning of the lynchings, dispatched two companies of the Minnesota National Guard from Fort Snelling after midnight. As the president of St. Paul's branch of the NAACP, Burnquist felt a special need to respond and thought only troops, equipped with machine guns, rifles, and pistols, could restore order. The mob dispersed before the troops arrived, but it was not long before calls came for the lynch mob participants to be brought to justice. The morning after the lynching, Burnquist received a telegram from the NAACP's national field secretary offering all possible assistance. The telegram said that the "apprehension and rigorous punishment of lynchers" would have a "wholesome and salutary effect" throughout the nation. The NAACP's St. Paul branch also stepped into action by hiring J. Louis Ervin, an attorney and former Duluth resident, to investigate the lynching along with a private detective agency.[24]

On June 17 and 18, Ervin obtained affidavits from the frightened and mostly illiterate black men still held in custody. The NAACP investigator found that all of the jailed men maintained their innocence, but it was noted that many of the men "cannot write their names." The affidavits—all typewritten but signed with an *X* or left unsigned—told a much different story than that of Irene Tusken and Jimmie Sullivan. Seventeen-year-old Clarence Green, of Louisiana, said that "he saw a white boy and girl going down toward the Big Top" followed by "six colored fellows." He identified three of the men as "Miller," "Ironjaw," and "Louis" but did not know the other three. "I did not see them when they came back and do not know what they did," Green attested with an

X. Loney Williams, of Tennessee, also attested with an *X* that he was loading wagons at the time of the alleged rape. He said "Ironjaw" and "Lewis"—a reference to Louis Hayes—told him that they and William Miller and Isaac McGhie had been "out" with a "white girl" but did not tell him "what they did with her." A Kentucky man, Nate Graves, also attested that he had been loading a wagon at about 8:15 P.M. on the night in question when Miller told him that "Ironjaw and him" had "a jaz out in the woods" with a girl. "I was working and did not have anything to do with it," the affidavit said.[25]

The still-alive men identified in these affidavits, William Miller, Louis Hayes, and Frank "Ironjaw" Spicer, all denied committing any crime. Miller's affidavit, written in the third-person, said he "was not across in the woods with any bunch of boys or any girl and does not know what was done in the woods," and that he "did not assault the girl and does not know who did." Hayes's affidavit, captioned at the top, "Can read and write a little," also insisted that he "was not with any bunch that went out and assaulted a white girl," and that he knows "nothing about it." He was "standing off at a distance and heard a fellow they call Mat tell a bunch of boys that they had a girl over in the woods," the affidavit recites, with Hayes stating he did not know if it was "a white or colored girl." Twenty-year-old Frank Spicer, alias Ironjaw, signed his affidavit with an *X* under the caption, "Cannot read or write." It attested that he was from Mississippi, worked in a dressing room, and was waiting on performers on the night of June 14. He was not with "any bunch that assaulted any girl," he asserted, saying he "does not know anything about it," and that "officers in Virginia tried to make me tell a lie on somebody but I would not do that." The other circus workers' affidavits also denied any wrongdoing.[26]

After the lynching, Irene Tusken said she was fairly certain that those lynched had been the guilty ones. "Their faces all looked alike to me as they were lined up for identification but from their voices and their build I'm sure they were some of the right ones," she declared. Her father, however, was not so sure. "For fear of committing a crime against an innocent person I hope there will be no more mob violence," he told a newspaper reporter. "The courts and the law should be allowed to take their course," he said, thanking the police and circus officials "in helping my daughter and the boy while they were identifying the men whom they thought committed the assault." In the lynching's aftermath, only one newspaper, the *Duluth Ripsaw*, was willing to call the young couple's story a fabrication. "NEGROES DID NOT RAPE GIRL," its June 26th front-page headline screamed in extra-large type. "Any man or any woman who knows anything about human anatomy and, especially, the anatomy of a young girl and husky young Negro boys," it printed, "firmly will believe that such a girl, undergoing rape by six lusty young fellows, would have to be taken to a hospital, if not a morgue, instead of walking to a street car, going to bed without attention and then getting up a few hours later, apparently in normal physical condition." The tiny *Duluth Ripsaw* also proclaimed that young Jimmie Sullivan had "an intimate acquaintance with Old John Barleycorn, the mysteries of sex and various forms of low moral endeavor."[27]

The NAACP's private investigator found most people "close-mouthed" about Jimmie Sullivan and his girlfriend. The police chief simply told the investigator that Tusken was, as far as he knew, "a woman of strictly moral character and very highly regarded in the neighborhood." Yet, the NAACP investigation unearthed much evidence that closely tracked the *Duluth Ripsaw*'s conclusions. Albert Busch, a drugstore clerk who lived a block away from Tusken, for instance, told the investigator that he had heard rumors that Sullivan had been "taking liberties with the girl at the time the negroes were supposed to have assaulted her." Also, the detective was told by a shoe store owner that Sullivan was "a wild, vicious character" who, with other boys and girls, had broken into his summer cottage on Lake Superior and had smashed furniture, torn bed linens, and slept there. The store owner called Sullivan "a young man of evil repute," and said that a shoe salesman, George Hargrave, had told him that Tusken had been "running around with men" and was "of loose morals." Another man said Sullivan was always chasing women and drank excessively, and that at the broken-in cottage, he had seen empty beer and whiskey bottles lying everywhere. Unfortunately, because Hargrave was out of town, the investigator never managed to talk to him before he finished writing his report.[28]

In its detailed report, the NAACP-hired Employers Detective Service relayed that its private investigator had, "after considerable difficulty," actually interviewed the alleged rape victim. Irene Tusken told the detective that she and Jimmie Sullivan had walked down to the circus grounds, met acquaintances from West Duluth, and then walked to the rear of the main tent as the roustabouts were taking down the cook and animal tents. She and Sullivan, she said, had been watching the loading of wagons but were confronted with "a crowd of negroes," one with a gun, when they turned to walk away. After saying that the gun was put to Sullivan's head and that she was grabbed, her mother interrupted the interviewer to say, "Irene did not know just what happened then." The detective told Mrs. Tusken to let her daughter tell her own story, but Irene thereupon told the detective that she must have fainted as she could not remember what happened next. She said only that when she regained consciousness, "the negroes were walking away." Before Irene's mother terminated the interview, the girl told the detective she yelled once before her mouth was covered, did not know the names of the people she met at the circus, and could identify the "negroes" only by their "size and physique." The detective service also reported that the boy's father, Patrick Sullivan, "would not discuss the matter at all" and "brusquely remarked" that "he had an appointment and walked away."[29]

When NAACP leader William Francis read this report at a Twin Cities NAACP meeting, the packed-to-capacity crowd became convinced of the lynched men's innocence. One of only a few black lawyers in St. Paul, Francis disbelieved Sullivan and Tusken's story from the start, writing just a few days after the lynching to say that neither "had told the truth about what happened that night." His views were almost certainly shared by those at the meeting. When a collection was taken up, over $150 was raised to defray ongoing investigative costs even as the NAACP's national office considered using the investigator's report as publicity for its national anti-lynching campaign. One local NAACP leader, Dr. Valdo Turner, was so impressed with the investigator's report that he wanted to reprint it right away and release it to the public. However, the NAACP's national office had second thoughts, fearing a libel suit because, while the report had plenty of hearsay evidence, it lacked sufficient direct evidence regarding Tusken's and Sullivan's characters.[30]

That bigotry fueled the lynching is clear. The city had witnessed Ku Klux Klan cross burnings, and racial tensions existed in northern Minnesota as in other parts of the country. Blacks had come to the Duluth area from southern states and as far away as Haiti in search of jobs, and in 1920, the city's black population numbered just five hundred. "It was the color of the three prisoners that made them victims of the mob," the *Minneapolis Journal* wrote, calling the lynching a disgrace. "Had they been white," it said, "they might have been the objects of reprobation for the crime for which they were charged, but would no doubt have been left to the processes of the law." The Iron Range's *Ely Miner*, in contrast, said the lynching was "to be regretted by all lovers of law and order," but stated that the "consensus of opinion throughout the county is that while the thing was wrong in principle," it was "most effective" in deterring assaults on "more young girls." A *Mankato Free Press* editorial derided "black rascals" who "pounce like fiends on white women," and then said that just as "mad dogs are shot to death without ceremony," "[b]easts in human shape are entitled to but scant consideration."[31]

After the lynching, troops were stationed in black neighborhoods to protect black Duluthians and to keep the peace. Duluth's Kiwanis and Rotary clubs denounced the lynchings, but thirteen blacks brought to Duluth's St. Louis County Jail were held for investigation nonetheless. The circus workers would be held indefinitely and would stay behind bars for weeks until the county attorney's office decided what to do with them. "It is not necessary for us to have complaints or warrants against them," Sheriff Frank Magie said flatly. In the following days, black families had bricks thrown through their windows and received anonymous threats. A Republican gubernatorial candidate, J. A. O. Preus, on the other hand, called for tougher treatment of sex offenders while campaigning in Duluth. "If I am elected governor, I will do all in my power to increase the penalty," he pledged. Meanwhile, other officeholders promised to do their duty. Veteran St. Louis County Attorney Warren Greene, calling the "original crime" one of the "most atrocious" ever, publicly said that lynch mob participants would be brought to justice, and that no crime justifies resorting to mob law. As for William Murnian, the city's public safety commissioner, he tried to take credit for the fact that no whites had lost their lives in the attack on the jail. "I gave strict orders to all men to use firearms under no consideration, and I believe this had a great deal to do with the lack of serious injuries," he told the press.[32]

Almost everyone had something to say to the media, but government probes—compelling testimony—were started too in the wake of the lynchings. On June 17, members of Duluth's police department, including Lieutenant Barber and Sergeant Olson, were called before a special grand jury convened in Duluth to investigate the mob's work. The grand jury was needed, Judge William Cant explained, to "discover and punish" the lynchers. A military investigation into the police's handling of the affair was also launched on Governor Burnquist's orders, and the county attorney, too, initiated his own investigation. While some wanted to sweep the whole affair under the rug, Greene promised to bring all guilty parties to justice. In prosecuting lynch mob leaders, he declared, "no half way measures" would be taken. "I am going through with this thing," he said. "It is started now and I am going to finish it."[33]

As part of its month-long probe, grand jurors heard from Commissioner Murnian, a dozen police officers, and the thirteen black prisoners. Other key witnesses, Dr. Graham, Irene Tusken and her mother, and James Sullivan and his father, also testified along with newspapermen and attorney Hugh McClearn. Handing out indictments as it did its work, the grand jury issued twenty-five indictments for the crime of rioting or instigating a riot and, in some instances, indicted lynch mob participants for murder. The first indictments were handed out just over a week after the lynching, and more than ten men, all of whom pled not guilty, would face the most serious charge: first-degree murder. Although Duluth officials denounced the lynching, some city residents set up a

legal defense fund to pay attorneys to defend those indicted for rioting and murder and to gain their pre-trial release by posting bonds. To
avoid prosecution, some lynch mob members simply fled Duluth, leading prosecutor Greene to warn that lawbreakers "can't evade the law by
leaving the city." "It is our intention to bring before the grand jury every
person who had a part in the lynching," he said.[34]

In mid-July, the grand jury issued its findings, taking care to refer
only to the "alleged attack upon the young girl" and Sullivan's "version
of the affair." No criminal cases had yet been tried, and the grand jury's
report focused solely on the police department's failures and the lynch
mob's activities, not on whether a rape had occurred in the first place.
While sidestepping that central issue, grand jurors called rape "a most
horrible and brutal crime—a crime that to many of us is worse than
murder." The grand jury decried the mob's jailhouse "kangaroo court,"
concluding that if thirty-year sentences for rape were not severe enough,
the remedy was to go to the state legislature and not to resort to violence. Blaming Commissioner Murnian for the lynching, grand jurors
found that Murnian's lack of action had placed "the foulest blot" upon
Duluth ever known.[35]

The grand jury's final report indicted seven blacks, Max Mason,
William Miller, Clarence Green, Frank Spicer, Louis Hayes, Loney
Williams, and Nate Gray, for rape. However, the report exonerated the
six other men still held in custody, leading to their release, as well as
Isaac McGhie, one of the lynched men. The grand jury's posthumous
exoneration of McGhie was sweeping in breadth; it found no evidence
McGhie had "any part in the crime." "[H]e was merely being held at
police headquarters as an important witness," the report found. The
NAACP's investigation reached an even broader conclusion. "[E]vidence
secured since the Duluth lynching," the NAACP wrote to Governor
Burnquist on July 23, 1920, "clearly established the fact that the three
Negroes lynched in that city in June were not guilty of criminal assault
upon the young white girl." "[T]he girl's companion and she," the
NAACP's Walter White wrote, "made up the story to cover misdeeds
of their own."[36]

As the trial dates of lynch mob participants neared, prosecutor Warren Greene had to prioritize his office's resources because over 1,600 fire damage suits, the result of a deadly, destructive forest fire near Duluth, were already clogging the courts. Greene decided to try only a few cases of the lynch mob participants first, the trials taking place simultaneously before three different judges. With crowds of spectators thronging the court's corridors, the first trial, of alleged mob ringleader Henry Stephenson, started on August 30. Accused of rioting, Stephenson was charged with helping to batter the cell room's outer and inner steel doors. Sergeant Olson testified first about the mob's actions, and another policeman said Stephenson threatened his life with a sledgehammer. Nate Natelson, himself under indictment, also turned state's evidence and testified against Stephenson, saying he had seen Stephenson, in overalls, use a fire hose against police and swing a sledgehammer at the hinges of the outer jail doors. After just fifty-five minutes of deliberation, Stephenson was convicted of rioting and sentenced to not more than five years in prison.[37]

But after that, the prosecution got mixed results. The trial of William Rozon ended in a hung jury after more than thirty-one hours of deliberations, even though Lieutenant Barber, the prosecution's star witness, identified Rozon as a mob participant. While truck driver Louis Dondino and nineteen-year-old Carl Hammerberg, who helped the mob in its water fight, were both convicted of rioting on September 13, that ended the prosecution's limited success. No murder convictions against lynch mob participants were ever obtained, and the acquittals of other men took the steam out of the prosecutions. In the trials, jurors often overlooked the most damaging testimony. For example, attorney Hugh McClearn testified that Leonard Hedman, accused of making inflammatory speeches on June 15, had stood on an automobile fender and demanded that the mob "get the niggers." Instead, the jury credited Hedman's flimsy claim that he actually spoke against lynching and only rode downtown in Louis Dondino's truck because he was going downtown anyway. In an impassioned, nearly two-hour closing argument, Hedman's lawyer claimed a conviction would ruin the young defendant's life and stain his family's name, an argument the jury, after twenty-eight hours of deliberation, apparently found appealing.[38]

The jailed circus workers' rape trials did not get started until Max Mason's trial in late November 1920. Leery of trying sexual assault cases with no concrete eyewitness identifications, Greene had, on two prior nights, July 10 and 11, brought the jailed blacks back to the area of the circus grounds. While nearly a month had elapsed since the alleged rape, this gave Irene Tusken and Jimmie Sullivan, up to then unable to pick out any suspect with any specificity, another chance to identify their alleged assailants. Lo and behold, at those mid-July, late-night rendezvous, Tusken and Sullivan both identified—by voice—Max Mason as the man holding the gun in the reported assault, as well as William Miller as an accomplice. To further aid Greene's case preparation, the jailed circus workers had also been brought before grand jurors on July 12 without either the benefit of counsel or being advised of their rights. Also, Greene ordered venereal disease testing for all of the black prisoners. When Dr. M. A. Nicholson reported that Mason was infected with gonorrhea, local prosecutors, still unable to secure any confession, decided to move forward and try Mason for rape. Dr. William Coventry, assigned to examine Tusken, had already concluded that she had a case of gonorrhea too, allowing the prosecution to argue that Mason was a rapist.[39]

Unwilling to fathom the possibility that two white teenagers might be lying, Duluth prosecutors embraced the teenagers' story of rape. In a written report to Minnesota's governor, Greene said that "some five or six negroes" confronted Tusken and Sullivan at the circus grounds after dark, and that a gun was placed to Sullivan's head, even though no gun was ever found. The assailants, Greene said, had taken a ring from the "young lady's finger" but later returned it and put their hands in Sullivan's pocket but obtained no money. According to Greene, the gang of circus workers had then taken the couple westerly across the grounds to a nearby ravine. Greene told the governor that "some of the negroes" then "threw the young lady to the ground while one held the young man with the gun some eight or ten feet away." "The young lady thereupon fainted," Greene relayed, adopting in toto the girl's story. Greene said that while Tusken was in that condition, "three or four of the negroes pulled up her dresses and got on top of her in succession, going away as they finished." Greene claimed that Mason was the man who held the gun to the boy's head, and that two men had "admitted complicity in the affair" even though the girl's family physician found no evidence of physical violence. Miller, Greene reported, was the man who placed his hand over the girl's mouth, threw her to the ground, and was attempting to have intercourse with her when she revived.[40]

At Mason's trial, Tusken testified she had known Sullivan "intimately" for over a year and had unexpectedly bumped into him at the circus grounds, where, near the menagerie, they watched "colored men" taking down tents and moving animals before realizing nearly everyone was gone. "When we turned around," Tusken testified, "there were five or six negroes stopped us" and "wouldn't let us go by." She said that "the shortest of the bunch" pointed a gun at Sullivan's head, and that "one took away my ring" and then gave it back before they carried her across a field and threw her down. Tusken told the jury she screamed when first grabbed but was threatened with the words, "Don't scream or I will shoot—." "[T]he tall one"—"I think it was Miller, his name was," Tusken testified—was said to have put a hand over her mouth. Tusken told the all-male jury that once on the ground, she fainted. Saying the next thing she remembered was waking up to find a man on top of her, Tusken said she "fought and pushed" off that man before Sullivan and she took the streetcar home. "I went right upstairs," and "I bathed myself there in the bathroom," Tusken testified. After Tusken said she wore a "union suit" that night, Greene put into evidence a torn, dirty suit. "Were those tears there before this encounter with these negroes out in the ravine, or not?" Greene asked. "They were not," Tusken replied twice.[41]

After her father spoke with Mr. Sullivan by telephone, Tusken added, her mother woke her up, and she and her parents went down to the police station at about three o'clock. Outside the circus train, Tusken noted, "I picked out just the ones that I thought were the ones that were there that night." Greene merely perfunctorily confirmed the time—9:30 A.M. on June 15—that Dr. Graham examined Irene before zeroing in on her identification of Mason in mid-July at the circus grounds. "I will ask you," Greene said, looking into Tusken's eyes, "whether or not you saw this defendant down there on either of those nights?" "I did," Tusken replied unequivocally but then had trouble with Greene's next question: "Which night was he down there?" Tusken replied not with an answer but with a question of her own: "He was down there the last night?" Caught off-guard, Greene turned to a new question altogether so the girl would not have to respond at all to his initial one. "I will ask you whether or not you recognized him?" Greene asked instead. "I did," Tusken replied. "I recognized him as the one that held the gun," she said.[42]

When Greene finished, Max Mason's African American lawyer, Ferdinand Lee Barnett, cross-examined her. The stepson of Ida Wells Barnett, a nationally known anti-lynching crusader, the able Illinois lawyer had been hired by the NAACP after defending blacks accused of murder in Chicago's 1919 race riots. After Tusken failed to answer two of Barnett's questions, one of which was, "What was done to you?" Barnett asked Mason's accuser a new question: "Anyone put their hands on you?" "I know two of them did," she replied. Although Tusken claimed there were six assailants during her direct examination, she told Barnett during his questioning that there were "five or six." "One was Mason and the other was Miller," she said, unable to identify any others. "Did you see the face of any of the men well enough to know them?" Barnett asked. "No, sir," she replied, telling Barnett she could not identify anyone's face because it had been too dark. Tusken also admitted that she failed to identify any of her alleged assailants at the train yard in the wee hours of the morning.[43]

After that, Barnett went for the jugular, asking what happened between the date of the alleged rape and the middle of July that enabled her to identify her asserted assailants. "Well, I don't know; I think it was on account of my condition," Tusken stumbled. "Anything else?" Barnett asked. "I think not," the teenage stenographer replied. To convey to the jury the highly suggestive nature of the mid-July outdoor identification procedure, Barnett asked another cut-to-the-chase question: "How did you come to hear the name of Mason and Miller out there?" "When they were brought up for identification they were asked their names," Tusken told him, affirming that it was the prosecutor, Warren Greene, who had asked the men to give their names at that time. When Barnett asked Tusken whether there were any distinguishing features of his client that made him stand out, Tusken said, "there was." The court reporter took down Tusken's fragmented answer: "The man that was Max Mason was—his face was darker than—and black; and his size,—he was shorter than—than quite a few brought before me. And he had—his build was just about like that one that held the gun." "That was all that helped you fix the identification?" Barnett asked incredulously. "Yes," Tusken replied curtly, adding later that Mason had "a peculiar walk" too, though she could not remember the clothes he had on that night. Barnett's last question simply highlighted the fact that Tusken had not reported a rape to police before going to bed.[44]

After Irene Tusken stepped down from the witness box, eighteen-year-old James Sullivan, her escort, was sworn as the prosecution's next witness. The courtroom, from which the public had been excluded during Tusken's testimony because of its sensitive nature, was now packed, with "[h]alf the audience composed of negro men and women" and "every inch of sitting and standing room" filled to capacity. Sullivan testified that he and Tusken were "held up by some colored men" after they split off from two girls and two boys at the circus. One man "put a gun to my head and told me to keep still or he would blow my brains out," Sullivan told jurors, saying they grabbed hold of Tusken, at which point she hollered once. "[O]ne of them put his hand over her mouth," he said, "and one of them I think took her ring off but gave it back to her again." After being led into a ravine at gunpoint, Sullivan said, "five or six in the bunch" forced Irene to the ground. "I saw one of them get on top of her at a time," he testified. "Did you see what was done with her dresses, if anything?" Greene asked. "The dresses were pulled up," Sullivan replied, noting that "I saw about four get on her at that time." He also recounted how he had later met up with Tusken and her father at the

Canadian Northern yards, where the circus workers were lined up and police were questioning them. "[W]e picked out the ones we thought was about the size of the ones that were in the bunch," Sullivan told the jury.[45]

When Sullivan described the mid-July identification procedure, his memory was less than clear. "I think it was the latter part of July, or August, but I am not sure," he said. "Who was with you?" Greene asked. "My father," Jimmie said. "Just tell the jury what happened out there, just how that was done?" Greene directed. "They brought one man out at a time and you asked him questions and I stated whether I thought he was in the bunch, or not," Sullivan explained. When asked if he recognized the man that held the gun to his head, Sullivan replied, "Yes, sir." "Which one was that?" Greene followed up. "That man sitting there," Jimmie said, pointing his finger at Max Mason.[46]

Barnett's cross-examination sought to undermine the boy's dramatic identification of his client from the witness box. "Did you see his face?" Barnett quizzed of the man Sullivan said put a gun to his head. "No," Sullivan conceded, "I didn't get a good look at his face." "At that time you did not recognize him?" and "You were not able to recognize him the next morning, were you?" Barnett asked next. "No, sir," Sullivan answered both times, saying, "I picked them out by their size." "Size and voice," he clarified. When asked about the morning of June 15 at the railroad yard, Sullivan said he had trouble identifying anyone because he was "excited" and "nervous." "I had been up all night long," he said, adding, "They all looked the same to me," and "I couldn't tell their faces." Sullivan said he only picked out "the ones I thought were about the size" because the police asked him to. "I told them I could not tell by their faces," Sullivan admitted. "They didn't want to take them all down," he noted later, saying, "I picked out some, and the girl picked out some, and the Captain picked out some."[47]

Two police officers on duty the night of the lynching testified next. The police officer in charge that night, John Murphy, recounted how he had arrested men at the Canadian Northern freight depot—"I believe we picked out thirteen men," he said—and how he drove to Virginia to arrest others. "Whereabouts did you get hold of this man Mason?"

Greene asked. "At Virginia," Murphy answered. "I believe we picked out nine more men at Virginia," he began, then modified his answer: "It was eight or nine, I don't just exactly remember the number now, it was something like that." When Police Captain A. G. Fiskett testified, he described in greater detail how the thirteen detainees from the train depot were identified: "I questioned the colored people and the girl would say: 'This is one.' We put him aside." "Some others of them she wasn't so positive," Fiskett said. Noting Tusken would say things like, "Looks like him" and "Sounds like him," Fiskett testified that they finally selected thirteen. "Did you people select some yourselves?" Greene asked. "Yes," Fiskett said, explaining why: "Because we thought the way they acted,—acted suspicious, that is, they didn't give a direct answer or else they contradicted themselves when questioned. So we picked them up—took them up to the police headquarters." On cross-examination, Barnett asked Fiskett about the lineup at the train depot, "Well, now, whom did you pick out?" "I couldn't recollect who I picked out now," Fiskett conceded.[48]

The Tuskens' family physician, Dr. David Graham, took the witness stand next, testifying that he examined Irene Tusken on the morning of June 15 while she lay in bed. "And did you examine her private parts at that time?" Greene asked. "Yes, sir," the doctor replied, saying he found "a normal condition" and no rupture of the girl's hymen. The medical testimony was so weak that Barnett asked only a few questions. "[W]hat was her general condition mentally and physically, as far as you could tell?" Barnett inquired. "She seemed slightly nervous," Dr. Graham replied, noting that her physical condition was good. After Dr. Graham said he performed both a digital and speculum examination, Barnett asked more specifically about that vaginal examination. "When you made the examination by the speculum," Barnett questioned, "did any tears, wounds or abrasions appear?" "No, sir," Dr. Graham replied, saying his digital examination found no evidence of soreness, sensitivity, or injury. "Doctor," Barnett asked next, "in case a violent assault and rape were committed on a female about the age of eighteen years, would or would there not be physical evidence of the rape?" "That would be hard to answer," Dr. Graham said evasively, admitting only that he could not remember prescribing any medicine for the girl on the morning of her examination.[49]

Dr. William Coventry and Dr. M. A. Nicholson wrapped up the state's case. Dr. Coventry testified he examined Tusken on July 10 and that his examination showed she had gonorrhea. "I found a very profuse vaginal discharge around the opening that the urine comes out of," Dr. Coventry told jurors, adding that "the case was acute—a recent case." Dr. Nicholson also described examining the jailed circus workers for venereal disease. "No. 8, Max Mason," he testified, "showed a large number of gonococci present, and the others were negative." "What I want to know is this," Greene ended, "as to whether or not the man had the case a month before that time?" "Probably," Dr. Nicholson conjectured. On cross-examination, Barnett asked Nicholson if he was sure. "Could you tell, doctor, from what you saw, when that disease was contracted?" Nicholson thought. "Well," he answered, "you couldn't tell accurately; it was more than two weeks." "How much longer standing than two weeks—could you tell that?" Barnett followed up. "No," Dr. Nicholson admitted.[50]

After calling jailed circus worker Louis Hayes to show the intimidating interrogation tactics of Duluth's police, Barnett recalled Dr. David Graham as a witness—this time for the defense. "I made an examination of the girl, a vaginal examination with a speculum and a digital, as it is called, with a finger. Found the girl clean looking in every way at that time," Dr. Graham testified. Barnett then asked a series of rapid fire questions: "[W]ere there then any tears in the vagina?" "Any abrasions?" "Were there any bruises?" "Was there any inflammation of the parts?" "Was any soreness complained of?" "[D]id the patient flinch at all?" "No, sir," Dr. Graham answered each time. The medical testimony finished, Barnett then called Max Mason to the stand before resting his case.[51]

Facing a long prison sentence if convicted, Mason testified that he joined John Robinson's Circus in late April 1920, working in the cookhouse by day and at the big top by night. He had arrived in Duluth on Sunday at about three o'clock, had done some work that day, and then had helped serve breakfast the next morning, the same day as the alleged assault. "[W]hat did you do in the cook house?" Barnett asked. "Waiting table; peeled spuds, potatoes," Mason answered, saying he finished those duties at around 6:30 P.M. "I got through with the tables, pulled off my apron and coat and put on my overalls, got ready to take down the cook house," Mason testified, saying he had helped take it down and load it in the wagon before going to the big top to work until ten o'clock. "[W]ere you at any time away from that work" and with "four, five or six other men" to "hold up or make an assault or attack upon a young woman named Irene Tusken?" Barnett asked point-blank. "No, sir," Mason replied.[52]

When Barnett asked Mason about Dr. Nicholson's visit to the jail, Mason said the doctor's examination was coercive. "If you don't be examined," Mason said Dr. Nicholson told him, the jailer would put him in "the dungeon" on "bread and water." To avoid that, Mason testified, "I went on and was examined." Mason admitted to being treated for gonorrhea in December 1919 when he was in Louisville, Kentucky, but said he used some medicine for about three weeks until, as Mason testified, "the doctor pronounced me well and I quit using it." "During all the time you have been in the jail," Barnett asked, "have you had any discharge?" "No, sir," Mason replied. On cross-examination, Greene tried to portray Mason as a liar. "Your claim is that you did not have any disease at that time?" Greene asked point blank. "That is my claim," Mason answered. Greene then tried to get the jury to infer guilt from Mason's initial refusal to be examined. "You say that at the time Doctor Nicholson was up at the jail that you protested vigorously against being examined at all?" Greene asked. "I refused to be examined," Mason admitted, saying later in response to another line of questioning that he had only one week of formal schooling.[53]

The closing arguments in the case were contentious. "Something did happen at the circus grounds in West Duluth, June 14," Barnett told the jury, conceding that "[t]he girl's ring may have been stolen and the boy's watch taken." But, Barnett argued, "the offense charged in the indictment against this defendant was not committed." Barnett accused prosecutor Warren Greene of having coached both Tusken and Sullivan to identify Max Mason by his stride, voice, and form. "Is it fair to send a man to the penitentiary for 20 years on that identification?" Barnett asked. Appealing to jurors to consider the truth, Barnett asked jurors whether they were going to believe his client or the prosecution's "cock-and-bull story." "I don't ask any favor for a black man—only justice," Barnett argued. His ethics questioned, an angry Greene closed by making a law-and-order appeal. "You will decide the most important case that has ever come before this court," Greene told jurors. "Why do we have mobs?" he pondered aloud. "It's because people think the negroes won't be convicted: That's why they take the law in their own hands." "The people of Duluth," Greene emphasized, "want to know through your verdict that when a white girl is ravished by a black or white man and the man is proven guilty, as in this case, the man is going to be found guilty."[54]

The trial judge, L. S. Nelson, instructed the jury on the morning of November 27, 1920. The instructions were neutral at first but then quickly drifted away from instructing on the law to strongly hinting at what the jury's verdict should be. "Gentleman of the Jury," the instructions began, "it is the claim of the State that on the 14th day of June" Max Mason "did wrongfully, unlawfully, wilfully and feloniously have sexual intercourse with one Irene Tusken against her will and without her consent." "It is the claim of the defendant that he is not guilty of the offense," the judge said, before recapping the state's case in a very tilted fashion. "[E]vidence has been introduced tending to show that while Irene Tusken and her escort, James Sullivan, were upon the circus grounds," the judge told jurors before their deliberations, "this defendant, with three or four others, stopped them as they turned to leave the grounds, held a gun to the head of Sullivan" and that "these men had sexual intercourse with her and that the defendant was one of them."[55]

After five hours of deliberation, the jury found Mason guilty of rape, and he was sentenced to "not more than thirty years" in prison. The *Duluth News Tribune* reported that "Mason received the verdict calmly, though his face bore a troubled expression as he elbowed his way through the crowd and out of the courtroom." The medical testimony at trial had given jurors all they needed to hear in order to convict. "It was the gonorrhea thing that clinched it," one juror recalled later. Defense lawyer Ferdinand Lee Barnett could not believe it. "I don't see how the jury could arrive at that decision based on the evidence presented in this case," he said, saying the defense was prepared to appeal. Attorney R. C. McCullough, another attorney assisting with Mason's defense, was equally upset. "There might have been a robbery," he said, but contended Tusken and Sullivan had concocted a tale of rape after they left the ravine. "I can see how they could have planned this rape story then in order to get even for being robbed," McCullough told the press.[56]

The jury's verdict dealt a shocking blow to the NAACP, which relied mostly on small donations—from church collections to contributions from the John Robinson's Circus and its employees to monies from the jailed men's families—to fund its defense efforts. With William Miller's trial only two days away, a new African American lawyer, Charles Scrutchin, took over as lead counsel. St. Paul attorney William Francis liked Scrutchin, a respected Bemidji lawyer and University of Michigan Law School graduate, and had wanted him to be retained from the start. As close friends, Francis and Scrutchin had corresponded about the rape allegations early on, and after hearing the jailed men had been taken out to the circus grounds in mid-July, Francis thought Scrutchin's services were needed. Amos Scruggs, another black lawyer who had delivered paychecks to the jailed circus workers, had told Francis that Warren Greene had taken the jailed men out to the circus grounds four to six at a time, and then had them move about and talk in Tusken's and Sullivan's presence, enabling them to later identify the men by their forms, voices, or movements. "It appears to me, if this is true," Francis wrote Duluth's NAACP president at the time, "that it is taking an unfair advantage of the men and they ought to have some advice along that line."[57]

Miller's trial went much differently. Scrutchin—married to a white woman—wasted no time in pummeling Jimmie Sullivan with questions as to why he and Irene Tusken came within three blocks of West Duluth's police station yet failed to report the assault right away. "I wanted to talk to my father first because he knew more what to do than I did," was all Sullivan could say. Another circus worker, Louis Hayes, testified Miller was busy working at the time in question, and Scrutchin's cross-examination of Dr. Graham was very effective. "Assuming the girl's story is true, and that she had fainted at the time the assault took place, would not an attack by six Negroes upon the girl have left physical evidence of tears or lacerations?" Miller's lawyer inquired. "I do not think I would have found her in a normal condition the next morning," Dr. Graham replied, unable, in good conscience, to say anything else. By the time of Warren Greene's closing argument, the county attorney was appealing to the jury's sympathies, trying to sway jurors not with evidence, but by telling them that if they acquitted Miller, they would be labeling the young girl—"a virgin," Greene said—"a falsifier and a prostitute." "God knows she has suffered enough already without having a jury say to her that she is not only a liar, but that she contracted the disease communicated to her by Mason from some other person," Greene pitched the jurors. But the trail-blazing and fearless Scrutchin did not back down. "If this girl was ravished as she claims to have been, she would have been taken to a morgue instead of her home," he argued, pleading for an acquittal to show that Duluth still had "a little spark of justice burning."[58]

The jury's acquittal of Miller after six hours of deliberation set him free. It also set off a chain of events, leading to the dismissal of the prosecution's remaining cases. "I understand from the Jury," Greene wrote after Miller's trial, "that they did not feel satisfied with the identification." Greene indicated he would request the dismissal of the remaining rape cases because Tusken and Sullivan were unable to identify anyone else, and "the negroes who informed the police as to their complicity in the crime were hung by the mob." In moving to dismiss the charges, Greene explained in open court that as "there is no evidence to take the place of that destroyed by the mob, I do not feel that the state is justified in holding these defendants longer." "That a rape of a most revolting type took place at the circus grounds in West Duluth last June is a fact that is clear to those who are familiar with all the details of the case,"

Greene told the court, adding that on the morning after the alleged rape, Eli Clayton and Elmer Jackson "confessed their part in it to the police," and that, with Isaac McGhie, "gave the police information upon which others were apprehended." "There is no question but that Clayton and Jackson would have turned state's evidence," Greene said, lamenting only that the mob hung his witnesses.[59]

The NAACP, which saw the "spreading of the lynching evil to a point so far North as Duluth" as a calamity for race relations, celebrated Miller's acquittal, and the national office wrote to Scrutchin to thank him for his splendid work in the case. The victory was particularly significant because 1920s Duluth was a place where any kind of perceived sexual misconduct—even risqué dancing—was frowned upon. In a 1920 Duluth newspaper article, for example, the police called for the adoption of a "daylight law" requiring a six-inch distance between dance partners and banning outright "[t]he shimmy, bunny-hug, angle-worm twist, frog hog, cheek-to-cheek dancing and other steps." It was feared by the NAACP that in this intolerant atmosphere, the mere allegation of a black-on-white gang rape would lead to a conviction of any African American, something the Miller acquittal disproved.[60]

As a result of the Duluth lynchings, there was an exodus of blacks from Duluth even as an NAACP branch was formed in that city. The NAACP's statewide membership also lobbied hard at the state capitol for an anti-lynching bill, which was the brainchild of William Francis's wife, Nellie, a leader in Baptist organizations and the women's suffrage movement. Nellie Francis wrote the anti-lynching legislation with the help of her husband, one of a handful of black St. Paul attorneys. Having worked for the Northern Pacific Railroad's legal department and been in private practice, William Francis had done everything from probate proceedings to adoptions to criminal defense work. He and Nellie, first a stenographer and then a ten-year West Publishing Company employee, were married in 1893. A sophisticated woman, Nellie was the only black among eighty-four high school graduates; her essay on "Race Problems" won second prize in fact in an annual oratorical contest. Her husband, who made two failed but pioneering bids for public office, traveled frequently and won many of his cases. Civil rights leader Roy Wilkins described him as an "elegant" man who "parted his hair in the middle, wore high white wing collars, soft silk ties, and a red rose in his lapel."[61]

As a local NAACP leader, William Francis wrote to Dr. W. E. B. Du Bois at the NAACP's national office for information about lynchings. The national office immediately sent him a packet of materials, including a copy of Kentucky's anti-lynching law. He and Nellie then worked hard to gain public support for their own legislation. Mass meetings were held, and Du Bois himself traveled to St. Paul and Duluth churches in March 1921 as part of the effort. Attended by state legislators sponsoring the anti-lynching bill, these events were interspersed with Bible readings, folk songs, and choir music. At one rally, there was dancing until midnight. The Francises' views on race relations, influenced by the prejudice they experienced themselves, could be summed up in William Francis's own words. "The solution of the whole problem," he said, "is simple justice, a recognition of the fact that the rights of the humblest citizens are as worthy of protection as the highest."[62]

Though fewer than nine thousand blacks lived in Minnesota, the husband-and-wife team of William and Nellie Francis, both on their local NAACP board, had considerable political clout. William was a member of the Minnesota Republican Central Committee and a presidential elector in 1920, and penned a personal letter to Governor Burnquist in early July 1920, enclosing the NAACP's investigative report on the Duluth lynchings, to which the governor wrote back, thanking him. Like her husband, Nellie was a leader in local civic organizations, serving, among other positions, as the director of the Republican Colored Women for Minnesota campaign. A leader of Minnesota's women's suffrage movement, Clara Ueland, called Nellie a "star" with the "spirit" of "a flame," and Nellie spoke out against lynchings at every opportunity at League of Women Voters' meetings as part of her lobbying campaign.[63]

The Francises' bill easily cleared the Minnesota Legislature and was signed into law in April 1921. The vote in the senate was forty-one to zero, and the house vote, eighty-one to one, was nearly unanimous too.

William Francis. Photograph courtesy of the Minnesota Historical Society.

Nellie Francis. Photograph courtesy of the Minnesota Historical Society.

Governor Preus had stated even before the bill's passage that it would be a pleasure to sign it. The new Minnesota law made any county in which a lynching occurred liable for damages in a civil suit to the dependents of the person lynched. The maximum amount that could be recovered under the law was $7,500, the same amount, not coincidentally, that had been unsuccessfully sought in 1920 from the City of Duluth in a wrongful death suit brought by Elmer Jackson's father. That negligence lawsuit had alleged that Clifford Jackson's lynched son had never been arrested before in his hometown of Topeka, Kansas, and that the Duluth police department was liable for Jackson's death. The lawsuit was filed by Elisha Scott, a young black lawyer from Topeka who later played a key role in the landmark case of *Brown v. Topeka Board of Education*. The new anti-lynching law also provided that any sheriff or other law enforcement officer who should "fail or neglect to use all lawful means to resist" a lynching "shall be removed from office by the Governor." The new Minnesota law resembled anti-lynching laws in other states.[64]

In St. Paul, a fitting public testimonial was thrown in Nellie Francis's honor in May 1921 at the Pilgrim Baptist Church. Proclaimed by NAACP activist James Loomis "as the most important piece of legislation affecting our race that has ever been passed in our state," Minnesota's new anti-lynching law, Loomis said, would persuade other states to follow suit and might even help secure the passage of a federal law "to stop the awful American crime of lynching." Nellie, who was presented with an engraved "loving cup" for her "untiring efforts" in the campaign for the state's new law, was praised for her devotion to ending racial prejudice. Visibly affected, Nellie told the large church audience, "Your children will reap the harvest of our solidarity—of our determination to stand together, to fight together, and, if needs be, to die together; for they are dying, every day, the men and women of our race, martyrs to lynch-law." While lynchings in America did not stop in 1920, Minnesota never witnessed another lynching after that time.[65]

Despite the passage of Minnesota's anti-lynching law, one sore spot remained for the NAACP: Max Mason's rape conviction. The NAACP had fought hard at Mason's trial to prove his innocence, and the guilty

verdict was met with disbelief. The NAACP's Duluth branch, fraction-
alized by a power struggle for control of it, had scant resources but still
managed to piece together enough money to pay for an appeal. Letters
like one from St. Paul resident Andrew Jackson ensured that everything
possible that could be done would be done on Mason's behalf. While
in Winnipeg, where the John Robinson's Circus performed shortly after
the lynchings, Jackson spoke to some of the black circus workers in the
troupe about the alleged rape. In a letter to his wife, later sent to the
NAACP, Jackson said he learned that "there was a white man selling
whiskey on the grounds" who had his whiskey taken away from him, and
that the man "had some women hustling at the same time and he caused
the woman to holla rape." In December 1920, the president of the
NAACP's Duluth branch wrote to the organization's national headquarters: "Max Mason was convicted largely on the doctor's statement that
he had infected the girl," the letter said, hoping for a reversal of Mason's
conviction because "a subsequent examination by a specialist shows no
trace of disease." To raise the $400 needed for the trial record's tran-
scription, Mason's attorney, Ferdinand Lee Barnett, traveled the state
and spoke at churches, with NAACP-sponsored flyers proclaiming,
"Come! And Show Your Race Loyalty."[66]

After cobbling together the money to perfect the appeal and enlist-
ing William Francis's help with it, the NAACP eventually took Mason's
case to the state's highest court. The argument of the NAACP's lawyers
was simple. "The most casual study of the evidence," Mason's appellate
brief read, "shows that the State absolutely failed to prove that the crime
of rape was committed." "Not a word of direct evidence is shown in the
record," the brief argued, "because the prosecuting witness—the victim
of the alleged rape, testified that she was unconscious from the time she
was thrown to the ground . . . and did not testify whether or not there
was penetration." "A few hours after the alleged assault," it continued,
Tusken "looked him in the face and did not identify him." Mason's brief
concluded by saying that "calm consideration of the evidence as shown
by the transcript, forces the conclusion that whatever may have happened
on the night of June 14th at the circus grounds, certainly the evidence

fails to show beyond a reasonable doubt that the crime of rape was committed by the defendant."[67]

In June 1922, however, the Minnesota Supreme Court upheld Mason's rape conviction. The court acknowledged that neither the girl nor her escort could identify the "negroes" after their initial arrests, but picked out Mason only in mid-July. Though identified only "from his size, his general appearance, his talk and his walk," the court found Mason's identification "sufficient." The state's highest court saw the medical testimony of venereal disease as corroborating a rape and credited Tusken's testimony that she had never had intercourse with any other man. "This testimony taken all together," the court opined, "made out a chain of circumstantial evidence corroborative of the testimony of the young man and woman." The court conceded that no one testified as to vaginal penetration and that "[t]he complaining witness was unconscious at the time of the assault." But it ruled that "[t]he evidence of a physician who examined complainant that he could not say there had been penetration is not conclusive that penetration had not taken place."[68]

A blistering dissent, authored by Duluth native Justice Homer Dibell, said the "story upon which the conviction rests" is "strange" and "strikingly improbable." The alleged rape victim upon returning home, he noted, "went upstairs, passing her father with the remark, 'I am going to bed,'" then "stopped at her mother's room, saying 'Mama, I met Jimmie tonight and we went to the circus.'" After receiving "the kindly response, 'All right, dear, go to bed now,'" Dibell wrote, the girl "went to her room, then to the bathroom, and then to bed and to sleep." "She made no complaint," Justice Dibell emphasized. He also pointed to Mason's denial of guilt and the treating physician's examination of her shortly after the alleged assault. The doctor found "a normal condition" with "no abrasions nor bruises nor inflammation nor evidence of soreness or tenderness." A former district judge in Duluth before his elevation to the Minnesota Supreme Court in 1918, Dibell was not one to mince words. "There is perhaps a possibility that six negroes committed the crime just as charged," he said, but concluded that "[c]onvictions are not rested on possibilities."[69]

On the identification issue, Dibell pointed out that when Mason was first brought before the girl at about 5:00 A.M. on June 15, she did not identify him. Finding the evidence legally insufficient, Dibell concluded that "[i]t is common knowledge that colored men are not easily distinguished in daytime and less readily in the dark" and that "[y]oung southern negroes, such as these, look much alike to the northerner." "That the girl was diseased on July 10 and Mason on July 19," Dibell added, proved little. "[A]bout all that can be said is that the condition of Mason was consistent with guilt, if a crime was committed," Dibell said. "It was not inconsistent with his innocence." "A like condition in any other man in Duluth that night, white or black," Dibell wrote, was consistent with either guilt or innocence, and thus the disease did not prove Mason was a rapist. Dibell concluded that it was only "a chance guess" by the majority of the court that Mason was connected with any offense.[70]

In the end, although his sentence called for up to thirty years behind bars, Mason was discharged from prison in September 1925 after serving approximately five years for his rape conviction. Although the new St. Louis County Attorney, Mason Forbes, and Max Mason's trial judge, L. S. Nelson, both supported Mason's release, he was nonetheless ordered to return to Alabama and remain out of Minnesota until November 1941. Forbes told the Board of Pardons that he "never felt that the evidence in the case was any too strong" and stated his opinion that "if the defendant had been a white man he would not have been convicted"; Judge Nelson wrote the pardon board to say, "I have always had some doubt about his guilt," that "the evidence of identification was far from satisfactory," and that Irene Tusken and Jimmie Sullivan's story "did not appear to be probable." Louis Dondino and Henry Stephenson, on the other hand, were paroled after spending just over a year behind bars. Carl Hammerberg, the only other person convicted of participating in the riot, was paroled in June 1922 but died less than two years later when he got trapped in a railroad refrigeration car while trying to hitch a ride from Minneapolis to Duluth. While most of the lynch mob participants would escape any form of punishment, the Duluth lynchings did help galvanize the nation's resolve to fight racial prejudice. St. Paul's Roy Wilkins, then a college student, felt "sick, scared, and angry" when he read about the lynchings, but later, incensed by them, became a national leader in America's civil rights movement. Not only did the Duluth lynchings force the nation to realize that racism was not just a southern phenomenon, but the NAACP's crusade against lynchings, one of the organization's early causes, would propel the issue of civil rights onto the American stage.[71]

The Duluth lynchings, no doubt, were a taboo subject for far too long in Minnesota, at least until the publication of Michael Fedo's book on the subject in the 1970s. Some people refused to talk about them at all, and others simply felt shame over what had happened. "Duluthians," one Duluth history wrote of the lynchings, "prefer not to hear the rattle of the skeleton in the closet." But things are changing. The graves of the three lynching victims were finally marked at a ceremony in 1991, and in 2001, city leaders gathered on the street corner where the three men were lynched to announce a "Week of Remembrance." "I find it difficult to believe it could happen in Duluth, Minnesota, but it did," Mayor Gary Doty said at the time, "but we hope to use it as a stepping-off point toward better race relations in this community." If the racial divisions created by America's past are ever to fully heal, human tragedies like the Duluth lynchings certainly can no longer be shelved in a closet or forgotten. Duluthians—indeed, all Americans—must never forget the horror and injustice wrought by extrajudicial killings in the past century, be they in Mississippi or Minnesota.[72]

Conclusion

The popularity of America's death penalty has ebbed and flowed. The anti-gallows movement in the United States gathered momentum in the 1830s, but those reform efforts, continuing into the 1850s, were quashed by a concurrent push for private executions and, ultimately, by the outbreak of the Civil War. When tens of thousands of innocent lives were being lost in the bloodiest conflict in American history, anti–death penalty reformers held out little hope for their cause. The Progressive Era brought the death penalty's abolition in Minnesota and elsewhere, but the eruption of World War I brought that penal reform movement to a standstill once more. The national anti-gallows movement lost its momentum during that war, and many American states actually reinstated death penalty laws. While the number of executions steadily declined from the mid-1930s to the late 1960s, state-sanctioned executions in America rose in the 1980s and 1990s.[1]

Minnesota has bucked the national trend toward more and more executions. Indeed, no death penalty law has been on the state's statute books since 1911 when George MacKenzie led the fight to abolish capital punishment. What is remarkable about non–death penalty states like Minnesota is that they did away with lynchings and executions while achieving some of the nation's lowest violent crime rates. A recent *New York Times* study examining FBI data found that during the past twenty years, the homicide rates in death penalty states have been, on a per capita basis, an astonishing 48 percent to 101 percent higher than in states without capital punishment. Even in 1995 when Minneapolis had ninety-five homicides—leading the *New York Times* to dub it "Murder-apolis" for its atypical rash of homicides—Minnesota's statewide murder rate was under four killings per one hundred thousand people. That figure nowhere even approaches the murder rates of active death penalty states like Texas and Louisiana; in 1995, Texas had nine murders per one hundred thousand people, and Louisiana saw seventeen murders per one hundred thousand state residents.[2]

What the Minnesota example teaches the nation is that we must stop thinking of America's death penalty as a "crime-fighting" tool and start thinking of it for what it is: just another form of violence in American society. The lessons of Minnesota's nineteenth-century transition from public executions at midday to private, after-dark killings must not be forgotten either. While Minneapolis legislator John Day Smith held out hope that ending public executions would lead to the death penalty's abolition, the "midnight assassination law" only drew the ire of journalists and failed to bring about abolition until after that law, at William Williams's execution, was blatantly violated. What Smith's law did, quite unexpectedly, was shape the course of American history. The U.S. Supreme Court's 1890 ruling that the Smith law was constitutional, followed by the Minnesota Supreme Court's 1907 ruling to that effect, allowed state legislators to mandate private, after-dark executions and bar news coverage of them.[3]

These two landmark decisions—one at the state, and one at the federal level—led to the proliferation of private, nighttime execution laws across the country. In 1893, Connecticut mandated that executions be carried out at night at the state prison, and in 1898, a Massachusetts law required nighttime executions within an enclosure. One of Minnesota's neighbors, North Dakota, passed its own law in 1903 requiring before-sunrise executions, as did Wyoming in 1905, and Texas and Alabama in 1923. South Dakota enacted a law in 1939 requiring executions between 12:01 A.M. and 6:00 A.M., Kentucky mandated before-sunrise executions in 1944, and Louisiana and Delaware later passed laws requiring executions between midnight and 3:00 A.M. Just a year after the Minnesota Supreme Court's ruling, Virginia enacted a law virtually identical to the Smith law, and Washington and Arkansas soon followed suit with gag laws of their own that forbade newspapers from printing execution details.[4]

The history behind Minnesota's "midnight assassination law," part of the larger national movement toward private executions that ended with America's last public execution in the 1930s, helps explain why state-sanctioned killing in the United States remains so shrouded in secrecy. The legacy of Smith's law and other laws like it certainly sheds light on why American executions have so often been conducted in the middle of the night, and why TV cameras are rigidly excluded from execution chambers. From 1977 to 1995, an astonishing 82 percent of all American executions were carried out between 11:00 P.M. and 7:30 A.M., and of those 313 executions, over 50 percent of them took place between midnight and 1:00 A.M., when many Americans were fast asleep. Americans no longer execute people in public squares at high noon, as they did a century ago, but executions now take place out of sight and often under cover of darkness. As a result, the violence of executions, seen by ordinary citizens more than a century ago, is masked.[5]

The shelves and stacks of St. Paul's Minnesota History Center hold other valuable lessons for all Americans. The demise of public executions in the North Star State was brought about, as in other places, because state lawmakers realized that executions were, far from deterring crime, actually brutalizing society and harming public morals. This conclusion is inescapable from even a cursory review of contemporaneous newspaper accounts. Public executions, once a fixture of the frontier, fell by the wayside as civic leaders increasingly came to abhor these gruesome spectacles and realized that execution-day crowds were not coming to hangings to honor the sanctity of life. Attendees, community leaders saw, were coming out of "morbid curiosity" or, worse yet, for entertainment, and alcohol consumption and crowd control were often major problems at these events. As public executions came to be seen as incongruous with societal values, county sheriffs and state legislators were pressured to privatize executions. When that happened, the general public no longer saw the gallows in operation, and newspapers became the primary way in which people learned about hangings.

As the national trend toward private executions accelerated, information about American executions became even less reliable when state legislatures passed gag laws like Minnesota's "midnight assassination law." Smith's law ensured that no public execution would ever occur in Minnesota again and, like other laws, made it a crime to publish any execution details. While most newspapers blatantly ignored the press-muzzling provision of Smith's law, others altered their news coverage of executions to comply with it or sanitized the news. When William Williams was hanged in 1906, the *St. Paul Pioneer Press* failed to even report at first that the sheriff bungled the hanging, saying only that it took Williams fourteen and a half minutes to die. Regardless of editorial decisions, the Smith law and others like it certainly hindered reporters' efforts to cover executions, much as the lack of TV cameras at American executions today makes full news coverage impossible.

In the end, Williams's horrific death and the successful prosecution of three St. Paul newspapers sparked serious questions by state legislators about the death penalty's use. While the newspapers lost their freedom-of-the-press court challenge, their blatant violations of the Smith law and their exposure of Williams's grisly death made Williams the last person to legally hang in the state. After a full account of Williams's strangulation was printed, Governor John A. Johnson announced he wanted to abolish capital punishment, and state legislators intensified their anti–death penalty efforts. Ironically, if newspapers had not violated the Smith law by printing the details of Williams's execution, the death penalty might not have been abolished as quickly as it was by the legislature.[6]

The intriguing tale of Minnesota's "midnight assassination law" and its abolitionist movement serves as a stern reminder about the dangers of regulating press access to executions. After all, if ordinary Americans were to see executions, as they did long ago, would they not come to see for themselves the violence and inhumanity of capital punishment? For, if Americans were to see state-sanctioned killings up close, as they did back in the heyday of lynchings and public executions, might not they see the death penalty as just a direct descendant and vestige of the bygone era of lynchings? When press freedoms are curtailed by statute, as they were under the Smith law, one thing is clear: the public is either misinformed or left uninformed about the state's ultimate sanction, the taking of human life.[7]

Minnesota's past, with all its murders and executions and lynchings, is a microcosm of the nation's history of violence. Like the carnage of the Civil War or the Dakota Conflict's bloodlust, the violent legacy left behind by state-sanctioned and extrajudicial killings in Minnesota must never be forgotten. Americans must learn from the past, realize that the government teaches by its example, and work together for a more educated and less violent society. When George MacKenzie saw men's lives taken, he did not sit idly by in the face of what he had seen. Instead, he built a coalition of legislators under Cass Gilbert's capitol dome and succeeded in having Minnesota's death penalty taken off the statute books. Nor did Nellie and William Francis stay silent after Duluth's tragic lynchings. After contacting the NAACP's national office, they drafted an anti-lynching bill and lobbied the public to ensure its passage. Only through the collective acts and raised voices of determined individuals did Minnesota abolish capital punishment and bring an end to the repugnant, often racially motivated practice of lynching.

Minnesota is, to be sure, far from a perfect place. Murders, rapes, and random shootings still occur, and a host of social ills, from child poverty to drug abuse and domestic violence to homelessness, still need to be overcome. However, Minnesotans should take solace from the fact that at least two forms of violence—executions and lynchings—are no longer a part of the state's fabric of life. While Minnesota lawyers now regularly represent death row inmates in other states, Minnesota itself has no death row. In Minnesota, law has triumphed over lawlessness, and in the criminal justice system, nonviolence has replaced executions, the violent means so prevalent in the state's distant past. Today, life imprisonment without the possibility of parole—not death—is Minnesota's maximum penalty for first-degree murder.[8]

Every time a murder happens, the rage of the murder victim's family, and that of the larger community, is palpable. Over a dozen calls for the death penalty's reinstatement by the Minnesota Legislature have, in fact, occurred since the state's abolition of capital punishment in 1911, often sparked by a gruesome homicide. These efforts have all failed, however, as lawmakers like Allan Spear and Wes Skoglund have wisely resisted efforts to bring back Minnesota's death penalty. Instead of resorting to executions, in what would be a misguided attempt to try to reduce violent crime through violent means, legislators have toughened prison sentences for violent and repeat offenders to protect the public and combat violence.[9]

A Minnesota native, Hubert H. Humphrey, once urged Americans "to get out of the shadow of states' rights and walk forthrightly into the bright sunshine of human rights." Many decades ago, the people of the North Star State did just that by coming together at the state capitol to outlaw capital punishment and to decry lynchings. If that could happen then, Martin Luther King Jr.'s unfulfilled dream—a colorblind society based on the principles of nonviolence, equality, and respect for human rights—must hold promise still for America's democracy. The chilling legacy left behind by state-sanctioned and extrajudicial violence is a pox on Dr. King's dream, and Minnesota's violent past shows just how ill-conceived it is to use violence to try to curtail violent crime. If people of character continue to speak out, perhaps one day the death penalty will be abolished not just in a handful of American states but worldwide. If that happens, then one midwestern state—Minnesota—will undoubtedly be remembered as having led America by its example, carrying the banner of nonviolence and international human rights into the twenty-first century.[10]

Notes

Introduction

1. Thomas O'Sullivan, *North Star Statehouse: An Armchair Guide to the Minnesota State Capitol* (St. Paul: Pogo Press, 1994), 1, 3–4, 9–10, 50, 62, 100; John D. Bessler, "The 'Midnight Assassination Law' and Minnesota's Anti–Death Penalty Movement, 1849–1911," *William Mitchell Law Review* 22 (1996): 577, 688; "Partial Autobiography of George MacKenzie" (unpublished manuscript obtained from Malcolm MacKenzie), 57.

2. Larry Millett, *Twin Cities: Then and Now* (St. Paul: Minnesota Historical Society Press, 1996), 160–61; O'Sullivan, *North Star Statehouse*, xiii, 3, 12, 17–18, 21, 25, 27, 31–33, 37, 46, 50, 52–53, 69–70, 75–78, 80, 84; Bessler, "'Midnight Assassination Law,'" 595–96, 599, 637, 697; Jane Davis, "Two Sioux War Orders: A Mystery Unraveled," *Minnesota History* 41 (Fall 1968): 117.

3. William Watts Folwell, *A History of Minnesota* (St. Paul: Minnesota Historical Society Press, 1961), 2:314; "Biographies of Black Pioneers," *Gopher Historian* (Winter 1968–69): 20.

4. LaLonnie Erickson, "Minnesota Homicides 1985 to 1997," *Minnesota Planning* (May 1999), 1, 3; http://www.deathpenaltyinfo.org/deter.html.

5. Lynching has, over time, had many definitions. Christopher Waldrep, "War of Words: The Controversy over the Definition of Lynching, 1899–1940," *Journal of Southern History* 66 (Feb. 2000): 75–100. A lynching has been defined as "an activity in which persons not officers of the law, in open defiance of the law, administer punishment by death to an individual for an alleged offense or to an individual with whom some offense has been associated." Ibid., 97. Another source defines lynching as "the execution without process of the law,

by a mob, of any individual suspected or convicted of a crime or accused of an offense against the prevailing social customs." Frank Shay, *Judge Lynch: His First Hundred Years* (New York: Ives Washburn, 1938), 7.

6. "The Duluth Lynching," *Duluth Herald*, 19 June 1920, 8 (citing *Chicago Tribune* editorial). Of 4,743 persons lynched in America from 1882 to 1968, 3,446, or over 72 percent, were black; in 1920, when the Duluth mob did its ugly work, 53 of 61 U.S. lynchings were of blacks. Robert Zangrando, *The NAACP Crusade against Lynching, 1909–1950* (Philadelphia: Temple University Press, 1980), 4, 6.

7. O'Sullivan, *North Star Statehouse*, 99.

8. Victor Streib, "Emerging Issues in Juvenile Death Penalty Law," *Ohio Northern University Law Review* 26 (2000): 732.

9. O'Sullivan, *North Star Statehouse*, 10, 12, 13, 60.

1. Lynch Mobs and Public Hangings

1. Daniel Elazar, Virginia Gray, and Wyman Spano, *Minnesota Politics and Government* (Lincoln: University of Nebraska Press, 1999), xxix, 70.

2. 1849 Minn. Laws, ch. 10; 1851 Minn. Laws, ch. 100, § 2; 1853 Minn. Laws, ch. 2, § 7; Theodore Blegen, *Minnesota: A History of the State* (Minneapolis: University of Minnesota Press, 1975), 162–63, 230; Nancy Bonvillain, *The Santee Sioux* (Philadelphia: Chelsea House Publishers, 1997), 27; Royal Hassrick, *The Sioux: Life and Customs of a Warrior Society* (Norman: University of Oklahoma Press, 1964), 48–49; Mary Beth Lorbiecki, *Painting the Dakota: Seth Eastman at Fort Snelling* (Afton, Minn.: Afton Historical Society Press, 2000), 78; Marilyn Ziebarth, "Judge Lynch in Minnesota," *Minnesota History* 55 (Summer 1996): 72; "Double Murder," *Minneapolis Tribune*, 29 May 1893, 2; "Old Chief Murdered," *Daily Pioneer Press*, 29 May 1893, 1; "Lynching of an Indian," *Minneapolis Times*, 29 May 1893, 2; "Slew the Chief," *St. Paul Globe*, 29 May 1893, 1.

3. Jane Lamm Carroll, "Criminal Justice on the Minnesota Frontier, 1820–1857" (Ph.D. diss., University of Minnesota, 1991), 2:251, 279–81.

4. Blegen, *Minnesota*, 170–71; Carroll, "Criminal Justice," 2:281–84.

5. Blegen, *Minnesota*, 171; Carroll, "Criminal Justice," 2:284–85; *Daily Minnesota Pioneer*, 30 December 1854, 2; "Letter from Gov. Gorman," *Daily Minnesota Pioneer*, 3 January 1855, 2; *Minnesota Republican*, 4 January 1855, 2.

6. John D. Bessler, *Death in the Dark: Midnight Executions in America* (Boston: Northeastern University Press, 1997), 44–46; William Watts Folwell, *A History of Minnesota* (St. Paul: Minnesota Historical Society Press, 1961), 2:80,

82; "Hanging the Indian," *Daily Minnesotian*, 30 December 1854, 2; Merle Potter, "Major Fridley's Kingdom," *Journal Magazine*, 4 September 1932, 4.

7. "Hanging the Indian," *Daily Minnesotian*, 30 December 1854, 2; *Daily Minnesotian*, 3 January 1855, 2; Potter, "Major Fridley's Kingdom," 4.

8. George Hage, *Newspapers on the Minnesota Frontier 1849–1860* (St. Paul: Minnesota Historical Society Press, 1967), 47; *Daily Minnesota Pioneer*, 30 December 1854, 2; *Daily Minnesotian*, 3 January 1855, 2; "The Execution," *Minnesota Republican*, 4 January 1855, 2; "The Approaching Execution," *St. Paul Pioneer*, 10 November 1865, 1; Carroll, "Criminal Justice," 2:285.

9. Hage, *Newspapers on the Minnesota Frontier*, 48–49; *Daily Minnesotian*, 1 January 1855, 2; "Execution of U-ha-zy," *Daily Minnesota Pioneer*, 1 January 1855, 2; *Daily Minnesotian*, 3 January 1855, 2; "The Penalty of Death," *Daily Minnesotian*, 13 January 1855, 2; "The Penalty of Death—Is It Expedient?" *Daily Minnesotian*, 15 January 1855, 2.

10. Walter Trenerry, *Murder in Minnesota: A Collection of True Cases* (St. Paul: Minnesota Historical Society Press, 1985), 78–79; Warren Upham, *Minnesota Geographic Names* (St. Paul: Minnesota Historical Society Press, 1969), 351; "Upon the Scaffold High," *Little Falls Transcript*, 19 July 1889, 3; "Last Hours of Life," *Minneapolis Tribune*, 19 October 1894, 4; Carroll, "Criminal Justice," 2:288; Robert Pomeroy, "Morrison County's Only Lynching," 1966, unpublished manuscript, Minnesota Historical Society, St. Paul; Ziebarth, "Judge Lynch," 72.

11. Blegen, *Minnesota*, 228; Trenerry, *Murder in Minnesota*, 3–12; "Disgraceful Lawlessness in Le Sueur County," *Daily Pioneer and Democrat*, 31 December 1858, 2.

12. Folwell, *History of Minnesota*, 2:29; Trenerry, *Murder in Minnesota*, 15–16; "Oscar F. Jackson Hung," *Daily Pioneer and Democrat*, 29 April 1859, 3.

13. Trenerry, *Murder in Minnesota*, 17–18.

14. Ibid., 19; Folwell, *History of Minnesota*, 2:29.

15. Folwell, *History of Minnesota*, 2:29–30; Clarence French and Frank Lamson, *Condensed History of Wright County, 1851–1935* (Delano, Minn.: French and Lamson, 1935), 12–13; Merle Potter, *101 Best Stories of Minnesota* (Minneapolis: Harrison and Smith Co., 1931), 210–13; Trenerry, *Murder in Minnesota*, 13–24; "Escape of Mrs. Bilansky," *Daily Pioneer and Democrat*, 27 July 1859, 3; "Oscar F. Jackson Hung," *Daily Pioneer and Democrat*, 29 April 1859, 3.

16. "Anniversary of Terrible Murder of Jewett Family," *Mankato Review*, 7 May 1918, 3; "Jewett Family Massacred," *Mankato Free Press*, 2 May 1932, 9.

17. "Anniversary of Terrible Murder of Jewett Family," *Mankato Review*, 7 May 1918, 3, 6.

18. Ibid.; "The Anniversary of the Murder of the Jewett Family," *The Daily Review*, 2 May 1893, 2.

19. "Interesting Reminiscence," *Mankato Review*, 11 February 1897, 3; "Interesting Reminiscence," *Mankato Review*, 12 February 1897, 2; "Anniversary of Terrible Murder of Jewett Family," *Mankato Review*, 7 May 1918, 3; "Jewett Family Massacred," *Mankato Free Press*, 2 May 1932, 9.

20. Folwell, *History of Minnesota*, 2:346–48; Trenerry, *Murder in Minnesota*, 43–44; "Indians inside the Lines," *Mankato Weekly Record*, 6 May 1865, 2; "The Hanging of John Campbell," *Mankato Review*, 3 May 1893, 2; "Anniversary of Terrible Murder of Jewett Family," *Mankato Review*, 7 May 1918, 3, 6.

21. "The Anniversary of the Murder of the Jewett Family," *The Daily Review*, 2 May 1893, 2; "The Hanging of John Campbell," *Mankato Review*, 3 May 1893, 2; "Anniversary of Terrible Murder of Jewett Family," *Mankato Review*, 7 May 1918, 6; "Mob Hanged Jewett Slayer," *Mankato Free Press*, 27 June 1952, 19.

22. Trenerry, *Murder in Minnesota*, 45–47, 51–52; *Redwood: The Story of a County* (Redwood County Board of Commissioners, 1964), 470–73; "The New Ulm Murders," *St. Paul Daily Pioneer*, 4 February 1868, 1; "John Gut to Be Hanged," *St. Paul Dispatch*, 25 February 1869, 4. Charles Campbell is also referred to as Alexander Campbell. *Redwood*, 470.

23. Trenerry, *Murder in Minnesota*, 45–47, 51–52; *Redwood*, 470–73; "The New Ulm Murders," *St. Paul Daily Pioneer*, 4 February 1868, 1; "John Gut to Be Hanged," *St. Paul Dispatch*, 25 February 1869, 4.

24. "Execution of Henry Kriegler," *Freeborn County Standard*, 2 March 1861, 2; "Execution at Albert Lea," *Daily Pioneer and Democrat*, 8 March 1861, 1.

25. Paul Nelson, *Fredrick L. McGhee: A Life on the Color Line, 1861–1912* (St. Paul: Minnesota Historical Society Press, 2002), 54–55; "He Was Strung Up," *Glencoe Enterprise*, 6 August 1896, 3; "A Lynching Was Averted," *Carlton County Vidette*, 15 October 1920, 1; "District Court Is Adjourned," *Carlton County Vidette*, 29 October 1920, 1; "Chap Who Raped Wrenshall Girl to Have Lots of Time to Regret," *Carlton County Vidette*, 5 November 1920, 1; "Victory over Lynchers in Minneapolis," *Labor Defender* 1, 10 (January 1934): 4.

26. *East Otter Tail County History* (Dallas, Tex.: Taylor Pub. Co., 1978), 28; "The Perham Murder," *Fergus Falls Independent*, 7 June 1882, 1; "Speedy

Retribution," *Fergus Falls Independent*, 14 June 1882, 2; *Fergus Falls Independent*, 21 June 1882, 1; "Otter Tail's Only Lynching," *Fergus Falls Daily Journal*, 11 March 1922, 2; Ziebarth, "Judge Lynch," 72.

27. Trenerry, *Murder in Minnesota*, 61–84; Edwin Chittenden, "The Blueberry War: Its Contemporary History," 1902, unpublished paper, Minnesota Historical Society, St. Paul; Lynching photo, July 23, 1872, MHS Cat. HV8.4/r1, Minnesota Historical Society, St. Paul; Ziebarth, "Judge Lynch," 72.

28. Blegen, *Minnesota*, 283; Chittenden, "The Blueberry War."

29. "Mob-Law in Minnesota," *Minneapolis Tribune*, 10 November 1879, 1; "Murders in Todd County," *Pioneer Press*, 10 November 1879, 1; "Blood for Blood," *Pioneer Press*, 11 November 1879, 2.

30. *The Minneapolis Tragedy: Full Account of the Crime of the Fiend Frank McManus, and the Swift Retribution of an Outraged Community* (Minneapolis: Haywood and Kruckeberg, 1882).

31. Ibid.; Isaac Atwater, ed., *History of the City of Minneapolis, Minnesota* (New York: Munsell, 1893), 1:324.

32. *The Minneapolis Tragedy*.

33. Ibid.

34. Ibid.

35. "Sheriff Rogers Shot!" *Glencoe Register*, 25 June 1896, 1; "Cold Blooded Murder!" *Glencoe Enterprise*, 25 June 1896, 4; "Sheriff Rogers," *Hutchinson Leader*, 26 June 1896, 5; "Dorman Musgrove," *Glencoe Enterprise*, 3 September 1896, 4; "Law and Order Outraged," *Minneapolis Tribune*, 7 September 1896, 1–2; "Partial Autobiography of George MacKenzie" (unpublished manuscript obtained from Malcolm MacKenzie), 49–50.

36. "Law and Order Outraged," *Minneapolis Tribune*, 7 September 1896, 1–2; "Partial Autobiography of George MacKenzie," 50.

37. "Law and Order Outraged," *Minneapolis Tribune*, 7 September 1896, 1–2.

38. Ibid.; Trenerry, *Murder in Minnesota*, 126; "Partial Autobiography of George MacKenzie," 50.

39. "Law and Order Outraged," *Minneapolis Tribune*, 7 September 1896, 1–2; "Murderers Are Lynched," *Glencoe Enterprise*, 10 September 1896, 2.

40. Ibid.

41. "The Glencoe Lynching," *Minneapolis Tribune*, 7 September 1896, 4; "Lynched at Midnight!" *Glencoe Enterprise*, 10 September 1896, 5.

42. Dwight E. Woodbridge and John S. Pardee, eds., *History of Duluth and St. Louis County: Past and Present* (Chicago: C. F. Cooper and Co., 1910), 2:735–36; "Awful Deed of a Fiend," *Duluth Evening Herald*, 5 May 1893, 1; "Deed of a Fiend," *Duluth News Tribune*, 6 May 1893, 1; "He Was Lynched," *Duluth Evening Herald*, 6 May 1893, 1; "Quick but Sure," *Duluth News Tribune*, 7 May 1893, 1; "Judge Lynch," *Duluth Evening Herald*, 8 May 1893, 4; "Crime of Belange," *Duluth News Tribune*, 8 May 1893, 8; "Inquiry to Be Made," *Duluth News Tribune*, 9 May 1893, 8; "Victim of Tar Party in Duluth Suicide, Belief," *Duluth News Tribune*, 1 October 1918, 1; "Three Mystery Deaths Baffle Duluth Officials," *Duluth News Tribune*, 2 October 1918, 8; "Governor Asked to Aid in Solving Death Mystery," *Duluth News Tribune*, 3 October 1918, 3; "Meining to Make Another Arrest in Murder Case," *Duluth News Tribune*, 6 October 1918, 9; "Intolerance, Ignorance Also Scarred the Lives of Local Finn Community," *Superior Evening Telegram* (undated newspaper clipping).

43. *Duluth (Minnesota) Lynchings of 1920: An Inventory of the Selected Materials* (St. Paul: Minnesota Historical Society, microfilm publication), 7.

2. On Lincoln's Orders

1. Philip B. Kunhardt Jr., Philip B. Kunhardt III, and Peter W. Kunhardt, *Lincoln: An Illustrated Biography* (New York: Gramercy Books, 1999), 184; David Nichols, *Lincoln and the Indians: Civil War Policy and Politics* (Columbia: University of Missouri Press, 1978), 132–34; John Day Smith, *The History of the Nineteenth Regiment of Maine Volunteer Infantry 1862–1865* (Minneapolis: Great Western Printing Co., 1909), 7–9; Henry Benjamin Whipple, *Lights and Shadows of a Long Episcopate, Being Reminiscences and Recollections of the Right Reverend Henry Benjamin Whipple, D.D., L.L.D., Bishop of Minnesota* (New York: Macmillan, 1912), 1, 31–33, 51, 60–62, 66, 100, 510–14; "Chief Big Eagle's Story," *Minnesota History* 38 (Sept. 1962): 136 n. 29.

2. Gary Clayton Anderson, *Little Crow: Spokesman for the Sioux* (St. Paul: Minnesota Historical Society Press, 1986), 78, 92, 113, 116, 118; Kenneth Carley, *The Sioux Uprising of 1862* (St. Paul: Minnesota Historical Society Press, 1976), 4–5; Nichols, *Lincoln and the Indians*, 134–35; Whipple, *Lights and Shadows*, 66, 99, 510–14; "Henry B. Whipple: 'At Whose Door Is the Blood of These Innocent Victims?'" *Star Tribune*, 28 May 2000, A21. The term *Sioux*, meaning "enemy" or "snake," originates from the Algonquin-speaking Ojibwe, while the term *Dakota*, meaning "league" or "ally" or "friend," is often used today.

Anderson, *Little Crow*, 6; Nancy Bonvillain, *The Santee Sioux* (Philadelphia: Chelsea House Publishers, 1997), 14; Sarah Wakefield, *Six Weeks in the Sioux Tepees: A Narrative of Indian Captivity*, ed. June Namias (Norman: University of Oklahoma Press, 1997), 9.

    3. David Herbert Donald, *Lincoln* (New York: Simon and Schuster, 1995), 57, 87–88, 163–64, 198; W. Emerson Reck, *A. Lincoln: His Last 24 Hours* (Columbia: University of South Carolina Press, 1987), 9.

    4. Anderson, *Little Crow*, 111–12; Dee Brown, *Bury My Heart at Wounded Knee: An Indian History of the American West* (New York: Henry Holt and Co., 1970), 38; Carley, *Sioux Uprising*, 2–4; Kunhardt, Kunhardt, and Kunhardt, *Lincoln*, 180; Duane Schultz, *Over the Earth I Come: The Great Sioux Uprising of 1862* (New York: St. Martin's Press, 1992), 23; Theodore C. Blegen and Philip D. Jordan, eds., *With Various Voices: Recordings of North Star Life* (St. Paul: Itasca Press, 1949), xiv; Karin Thiem, "The Minnesota Sioux War Trials" (master's thesis, Mankato State University, 1979), 5.

    5. Anderson, *Little Crow*, 222; Carley, *Sioux Uprising*, 4–5; Roy Meyer, *History of the Santee Sioux: United States Indian Policy on Trial* (Lincoln: University of Nebraska Press, 1993), 107; Nichols, *Lincoln and the Indians*, 134–35; Schultz, *Over the Earth I Come*, 13–15; Whipple, *Lights and Shadows*, 106; Carol Chomsky, "The United States–Dakota War Trials: A Study in Military Injustice," *Stanford Law Review* 43 (1990): 13, 15–17.

    6. Anderson, *Little Crow*, 123; Peg Meier, comp., *Bring Warm Clothes: Letters and Photos from Minnesota's Past* (Minneapolis: Minneapolis Tribune, 1981), 98; Carley, *Sioux Uprising*, 5–6; *Minnesota in the Civil and Indian Wars 1861–1865* (St. Paul: Pioneer Press Co., 1890), 1:731; Doane Robinson, *A History of the Dakota or Sioux Indians* (Minneapolis: Ross and Haines, 1967), 267; Gary C. Anderson and Alan R. Woolworth, eds., *Through Dakota Eyes: Narrative Accounts of the Minnesota Indian War of 1862* (St. Paul: Minnesota Historical Society Press, 1988), 9.

    7. Anderson, *Little Crow*, 9–10, 15–16, 23, 29–31, 38, 40, 63, 78–79, 108–9, 127; Robinson, *History of the Dakota*, 254, 256–59; Anderson and Woolworth, eds., *Through Dakota Eyes*, 20; John Nicolay, "The Sioux War," *Continental Monthly* (Feb. 1863): 196. The 1851 treaty was signed by Alexander Ramsey and Little Crow, among others, on August 5, 1851.

    8. Anderson, *Little Crow*, 37–39, 53–54, 69–71, 100, 113, 119, 121, 127–29, 132–34; Carley, *Sioux Uprising*, 5–6; Mark Diedrich, *Famous Chiefs of the*

Eastern Sioux (Minneapolis: Coyote Books, 1987), 67; William Watts Folwell, *A History of Minnesota* (St. Paul: Minnesota Historical Society, 1961), 2:147–48; C. M. Oehler, *The Great Sioux Uprising* (New York: Da Capo Press, 1997), 27; Anderson and Woolworth, eds., *Through Dakota Eyes*, 25; Chomsky, "United States–Dakota War Trials," 17.

9. Anderson, *Little Crow*, 113, 119, 121, 132–34; Bonvillain, *Santee Sioux*, 24; Carley, *Sioux Uprising*, 5–9; Michael Clodfelter, *The Dakota War: The United States Army versus the Sioux, 1862–65* (Jefferson, N.C.: McFarland and Co., 1998), 53; Donald, *Lincoln*, 367; *Minnesota in the Civil and Indian Wars*, 1:246; Nichols, *Lincoln and the Indians*, 137; Robinson, *History of the Dakota*, 264; Chomsky, "United States–Dakota War Trials," 17; Education Supplement— "The Great Dakota Conflict," 7, 10, 12, undated collection of *St. Paul Pioneer Press* articles, first printed as a five-part series on July 19, August 16, October 11, November 29, and December 27, 1987.

10. Anderson, *Little Crow*, 24, 33–36, 44–46, 52, 56, 75–76, 82–87, 101–3, 106, 184; Bonvillain, *Santee Sioux*, 29; Diedrich, *Famous Chiefs*, 43, 47–50, 55–57, 61, 65–66, 68; Robinson, *History of the Dakota*, 266; Anderson and Woolworth, eds., *Through Dakota Eyes*, 23; Chomsky, "United States–Dakota War Trials," 18, n. 25.

11. Anderson, *Little Crow*, 38, 65, 71–72, 94–95, 103–6, 131–32; Carley, *Sioux Uprising*, 10–12; Oehler, *Great Sioux Uprising*, 21, 32–33; Anderson and Woolworth, eds., *Through Dakota Eyes*, 23; Schultz, *Over the Earth I Come*, 42–44; Chomsky, "United States–Dakota War Trials," 18, n. 25; "Chief Big Eagle's Story," *Minnesota History* 38 (Sept. 1962): 134.

12. Anderson, *Little Crow*, 58, 91, 122, 135–36, 222; Meier, comp., *Bring Warm Clothes*, 100; Carley, *Sioux Uprising*, 11–16; Mark Diedrich, *Dakota Oratory: Great Moments in the Recorded Speech of the Eastern Sioux, 1695–1874* (Rochester, Minn.: Coyote Books, 1989), 63; Diedrich, *Famous Chiefs*, 62; Folwell, *History of Minnesota*, 2:109–15; *Minnesota in the Civil and Indian Wars*, 1:249, 2:179–81; Oehler, *Great Sioux Uprising*, 76; Schultz, *Over the Earth I Come*, 40–41.

13. Anderson, *Little Crow*, 98, 105, 139–43, 190; Carley, *Sioux Uprising*, 17–19, 22–23; Folwell, *History of Minnesota*, 2:111, 115–18, 128; Schultz, *Over the Earth I Come*, 64, 74–77, 219; Anderson and Woolworth, eds., *Through Dakota Eyes*, 74–75, 77; Whipple, *Lights and Shadows*, 120–21; Wakefield, *Six Weeks in the Sioux Tepees*, 25, 66, 125; Blegen and Jordan, eds., *With Various Voices*, 67.

14. Carley, *Sioux Uprising*, 21–25, 50–55; Donald, *Lincoln*, 310; Folwell, *History of Minnesota*, 2:123–24, 161; *Minnesota in the Civil and Indian Wars*, 2:202; Nichols, *Lincoln and the Indians*, 5, 17–18, 34, 86.

15. Anderson, *Little Crow*, 93, 144–46; Carley, *Sioux Uprising*, 25–39; Charles Flandrau, *The History of Minnesota and Tales of the Frontier* (St. Paul: E. W. Porter, 1900), 143; Folwell, *History of Minnesota*, 2:129–31, 134–44; Thomas Hughes, *Old Traverse des Sioux* (St. Peter, Minn.: Nicollet County Historical Society, 1993), 117–19; *Minnesota in the Civil and Indian Wars*, 2:173, 206; Russell Fridley, "Charles E. Flandrau: Attorney at War," *Minnesota History* 38 (Sept. 1962): 116–18.

16. Anderson, *Little Crow*, 37–39, 53–54, 69–71, 209; Clodfelter, *Dakota War*, 50–51; Folwell, *History of Minnesota*, 2:147–48, 168–70; Hughes, *Old Traverse des Sioux*, 117; Nichols, *Lincoln and the Indians*, 65–66, 77; Oehler, *Great Sioux Uprising*, 14; Schultz, *Over the Earth I Come*, 140; Nathaniel West, *The Ancestry, Life, and Times of Hon. Henry Hastings Sibley* (St. Paul: Pioneer Press Pub. Co., 1889), 254; Blegen and Jordan, eds., *With Various Voices*, 53, 58; "Harvest of Death," *St. Paul Daily News*, 18 February 1891, 1; Jane Spector Davis, *Guide to a Microfilm Edition of the Henry Hastings Sibley Papers* (St. Paul: Minnesota Historical Society, 1968), 2–5; Marx Swanholm, "Alexander Ramsey and the Politics of Survival," Minnesota historic sites pamphlet series, no. 13 (St. Paul: Minnesota Historical Society, 1977), 7–11; John Russell Wilkerson, "Henry Hastings Sibley: Frontier Politician, 1846–1857" (master's thesis, Mankato State College, 1970), 63, 66–67, 74. In the nineteenth century, it was common for Indians to refer to America's president as "the Great Father." Francis Paul Prucha, *The Great Father: The United States Government and the American Indians* (Lincoln: University of Nebraska Press, 1984), xxviii.

17. Carley, *Sioux Uprising*, 73; Donald, *Lincoln*, 199, 200–201, 310; Folwell, *History of Minnesota*, 2:84; West, *Ancestry, Life, and Times*, 257; Whipple, *Lights and Shadows*, 96, 105, 122.

18. Donald, *Lincoln*, 20–21, 44–45, 115, 129, 245, 392, 520–21; Kunhardt, Kunhardt, and Kunhardt, *Lincoln*, 186; Nichols, *Lincoln and the Indians*, 3.

19. Carley, *Sioux Uprising*, 59; Ray P. Basler et al., eds., *The Collected Works of Abraham Lincoln* (Springfield, Ill.: Abraham Lincoln Association, 1953), 5:396–97; Donald, *Lincoln*, 363; Folwell, *History of Minnesota*, 2:62, 103; Thomas Lowry, *Don't Shoot That Boy! Abraham Lincoln and Military Justice* (Mason City, Iowa: Savas Publishing Co., 1999), 14; *Mankato: Its First Fifty Years* (Mankato,

Minn.: Free Press Printing Co., 1903), 334; Nichols, *Lincoln and the Indians*, 41–42, 65, 80–82.

20. Anderson, *Little Crow*, 151–55; Carley, *Sioux Uprising*, 30–31, 40–50; Diedrich, *Famous Chiefs*, 69–70; Flandrau, *History of Minnesota*, 161; Folwell, *History of Minnesota*, 2:149–55, 162, 176; William G. Gresham, *History of Nicollet and LeSueur Counties* (Indianapolis: B. F. Bowen, 1916), 1:134; *Minnesota in the Civil and Indian Wars*, 1:305, 308; Nichols, *Lincoln and the Indians*, 19, 66, 87; West, *Ancestry, Life, and Times*, 267; "Hon. H. H. Sibley, and the Indian Expedition," *Mankato Independent*, 4 September 1862, 2.

21. Kunhardt, Kunhardt, and Kunhardt, *Lincoln*, 176; *Lincoln Day by Day: A Chronology, 1809–1865* (Washington, D.C.: Lincoln Sesquicentennial Commission, 1960), 3:139–42; Smith, *History of the Nineteenth Regiment*, 7–9; "Lincoln's Summer Retreat Now a Monument," *Star Tribune*, 8 July 2000, A6.

22. Donald, *Lincoln*, 252, 258, 285, 309, 311, 358; Kunhardt, Kunhardt, and Kunhardt, *Lincoln*, 278–79; Ray Morris Jr., *The Better Angel: Walt Whitman in the Civil War* (New York: Oxford University Press, 2000), 49, 88–89; Nichols, *Lincoln and the Indians*, 54–56, 104; Whipple, *Lights and Shadows*, 136–37.

23. Donald, *Lincoln*, 153–54, 159–60, 335–37; Kunhardt, Kunhardt, and Kunhardt, *Lincoln*, 90, 174–75, 278–79, 291; Harold Holzer, ed., *Lincoln as I Knew Him: Gossip, Tributes, and Revelations from His Best Friends and Worst Enemies* (Chapel Hill, N.C.: Algonquin Books of Chapel Hill, 1999), 75.

24. Carley, *Sioux Uprising*, 59–62; Clodfelter, *Dakota War*, 45–46; Basler et al., eds., *Collected Works of Abraham Lincoln*, 5:432; Donald, *Lincoln*, 307, 329, 361, 370, 393; Kunhardt, Kunhardt, and Kunhardt, *Lincoln*, 186; *Lincoln Day by Day*, 3:132, 134, 136–41, 150, 155; E. B. Long, *The Civil War Day by Day: An Almanac 1861–1865* (New York: Da Capo Press, 1971), 239; *Minnesota in the Civil and Indian Wars*, 1:154, 158, 2:195–96; Morris, *Better Angel*, 15; Nichols, *Lincoln and the Indians*, 84, 87, 89; T. Harry Williams, *Lincoln and His Generals* (New York: Gramercy Books, 2000), 120, 151–52; Chomsky, "United States–Dakota War Trials," 22 n. 53; Thiem, "Minnesota Sioux War Trials," 28–29, 32.

25. Anderson, *Little Crow*, 156–57; Carley, *Sioux Uprising*, 60–61; Folwell, *History of Minnesota*, 2:172–73; Isaac V. D. Heard, *History of the Sioux War and Massacres of 1862 and 1863* (New York: Harper and Brothers, 1863), 147–50; West, *Ancestry, Life, and Times*, 265; Whipple, *Lights and Shadows*, 61.

26. Carley, *Sioux Uprising*, 61; Heard, *History of the Sioux War*, 158–59;

Schultz, *Over the Earth I Come*, 215; Chomsky, "United States–Dakota War Trials," 22.

27. Anderson, *Little Crow*, 159; Brown, *Bury My Heart at Wounded Knee*, 56–67; Carley, *Sioux Uprising*, 59, 62–63; Folwell, *History of Minnesota*, 2:181–82; Heard, *History of the Sioux War*, 175, 177–78; *Minnesota in the Civil and Indian Wars*, 1:159, 351, 2:233–34, 250; Nichols, *Lincoln and the Indians*, 88; Robinson, *History of the Dakota*, 293–94; Schultz, *Over the Earth I Come*, 232.

28. Anderson, *Little Crow*, 160–61, 163; Carley, *Sioux Uprising*, 63–65; Folwell, *History of Minnesota*, 2:183; Schultz, *Over the Earth I Come*, 237–38.

29. Anderson, *Little Crow*, 163; Carley, *Sioux Uprising*, 65–67; Folwell, *History of Minnesota*, 2:184–85; *Minnesota in the Civil and Indian Wars*, 2:238–39, 267; Nichols, *Lincoln and the Indians*, 89–90; Schultz, *Over the Earth I Come*, 239; Anderson and Woolworth, eds., *Through Dakota Eyes*, 194, 256; Thiem, "Minnesota Sioux War Trials," 30, 51.

30. Anderson, *Little Crow*, 168–75; Carley, *Sioux Uprising*, 67–69; Clodfelter, *Dakota War*, 57; Donald, *Lincoln*, 374–76, 380; Heard, *History of the Sioux War*, 251; Kunhardt, Kunhardt, and Kunhardt, *Lincoln*, 188; *Minnesota in the Civil and Indian Wars*, 2:250; Morris, *Better Angel*, 78; Oehler, *Great Sioux Uprising*, 224–28; Chomsky, "United States–Dakota War Trials," 15, 19.

31. Carley, *Sioux Uprising*, 67–69; Folwell, *History of Minnesota*, 2:177; Heard, *History of the Sioux War*, v; *Minnesota in the Civil and Indian Wars*, 1:313, 353, 2:246–47, 277; Oehler, *Great Sioux Uprising*, 39, 203; Schultz, *Over the Earth I Come*, 144; Chomsky, "United States–Dakota War Trials," 24, 50–51, nn. 61–62; Thiem, "Minnesota Sioux War Trials," 36, 46–47, 50, 52, 54–56, 70.

32. Carley, *Sioux Uprising*, 72; Nichols, *Lincoln and the Indians*, 104; Whipple, *Lights and Shadows*, 123, 125–29.

33. Carley, *Sioux Uprising*, 69; Heard, *History of the Sioux War*, 255, 261, 267, 269; *Minnesota in the Civil and Indian Wars*, 1:313–14; Nichols, *Lincoln and the Indians*, 94–95; Whipple, *Lights and Shadows*, 515; Chomsky, "United States–Dakota War Trials," 23, 25–28, 30, 93, n. 71; Thiem, "Minnesota Sioux War Trials," 29, 66.

34. Carley, *Sioux Uprising*, 69, 72; Nichols, *Lincoln and the Indians*, 7, 23, 98, 104–5; Chomsky, "United States–Dakota War Trials," 13, 26–28, 30, n. 494; Thiem, "Minnesota Sioux War Trials," 54.

35. Basler et al., eds., *Collected Works of Abraham Lincoln*, 5:493; Donald, *Lincoln*, 150–51; Folwell, *History of Minnesota*, 2:197; Kunhardt, Kunhardt, and

Kunhardt, *Lincoln*, 190–91, 277; *Minnesota in the Civil and Indian Wars*, 2:289; Nichols, *Lincoln and the Indians*, 95–96, 98; Schultz, *Over the Earth I Come*, 252; Chomsky, "United States–Dakota War Trials," 27; Thiem, "Minnesota Sioux War Trials," 66.

36. Donald, *Lincoln*, 150–51, 384, 390, 394; Kunhardt, Kunhardt, and Kunhardt, *Lincoln*, 192–93; Nichols, *Lincoln and the Indians*, 99.

37. Carley, *Sioux Uprising*, 70; *Minnesota in the Civil and Indian Wars*, 2:290; Nichols, *Lincoln and the Indians*, 101; Chomsky, "United States–Dakota War Trials," 26–27, 29–31, nn. 94, 107; A. Katherine Hughes, "The Developmental Stages of a Frontier Town: Mankato, Minnesota, from Inception to Maturity, 1852–1868" (master's thesis, Mankato State University, 1991), 101.

38. Presidential Message, 37th Congress, 3d sess., Executive Doc. No. 7 (Dec. 11, 1862), 4–5; Donald, *Lincoln*, 476; *Minnesota in the Civil and Indian Wars*, 2:290; Nichols, *Lincoln and the Indians*, 102; Chomsky, "United States–Dakota War Trials," 29–30; Thiem, "Minnesota Sioux War Trials," 93; *Mankato Independent*, 15 November 1862, 2; "The Sioux War," *Mankato Weekly Record*, 20 December 1862, 1.

39. Carley, *Sioux Uprising*, 71; Basler et al., eds., *Collected Works of Abraham Lincoln*, 5:493; Folwell, *History of Minnesota*, 2:204; Kunhardt, Kunhardt, and Kunhardt, *Lincoln*, 191; Nichols, *Lincoln and the Indians*, 106–7.

40. Basler et al., eds., *Collected Works of Abraham Lincoln*, 6:357; Donald, *Lincoln*, 314–15, 317, 489; Kunhardt, Kunhardt, and Kunhardt, *Lincoln*, 214.

41. Basler et al., eds., *Collected Works of Abraham Lincoln*, 5:518–19, 522, 525–26; *Minnesota in the Civil and Indian Wars*, 1:162; Chomsky, "United States–Dakota War Trials," 21.

42. Kunhardt, Kunhardt, and Kunhardt, *Lincoln*, 207; *Lincoln as I Knew Him*, 43; Stephen Oates, *With Malice toward None: A Life of Abraham Lincoln* (New York: HarperPerennial, 1994), 368; Prucha, *Great Father*, 472.

43. Robert Alotta, *Civil War Justice: Union Army Executions under Lincoln* (Shippensburg, Pa.: White Mane Pub. Co., 1989), 4; Basler et al., eds., *Collected Works of Abraham Lincoln*, 5:537–38.

44. "The Case of the Minnesota Indians," *St. Paul Pioneer*, 13 December 1862, 1.

45. Ibid.; Folwell, *History of Minnesota*, 2:203 n. 25.

46. Daniel Buck, *Indian Outbreaks* (Mankato, Minn., 1904), 224; Carley, *Sioux Uprising*, 70; Basler et al., eds., *Collected Works of Abraham Lincoln*, 5:540–41;

Minnesota in the Civil and Indian Wars, 1:353; Schultz, *Over the Earth I Come*, 254–55; Nichols, *Lincoln and the Indians*, 111; West, *Ancestry, Life, and Times*, 285–86; Chomsky, "United States–Dakota War Trials," 30–32; Jane Davis, "Two Sioux War Orders: A Mystery Unraveled," *Minnesota History* 41 (Fall 1968): 118; "The Trouble at Mankato," *St. Paul Pioneer*, 10 December 1862, 1; John Haack, "Army Recruit's Diary Records the Day of the Death-Dance," *Mankato Free Press*, 27 December 1971, 34.

47. Donald, *Lincoln*, 80–82, 91–93; Kunhardt, Kunhardt, and Kunhardt, *Lincoln*, 194; Abraham Lincoln, *The Political Thought of Abraham Lincoln*, ed. Richard N. Current (Indianapolis: Bobbs-Merrill, 1967), 11–21.

48. Alotta, *Civil War Justice*, 4, 10, 13, 17, 28, 43, 109; Basler et al., eds., *Collected Works of Abraham Lincoln*, vols. 5–8; Lowry, *Don't Shoot That Boy!* 85, 93–94, 235–44, 246, 259–61; West, *Ancestry, Life, and Times*, 286; Davis, "Two Sioux War Orders," 119.

49. Basler et al., eds., *Collected Works of Abraham Lincoln*, 6:414–15; Donald, *Lincoln*, 489, 513–14; William Herndon and Jesse Weik, *Herndon's Life of Lincoln* (New York: A. and C. Boni, 1930), 430; Ward Hill Lamon, *Recollections of Abraham Lincoln* (Lincoln: University of Nebraska Press, 1994), 102–3; Kunhardt, Kunhardt, and Kunhardt, *Lincoln*, 330; Lowry, *Don't Shoot That Boy!* i–iii, 4, 18, 21, 75, 86–87, 90–92, 97–110, 116–24, 127–32, 139–40, 145–47, 150–56, 158–61, 164–66, 169, 172–81, 185–94, 196–202, 204–11, 214, 219–21, 232; Reck, *A. Lincoln*, 43.

50. Presidential Message, 37th Congress, 3d sess., Executive Doc. No. 7 (Dec. 11, 1862), 2; Alotta, *Civil War Justice*, 64; Basler et al., eds., *Collected Works of Abraham Lincoln*, 5:542–43; Donald, *Lincoln*, 270, 394, 399, 548; Kunhardt, Kunhardt, and Kunhardt, *Lincoln*, 301; *Minnesota in the Civil and Indian Wars*, 2:291; Nichols, *Lincoln and the Indians*, 112; Reck, *A. Lincoln*, 15; Chomsky, "United States–Dakota War Trials," 86; Davis, "Two Sioux War Orders," 117, 119–21; "The Report on the Condemned Indians to the President," *Mankato Free Press*, 29 August 1987, 6.

51. Gary Clayton Anderson, *Kinsmen of Another Kind: Dakota-White Relations in the Upper Mississippi Valley, 1650–1862* (St. Paul: Minnesota Historical Society Press, 1997), 268; Anderson, *Little Crow*, 229–30; Basler et al., eds., *Collected Works of Abraham Lincoln*, 5:550–51; Nichols, *Lincoln and the Indians*, 103–4; Wakefield, *Six Weeks in the Sioux Tepees*, 5–6; Chomsky, "United States–Dakota War Trials," 32, n. 118; Thiem, "Minnesota Sioux War Trials," 51, 57–58.

52. Basler et al., eds., *Collected Works of Abraham Lincoln*, 6:6–7; Davis, "Two Sioux War Orders," 121; "There Was Lack of Rope in Mankato When the Indians Were to Be Hanged," *Mankato Free Press*, 26 January 1921, 9; Henry Hastings Sibley Papers, Correspondence and Miscellaneous Papers, Roll No. 11, Frames 754 and 774, Minnesota Historical Society, St. Paul; John Nicolay to Henry Sibley, 9 December 1862, Abraham Lincoln Papers, Reel 96, Frames 42426–27, Library of Congress.

53. Theodore Blegen, *Minnesota: A History of the State* (Minneapolis: University of Minnesota Press, 1975), 250; Carley, *Sioux Uprising*, 72; *Chaska: A Minnesota River City* (Chaska, Minn.: Chaska Bicentennial Committee, 1976), 33; Clodfelter, *Dakota War*, 57; Heard, *History of the Sioux War*, 272, 285, 288; Hughes, *Old Traverse des Sioux*, 140; Nichols, *Lincoln and the Indians*, 123–24; West, *Ancestry, Life, and Times*, 294; Chomsky, "United States–Dakota War Trials," 34, 39, 54, n. 155; Thiem, "Minnesota Sioux War Trials," 64; Henry Hastings Sibley Papers, Correspondence and Miscellaneous Papers, Roll 11, Frame 776, Minnesota Historical Society, St. Paul.

54. Buck, *Indian Outbreaks*, 254, 267; Diedrich, *Dakota Oratory*, 82; Heard, *History of the Sioux War*, 276–78, 284, 287; Thomas Hughes, *History of Blue Earth County* (Marceline, Mo.: Walsworth Pub. Co., 1976), 132; *Lincoln Day by Day*, 3:158; Jacob Nix, *The Sioux Uprising in Minnesota, 1862: Jacob Nix's Eyewitness History*, trans. Gretchen Steinhauser, Don Heinrich Tolzmann, and Eberhard Reichmann, ed. Don Heinrich Tolzmann (Indianapolis, Ind.: Deutsches Haus-Athenaeum, 1994), ix-xi, 133–34; Anderson and Woolworth, eds., *Through Dakota Eyes*, 27, 217; West, *Ancestry, Life, and Times*, 289; Chomsky, "United States–Dakota War Trials," 35; Hughes, "Developmental Stages of a Frontier Town," 104.

55. Hughes, *History of Blue Earth County*, 134.

56. Anderson, *Little Crow*, 164; Carley, *Sioux Uprising*, 72; Donald, *Lincoln*, 407–8; Heard, *History of the Sioux War*, 289, 291, 294; Hughes, *History of Blue Earth County*, 133; Morris, *Better Angel*, 78; Schultz, *Over the Earth I Come*, 2; Wakefield, *Six Weeks in the Sioux Tepees*, 95; Anderson and Woolworth, eds., *Through Dakota Eyes*, 97; Wilhelm von Festenberg-Pakisch, *The History of SS. Peter and Paul's Parish in Mankato, Minnesota 1854–1899* (Mankato, Minn.: Mankato Post, 1899), 50; West, *Ancestry, Life, and Times*, 290; Davis, "Two Sioux War Orders," 124; Haack, "Army Recruit's Diary Records," 34; Thiem, "Minnesota Sioux War Trials," 59–63, 96; "The Execution of the Sioux Murderers,"

St. Paul Pioneer, 28 December 1862, 4; "The Report on the Condemned Indians to the President," *Mankato Free Press*, 29 August 1987, 6; Trial Transcript, Case No. 15, Records of the U.S. Senate, 1862 (S 144, Group 46), National Archives, Washington, D.C.

57. Carley, *Sioux Uprising*, 75; Clodfelter, *Dakota War*, 58–59; Heard, *History of the Sioux War*, 292–93; Hughes, *History of Blue Earth County*, 132, 134; Nix, *The Sioux Uprising*, 136; Schultz, *Over the Earth I Come*, 2–4; A. P. Connolly, *A Thrilling Narrative of the Minnesota Massacre and the Sioux War of 1862–63* (Chicago: A. Connolly, 1896), 172–73; Chomsky, "United States–Dakota War Trials," 37 n. 144; "Army Captain Describes Burial of Hanged Indians," *Mankato Free Press*, 25 January 1937; Education Supplement—"The Great Dakota Conflict," 38, 47. Another source says it was Cut Nose who fell to the ground and had to be strung up a second time. Meyer, *History of the Santee Sioux*, 132 n. 36.

58. Clodfelter, *Dakota War*, 58; Basler et al., eds., *Collected Works of Abraham Lincoln*, 6:7; Stephen Riggs, *Mary and I: Forty Years with the Sioux* (Williamstown, Mass.: Corner House Pub., 1971), 221; Wakefield, *Six Weeks in the Sioux Tepees*, 4, 27, 34, 68, 84–85, 115–16, 118, 121–22; West, *Ancestry, Life, and Times*, 292; Whipple, *Lights and Shadows*, 131–32, 528; Chomsky, "United States–Dakota War Trials," 34, 92, n. 124; Trial Transcripts, Case Nos. 3 and 121, Records of the U.S. Senate, 1862 (S 144, Group 46), National Archives, Washington, D.C.

59. "Execution of 39 Sioux," *Mankato Weekly Record*, 26 December 1862, 1–2; "The Execution of the Sioux Murderers," *St. Paul Pioneer*, 28 December 1862, 1, 4.

60. Anderson, *Little Crow*, 165; Buck, *Indian Outbreaks*, 221–23; Clodfelter, *Dakota War*, 59–60; Folwell, *History of Minnesota*, 2:200–201; *Minnesota in the Civil and Indian Wars*, 1:353, 747; Nichols, *Lincoln and the Indians*, 121–24; Riggs, *Mary and I*, 220–22, 224; Anderson and Woolworth, eds., *Through Dakota Eyes*, 227, 261–62; Chomsky, "United States–Dakota War Trials," 37–39, n. 145; Thiem, "Minnesota Sioux War Trials," 89–90, 96.

61. Basler et al., eds., *Collected Works of Abraham Lincoln*, 6:7, 7:325–26; Diedrich, *Dakota Oratory*, 95; Heard, *History of the Sioux War*, 270; Hughes, *History of Blue Earth County*, 135; Hughes, *Old Traverse des Sioux*, 139–40; Lowry, *Don't Shoot That Boy!* 170; Nichols, *Lincoln and the Indians*, 113; Schultz, *Over the Earth I Come*, 144, 263; Anderson and Woolworth, eds., *Through Dakota Eyes*, 21; Chomsky, "United States–Dakota War Trials," 39–40; Thiem, "Minnesota Sioux

War Trials," 52, 81–82, 98, 100; Trial Transcript, Case No. 163, Records of the U.S. Senate, 1862 (S 144, Group 46), National Archives, Washington, D.C.

62. Basler et al., eds., *Collected Works of Abraham Lincoln*, 7:111–12, 152, 208, 359, 436, 522; Donald, *Lincoln*, 394–95, 489, 514; Lowry, *Don't Shoot That Boy!* iii, 88; Morris, *Better Angel*, 200; Nichols, *Lincoln and the Indians*, 117–19, 123; Reck, *A. Lincoln*, 22, 44; Whipple, *Lights and Shadows*, 289; Chomsky, "United States–Dakota War Trials," 37 n. 146.

63. Anderson, *Little Crow*, 7–8, 63, 91, 176–78, 181; Brown, *Bury My Heart at Wounded Knee*, 64; Clodfelter, *Dakota War*, 62–65; *Minnesota in the Civil and Indian Wars*, 1:749, 2:266; Oehler, *Great Sioux Uprising*, 238; Whipple, *Lights and Shadows*, 250–51; Chomsky, "United States–Dakota War Trials," 41–43, 45–46; Thiem, "Minnesota Sioux War Trials," 105–14; "The Execution," *St. Paul Weekly Pioneer*, 12 November 1865, 4.

64. *Blue Book of the State of Illinois* (1934–35), 565; Donald, *Lincoln*, 574, 582–83, 585–86, 597; Kunhardt, Kunhardt, and Kunhardt, *Lincoln*, 342, 346, 348, 350, 352–53, 366, 378, 392; Reck, *A. Lincoln*, 37, 55, 63–65, 74, 82, 102–3, 107, 114, 134; "Origins of Marble in the Lincoln Tomb," unpublished document from information center at Lincoln's tomb, Springfield, Illinois.

65. Anderson, *Little Crow*, 139; Brown, *Bury My Heart at Wounded Knee*, 439–45; Carley, *Sioux Uprising*, 53–58; Clodfelter, *Dakota War*, 66, 72–73, 95–97, 99, 101, 113, 116–17, 141, 160–61, 171, 174, 220; William Coleman, *Voices of Wounded Knee* (Lincoln: University of Nebraska Press, 2000), 295–324; *Minnesota in the Civil and Indian Wars*, 1:312; Elaine Goodale Eastman, *Sister to the Sioux: The Memoirs of Elaine Goodale Eastman 1885–91*, ed. Kay Graber (Lincoln: University of Nebraska Press, 1978), 159–67; Chomsky, "United States–Dakota War Trials," 14; Chuck Haga, "Another Burial for Dakota Leader," *Star Tribune*, 16 July 2000, B1, B7; "Treatment of Indian Remains a Disgrace," *Mankato Free Press*, 18 July 2000, 6A.

3. The Execution of Ann Bilansky

1. Elizabeth Rapaport, "Equality of the Damned: The Execution of Women on the Cusp of the 21st Century," *Ohio Northern University Law Review* 26 (2000): 581, 590–92, 600; *Tucker v. Johnson*, 115 F.3d 276, 278–79 (5th Cir. 1997).

2. Matthew Cecil, "Justice in Heaven: The Trial of Ann Bilansky," *Minnesota History* 55 (Winter 1997–98): 351–54; Alexander Ramsey Papers and

Records, 1860–1863, Roll 12A (Microfilm Edition), Minnesota State Archives (Copies of Letters Sent—Pardon and Other Criminal Papers—Bilansky, A.), 00639, 00656.

3. Cecil, "Justice in Heaven," 354; "Death of an Old Resident," *Pioneer and Democrat*, 12 March 1860, 3; Ramsey Papers, 00500.

4. Cecil, "Justice in Heaven," 354; "Supposed Case of Poisoning," *Pioneer and Democrat*, 15 March 1859, 3.

5. Cecil, "Justice in Heaven," 354–55; *Commercial Advertiser Directory for the City of St. Paul* (1858), 153; J. Fletcher Williams, *A History of the City of St. Paul to 1875* (St. Paul: Minnesota Historical Society Press, 1983), 391.

6. Cecil, "Justice in Heaven," 350, 356–58; Ramsey Papers, 00482.

7. Cecil, "Justice in Heaven," 353, 356; "The Bilanski Case," *Pioneer and Democrat*, 24 May 1859, 3; Ramsey Papers, 00482–86, 00495–96, 00501, 00504–5, 00638–40.

8. Cecil, "Justice in Heaven," 355–57; "The Bilanski Case," *Pioneer and Democrat*, 24 May 1859, 3; "Second Day's Proceeding," *Pioneer and Democrat*, 25 May 1859, 3; Ramsey Papers, 00488–91, 00640.

9. Cecil, "Justice in Heaven," 357; "Second Day's Proceeding," *Pioneer and Democrat*, 25 May 1859, 3; Ramsey Papers, 00507–8, 00512, 00518, 00641–43.

10. Cecil, "Justice in Heaven," 357; "Second Day's Proceeding," *Pioneer and Democrat*, 25 May 1859, 3.

11. Cecil, "Justice in Heaven," 357; Ramsey Papers, 00503, 00506–10, 00513, 00515, 00641–43.

12. Ramsey Papers, 00519–29, 00644–45; "Third Day's Proceedings," *Daily Pioneer and Democrat*, 26 May 1859, 3.

13. Ramsey Papers, 00530–33.

14. Ibid., 00534–39, 00645–46.

15. Ibid., 00540–46, 00647.

16. Ibid., 00546–56, 00648–49; Williams, *History of the City of St. Paul*, 360–61; "The Bilansky Case—Fourth Day," *Pioneer and Democrat*, 27 May 1859, 3.

17. C. C. Andrews, ed., *History of St. Paul, Minn.* (Syracuse, N.Y.: D. Mason and Co., 1890), 299; Ramsey Papers, 00557–73, 00649–53.

18. Cecil, "Justice in Heaven," 357–58; "Fifth Day's Proceedings," *Daily Pioneer and Democrat*, 28 May 1859, 3; Ramsey Papers, 00557–73, 00649–53.

19. Cecil, "Justice in Heaven," 358–59; "Fifth Day's Proceedings," *Daily*

Pioneer and Democrat, 28 May 1859, 3; "Sixth Day's Proceedings," *Daily Pioneer and Democrat*, 1 June 1859, 3; Ramsey Papers, 00573–74, 00653, 00658.

20. Ramsey Papers, 00576–80, 00654.

21. Williams, *History of the City of St. Paul*, 360; Cecil, "Justice in Heaven," 353, 358–59; Ramsey Papers, 00580–87, 00596–97, 00654–55, 00658.

22. Ramsey Papers, 00586–96, 00656–57.

23. Cecil, "Justice in Heaven," 358–59; Ramsey Papers, 00597–00618, 00658–60.

24. Cecil, "Justice in Heaven," 356, 359; "The Freshet," *Daily Pioneer and Democrat*, 3 June 1859, 3; "Conviction of Anne Bilansky," *Pioneer and Democrat*, 4 June 1859, 3.

25. Cecil, "Justice in Heaven," 356, 359; "The Freshet," *Daily Pioneer and Democrat*, 3 June 1859, 3; "Conviction of Anne Bilansky," *Pioneer and Democrat*, 4 June 1859, 3.

26. *State v. Bilansky*, 3 Minn. 169, 171, 177, 179, 181 (1859); *State v. Bilansky*, 3 Minn. 313, 314, 317 (1859); Cecil, "Justice in Heaven," 359.

27. *State v. Bilansky*, 3 Minn. 169, 181 (1859); Walter Trenerry, *Murder in Minnesota: A Collection of True Cases* (St. Paul: Minnesota Historical Society Press, 1985), 39; Cecil, "Justice in Heaven," 360; "New Trial Refused in Bilansky Case—The Prisoner Let Out of Jail!" *Daily Pioneer and Democrat*, 26 July 1859, 3; "Escape of Mrs. Bilansky," *Daily Pioneer and Democrat*, 26 July 1859, 3; "Escape of Mrs. Bilansky," *Daily Pioneer and Democrat*, 27 July 1859, 3; "The Bilansky Murder," *Daily Pioneer and Democrat*, 24 March 1860, 3.

28. Theodore Blegen, *Minnesota: A History of the State* (Minneapolis: University of Minnesota Press, 1975), 226; William Watts Folwell, *A History of Minnesota* (St. Paul: Minnesota Historical Society, 1961), 2:1–4; *Minnesota Legislative Manual* (1911), 87, 100; Trenerry, *Murder in Minnesota*, 37–38; Ramsey Papers, 00633–34; Karin Thiem, "The Minnesota Sioux War Trials" (master's thesis, Mankato State University, 1979), 33.

29. *Minnesota House Journal* (1860), 50–51, 154–55; *Minnesota Legislative Manual* (1879), 169; Trenerry, *Murder in Minnesota*, 38; "Senate," *Daily Pioneer and Democrat*, 8 December 1859, 2; "House of Representatives," *Daily Pioneer and Democrat*, 14 December 1859, 2; "House of Representatives," *Daily Pioneer and Democrat*, 1 January 1860, 2; "The Bilansky Murder," *Daily Pioneer and Democrat*, 24 March 1860, 3.

30. *Minnesota House Journal* (1860), 290; *Minnesota Legislative Manual*

(1879), 169; *Minnesota Senate Journal* (1860), 220, 224; "Senate," *Daily Pioneer and Democrat*, 8 December 1859, 2; "State Legislature—Second Session," *Daily Pioneer and Democrat*, 19 January 1860, 2; *Daily Pioneer and Democrat*, 19 January 1860, 2; "House," *Daily Pioneer and Democrat*, 24 January 1860, 2; "Execution of Anne Bilansky," *Daily Pioneer and Democrat*, 26 January 1860, 3; "State Legislature," *Daily Pioneer and Democrat*, 10 February 1860, 2; "Capital Punishment," *Daily Pioneer and Democrat*, 8 March 1860, 3; "Execution of Mrs. Bilansky," *Daily Pioneer and Democrat*, 24 March 1860, 2.

31. Cecil, "Justice in Heaven," 360; "Coroner's Inquest," *Daily Pioneer and Democrat*, 10 January 1860, 3.

32. Folwell, *History of Minnesota*, 2:33–36, 53; George Hage, *Newspapers on the Minnesota Frontier 1849–1860* (St. Paul: Minnesota Historical Society Press, 1967), 81–91; "Opposed to Hanging," *Daily Pioneer and Democrat*, 23 December 1859, 1.

33. Hage, *Newspapers on the Minnesota Frontier*, 81–91; Jesse Jackson, *Legal Lynching: Racism, Injustice and the Death Penalty* (New York: Marlowe and Company, 1996), 178–85; "Opposed to Hanging," *Daily Pioneer and Democrat*, 23 December 1859, 1.

34. Jane Grey Swisshelm, *Crusader and Feminist, Letters of Jane Grey Swisshelm 1858–1865*, ed. Arthur J. Larsen (St. Paul: Minnesota Historical Society, 1934), 1, 5, 9, 26–27, 30, 180–84, 192–93, 224–27; Trenerry, *Murder in Minnesota*, 39; Cecil, "Justice in Heaven," 360; "Death Warrant for Hayward," *St. Paul Pioneer Press*, 8 December 1895, 6; Education Supplement—"The Great Dakota Conflict," 27, undated collection of *St. Paul Pioneer Press* articles, first printed as a five-part series on July 19, August 16, October 11, November 29, and December 27, 1987.

35. *Minnesota House Journal* (1860), 361–62; "State Legislature," *Daily Pioneer and Democrat*, 1 February 1860, 2.

36. *Minnesota House Journal* (1860), 155, 368, 407, 443–45; "State Legislature," *Daily Pioneer and Democrat*, 2 February 1860, 2; "State Legislature," *Daily Pioneer and Democrat*, 9 February 1860, 2; "Revising the Verdicts of Juries—Pious Skullduggery," *Daily Pioneer and Democrat*, 11 February 1860, 2.

37. *Minnesota House Journal* (1860), 500, 502, 606, 660–61, 699–700; *Minnesota Senate Journal* (1860), 402, 410, 525–27; "Mrs. Bilansky," *Daily Pioneer and Democrat*, 9 February 1860, 3; "State Legislature," *Daily Pioneer and Democrat*, 10 February 1860, 2; "Revising the Verdicts of Juries—Pious Skullduggery,"

Daily Pioneer and Democrat, 11 February 1860, 2; "State Legislature," *Daily Pioneer and Democrat*, 12 February 1860, 2; "State Legislature," *Daily Pioneer and Democrat*, 15 February 1860, 2; "State Legislature," *Daily Pioneer and Democrat*, 29 February 1860, 2; "Mrs. Bilansky," *Daily Pioneer and Democrat*, 7 March 1860, 2.

38. *Minnesota Senate Journal* (1860), 423, 644; "State Legislature," *Daily Pioneer and Democrat*, 12 February 1860, 2; "Mrs. Bilansky," *Daily Pioneer and Democrat*, 7 March 1860, 2; "Capital Punishment," *Daily Pioneer and Democrat*, 8 March 1860, 3; "State Legislature," *Daily Pioneer and Democrat*, 8 March 1860, 2; "The Bilansky Murder," *Daily Pioneer and Democrat*, 24 March 1860, 3.

39. *Minnesota House Journal* (1860), 697–700; "State Legislature," *Daily Pioneer and Democrat*, 9 March 1860, 2; "Veto by Governor Ramsey," *Daily Pioneer and Democrat*, 9 March 1860, 2.

40. Cecil, "Justice in Heaven," 361–63; Ramsey Papers, 00668–72, 00697–701, 00705–9, 00717–21.

41. "Mrs. Bilansky," *Daily Pioneer and Democrat*, 18 January 1860, 3; "The Bilansky Murder," *Daily Pioneer and Democrat*, 24 March 1860, 3; "Execution of Mrs. Bilansky," *Daily Pioneer and Democrat*, 24 March 1860, 2; "Expiated by the Rope," *St. Paul Pioneer Press*, 29 August 1885, 2.

42. John D. Bessler, *Death in the Dark: Midnight Executions in America* (Boston: Northeastern University Press, 1997), 41–46, 64; Ramsey Papers, 00703.

43. "The Bilansky Murder," *Daily Pioneer and Democrat*, 24 March 1860, 3.

44. Ibid.; Cecil, "Justice in Heaven," 350; "Mrs. Bilansky—Correction," *Daily Pioneer and Democrat*, 25 March 1860, 3.

45. Trenerry, *Murder in Minnesota*, 219; Cecil, "Justice in Heaven," 351; "The Bilansky Murder," *Daily Pioneer and Democrat*, 24 March 1860, 3; "Execution of Mrs. Bilansky," *Daily Pioneer and Democrat*, 24 March 1860, 2; "Mrs. Bilansky—Correction," *Daily Pioneer and Democrat*, 25 March 1860, 3.

46. "The Bilansky Poison Case," *Daily Pioneer and Democrat*, 5 June 1859, 2; "Execution of Mrs. Bilansky," *Daily Pioneer and Democrat*, 24 March 1860, 2–3; *Daily Pioneer and Democrat*, 25 March 1860, 3; "Capital Punishment," *Daily Pioneer and Democrat*, 27 March 1860, 3.

47. Cecil, "Justice in Heaven," 350; "The Bilansky Poison Case," *Daily Pioneer and Democrat*, 5 June 1859, 2; Noel Holston, "Scandalous Noose," *Star*

Tribune, 10 March 2000, F18–19; "History Theater Yearns for More of That Murderous Lore," *Star Tribune*, 21 March 2000, B4.

48. Randall Coyne and Lyn Entzeroth, *Capital Punishment and the Judicial Process* (Durham, N.C.: Carolina Academic Press, 1994), 157, 162; Cecil, "Justice in Heaven," 351; Rapaport, "Equality of the Damned," 581.

4. The Gallows Reconsidered

1. John D. Bessler, *Death in the Dark: Midnight Executions in America* (Boston: Northeastern University Press, 1997), 33; Randall Coyne and Lyn Entzeroth, *Capital Punishment and the Judicial Process* (Durham, N.C.: Carolina Academic Press, 1994), 1–2; Hugo Adam Bedau, ed., *The Death Penalty in America: Current Controversies* (New York: Oxford University Press, 1997), 3–4; http://www.biography.com, listing for "Boleyn, Anne."

2. Bedau, *Death Penalty in America*, 4, 8; *Minnesota Legislative Manual* (1995), 22; *State v. Bilansky*, 3 Minn. 169, 175 (1859); Brief No. 32, "Capital Punishment in Wisconsin," LRL-B-532 (Nov. 1955), Wisconsin Legislative Reference Library, Madison, Wis., 1.

3. *Minnesota House Journal* (1861), 3, 61, 139, 151, 156, 203, 207, 217, 226–27, 237; *Minnesota House Journal* (1865), 150, 209, 434; *Minnesota Legislative Manual* (1875), 66; *Minnesota Senate Journal* (1861), 103, 109, 124, 372; Richard Moe, *The Last Full Measure: The Life and Death of the First Minnesota Volunteers* (New York: Henry Holt, 1993), 296; Geoffrey Ward, *The Civil War: An Illustrated History* (New York: Knopf, 1990), 225; "House of Representatives," *Daily Pioneer and Democrat*, 16 January 1861, 2; "Capital Punishment," *Daily Pioneer and Democrat*, 7 February 1861, 1; "House of Representatives," *St. Paul Weekly Pioneer and Democrat*, 8 February 1865, 4; "Death Calls Minnesota's War Hero," *St. Paul Pioneer Press*, 14 June 1905, 1; Judge Bert Fesler, "Reminiscences of Col. Colvill," Eighth Annual Meeting of the North Shore Historical Assembly, 22 August 1936, www.arthes.com/gdg/wcolvill.html.

4. Marvin Bovee, *Christ and the Gallows* (New York: Masonic Pub. Co., 1870), 282–83; *Minnesota House Journal* (1868), 82, 118–19; "Legislative Topics," *St. Paul Daily Pioneer*, 31 January 1868, 1; "Legislative Topics," *St. Paul Daily Pioneer*, 4 February 1868, 1; "Abolishing Capital Punishment," *St. Paul Daily Pioneer*, 9 February 1868, 1; "Capital Punishment," *Red Wing Argus*, 13 February 1868, 1.

5. Elwood McIntyre, "Farmer Halts the Hangman: The Story of Marvin

Bovee," *Wisconsin Magazine of History* (Autumn 1958): 3, 6–7, 9; "Capital Punishment in Minnesota," *St. Paul Daily Pioneer*, 9 February 1868, 1; "Legislative Topics," *St. Paul Daily Pioneer*, 12 February 1868, 1; "Address on Capital Punishment," *St. Paul Daily Pioneer*, 19 February 1868, 1; "Silver Wedding of Mr. and Mrs. Marvin H. Bovee," *Whitewater Register*, 20 October 1887, 3; "Sketch of Marvin H. Bovee," State Historical Society of Wisconsin, WPA, SHSW Archives WIS/MSS/MM (Dec. 3, 1940); Brief No. 32, "Capital Punishment in Wisconsin," 2.

6. Theodore Blegen, *Minnesota: A History of the State* (Minneapolis: University of Minnesota Press, 1975), 288–89; Bovee, *Christ and the Gallows*, 282; William Everts, *Stockwell of Minneapolis: A Pioneer of Social and Political Conscience* (St. Cloud, Minn.: North Star Press of St. Cloud, 1996), 40; *Minnesota House Journal* (1868), 26, 33–34, 165; *Minnesota Senate Journal* (1868), 19, 23; McIntyre, "Farmer Halts the Hangman," 4, 9; "Legislative Topics," *St. Paul Daily Pioneer*, 18 February 1868, 1; "Address on Capital Punishment," *St. Paul Daily Pioneer*, 19 February 1868, 1.

7. McIntyre, "Farmer Halts the Hangman," 3; "Capital Punishment," *St. Paul Daily Pioneer*, 20 February 1868, 4; "To the Public," *St. Paul Dispatch*, 2 March 1868, 2; "The Gallows in Minnesota," *St. Paul Dispatch*, 24 March 1868, 1.

8. Bovee, *Christ and the Gallows*, 283; *Minnesota House Journal* (1868), 299, 302–3, 313–14, 337–39; *Minnesota Senate Journal* (1868), 245, 273–74, 284; 1868 Minn. Laws, ch. 88, § 6; "Minnesota Legislature," *St. Paul Dispatch*, 5 March 1868, 4; "The Gallows in Minnesota," *St. Paul Dispatch*, 24 March 1868, 1.

9. Walter Trenerry, *Murder in Minnesota: A Collection of True Cases* (St. Paul: Minnesota Historical Society Press, 1985), 72–74, 219–20; "Execution!" *St. Paul Dispatch*, 6 March 1868, 1; 1868 Minn. Laws, ch. 88, § 4.

10. "Murderer to Be Executed at St. Peter," *St. Paul Daily Pioneer*, 26 January 1868, 1; "The Poor Murderer," *St. Peter Tribune*, 29 January 1868, 3; "The Death Penalty in Nicollet County," *St. Peter Tribune*, 29 January 1868, 2; "The St. Peter Murderer," *St. Paul Daily Pioneer*, 30 January 1868, 1; "The Execution of Roesch Postponed," *St. Peter Tribune*, 5 February 1868, 2; "Roesch," *St. Peter Tribune*, 12 February 1868, 3; "Execution!" *St. Paul Dispatch*, 6 March 1868, 1; "The Gallows," *St. Paul Daily Pioneer*, 7 March 1868, 4.

11. "The Execution of Roesch," *St. Peter Tribune*, 19 February 1868, 3; "The Execution," *St. Peter Tribune*, 26 February 1868, 3; "The Execution of

Andreas Roesch," *St. Peter Tribune*, 4 March 1868, 3; "Execution!" *St. Paul Dispatch*, 6 March 1868, 1; "The Gallows!" *St. Paul Daily Pioneer*, 7 March 1868, 4; "Expiated by the Rope," *St. Paul Pioneer Press*, 29 August 1885, 2.

12. "Execution!" *St. Paul Dispatch*, 6 March 1868, 1; "The Gallows!" *St. Paul Daily Pioneer*, 7 March 1868, 4; "Execution," *St. Peter Tribune*, 11 March 1868, 3.

13. *Minnesota Senate Journal* (1869), 149, 180–81, 389; Penny Petersen, *Hiding in Plain Sight: Minneapolis' First Neighborhood* (Minneapolis: Marcy-Holmes Neighborhood Association/NRP, 1999), 34; "Judge William Lochren, Old Soldier, Pioneer Resident and Eminent Jurist, Dead," *Minneapolis Journal*, 28 January 1912, 1, 4; "Minnesota Legislature," *St. Paul Daily Pioneer Press*, 24 February 1869, 4; "Legislative Topics," *St. Paul Daily Pioneer Press*, 26 February 1869, 1.

14. Messages of the Governors to the Legislature of Minnesota, Gov. Cushman K. Davis, Annual Legislative Message, 8 January 1875; *Minnesota House Journal* (1875), 141, 190, 298, 363; *Minnesota House Journal* (1876), 243, 360–61; *Minnesota Senate Journal* (1875), 423–24; *Minnesota Senate Journal* (1876), 434; Trenerry, *Murder in Minnesota*, 100–101; *Minneapolis Tribune*, 7 February 1872, 2; "House," *St. Paul Daily Pioneer Press*, 4 February 1875, 2; "Capital Punishment," *St. Paul Pioneer Press*, 25 February 1876, 4; "Afternoon Session," *St. Paul Pioneer Press*, 27 February 1876, 4; "Restoring Death Penalty," *Minneapolis Daily Tribune*, 27 February 1876, 1; "Minnesota Legislature," *St. Paul Pioneer*, 2 March 1875, 2; "Minnesota Legislature," *St. Paul Pioneer*, 5 March 1875, 2; "Expiated by the Rope," *St. Paul Pioneer Press*, 29 August 1885, 2; *St. Paul Pioneer Press*, 29 August 1885, 4; Orville Quackenbush, "The Development of the Correctional, Reformatory, and Penal Institutions of Minnesota: A Sociological Interpretation" (Ph.D. thesis, University of Minnesota, 1956), 29, 47 n. 2.

15. George Huntington, *Robber and Hero: The Story of the Northfield Bank Raid* (Northfield, Minn.: Northfield Historical Society Press, 1994), x–xi, xiv, xvii, 3, 58; John Koblas, *The Jesse James Northfield Raid: Confessions of the Ninth Man* (St. Cloud, Minn.: North Star Press of St. Cloud, 1999), 2, 4–5, 20, 40, 46, 60, 62–68, 71–73, 102–4.

16. Koblas, *Jesse James Northfield Raid*, 68, 92–93, 99, 101, 106–10.

17. Ibid., 62, 117–18; Huntington, *Robber and Hero*, 78; "The Robbers," *Faribault Democrat*, 17 November 1876, 3; "The Youngers," *Faribault Democrat*, 24 November 1876, 3.

18. Messages of the Governors to the Legislature of Minnesota, Gov. John S. Pillsbury, Annual Legislative Message, 4 January 1877, 32–34; Blegen, *Minnesota*, 294–95; William Watts Folwell, *A History of Minnesota* (St. Paul: Minnesota Historical Society, 1961), 2:113–14; Koblas, *Jesse James Northfield Raid*, 83–84; Petersen, *Hiding in Plain Sight*, 78; Trenerry, *Murder in Minnesota*, 100–101; Quackenbush, "Penal Institutions of Minnesota," 29, 47.

19. *Minnesota House Journal* (1877), 41, 152–53, 214–15, 269–70, 335, 368, 388, 446, 570, 607; *Minnesota Senate Journal* (1877), 66, 188–89, 246–47, 249, 310, 338, 340–41, 388, 390, 444, 505, 523; "House of Representatives," *St. Paul Pioneer Press*, 13 January 1877, 4; "The Legislature," *St. Paul Pioneer Press*, 23 January 1877, 4; "House of Representatives," *St. Paul Pioneer Press*, 3 February 1877, 5; "House of Representatives," *St. Paul Pioneer Press*, 10 February 1877, 4; "The Legislature," *St. Paul Pioneer Press*, 11 February 1877, 4; "The Death Penalty," *St. Paul Pioneer Press*, 20 February 1877, 4; "The House," *St. Paul Pioneer Press*, 22 February 1877, 3; "The Death Penalty," *St. Paul Pioneer Press*, 24 February 1877, 3.

20. Huntington, *Robber and Hero*, 78; *Minnesota House Journal* (1879), 127, 258; *Minnesota House Journal* (1881), 19, 178–79; *Minnesota Legislative Manual* (1868), 9, 79; *Minnesota Legislative Manual* (1879), 362; "The House," *St. Paul Pioneer Press*, 28 January 1879, 7; "The House," *St. Paul Dispatch*, 28 January 1879, 7; "The Legislature," *St. Paul Dispatch*, 28 January 1879, 4; "The House," *St. Paul Pioneer Press*, 4 February 1879, 2; "House," *St. Paul Dispatch*, 4 February 1879, 4; "The House," *St. Paul Pioneer Press*, 5 February 1879, 3; "The House," *St. Paul Pioneer Press*, 19 February 1879, 3; "The House," *St. Paul Dispatch*, 19 February 1879, 2; "The House," *St. Paul Pioneer Press*, 19 February 1879, 5; "Prohibitory Legislation," *Minneapolis Tribune*, 20 February 1879, 2; *St. Paul Pioneer Press*, 11 January 1881, 2; "The Legislature," *St. Paul Pioneer Press*, 11 January 1881, 2; "Routine Report," *Minneapolis Tribune*, 22 January 1881, 2; *Minneapolis Journal*, 4 February 1906, 12; Messages of the Governors to the Legislature of Minnesota, Gov. John S. Pillsbury, Annual Legislative Message, 6 January 1881.

21. Blegen, *Minnesota*, 244–47, 386, 435; *Minnesota House Journal* (1883), 142, 216–17, 227, 538, 603; *Minnesota Senate Journal* (1883), 3, 13, 59–60, 77, 83, 456, 467, 508; "A Leper Lynched," *Daily Pioneer Press*, 28 April 1882, 6; "First and Second Thoughts," *Daily Pioneer Press*, 29 April 1882, 4; "Introduction of Bills," *St. Paul Pioneer Press*, 10 January 1883, 5; *St. Paul Pioneer Press*, 26

January 1883; *St. Paul Pioneer Press*, 31 January 1883, 4–5; S.F. 14, 23rd Leg., 1st sess., Minn. (1883); 1883 Minn. Laws, ch. 122; Lynching photo, 28 April 1882, MHS Cat. HV8.14 r2, Minnesota Historical Society, St. Paul.

22. Penal Code of the State of Minnesota §§ 156, 542 (1886); *Holden v. Minnesota*, 137 U.S. 483, 489–90 (1890); "Expiated by the Rope," *St. Paul Pioneer Press*, 29 August 1885, 2; "The Hanging at Duluth," *St. Paul Pioneer Press*, 3 September 1885, 4.

23. *Minnesota Legislative Manual* (1883), 278; "Expiated by the Rope," *St. Paul Pioneer Press*, 29 August 1885, 1–2.

24. Trenerry, *Murder in Minnesota*, 220; "Meets His Doom To-Day," *St. Paul Pioneer Press*, 28 August 1885, 1; "Owned His Guilt," *Minneapolis Journal*, 28 August 1885, 1; "Expiated by the Rope," *St. Paul Pioneer Press*, 29 August 1885, 1–2.

25. Alvin H. Wilcox, *A Pioneer History of Becker County, Minnesota* (St. Paul: Pioneer Press Co., 1907), 348–49; "Quick Work," *Minneapolis Tribune*, 24 June 1886, 1; "A Minnesota Lynching," *St. Paul Pioneer Press*, 24 June 1886, 1; "A Disgrace in Minnesota," *Minneapolis Tribune*, 25 June 1886, 4; "Murder Most Foul!" *Detroit Record*, 26 June 1886, 3; "Witness Relates Murder of City Marshal in 1886," *Detroit Lakes Tribune*, 19 November 1936, 3; Lynching Photo, 23 June 1886 (St. Paul: Minnesota Historical Society).

26. Trenerry, *Murder in Minnesota*, 220; "No Hope for Holong," *Fergus Falls Weekly Journal*, 12 April 1888, 1; "All Is Over," *Fergus Falls Weekly Journal*, 19 April 1888, 1–2; "Through a Trap," *St. Paul Globe*, 23 October 1891, 1.

27. "All Is Over," *Fergus Falls Weekly Journal*, 19 April 1888, 1.

28. "Martin Moe and John Lee, on the 15th, Their Maker Will See," *Alexandria Post*, 25 January 1889, 4; "The Drop to Death!" *Alexandria Post*, 15 February 1889, 1; "Hanging It Will Be," *St. Paul Pioneer Press*, 22 February 1889, 6; "Down to Death!" *Minneapolis Journal*, 22 March 1889, 1; "A Fight for Life," *St. Paul Pioneer Press*, 22 March 1889, 1; "A Dark Drama of Death," *Minneapolis Journal*, 22 March 1889, 3; "A Lioness and Her Cubs," *Minneapolis Journal*, 22 March 1889, 2.

29. *Minnesota Legislative Manual* (1889), 293; "Martin Moe and John Lee, on the 15th, Their Maker Will See," *Alexandria Post*, 25 January 1889, 4; "The Gallows in Sight," *St. Paul Pioneer Press*, 10 February 1889, 2; "Lee Is Launched," *St. Paul Pioneer Press*, 16 February 1889, 1.

30. "Doomed to Death," *St. Paul Pioneer Press*, 14 February 1889, 1;

"Merciful to Moe," *St. Paul Pioneer Press*, 15 February 1889, 1; "The Drop to Death!" *Alexandria Post*, 15 February 1889, 1; "Lee Is Launched," *St. Paul Pioneer Press*, 16 February 1889, 1; "An Old Time Hanging," *Mapleton Enterprise*, 6 November 1896, 20.

31. *Minnesota Legislative Manual* (1889), 295; "Invitations to the Hanging," *St. Paul Pioneer Press*, 12 March 1889, 6; "Pleading for Her Sons," *St. Paul Pioneer Press*, 15 March 1889, 6; "A Quiet Day," *St. Paul Pioneer Press*, 19 March 1889, 6; "No Interference," *St. Paul Pioneer Press*, 21 March 1889, 1; "A Fight for Life," *St. Paul Pioneer Press*, 22 March 1889, 2.

32. "A Fight for Life," *St. Paul Pioneer Press*, 22 March 1889, 2; "Down to Death!" *Minneapolis Journal*, 22 March 1889, 1; "Death's Discount," *St. Paul Pioneer Press*, 23 March 1889, 1; "Time Heals All Wounds," *Minneapolis Journal*, 23 March 1889, 1.

33. Louis Masur, *Rites of Execution: Capital Punishment and the Transformation of American Culture, 1776–1865* (New York: Oxford University Press, 1989), 98–100; "Can See the Scaffold," *Minneapolis Journal*, 23 March 1889, 2; *St. Paul Pioneer Press*, 24 March 1889, 3; "The Sorrow of a Mother," *St. Paul Pioneer Press*, 24 March 1889, 6; *Minneapolis Journal*, 25 March 1889, 4; "All Sorts of Cranks," *St. Paul Pioneer Press*, 25 March 1889, 6; "The Morals of Hanging," *St. Paul Pioneer Press*, 25 March 1889, 6; *Minneapolis Journal*, 25 March 1889, 4; "Viewing the Scaffold," *Minneapolis Journal*, 26 March 1889, 2; *Minneapolis Journal*, 29 March 1889, 4; "The Barrett Bills," *St. Paul Pioneer Press*, 31 March 1889, 2; "Echoes of the Barrett Execution," *Minneapolis Journal*, 4 April 1889, 4; "The Barrett Hanging," *Minneapolis Journal*, 4 April 1889, 2; *Minneapolis Journal*, 27 April 1889, 5; "Scientific Phrenology," *Minneapolis Journal*, 15 May 1889, 2.

5. The "Midnight Assassination Law"

1. John D. Bessler, *Death in the Dark: Midnight Executions in America* (Boston: Northeastern University Press, 1997), 46–47.

2. Ibid., 47–52; Louis Masur, *Rites of Execution: Capital Punishment and the Transformation of American Culture, 1776–1865* (New York: Oxford University Press, 1989), 93–116; Michael Madow, "Forbidden Spectacle: Executions, the Public and the Press in Nineteenth-Century New York," *Buffalo Law Review* 43 (1995): 461.

3. Bessler, *Death in the Dark*, 52; 1885 Ohio Laws 169; 1889 Ind. Acts 192; 1889 Colo. Sess. Laws 118.

4. *Minnesota Legislative Manual* (1889), 631, 637–38; "Capital Punishment," *St. Paul Pioneer Press*, 13 March 1889, 1; "The House Decides That Capital Punishment Is Proper and Postpones Mr. Davis' Bill," *St. Paul Pioneer Press*, 13 March 1889, 1.

5. Bessler, *Death in the Dark*, 52; *Minnesota Legislative Manual* (1889), 615; *Minnesota Senate Journal* (1889), 483, 707, 1068; *Portrait Gallery of the Twenty-Ninth Legislature of the State of Minnesota* (Minneapolis: Bramblett and Beygeh, 1895), 7; "The Death Penalty," *St. Paul Pioneer Press*, 19 March 1889, 1; "Minnesota Legislature," *Martin County Sentinel*, 29 March 1889, 3; "Senator Day Is President," *St. Paul Pioneer Press*, 26 January 1895, 1; 1888 N.Y. Laws, ch. 489.

6. *Minnesota Legislative Manual* (1911), 103; "Shall It Be Hanging?" *St. Paul Pioneer Press*, 7 February 1889, 6; *Martin County Sentinel*, 29 March 1889, 2; *Martin County Sentinel*, 12 July 1889, 4.

7. *Minnesota Senate Journal* (1889), 483, 707, 1068; "The Death Penalty," *St. Paul Pioneer Press*, 19 March 1889, 1; "Death by Lightning," *St. Paul Pioneer Press*, 21 March 1889, 5; "Sunday Saunterings," *St. Paul Pioneer Press*, 24 March 1889, 11; "Dispense with the Rope," *Minneapolis Tribune*, 3 April 1889, 4; "A Barbarous Penalty," *St. Paul Pioneer Press*, 17 October 1891, 4; "Barbarism of the Gallows," *Minneapolis Tribune*, 17 October 1891, 4; "The Execution of Rose," *St. Paul Globe*, 17 October 1891, 4; "Another Strangling," *St. Paul Pioneer Press*, 24 October 1891, 4; "Introduction of Electrocution," *St. Paul Dispatch*, 5 January 1899, 9.

8. Isaac Atwater, *History of the City of Minneapolis* (New York: Munsell, 1893), 484c–484f; *Minnesota Legislative Manual* (1889), 637; "Murderers Must Hang," *Minneapolis Journal*, 2 April 1889, 1; "Hanging Will Do," *Minneapolis Tribune*, 3 April 1889, 2; "Echoes of the Barrett Execution," *Minneapolis Journal*, 4 April 1889, 4; *St. Paul Pioneer Press*, 5 April 1889, 6; "John Day Smith–Part I," *ECCO News*, July 1979, 12–13 (available at Minneapolis Public Library, Special Collections); "John Day Smith–Part II," *ECCO News*, September 1979, 10–11; "Capital Punishment," *St. Paul Pioneer Press*, 3 April 1889, 1.

9. *Minnesota Legislative Manual* (1889), 636–37; "Murderers Must Hang," *Minneapolis Journal*, 2 April 1889, 1; "Capital Punishment," *St. Paul Pioneer Press*, 3 April 1889, 1; "Dispense with the Rope," *Minneapolis Tribune*, 3 April 1889, 4.

10. *History of Litchfield and an Account of Its Centennial Celebration 1895* (Augusta, Maine: Kennebec Journal Print, 1897), 308; *Minnesota Legislative Manual* (1911), 104, 629; John Day Smith, *Cases on Constitutional Law* (St. Paul:

West Publishing Co., 1897); John Day Smith, *The History of the Nineteenth Regiment of Maine Volunteer Infantry 1862–1865* (Minneapolis: Great Western Printing Company, 1909), 16, 43, 61–62, 69–75, 83, 108, 116–17, 206–7, 226; *The Gopher* 12 (1899): 66–67 (available at Minneapolis Public Library, Special Collections); "His Idea Started Glen Lake Farm," *Minneapolis Journal*, 27 September 1931, 3; "Judge J. D. Smith Dies at 88, Funeral Tuesday," *Minneapolis Journal*, 6 March 1933, 9; "John Day Smith Succumbs at 88," *Minneapolis Tribune*, 6 March 1933, 2; "Judge John Day Smith, 1845–1933," memorial prepared by E. F. Waite and presented February 3, 1934, Minneapolis Bar Association Papers, 1916–1934, Minnesota Historical Society, St. Paul.

 11. Robert Alotta, *Civil War Justice: Union Army Executions under Lincoln* (Shippensburg, Pa.: White Mane Publishing Company, 1989), 30–31, 76–77, 86, 107–8, 112–14, 186–211; Smith, *History of the Nineteenth Regiment*, v, 1–2, 6, 25, 42, 56, 70, 73, 79–81, 86–88, 91, 93–94, 103–5, 123–24, 133, 135, 172–73, 193, 211, 255, 289–90, 309, 314, 317, 336; Philip B. Kunhardt Jr., Philip B. Kunhardt III, and Peter W. Kunhardt, *Lincoln: An Illustrated Biography* (New York: Knopf, 1992), 192–93; John Day Smith, *What War Meant to a Maine Soldier 1861–1865* (Washington, D.C.), 6 January 1927 (available at Minnesota Historical Society, St. Paul); "*John Day Smith–Part I*," *ECCO News*, July 1979, 12–13.

 12. *Minnesota House Journal* (1889), 818, 907, 917, 1045, 1062–63, 1222, 1418; *Minnesota Senate Journal* (1889), 777, 797, 835, 845, 856, 878, 915; H.F. 1185, 26th Leg., 1st sess., Minn. (1889); 1889 Minn. Laws, ch. 20, § 8; "Dispense with the Rope," *Minneapolis Tribune*, 3 April 1889, 4; "Will It Work?" *Minneapolis Journal*, 24 April 1889, 8.

 13. Bessler, *Death in the Dark*, 4; 1889 Minn. Laws, ch. 20, §§ 3–6.

 14. "Bills That Have Passed," *St. Paul Pioneer Press*, 23 April 1889, 9; "Hard on the Reporters," *St. Paul Pioneer Press*, 24 April 1889, 3; "Will It Work?" *Minneapolis Journal*, 24 April 1889, 8; "A Change Required," *Minneapolis Tribune*, 24 October 1891, 4; *Martin County Sentinel*, 10 May 1889, 4; "John Day Smith–Part I," *ECCO News*, July 1979, 13.

 15. "Upon the Scaffold High," *Little Falls Transcript*, 19 July 1889, 3; "The Drop Falls," *St. Paul Pioneer Press*, 19 July 1889, 1; "Hanged in Private," *St. Paul Dispatch*, 19 July 1889, 1; "The Last of Bulow," *Little Falls Transcript*, 26 July 1889, 3; "Last Hours of Life," *Minneapolis Tribune*, 19 October 1894, 1; "Sheriff's Tea Party," *St. Paul Dispatch*, 14 February 1906, 10; "The Smith Execution Law," *Minneapolis Journal*, 14 February 1906, 4.

16. "Hanged in Private," *St. Paul Dispatch*, 19 July 1889, 1; *Little Falls Transcript*, 19 July 1889, 3; "The Last of Bulow," *Little Falls Transcript*, 26 July 1889, 4; *Alexandria Post*, 26 July 1889, 1.

17. "The Drop Falls," *St. Paul Pioneer Press*, 19 July 1889, 1; "Hanged in Private," *St. Paul Dispatch*, 19 July 1889, 1.

18. "A 'Morbid' Law," *St. Paul Dispatch*, 19 July 1889, 2.

19. Ibid.

20. "John Day and His Law," *Little Falls Transcript*, 26 July 1889, 2.

21. Ibid.; "John Day Smith Succumbs at 88," *Minneapolis Tribune*, 6 March 1933, 2.

22. "Disreputable Journalism," *Martin County Sentinel*, 26 July 1889, 4.

23. Ibid.; *Minnesota Legislative Manual* (1889), 524; "Two Lives Taken," *Martin County Sentinel*, 29 March 1889, 2.

24. "The Execution of Brown," *Moorhead Daily News*, 13 September 1889, 4; "Execution of Thomas Brown," *Moorhead Daily News*, 19 September 1889, 4; "Executed," *Moorhead Daily News*, 20 September 1889, 1; "Gone to His Doom," *St. Paul Dispatch*, 20 September 1889, 1.

25. Theodore Blegen, *Minnesota: A History of the State* (Minneapolis: University of Minnesota Press, 1975), 386–87; "Through the Trap," *St. Paul Pioneer Press*, 27 June 1890, 1; "Hanged Until Dead," *Redwood Reveille* (Redwood Falls), 17 October 1891, 3; "Rose's Footsteps," *Daily Pioneer Press*, 19 October 1891, 1; "Hanged Till Dead," *Minneapolis Tribune*, 23 October 1891, 1; Execution Records, Box 1, Minnesota Historical Society, St. Paul.

26. "Paid the Penalty," *Pine County Pioneer* (Pine City), 27 June 1890, 1, 4; "Through the Trap," *St. Paul Pioneer Press*, 27 June 1890, 1.

27. Wayne Webb, *Redwood: The Story of a County* (Minn.: Redwood County Board of Commissioners, 1964), 459–64; "The Rope Broke," *Redwood Gazette*, 22 October 1891, 1; "Watch Slover," *Redwood Gazette*, 22 October 1891, 2.

28. Webb, *Redwood*, 462; "Full of Horrors," *St. Paul Pioneer Press*, 16 October 1891, 1; "Dropped to Death," *St. Paul Globe*, 16 October 1891, 1; "Rose Twice Hanged," *St. Paul Pioneer Press*, 17 October 1891, 1.

29. *Sleepy Eye Dispatch*, 15 October 1891, 1; "Full of Horrors," *St. Paul Pioneer Press*, 16 October 1891, 1; "Hanged Until Dead," *Redwood Reveille* (Redwood Falls), 17 October 1891, 3; "Rose Twice Hanged," *St. Paul Pioneer Press*, 17 October 1891, 1; "Rose's Last Letter," *Redwood Gazette*, 22 October 1891, 3.

30. "The Death March," *Minneapolis Tribune*, 16 October 1891, 1; "Full of Horrors," *St. Paul Pioneer Press*, 16 October 1891, 1; "Dropped to Death," *St. Paul Globe*, 16 October 1891, 1; "Bungling, Shocking!" *St. Paul Globe*, 17 October 1891, 1; "More in Detail," *Minneapolis Tribune*, 17 October 1891, 1; "Rose Hanged Twice," *St. Paul Pioneer Press*, 17 October 1891, 1; "It Sometimes Happens," *St. Paul Pioneer Press*, 17 October 1891, 4; "John Day Smith, with Amendments," *Redwood Gazette*, 22 October 1891, 3; "Those Fresh Young Reporters," *Redwood Reveille* (Redwood Falls), 31 October 1891, 3; "Was a Confession Made," *Redwood Gazette*, 24 January 1900, 1.

31. "Caught in an Old Trick," *Minneapolis Tribune*, 17 October 1891, 4; "It Sometimes Happens," *St. Paul Pioneer Press*, 17 October 1891, 4; "News of the Hanging," *St. Paul Globe*, 18 October 1891, 4; "Getting Out of a Hole," *St. Paul Pioneer Press*, 19 October 1891, 4.

32. "Rose's Footsteps," *St. Paul Pioneer Press*, 19 October 1891, 1; "Hanged Till Dead," *Minneapolis Tribune*, 23 October 1891, 1; "Through a Trap," *St. Paul Globe*, 23 October 1891, 1; "Rosa Bray Avenged," *St. Paul Pioneer Press*, 23 October 1891, 1; "Goheen Is Buried," *St. Paul Globe*, 24 October 1891, 1.

33. *Pine County Pioneer* (Pine City), 4 July 1890, 1; "Rose Twice Hanged," *St. Paul Pioneer Press*, 17 October 1891, 1; "A Change Required," *Minneapolis Tribune*, 24 October 1891, 4; "Another Strangling," *St. Paul Pioneer Press*, 24 October 1891, 4.

34. William Everts, *Stockwell of Minneapolis: A Pioneer of Social and Political Conscience* (St. Cloud, Minn.: North Star Press of St. Cloud, 1996), 69; *Minnesota House Journal* (1897), 31, 107, 192, 202; *Minnesota Senate Journal* (1897), 186, 190; *Portrait Gallery of the Twenty-Ninth Legislature*, 110; H.F. 1, 30th Minn. Leg., 1st sess. (1897); "Four Bills Introduced," *St. Paul Pioneer Press*, 8 January 1897, 2; "Salaries Must Be Reduced," *St. Paul Pioneer Press*, 28 January 1897, 3; "The House," *St. Paul Pioneer Press*, 6 February 1897, 1; "Two Houses Get Together," *St. Paul Pioneer Press*, 6 February 1897, 2; "Prevented the Slaughter," *St. Paul Pioneer Press*, 7 February 1897, 10.

35. *Holden v. Minnesota*, 137 U.S. 483, 484–85 (1890); *Holden*, Transcript of Record, 1, 7; "Holden's Last Chance," *St. Paul Pioneer Press*, 10 December 1890, 10.

36. Bessler, *Death in the Dark*, 52–55; *In re* Medley, 134 U.S. 160 (1890); *In re* Savage, 134 U.S. 176 (1890); *Holden*, 137 U.S. at 487; *Holden*, Transcript of Record, 2, 7; "How About Clift Holden?" *St. Paul Pioneer Press*, 3 July 1890, 5.

37. *Holden*, Transcript of Record, 11, 17, and Appellant's Brief, 3.

38. *Holden*, Appellant's Brief, 4, 14, 15, 20.

39. *Holden*, Respondent's Brief, 3, 18.

40. *Holden*, 137 U.S. at 491, 493–95; "Holden Must Hang," *St. Paul Pioneer Press*, 9 December 1890, 4; "To Stretch Hemp," *Minneapolis Tribune*, 9 December 1890, 1; "Clifton Holden's Case," *St. Paul Pioneer Press*, 22 November 1890, 5; "The Holden Case," *Minneapolis Tribune*, 21 November 1890, 3; "Full of Horrors," *St. Paul Pioneer Press*, 16 October 1891, 1; Execution Records, Box 1, Minnesota Historical Society, St. Paul.

41. "Nearing Their End," *Duluth News Tribune*, 18 October 1894, 1; "The Debt Is Paid," *St. Paul Pioneer Press*, 19 October 1894, 4; "Ready for the Drop," *Duluth News Tribune*, 19 October 1894, 1; "The Gallows Tree Bears Its Fruit," *St. Paul Pioneer Press*, 19 October 1894, 1–2; "Last Hours of Life," *Minneapolis Tribune*, 19 October 1894, 1; "Paid the Penalty," *Minneapolis Tribune*, 20 October 1894, 3; "Well Rid of Gottschalk," *St. Paul Pioneer Press*, 22 July 1905, 1, 6; Execution Records, Box 1, Minnesota Historical Society, St. Paul.

42. "What to Do with Criminals," *Minneapolis Tribune*, 19 October 1894, 4; "Last Act of the Tragedy," *St. Paul Pioneer Press*, 20 October 1894, 2; "A 'Painless' Death," *St. Paul Pioneer Press*, 21 October 1894, 4; Execution Records, Box 1, Minnesota Historical Society, St. Paul.

43. *State v. Hayward*, 62 Minn. 474, 481, 65 N.W. 63, 64 (1895); "The Crime!" *Minneapolis Tribune*, 11 December 1895, 6.

44. Walter Trenerry, *Murder in Minnesota: A Collection of True Cases* (St. Paul: Minnesota Historical Society Press, 1985), 143–47; *Hayward*, 62 Minn. at 481, 485, 65 N.W. at 64–65; "The Crime!" *Minneapolis Tribune*, 11 December 1895, 6.

45. Trenerry, *Murder in Minnesota*, 148–49.

46. Ibid., 126, 149, 151, 154; *State v. Hayward*, 62 Minn. 114, 64 N.W. 90, *aff'd*, 62 Minn. 474, 76, 65 N.W. 63, 65 (1895); "One Juror in Addition," *St. Paul Pioneer Press*, 23 January 1895, 6; "Many Were Called," *St. Paul Pioneer Press*, 24 January 1895, 6; "Hayward's Salvation," *St. Paul Pioneer Press*, 30 January 1895, 6; "'He's a Liar,' Says Harry," *St. Paul Pioneer Press*, 3 March 1895, 3, 6; "Harry Expects Conviction," *St. Paul Pioneer Press*, 5 March 1895, 6; "Hemp for Hayward," *St. Paul Pioneer Press*, 9 March 1895, 1, 6; "Sentenced to Be Hanged," *St. Paul Pioneer Press*, 12 March 1895, 1; Execution Records, Box 1, Minnesota Historical Society, St. Paul; "Judge John Day Smith, 1845–1933."

47. "Hayward Hanging," *St. Paul Pioneer Press*, 3 December 1895, 6; "A Noose Ready for His Neck," *Minneapolis Tribune*, 8 December 1895, 1; "Hayward's Death Warrant," *Minneapolis Tribune*, 8 December 1895, 3; "Death Warrant for Hayward," *St. Paul Pioneer Press*, 8 December 1895, 6; "The Awful Curse of a Brother," *Minneapolis Tribune*, 9 December 1895, 2; "John Day Smith Pleads," *Minneapolis Tribune*, 10 December 1895, 4; "Hayward's Latest Trick," *St. Paul Pioneer Press*, 10 December 1895, 1.

48. Trenerry, *Murder in Minnesota*, 152; "Hayward's Latest Trick," *St. Paul Pioneer Press*, 10 December 1895, 2.

49. Trenerry, *Murder in Minnesota*, 152; "A Noose Ready for His Neck," *Minneapolis Tribune*, 8 December 1895, 11; "Has But a Single Day to Live," *Minneapolis Tribune*, 10 December 1895, 1; "Waning!" *Minneapolis Tribune*, 11 December 1895, 3; "Watchers Outside," *St. Paul Pioneer Press*, 11 December 1895, 2; "Hayward's Confession," *Minneapolis Tribune*, 19 December 1895, 1.

50. Atwater, *History of the City of Minneapolis*, 201–3, 484f; Smith, *History of the Nineteenth Regiment*, 73–74; "Close of a Chapter of Crime," *St. Paul Pioneer Press*, 11 December 1895, 1; "The Wages of Sin," *Minneapolis Tribune*, 11 December 1895, 1; "Judge John Day Smith, 1845–1933," 3, 6.

51. "Hanging Hayward," *St. Paul Pioneer Press*, 3 December 1895, 6; "The Wages of Sin," *Minneapolis Tribune*, 11 December 1895, 1; "'I Die Game,' Says Harry," *St. Paul Pioneer Press*, 11 December 1895, 1–2; "Hayward Is Laid to Rest," *St. Paul Pioneer Press*, 12 December 1895, 6; "The Sorrow of His Mother," *Minneapolis Tribune*, 12 December 1895, 1, 7; "The Hayward Gallows," *Minneapolis Tribune*, 15 December 1895, 16; "The Voice of Hayward," *Minneapolis Tribune*, 18 December 1895, 7.

52. "Exit Hayward," *St. Paul Pioneer Press*, 11 December 1895, 4; "A Good Law," *Minneapolis Tribune*, 12 December 1895, 6.

53. Blegen, *Minnesota*, 457–58; Trenerry, *Murder in Minnesota*, 223–26; James Taylor Dunn, "The Minnesota State Prison during the Stillwater Era, 1853–1914," *Minnesota History* 37 (December 1960): 137; "Crawford's Day of Doom," *St. Paul Pioneer Press*, 5 December 1905, 10; "The Revenge of a Newspaper," *Minneapolis Journal*, 5 December 1905, 1; "Hanged," *Minneapolis Tribune*, 5 December 1905, 1; "Crawford Calmly Goes to Execution," *St. Paul Pioneer Press*, 6 December 1905, 11; "Paid the Penalty," *Sherburne County Star News*, 7 December 1905, 11; "Sheriff to Obey the Law," *St. Paul Dispatch*, 10

February 1906, 24; *Sherburne County Star News* (Elk River), 14 December 1905, 5; "John Day Smith–Part II," *ECCO News*, September 1979, 11. Legislative attempts to move executions to the state prison at Stillwater always failed. *Minnesota House Journal* (1903), 263, 529–30, 536, 600–601, 621–22, 638, 1589; *Minnesota Senate Journal* (1903), 493–95, 840, 1369; "Murderers May Be Electrocuted," *Duluth News Tribune*, 6 March 1903, 1; "Publicity and Hangings," *St. Paul Pioneer Press*, 23 February 1907, 1, 6. For example, in 1899, a bill failed to pass that would have required executions at the state prison before sunrise. *Minnesota House Journal* (1899), 33, 212, 435; "Execution of Murderers," *St. Paul Dispatch*, 7 February 1899, 3; "Introduction of Electrocution," *St. Paul Dispatch*, 5 January 1899, 9.

54. "Pryde Will Hang," *Brainerd Dispatch*, 17 July 1896, 4; "John E. Pryde Is Hanged," *St. Paul Pioneer Press*, 23 July 1896, 4; "Execution of John E. Pryde," *Brainerd Dispatch*, 24 July 1896, 1; "Sentenced to Death," *St. Paul Pioneer Press*, 8 January 1897, 5; "Kelly's Expiation," *St. Paul Pioneer Press*, 23 March 1897, 1; "John Moshik Dies," *Minneapolis Journal*, 18 March 1898, 2; "Lemke's Murder Is Avenged," *St. Paul Pioneer Press*, 18 March 1898, 6; "Henderson Prays for Prisoners," *Duluth News Tribune*, 2 March 1903, 5; "Slayer of Ida M'Cormack Dies upon the Scaffold," *Duluth News Tribune*, 6 March 1903, 1; "Dies at End of Noose," *St. Paul Pioneer Press*, 6 March 1903, 1; "Must Hang After All," *St. Paul Pioneer Press*, 18 March 1903, 6; "Oleson Dies on the Gallows," *St. Paul Pioneer Press*, 20 March 1903, 6; "A Life for a Life," *Aitkin Age*, 24 March 1903, 4; "Chounard, A Wife Murderer, Dies," *Minneapolis Journal*, 30 August 1904, 5; Execution Records, Box 1, Minnesota Historical Society, St. Paul.

55. *Henderson Then and Now* (Hutchinson, Minn.: Crow River Press, 1995), 161; "Wallert Hanged," *Hub* (Gaylord), 29 March 1901, 4; "Wallert Is Hanged," *Minneapolis Times*, 29 March 1901, 1; "Dropped into Eternity," *Arlington Enterprise*, 4 April 1901, 1; "Wallert Hanged," *Hub* (Gaylord), 15 April 1901, 6; "Tapper Pays the Penalty," *St. Paul Pioneer Press*, 18 February 1902, 11; "Rosa Mixa Is Avenged," *Weekly Valley Herald* (Chaska), 20 February 1902, 1; "Gallows Too Slow a Method," *Weekly Valley Herald* (Chaska), 20 February 1902, 2; "John Day Smith–Part II," *ECCO News*, September 1979, 11; Execution Records, Box 1, Minnesota Historical Society, St. Paul; "Joe Ott Hung," *Granite Falls Journal*, 20 October 1898, 4; *Minneapolis Tribune*, 21 October 1898, 3; *Granite Falls Journal*, 27 October 1898, 4; "Ott Is Hanged," *Minneapolis Tribune*, 28 October 1898, 1.

6. The Botched Hanging of William Williams

1. D. J. Tice, *Minnesota's Twentieth Century: Stories of Extraordinary Everyday People* (Minneapolis: University of Minnesota Press, 1999), 11–14; "Gottschalk His Own Executioner," *St. Paul Pioneer Press*, 20 July 1905, 1; "Inquest To-Day for Gottschalk," *St. Paul Pioneer Press*, 21 July 1905, 2; "Well Rid of Gottschalk," *St. Paul Pioneer Press*, 22 July 1905, 6.

2. "Gottschalk's End to Be the Gallows," *St. Paul Pioneer Press*, 1 May 1905, 1; "Fix Early Date for Hanging," *St. Paul Pioneer Press*, 15 May 1905, 2; "Gottschalk to Be Hanged Aug. 8," *St. Paul Pioneer Press*, 16 May 1905, 2; "Sheriffs Are Coming," *St. Paul Pioneer Press*, 14 July 1905, 2; "Gallows Ready for Gottschalk," *St. Paul Pioneer Press*, 18 July 1905, 2; "No Last Resting Place for Gottschalk's Body," *St. Paul Pioneer Press*, 22 July 1905, 6; "Sheriffs Meet in Annual Convention," *St. Paul Pioneer Press*, 9 August 1905, 3; "State Executions," *St. Paul Pioneer Press*, 2 February 1907, 6.

3. "Well Rid of Gottschalk," *St. Paul Pioneer Press*, 22 July 1905, 6.

4. Ibid.; "Executions at Penitentiary," *St. Paul Pioneer Press*, 10 August 1905, 2.

5. *State v. Williams*, 96 Minn. 351, 354–55 (1905).

6. Ibid., 357.

7. Ibid., 357–60.

8. Ibid., 354, 360; Walter Trenerry, *Murder in Minnesota: A Collection of True Cases* (St. Paul: Minnesota Historical Society Press, 1985), 160; "Williams Is Hanged at County Jail," *St. Paul Pioneer Press*, 13 February 1906, 2.

9. *Williams*, 96 Minn. at 370–73; "Williams Is Doomed to Gallows," *St. Paul Pioneer Press*, 20 May 1905, 1.

10. *Williams*, 96 Minn. at 365–73.

11. Trenerry, *Murder in Minnesota*, 162–63; *Williams*, 96 Minn. at 353, 364–65; "Must Face the Gallows," *St. Paul Dispatch*, 12 February 1906, 7; "Governor Will Quiz Miesen," *St. Paul Pioneer Press*, 14 February 1906, 3; "Newspaper Indicted for Giving News," *St. Paul Pioneer Press*, 3 March 1906, 1.

12. "Sheriff to Obey the Law," *St. Paul Dispatch*, 10 February 1906, 24; "Must Face the Gallows," *St. Paul Dispatch*, 12 February 1906, 7.

13. "Sheriff to Obey the Law," *St. Paul Dispatch*, 10 February 1906, 24; "Sheriff Will Kill Williams," *St. Paul Pioneer Press*, 12 February 1906, 4; *St. Paul Dispatch*, 12 February 1906, 1; "Displayed His Nerve to the Very Last," *St. Paul Dispatch*, 13 February 1906, 3; "Goes to Gallows in Dead of Night,"

Minneapolis Journal, 13 February 1906, 6; Joseph E. Hennessey, "This Is Murder; I Am Innocent," *St. Paul Daily News*, 13 February 1906, 1; Affidavit of Anton Miesen, 14 February 1906.

14. "Williams Is Hanged at County Jail," *St. Paul Pioneer Press*, 13 February 1906, 1; Hennessey, "This Is Murder," 1.

15. "Displayed His Nerve to the Very Last," *St. Paul Dispatch*, 13 February 1906, 3.

16. Ibid.; "Sheriff's Tea Party," *St. Paul Dispatch*, 14 February 1906, 10; "The Smith Execution Law," *Minneapolis Journal*, 14 February 1906, 4.

17. "What Should Result," *St. Paul Dispatch*, 28 February 1906, 10; "An Unsafe Law and the Remedy," *St. Paul Pioneer Press*, 6 March 1906, 6; "Well Rid of Gottschalk," *St. Paul Pioneer Press*, 22 July 1905, 6; "Death by Electricity," *St. Paul Pioneer Press*, 24 February 1907, 1.

18. *Minnesota Legislative Manual* (1911), 5–6; "The Only Newspaper Man Who Witnessed the Hanging," *St. Paul Daily News*, 13 February 1906, 1; "Governor Will Quiz Miesen," *St. Paul Pioneer Press*, 14 February 1906, 3; "Newspaper Indicted for Giving News," *St. Paul Pioneer Press*, 3 March 1906, 1.

19. *Minnesota Legislative Manual* (1911), 5–6; "Won't Do a Thing to the Sheriff," *St. Paul Pioneer Press*, 15 February 1906, 3; "Death Penalty Decried by State's Executive," *Minneapolis Journal*, 25 February 1906, 7; "St. Paul Newspapers Procure Indictments," *Minneapolis Journal*, 4 March 1906, 5; *St. Paul Herald*, 16 March 1918, 1.

20. *Men of Minnesota* (St. Paul: Minnesota Historical Co., 1902), 53; *St. Paul City Directory* (1906) (listing Emil W. Helmes as "Asst Corporation Atty" in "City Hall"); Trenerry, *Murder in Minnesota*, 162–63; "Protest to Prosecutor," *St. Paul Dispatch*, 15 February 1906, 4; "Goes After Papers," *St. Paul Pioneer Press*, 20 February 1906, 2; "St. Paul Newspapers Procure Indictments," *Minneapolis Journal*, 4 March 1906, 5.

21. "Goes After Papers," *St. Paul Pioneer Press*, 20 February 1906, 2; "Newspaper Indicted for Giving News," *St. Paul Pioneer Press*, 3 March 1906, 1; "Newspapers Indicted," *Minneapolis Journal*, 3 March 1906, 7.

22. "Seeking to Curb Press," *St. Paul Dispatch*, 3 March 1906, 7; "Newspapers Indicted," *Minneapolis Journal*, 3 March 1906, 7; Indictments of *The Pioneer Press, State v. Pioneer Press Co.* (File No. 4695), *The Dispatch, State v. Dispatch Printing Co.* (File No. 4696), and *The Daily News, State v. Daily News Publishing Co.* (File No. 4697) (Criminal Register I, Ramsey County, Minnesota Historical

Society, St. Paul); "Newspaper Indicted for Giving News," *St. Paul Pioneer Press*, 3 March 1906, 1.

23. "St. Paul Newspapers Procure Indictments," *Minneapolis Journal*, 4 March 1906, 5; "An Unsafe Law and the Remedy," *St. Paul Pioneer Press*, 6 March 1906, 6.

24. "Newspaper Indicted for Giving News," *St. Paul Pioneer Press*, 3 March 1906, 1; "An Unsafe Law and the Remedy," *St. Paul Pioneer Press*, 6 March 1906, 6.

25. Ibid.

26. *St. Paul Pioneer Press*, 3 March 1906, 6; "Pioneer Press Enters Plea," *St. Paul Pioneer Press*, 4 March 1906, 1.

27. *State v. Pioneer Press Co.*, 100 Minn. 173, 110 N.W. 867 (1907), Appellant's Brief, 9; "Seeking to Curb Press," *St. Paul Dispatch*, 3 March 1906, 7; "Pioneer Press Enters Plea," *St. Paul Pioneer Press*, 4 March 1906, 1; "Papers Demur," *St. Paul Dispatch*, 5 March 1906, 6; "Papers to Test Law," *St. Paul Pioneer Press*, 6 March 1906, 7; "Validity of Law Attacked," *St. Paul Dispatch*, 10 March 1906, 9; "Muzzle Law Not Constitutional," *St. Paul Pioneer Press*, 11 March 1906, 1; Case Certification, File No. 4695 (Criminal Register I, Ramsey County); Demurrers to Indictments, File Nos. 4696, 4697 (Criminal Register I, Ramsey County).

28. *State v. Pioneer Press Co.*, 100 Minn. 173, 110 N.W. 867 (1907), Respondent's Brief, 15, 21; "Validity of Law Attacked," *St. Paul Dispatch*, 10 March 1906, 9; "Young Prisoner Affronts Court," *St. Paul Pioneer Press*, 10 March 1906, 5; "Muzzle Law Not Constitutional," *St. Paul Pioneer Press*, 11 March 1906, 1.

29. *Pioneer Press Co.*, Certified Case, 3; "Law Is Held to Be Legal," *St. Paul Dispatch*, 16 April 1906, 1; "Muzzle Law Is Sustained," *St. Paul Pioneer Press*, 17 April 1906, 2; "Validity of Law Upheld by Court," *St. Paul Daily News*, 16 April 1906, 1.

30. Trenerry, *Murder in Minnesota*, 165; *Pioneer Press Co.*, Certified Case/Report, 2–3, 9–16; File Nos. 4696, 4697 (Criminal Register I, Ramsey County).

31. *Pioneer Press Co.*, Appellant's Brief, 12–13, 15.

32. Ibid., 16, 24.

33. *Pioneer Press Co.*, Respondent's Brief, 7–8, 15, 21.

34. *State v. Pioneer Press Co.*, 100 Minn. 173, 175, 177, 110 N.W. 867,

868–69 (1907); "Must Not Tell about Hangings," *St. Paul Pioneer Press*, 22 February 1907, 5.

35. "Publicity and Hangings," *St. Paul Pioneer Press*, 23 February 1907, 1.

36. "Newspapers Lose Appeal," *St. Paul Dispatch*, 21 February 1907, 1; "Lid Forced Down on All Executions," *St. Paul Daily News*, 21 February 1907, 3; "Newspapers Lose Appeal," *St. Paul Dispatch*, 21 February 1907, 1; File Nos. 4695, 4696, 4697 (Criminal Register I, Ramsey County).

7. The Abolition of Capital Punishment

1. Hugo Adam Bedau, ed., *The Death Penalty in America: Current Controversies* (New York: Oxford University Press, 1997), 8–9, 411; D. J. Tice, *Minnesota's Twentieth Century: Stories of Extraordinary Everyday People* (Minneapolis: University of Minnesota Press, 1999), 15; John D. Bessler, "The 'Midnight Assassination Law' and Minnesota's Anti–Death Penalty Movement, 1849–1911," *William Mitchell Law Review* 22 (1996): 604–5; David Brion Davis, "The Movement to Abolish Capital Punishment in America, 1787–1861," *American Historical Review* 63 (1957): 22, 33.

2. William P. Everts Jr., *Stockwell of Minneapolis: A Pioneer of Social and Political Conscience* (St. Cloud, Minn.: North Star Press of St. Cloud, 1996), 57; *Minnesota House Journal* (1891), 149, 371; *Minnesota House Journal* (1893), 84, 302, 593–94, 644, 889, 931; *Minnesota Legislative Manual* (1891), 249; *Minnesota Legislative Manual* (1893), 578, 593; *Minnesota Senate Journal* (1893), 588, 620, 995; "In the House," *St. Paul Pioneer Press*, 3 February 1891, 2; "Capital Punishment," *St. Paul Pioneer Press*, 27 February 1891, 2; "To Abolish Capital Punishment," *St. Paul Dispatch*, 19 January 1893, 8; "Weary Legislators," *St. Paul Pioneer Press*, 20 January 1893, 1; "House Declines," *St. Paul Dispatch*, 24 February 1893, 1; "For Good Roads," *St. Paul Pioneer Press*, 24 February 1893, 2; "Necklaces of Hemp," *St. Paul Pioneer Press*, 24 March 1893, 2; "Capital Punishment," *Minneapolis Journal*, 24 March 1893, 4; *St. Paul Dispatch*, 24 March 1893, 3; "Senate Files," *St. Paul Pioneer Press*, 25 March 1893, 4; *St. Paul Dispatch*, 25 March 1893, 2; "To Abolish Capital Punishment," *St. Paul Pioneer Press*, 25 March 1893, 4; "The Death Penalty," *St. Paul Pioneer Press*, 27 March 1893, 6; "On Capital Punishment," *Minneapolis Journal*, 27 March 1893, 8; "No More New Bills," *St. Paul Pioneer Press*, 28 March 1893, 2, 7; *St. Paul Dispatch*, 28 March 1893, 2; "Judiciary Committee," *St. Paul Pioneer Press*, 29 March 1893, 2; "Lost, Strayed or Stolen," *St. Paul Pioneer Press*, 29 March 1893, 2; "Want a

New Bill," *St. Paul Pioneer Press*, 30 March 1893, 9; *St. Paul Pioneer Press*, 31 March 1893, 6; "John Day Smith–Part II," *ECCO News*, Sept. 1979, 10 (available at Minneapolis Public Library, Special Collections).

3. *Minnesota House Journal* (1895), 64, 367, 581; *Portrait Gallery of the Twenty-Ninth Legislature of the State of Minnesota* (Minneapolis: Bramblett and Beygeh, 1895), 137; "In the House," *St. Paul Pioneer Press*, 24 January 1895, 1; "Senator Day Is President," *St. Paul Pioneer Press*, 26 January 1895, 1; "Hemp for Hayward," *St. Paul Pioneer Press*, 9 March 1895, 1; "The Senate Approves," *St. Paul Pioneer Press*, 9 March 1895, 2; "Some May Be Woodchucks," *St. Paul Pioneer Press*, 31 March 1895, 8.

4. *Minnesota House Journal* (1895), 204, 221, 322–23, 330; *Portrait Gallery of the Twenty-Ninth Legislature*, 109, 120, 128, 131, 135, 194; H.F. 371, 29th Leg., 1st sess., Minn. (1895); "Will Please H. Hayward," *St. Paul Pioneer Press*, 17 February 1895, 2; "Hayward May Hang," *St. Paul Pioneer Press*, 5 March 1895, 6.

5. Everts, *Stockwell of Minneapolis*, 235, 245, 249–53, 256, 260, 392–93; *Minnesota House Journal* (1897), 58, 120, 219–20; *Minnesota Legislative Manual* (1897), 615; "House Will Work To-Day," *St. Paul Pioneer Press*, 16 January 1897, 1–2; "Arbitration Commended," *St. Paul Pioneer Press*, 29 January 1897, 3; "Busy Day for Stockwell," *St. Paul Pioneer Press*, 10 February 1897, 2; "We Will Still Hang," *St. Paul Pioneer Press*, 10 February 1897, 2.

6. *Minnesota House Journal* (1901), 104, 1007, 1119; *Minnesota Legislative Manual* (1901), 696; *Minnesota Legislative Manual* (1905), 661, 677; *Minnesota House Journal* (1905), 166, 799, 1061–62, 1141, 1662; *Minnesota Senate Journal* (1905), 98, 207–8, 238, 313, 1279; "New House Bills," *Minneapolis Journal*, 29 January 1901, 12; "To Remove Death Penalty," *Minneapolis Journal*, 29 January 1901, 12; "Senate Session Remarkable for Nothing but New Measures," *Minneapolis Journal*, 24 January 1905, 9; "Short Session," *Minneapolis Journal*, 7 February 1905, 4; "Think Death Penalty Wrong," *Minneapolis Journal*, 8 February 1905, 7; "May Abolish Hanging," *Minneapolis Journal*, 15 February 1905, 9; "Punishment for Murder," *Minneapolis Journal*, 21 February 1905, 5; "Legislative Doings Today," *Minneapolis Journal*, 2 March 1905, 4; "Legislative Proceedings," *Minneapolis Tribune*, 2 March 1905, 4; "Bills Passed," *St. Paul Pioneer Press*, 3 March 1905, 2; "Death Penalty Decried by State's Executive," *Minneapolis Journal*, 25 February 1906, 7; "Only Three Hangings," *St. Paul Pioneer Press*, 22 February 1907, 5.

7. *Minnesota House Journal* (1907), 161, 301, 1380–81, 1400, 1901; *Minnesota Legislative Manual* (1907), 671; "Bills Introduced," *St. Paul Pioneer Press*, 1 February 1907, 2; "Hangings at State Prison," *St. Paul Pioneer Press*, 1 February 1907, 2; "State Executions," *St. Paul Pioneer Press*, 2 February 1907, 6; "Bill to Abolish Death Penalty," *St. Paul Pioneer Press*, 6 March 1907, 4; "Sheriff the Hangman," *St. Paul Pioneer Press*, 13 April 1907, 5.

8. *Minnesota House Journal* (1907), 376, 1381–82, 1942; *Minnesota Legislative Manual* (1907), 672; "Murderers May Be Electrocuted," *Duluth News Tribune*, 6 March 1903, 1; "Bills Introduced," *St. Paul Pioneer Press*, 21 February 1907, 5; "In the House," *Minneapolis Tribune*, 21 February 1907, 8; "Death By Electricity," *St. Paul Pioneer Press*, 24 February 1907, 1; "Bill to Abolish Death Penalty," *St. Paul Pioneer Press*, 6 March 1907, 4.

9. *Minnesota House Journal* (1907), 551, 586–87; *Minnesota Legislative Manual* (1907), 675; "Bills Introduced," *St. Paul Pioneer Press*, 7 March 1907, 4; "Would Abolish Capital Punishment," *Minneapolis Tribune*, 7 March 1907, 9; "To Stop Hangings," *St. Paul Pioneer Press*, 8 March 1907, 2; "Gallows Stay in Minnesota," *St. Paul Pioneer Press*, 9 April 1907, 5.

10. *Gaylord: Hub of Sibley County* (Gaylord, Minn.: Gaylord History Committee, 1982), 259; *Minnesota House Journal* (1909), 101, 386, 783, 798, 1019; *Minnesota Legislative Manual* (1909), 721–22; "Hanged Until Dead," *Redwood Reveille* (Redwood Falls), 17 October 1891, 3; "Anti-Hanging Bill Again," *St. Paul Dispatch*, 19 January 1909, 5; "Would Abolish Death Penalty," *St. Paul Pioneer Press*, 20 January 1909, 6; "Would Abolish Hanging," *St. Paul Dispatch*, 11 February 1909, 3; "Death Penalty to Remain," *St. Paul Dispatch*, 9 March 1909, 3; "Will Not Abolish Hanging," *St. Paul Pioneer Press*, 10 March 1909, 8; "The Most Atrocious Crime," *St. Paul Pioneer Press*, 22 February 1998, 1; "Partial Autobiography of George MacKenzie" (unpublished manuscript obtained from Malcolm MacKenzie), 9, 55–56.

11. *Men of Minnesota* (St. Paul: R. L. Polk and Co., 1915), 186; Walter Trenerry, *Murder in Minnesota: A Collection of True Cases* (St. Paul: Minnesota Historical Society Press, 1985), 168–84; "To Abolish Death Penalty," *St. Paul Dispatch*, 10 December 1910, 9.

12. Carl Chrislock, *The Progressive Era in Minnesota 1899–1918* (St. Paul: Minnesota Historical Society, 1971), 14, 20, 36–37; *Minnesota House Journal* (1911), 19–20; *Minnesota Senate Journal* (1911), 14; "Eberhart Address Longest on Record," *Minneapolis Journal*, 4 January 1911, 1; Messages of the Governors

to the Legislature of Minnesota, Gov. Adolph O. Eberhart's Inaugural Message to the Minnesota Legislature, Jan. 4, 1911.

13. "Gaylord Mourns Death of George A. MacKenzie, 91, Attorney Here 62 Years," *Gaylord Hub*, 1 October 1948, 1, 4; "Partial Autobiography of George MacKenzie," 1–6, 8, 15, 25, 29–30, 38–40, 42, 54; Memorial of George A. MacKenzie, 6 December 1948, "MacKenzie Family" file, 3, Nicollet County Historical Society.

14. *Gaylord*, 259; John Koblas, *The Jesse James Northfield Raid: Confessions of the Ninth Man* (St. Cloud, Minn.: North Star Press of St. Cloud, 1999), 164–65, 168–80, 186, 189–90; *Minnesota House Journal* (1911), 44, 232–33; *Minnesota Legislative Manual* (1911), 674; "Facts about Minnesota Lawmakers," *Minneapolis Journal*, 8 January 1911, 2; "Opposes Death Sentence," *Minneapolis Journal*, 11 February 1911, 3; "Ask Inquiry into Governor's Delay," *Minneapolis Journal*, 23 February 1911, 1; "Daily News Calls Roll on House and Senate," *St. Paul Daily News*, 19 April 1911, 1; Memorial of George A. MacKenzie; "Partial Autobiography of George MacKenzie," 9–12.

15. *Minnesota Legislative Manual* (1911), 647; *Minnesota Senate Journal* (1911), 44, 1435; "Facts about Minnesota Legislators," *Minneapolis Journal*, 8 January 1911, 2; "New Senate Bills," *Minneapolis Journal*, 10 January 1911, 8; "Minnesota Politics," *Minneapolis Journal*, 11 January 1911, 18; "Ask Inquiry into Governor's Delay," *Minneapolis Journal*, 23 February 1911, 1.

16. *Minnesota House Journal* (1911), 471; "Ask Inquiry into Governor's Delay," *Minneapolis Journal*, 23 February 1911, 1; "Hear Governor Criticized," *Minneapolis Journal*, 24 February 1911, 1; "Death Penalty's Doom Seen," *Minneapolis Tribune*, 25 February 1911, 17.

17. *Gaylord*, 378; "Capital Punishment Rapped by the House," *Minneapolis Tribune*, 1 March 1911, 1; "House Votes to Abolish Hanging," *St. Paul Pioneer Press*, 1 March 1911, 8; "Death Penalty Abolished," *Minneapolis Journal*, 19 April 1911, 15; Joyce Peterson, "Bills to Restore Death Penalty Often Short-Lived," *Session Weekly* (Minnesota Legislature), 28 February 1992, 12; "Partial Autobiography of George MacKenzie," 56; 1911 Speech of George MacKenzie, obtained from Malcolm MacKenzie.

18. *Minnesota House Journal* (1911), 125, 145, 235–36, 471, 514, 1796; *Minnesota Legislative Manual* (1911), 684, 688, 698, 704; *Minnesota Senate Journal* (1911), 474, 476, 1553; "Facts about Minnesota Lawmakers," *Minneapolis Journal*, 8 January 1911, 2; "House Votes to Abolish Hanging," *Minneapolis*

Journal, 1 March 1911, 10; "Capital Punishment Rapped by the House," *Minneapolis Tribune*, 1 March 1911, 1; "House Votes to Abolish Hanging," *St. Paul Pioneer Press*, 1 March 1911, 8.

19. Franklyn Curtiss-Wedge, *History of McLeod County Minnesota* (Chicago: H. C. Cooper Jr. and Co., 1917), 299; *Minnesota House Journal* (1911), 512–13; "Wallert Bound Over," *Arlington Enterprise*, 6 September 1900, 1; "To Be Hanged," *Arlington Enterprise*, 13 December 1900, 1; "Condemned to Hang," *Gaylord Hub*, 14 December 1900, 1; "Must Hang," *Sibley County Independent*, 14 December 1900, 1; "Wallert's Crime," *Minneapolis Times*, 29 March 1901, 1; "House Votes to Abolish Hanging," *Minneapolis Journal*, 1 March 1911, 10; Memorial of George A. MacKenzie; "Partial Autobiography of George MacKenzie," 49, 54–55, 57.

20. "Kills Wife and Four Children," *Minneapolis Times*, 21 August 1900, 1; "Wallert Caught Admits Guilt," *Minneapolis Times*, 22 August 1900, 1–2; "Five Murdered," *Arlington Enterprise*, 23 August 1900, 1; "The Deed of a Fiend," *Sibley County Independent*, 24 August 1900, 1; "To Be Hanged," *Arlington Enterprise*, 13 December 1900, 1, 4; "Wallert's Crime," *Minneapolis Times*, 29 March 1901, 1; "Wallert Is Hanged," *Minneapolis Times*, 29 March 1901, 1.

21. *The Death Penalty in America*, 4; 1911 Speech of George MacKenzie.

22. "House Votes to Abolish Hanging," *St. Paul Pioneer Press*, 1 March 1911, 8; "Fear Bill May Set Murderers Free," *Minneapolis Journal*, 1 March 1911, 10; "O'Malley a Problem," *St. Paul Pioneer Press*, 7 March 1911, 4; "Quirk Is Near Parole," *Minneapolis Journal*, 20 April 1911, 7.

23. *Gaylord*, 362, 475; "Gaylord Mourns Death of George A. MacKenzie, 91, Attorney Here 62 Years," *Gaylord Hub*, 1 October 1948, 4; "Partial Autobiography of George MacKenzie," 22–24, 42–46, 57, 59, 68, 70–73, 75–78.

24. *Minnesota Senate Journal* (1911), 528, 951, 1366; "Death Penalty Abolished," *Minneapolis Journal*, 19 April 1911, 15.

25. "Many Prisoners Ask for Pardons," *Minneapolis Journal*, 8 January 1911, 6; "Plea to Save Two Lives," *St. Paul Pioneer Press*, 26 March 1911, 1; "Armed Deputies Guard O'Malley," *St. Paul Pioneer Press*, 4 April 1911, 1; "Pass Measure to Abolish Hanging," *St. Paul Pioneer Press*, 19 April 1911, 1.

26. *Minnesota Senate Journal* (1911), 1366; 1911 Minn. Laws 387; "End of Legislature Sees Surfeit of Bills," *Minneapolis Tribune*, 18 April 1911, 1; "Death Penalty Abolished," *Minneapolis Journal*, 19 April 1911, 15; "O'Malley's Life Saved; Hanging Is Abolished," *Minneapolis Tribune*, 19 April 1911, 7; "Pass

Measure to Abolish Hanging," *St. Paul Pioneer Press*, 19 April 1911, 1; "Important Bills Passed on Last Legislative Day," *St. Paul Pioneer Press*, 19 April 1911, 1; "Faint Praise by Governor," *St. Paul Daily News*, 19 April 1911, 2.

27. "Hanging Is Abolished," *St. Paul Pioneer Press*, 20 April 1911, 6; "Our Progress in Penology," *Minneapolis Journal*, 20 April 1911, 12.

28. "Hanging Is Abolished," *St. Paul Pioneer Press*, 20 April 1911, 6; "Our Progress in Penology," *Minneapolis Journal*, 20 April 1911, 12.

29. "O'Malley Escapes Noose," *St. Paul Daily News*, 19 April 1911, 2; "Quirk Is Near Parole," *Minneapolis Journal*, 20 April 1911, 7; "Death Sentences Commuted," *St. Paul Pioneer Press*, 22 April 1911, 6; "Partial Autobiography of George MacKenzie," 57.

30. Trenerry, *Murder in Minnesota*, 167; "Judge John Day Smith III: Jurist Suffers from a Nervous Breakdown," *Minneapolis Tribune*, 22 February 1911, 9; "Judge John Day Smith, 1845–1933," memorial prepared by E. F. Waite and presented February 3, 1934, Minneapolis Bar Association Papers, 1916–1934, Minnesota Historical Society, St. Paul.

31. *State ex. rel. Kelly v. Wolfer*, 119 Minn. 368, 375–76, 138 N.W. 315, 319 (1912).

32. John Galliher, Gregory Ray, and Brent Cook, "Abolition and Reinstatement of Capital Punishment during the Progressive Era and Early 20th Century," *Journal of Criminal Law and Criminology* 83 (1992): 538–39, 555, 560–67.

8. A Travesty of Justice

1. John Galliher, Larry Koch, David Keys, and Teresa Guess, *America without the Death Penalty* (Boston: Northeastern University Press, 2002), 79–99; *Minnesota Legislative Manual* (1913), 650; *Sibley County Independent*, 10 March 1911, 4; "Death Penalty Legislation in Minnesota since 1911," *Session Weekly*, 28 February 1992, 13; "Partial Autobiography of George MacKenzie" (unpublished manuscript obtained from Malcolm MacKenzie), 58.

2. "Hey, Skinnay! Circus Is Here," *Duluth News Tribune*, 14 June 1920, 4; "They're Here! Circus Folk," *Duluth Herald*, 14 June 1920, 7; *State v. Mason*, Case No. 22590 (Minn.), Trial Transcript/Record, 136–37, 146, 152.

3. Michael Fedo, *The Lynchings in Duluth* (St. Paul: Minnesota Historical Society Press, 2000), 3–4, 9–10, 13–18, 138; Dora MacDonald, *This Is Duluth* (Ashland, Wis.: Paradigm Press, 1999), 1; "Robinson Circus Shows to

Enormous Crowds," *Duluth Herald*, 15 June 1920, 2; "Attack on Girl Was Cause of Negro Lynching," *Duluth News Tribune*, 16 June 1920, 3; "Duluth Guarded from New Riots," *St. Paul Pioneer Press*, 17 June 1920, 1; "Negroes Did Not Rape Girl," *Duluth Ripsaw*, 26 June 1920, 1; "The Most Atrocious Crime," *St. Paul Pioneer Press*, 22 February 1998, 6G; *State v. Mason*, Case No. 22590 (Minn.), Record, 2, 63, 139, and State's Brief, 4.

4. Fedo, *Lynchings in Duluth*, 3, 18–21; W. F. Rhinow investigation, statement of John Murphy and Oscar Olson, Governor J. A. A. Burnquist Papers, File No. 648C, Box 83, Minnesota Historical Society, St. Paul; *State v. Mason*, Case No. 22590 (Minn.), Trial Transcript/Record, 159, 168, 184.

5. Fedo, *Lynchings in Duluth*, 13, 21–24, 140; *State v. Mason*, Case No. 22590 (Minn.), Trial Transcript/Record, 112, 169–70.

6. Fedo, *Lynchings in Duluth*, 24–26, 34; "Duluth Police Chief and Deputy Marshall Arrested on Liquor-Smuggling Charges; Chief Quits Office," *Duluth News Tribune*, 8 July 1920, 1; *State v. Mason*, Case No. 22590 (Minn.), Trial Transcript/Record, 112, 171.

7. Fedo, *Lynchings in Duluth*, 25–26, 62, 130, 138–39; "Physician, Girl Throw New Light on Assault Case," *Duluth News Tribune*, 17 June 1920, 9; H. J. Carling to Dr. Turner, June 28, 1920, 3–4, Burnquist Papers, correspondence and misc., Aug. 11, 1920–Nov. 1921, P448, Box 21.

8. Fedo, *Lynchings in Duluth*, 31–32, 35, 37, 42, 44, 46; "Alleged Rioter in Lynch Case Is Being Tried," *Duluth News Tribune*, 31 August 1920, 3; "The Most Atrocious Crime," *St. Paul Pioneer Press*, 22 February 1998, 6G.

9. Fedo, *Lynchings in Duluth*, 46–50; "West Duluth Girl Victim of Six Negroes," *Duluth Herald*, 15 June 1920, 1.

10. Fedo, *Lynchings in Duluth*, 44, 52–54; Rhinow investigation, Oscar Olson's statement, Burnquist Papers, File No. 648C, Box 83.

11. Fedo, *Lynchings in Duluth*, 3, 54–55, 58.

12. Ibid., 58–59, 61.

13. Ibid., 62–63; "Scope of Lynch Probe Extended on New Evidence," *Duluth News Tribune*, 6 July 1920, 3; Lynching–Duluth, Minn., June 14–29, 1920, NAACP Administrative File, NAACP Papers, Box C-359, Manuscript Reading Room, Library of Congress.

14. Fedo, *Lynchings in Duluth*, xxv, 66–68, 90; "Official Responsibility," *Duluth News Tribune*, 4 August 1920, 12; "Police Forbidden to Use Their Firearms to Withhold Rioters," *Duluth Herald*, 16 June 1920, 1; "Murnian Says

He Did Right," *Duluth Herald*, 17 June 1920, 1; Rhinow investigation, Oscar Olson's statement, Burnquist Papers, File No. 648C, Box 83.

15. Fedo, *Lynchings in Duluth*, 68–77; Report of the Grand Jury, July 13, 1920, reprinted in "The Shame of Duluth," undated pamphlet compiled by James C. Waters Jr., Hyattsville, Md., Manuscript Division, Library of Congress, 15.

16. Fedo, *Lynchings in Duluth*, 77–85; "Infuriated Mob Takes Three Negroes from Police Station and Hang Them," *Duluth Herald*, 16 June 1920, 14; "Make Penalty Fit Crime," *Duluth News Tribune*, 1 July 1920, 16; "Barber Tells of Lynching Scenes," *Duluth News Tribune*, 2 September 1920, 2; Report of the Grand Jury, July 13, 1920, reprinted in "The Shame of Duluth," 15, 17; *Mob Violence: A Photographic Review and Description of the Lynchings* (Duluth, Minn.: Duluth Publishing Company, 1920), 2 (available at Minnesota Historical Society, St. Paul).

17. Fedo, *Lynchings in Duluth*, 86–89, 92–94; "Police Recount Attack of Mob upon City Jail," *Duluth News Tribune*, 1 September 1920, 1–2; Rhinow investigation, Oscar Olson's statement, Burnquist Papers, File No. 648C, Box 83.

18. Fedo, *Lynchings in Duluth*, 95–97.

19. Ibid., 97–99; "Four-Hour Battle Overpowers Police Efforts against Lynching," *Duluth News Tribune*, 16 June 1920, 3.

20. Fedo, *Lynchings in Duluth*, 38, 99–100; "Infuriated Mob Takes Three Negroes from Police Station Hanging Them to Light Pole," *Duluth Herald*, 16 June 1920, 1.

21. Fedo, *Lynchings in Duluth*, 39, 100–106; "5,000 Persons Attack Jail; Blacks Dragged from Cells," *St. Paul Pioneer Press*, 16 June 1920, 1; "3 Dragged from Jail and Hanged at Street Corner," *Duluth News Tribune*, 16 June 1920, 1; "C. E. Jackson Believes His Son May Have Been Negro Hanged at Duluth," *Topeka Daily Capital*, 20 June 1920, 3; "Probe Deepens; Termination Is Not in Sight," *Duluth News Tribune*, 26 June 1920, 1; "Three Indicted in Duluth," *St. Paul Pioneer Press*, 30 June 1920, 1; "The Most Atrocious Crime," *St. Paul Pioneer Press*, 22 February 1998, 6G.

22. Fedo, *Lynchings in Duluth*, 106–9; "Topeka Youth May Be Victim of Duluth Mob," *Topeka Plain Dealer*, 18 June 1920; "Topeka, Kan., Had Ties to One of the Circus Workers," *Duluth News Tribune*, 26 October 1991, 1B.

23. *Duluth Directory* (Duluth, Minn.: R. L. Polk and Co., 1920), 142–43,

366, 390, 396–97; Fedo, *Lynchings in Duluth*, 109–11; "Negroes Lynched Despite Plea of Duluth Clergy," *Duluth News Tribune*, 16 June 1920, 3; "Pictures of Lynching Are Cause of Arrest," *Duluth News Tribune*, 18 June 1920, 6; "Displayed Photo; Ordered Arrested," *Mankato Free Press*, 19 June 1920, 8; "Pictures of Lynching Sell for 50 Cents Each," *Duluth News Tribune*, 19 June 1920, 5; "C. E. Jackson Believes His Son May Have Been Negro Hanged at Duluth," *Topeka Daily Capital*, 20 June 1920, 3; "Two Members of 'Jail Court' Held in Probe," *Duluth News Tribune*, 22 June 1920; 1, 3; "Photographer Fined $25 for Displaying Lynching Photos," *Duluth News Tribune*, 22 June 1920, 6; "Lynching Pictures," *Duluth News Tribune*, 9 July 1920, 12; Craig Grau, "The Past Can't Be Changed; We Can," *Duluth News Tribune*, 18 June 2000, 19A; Lynching–Duluth, Minn., news clippings, June 14–29, 1920, NAACP Branch Files, Duluth, Minn., 1920, Box G-103, and NAACP Administrative File, NAACP Papers, Box C-359.

24. Fedo, *Lynchings in Duluth*, 112–13, 115–17; "Troops Are Rushed to Lynching Scene," *St. Paul Pioneer Press*, 16 June 1920, 1; "Troops Sent Back to Guard Duluth," *St. Paul Pioneer Press*, 18 June 1920, 1; "Opposed to Rule of Mob," *Duluth Herald*, 19 June 1920, 4; "Reports Are Made on Duluth Lynching," *Appeal*, 10 July 1920, 3; Lynching–Duluth, Minn., June 14–29, 1920, NAACP Administrative File, NAACP Papers, Box C-359.

25. Lynching–Duluth, Minn., June 14–29, 1920, NAACP Administrative File, NAACP Papers, Box C-359. Loney Williams's first name is spelled "Lounie" in the affidavit but "Loney" or "Lonnie" in the newspapers and other sources. Fedo, *Lynchings in Duluth*, 24; "Attorneys End Pleas to Jury in Assault Case," *Duluth News Tribune*, 27 November 1920, 3.

26. Lynching–Duluth, Minn., June 14–29, 1920, NAACP Administrative File, NAACP Papers, Box C-359.

27. "Father of Negroes' Victim Deplores Lynching by Mob," *Duluth News Tribune*, 17 June 1920, 9; "Negroes Did Not Rape Girl," *Duluth Ripsaw*, 26 June 1920, 1; "Duluth," *Crisis* 20, 5 (Sept. 1920): 231; Lynching–Duluth, Minn., 1920, news clippings, June 14–29, 1920, July–Aug. 1920, NAACP Administrative File, Box C-359, and NAACP Branch Files, Minneapolis, Minn., 1920–1922, Box G-103, NAACP Papers.

28. Earl Spangler, *The Negro in Minnesota* (Minneapolis: T. S. Denison, 1961), 72, 86, 92, 102; *Standing Fast: The Autobiography of Roy Wilkins* (Cambridge, Mass.: Da Capo Press, 1994), 36, 115; "Memorial Mentionings," *Appeal*,

4 September 1920, 3; "Biographies of Black Pioneers," *Gopher Historian* (Winter 1968–69): 20; H. J. Carling to Dr. Turner, June 28, 1920, 1–2, Correspondence and Misc., Aug. 11, 1920–Nov. 1921, P448, Box 21, Burnquist Papers; Lynching–Duluth, Minn., June 14–29, 1920, NAACP Administrative File, NAACP Papers, Box C-359.

29. H. J. Carling to Dr. Turner, June 28, 1920, 2–5, Correspondence and Misc., Aug. 11, 1920–Nov. 1921, P448, Box 21, Burnquist Papers. Dr. Valdo Turner, who helped organize the NAACP's St. Paul branch in 1913, was the man who urged the private investigator's hiring.

30. "Duluth Lynching," *Appeal*, 3 July 1920, 3; "Micheaux Movie Hits Lynch Evil," *Appeal*, 3 July 1920, 2; "Reports Are Made on Duluth Lynching," *Appeal*, 10 July 1920, 3; "Within Our Gates," *Appeal*, 17 July 1920, 3; H. J. Carling to Dr. Turner, June 28, 1920, 2–5, Correspondence and Misc., Aug. 11, 1920–Nov. 1921, P448, Box 21, Burnquist Papers; Lynching–Duluth, Minn., July–Aug. 1920, NAACP Administrative File, Box C-359, and NAACP Branch Files, Duluth, Minn., 1915–1920/1920, Box G-103, NAACP Papers.

31. Fedo, *Lynchings in Duluth*, 6, 13, 27, 30, 117–19; Spangler, *Negro in Minnesota*, 101; "Three Black Hawks Swung from Poles," *Mankato Free Press*, 16 June 1920, 1, 9; "Start Lynching Probe," *Mankato Free Press*, 17 June 1920, 1; "The Duluth Tragedy," *Mankato Free Press*, 17 June 1920, 6; "National Press Raps Police for Duluth Lynching," *Duluth News Tribune*, 24 June 1920, 2; "Favors Death Penalty," *St. Paul Pioneer Press*, 22 July 1920, 8.

32. Fedo, *Lynchings in Duluth*, 121–25, 131; "Lynchers Will Be Prosecuted by Att'y Greene," *Duluth News Tribune*, 16 June 1920, 1; "Kiwanis Club and Duluth Citizens Deplore Lynchings," *Duluth Herald*, 16 June 1920, 2; "Duluth Guarded from New Riots," *St. Paul Pioneer Press*, 17 June 1920, 2; "Demand Quiz of Police Efforts to Defeat Mob," *Duluth News Tribune*, 17 June 1920, 1; "Troops Sent Back to Guard Duluth," *St. Paul Pioneer Press*, 19 June 1920, 1; "Soldiers Halt Mob's Desires for Lynching," *Duluth News Tribune*, 20 June 1920, 1; "Negroes Jailed Legally, Reply to Habeas Plea," *Duluth News Tribune*, 4 July 1920, 1, 6.

33. Fedo, *Lynchings in Duluth*, 128–30; "Officials Will Act after Quiz of Mob Leaders," *Duluth News Tribune*, 17 June 1920, 1, 9; "Police Tell of Lynching," *St. Paul Pioneer Press*, 18 June 1920, 1; "Trio of Police Force Examined by Grand Jury," *Duluth News Tribune*, 18 June 1920, 1; "Mob Flayed by Judge in Charge to Grand Jury," *Duluth News Tribune*, 18 June 1920, 8; "Military Probe

into Lynching Is Rhinow's Aim," *Duluth News Tribune*, 18 June 1920, 8; *Duluth News Tribune*, Supplement, 1 January 2000, 5; Lynching–Duluth, Minn., June 14–29, 1920, NAACP Administrative File, NAACP Papers, Box C-359.

34. Fedo, *Lynchings in Duluth*, 149; "Trio of Police Force Examined by Grand Jury," *Duluth News Tribune*, 18 June 1920, 1; "Grand Jury to Sift Stories of Police Defense," *Duluth News Tribune*, 19 June 1920, 3; "Grand Jury to Quiz 14 Negroes," *Duluth News Tribune*, 21 June 1920, 1; "Two Members of 'Jail Court' Held in Probe," *Duluth News Tribune*, 22 June 1920, 1; "Arrest Made in Connection with Lynching," *Duluth News Tribune*, 23 June 1920, 4; "Three, Alleged to Have Aided Mob, Indicted," *Duluth News Tribune*, 24 June 1920, 1, 12; "3 Indicted at Duluth," *St. Paul Pioneer Press*, 24 June 1920, 1; "Cannot Escape Law by Flight, Greene Avers," *Duluth News Tribune*, 25 June 1920, 1; "Youth Indicted in Lynching Free on $15,000 Bail," *Duluth News Tribune*, 27 June 1920, 1, 4; "Murnian Denies Rumor He Plans to Resign Office," *Duluth News Tribune*, 28 June 1920, 4; "Lawyers Renew Efforts to Get Bail for Youths," *Duluth News Tribune*, 29 June 1920, 8; "Murder Charge against Three More in Lynch Probe," *Duluth News Tribune*, 30 June 1920, 1; "Three Indicted in Duluth," *St. Paul Pioneer Press*, 30 June 1920, 1; "Grand Jury in Partial Report Indicts 5 Men," *Duluth News Tribune*, 2 July 1920, 1; "District Grand Jury to Resume Lynching Probe," *Duluth News Tribune*, 5 July 1920, 3; "New Evidence in Lynching Probe Prolongs Quiz; Girl Testifies," *Duluth News Tribune*, 8 July 1920, 1; "Thirteen Negroes Face Grand Jury," *Duluth News Tribune*, 9 July 1920, 1, 3; "Grand Jury Will Report Findings on Police Probe," *Duluth News Tribune*, 10 July 1920, 3; "Seven More Men Indicted in Probe; Names Secret," *Duluth News Tribune*, 14 July 1920, 1; "Special Grand Jury Returns 10 Indictments," *Duluth News Tribune*, 15 July 1920, 1; "Charge 2 with Aiding Lynching; Not Guilty, Plea," *Duluth News Tribune*, 18 July 1920, 9; "Two Grand Jury Bodies to Close Record Sessions," *Duluth News Tribune*, 19 July 1920, 3; "Greene Demands Immediate Trial for 30 Indicted in Lynching Probe," *Duluth News Tribune*, 20 July 1920, 1; "Seven Negroes File Petition to Quash Charges," *Duluth News Tribune*, 24 July 1920, 3; "Will Give Fund to Indicted Men," *Duluth News Tribune*, 31 July 1920, 1; "$8000 Sought for Lynching Trials," *Duluth News Tribune*, 3 August 1920, 4; "Fund for Defendants in Lynch Trials Now $450," *Duluth News Tribune*, 5 August 1920, 3; "Sheriff Makes One More Arrest in Lynching Case," *Duluth News Tribune*, 7 August 1920, 3; "Nine Arraigned Deny Charges in Lynching Probe," *Duluth News Tribune*, 10 August 1920, 3; "Order

of Trial in Lynch Cases Fixed by Greene," *Duluth News Tribune*, 15 August 1920, 8; "Special Venire of 72 Jurymen in Lynch Trials," *Duluth News Tribune*, 18 August 1920, 3; "Order of Trials in Lynch Cases Given by Greene," *Duluth News Tribune*, 26 August 1920, 3; *Duluth (Minnesota) Lynching of 1920: An Inventory of the Selected Materials* (St. Paul: Minnesota Historical Society, microfilm publication), 7.

35. "Grand Jury Calls Murnian Incompetent to Head Police Department," *Duluth News Tribune*, 14 July 1920, 8.

36. "Infuriated Mob Takes Three Negroes from Police Station Hanging Them to Light Pole," *Duluth Herald*, 16 June 1920, 1; "Negroes Did Admit Guilt," *Duluth Herald*, 17 June 1920, 13; "One of Lynched Negroes Innocent of Alleged Assault, Is Jury Report," *Duluth News Tribune*, 20 July 1920, 1; "Greene Demands Immediate Trial for 30 Indicted in Lynching Probe," *Duluth News Tribune*, 20 July 1920, 1; "Seven Negroes File Petition to Quash Charges," *Duluth News Tribune*, 24 July 1920, 3; "Evidence Taken on Petition to Quash Charges," *Duluth News Tribune*, 1 August 1920, 4; "Court Refuses Negroes' Claims for Dismissal," *Duluth News Tribune*, 22 August 1920, 3; Walter White to Gov. J. A. A. Burnquist, July 23, 1920, Correspondence and Misc., Aug. 11, 1920–Nov. 1921, P448, Box 21, Burnquist Papers; Lynching–Duluth, Minn., 1920, news clippings, NAACP Administrative File, NAACP Papers, Box C-359.

37. "Order of Trial in Lynch Cases Fixed by Greene," *Duluth News Tribune*, 15 August 1920, 8; "Special Venire of 72 Jurymen in Lynch Trials," *Duluth News Tribune*, 18 August 1920, 3; "Police Recount Attack of Mob upon City Jail," *Duluth News Tribune*, 1 September 1920, 1–2; "Barber Tells of Lynching Scenes," *Duluth News Tribune*, 2 September 1920, 1–2; "Witnesses Deny Alleged Proof Given Officials," *Duluth News Tribune*, 2 September 1920, 1, 3; "Verdict Obtained in 55 Minutes of Deliberation," *Duluth News Tribune*, 3 September 1920, 1, 3; "Second Group of Lynch Cases Ready for Trial," *Duluth News Tribune*, 7 September 1920, 3; "Close of Three New Riot Cases Will Halt Trials," *Duluth News Tribune*, 13 September 1920, 3; "Greene Ready to Prosecute Test Charges," *Duluth News Tribune*, 22 November 1920, 3.

38. Fedo, *Lynchings in Duluth*, 149–51; "Alleged Rioter in Lynch Case Is Being Tried," *Duluth News Tribune*, 31 August 1920, 1, 3; "Second of Lynch Cases May Go to Trial Jury Today," *Duluth News Tribune*, 3 September 1920, 4; "Fate of Rozon, Alleged Rioter, Still with Jury," *Duluth News Tribune*, 4 September 1920, 3; "Wrestles with Fate of Rozon for 31½ Hours," *Duluth News*

Tribune, 5 September 1920, 1, 3; "State to Close Case in Hedman Trial Tomorrow," *Duluth News Tribune*, 6 September 1920, 3; "State Tightens Net in Two New Lynching Cases," *Duluth News Tribune*, 8 September 1920, 1, 10; "Hedman's Fate May Be Decided Today," *Duluth News Tribune*, 9 September 1920, 3; "Attorneys Clash in Hedman Case; Ready for Jury," *Duluth News Tribune*, 10 September 1920, 1, 3; "Lynch Juries Retire Failing to Agree; Seek Further Facts," *Duluth News Tribune*, 11 September 1920, 1; "Defense Assails Men Higher Up in Lynch Trial," *Duluth News Tribune*, 11 September 1920, 3; "Two Not Guilty of Riot Charges in Lynch Trials," *Duluth News Tribune*, 12 September 1920, 1; "3 Lynch Cases Ready for Trial," *Duluth News Tribune*, 12 September 1920, 12; "Three New Riot Case Juries Hear Police Grilled," *Duluth News Tribune*, 15 September 1920, 1, 3; "Three More Riot Trials May Go to Juries Today," *Duluth News Tribune*, 16 September 1920, 1, 3; "One Convicted, Two Acquitted of Riot Charge," *Duluth News Tribune*, 17 September 1920, 1; "Counsel to Ask for New Trial of Hammerberg," *Duluth News Tribune*, 19 September 1920, 11; Steven Hoffbeck, "'Victories Yet to Win': Charles W. Scrutchin, Bemidji's Black Activist Attorney," *Minnesota History* 55 (Summer 1996): 71; Lynching–Duluth, Minn., 1920, news clippings, NAACP Administrative File, NAACP Papers, Box C-359.

39. Fedo, *Lynchings in Duluth*, 143–45, 155; "Attack on Girl Was Cause of Negro Lynching," *Duluth News Tribune*, 16 June 1920, 3; "New Arrests in Lynch Quiz Are Certain," *Duluth News Tribune*, 7 July 1920, 1; "Date for Trial of Lynch Cases Fixed by Court," *Duluth News Tribune*, 12 August 1920, 3; "Defense Quizzes Girl's Escort in Negro Trial," *Duluth News Tribune*, 24 November 1920, 1.

40. Warren Greene's Supplementary Statement, accompanying his December 14, 1920, letter to Gov. J. A. A. Burnquist, Correspondence and Misc., Aug. 11, 1920–Nov. 1921, P448, Box 21, Burnquist Papers.

41. "Courtroom Cleared While Witness Victim Tells of Circus-Day Attack," *Duluth News Tribune*, 23 November 1920, 1; "Defense Quizzes Girl's Escort in Negro Trial," *Duluth News Tribune*, 24 November 1920, 1; *State v. Mason*, Case No. 22590 (Minn.), Trial Transcript/Record, 3–20.

42. *State v. Mason*, Case No. 22590 (Minn.), Trial Transcript/Record, 20–24.

43. Ibid., 24–37; Hoffbeck, "'Victories Yet to Win,'" 60–71, 73–75; NAACP Branch Files, Duluth, Minn., 1915–1920/1920, NAACP Papers, Box G-103.

44. *State v. Mason*, Case No. 22590 (Minn.), Trial Transcript/Record, 41–44, 49.

45. Ibid., 50–60; "Defense Quizzes Girl's Escort in Negro Trial," *Duluth News Tribune*, 24 November 1920, 1.

46. *State v. Mason*, Case No. 22590 (Minn.), Trial Transcript/Record, 61–63.

47. Ibid., 63–85, 94–95, 97–105.

48. Ibid., 112–16, 121, 123–25.

49. Ibid., 127–31.

50. Ibid., 131–35.

51. Ibid., 138–45, 153–57.

52. Ibid., 159–65.

53. Ibid., 178–83, 185–88.

54. Fedo, *Lynchings in Duluth*, 153–54, 158–61; J. Royster, ed., *Southern Horrors and Other Writings: The Anti-Lynching Campaign of Ida B. Wells, 1892–1900* (Boston: Bedford Books, 1997), 39; Hoffbeck, "'Victories Yet to Win,'" 67, 71, 73; "Seven Negroes File Petition to Quash Charges," *Duluth News Tribune*, 24 July 1920, 3; "Evidence Taken on Petition to Quash Charges," *Duluth News Tribune*, 1 August 1920, 4; "Court Refuses Negroes' Claims for Dismissal," *Duluth News Tribune*, 22 August 1920, 3; "Attorneys End Pleas to Jury in Assault Case," *Duluth News Tribune*, 27 November 1920, 3; NAACP Branch Files, Duluth, Minn., 1920, NAACP Papers, Box G-103.

55. "Attorneys End Pleas to Jury in Assault Case," *Duluth News Tribune*, 27 November 1920, 3; *State v. Mason*, Case No. 22590 (Minn.), Trial Transcript/Record, 190–92.

56. Hoffbeck, "'Victories Yet to Win,'" 67, 71, 73; "First of Group in Assault Faces Jail Term," *Duluth News Tribune*, 28 November 1920, 1; *State v. Mason*, Case No. 22590 (Minn.), Trial Transcript/Record, 196–200.

57. Hoffbeck, "'Victories Yet to Win,'" 60, 66, 70–71, 73–74; "First of Group in Assault Faces Jail Term," *Duluth News Tribune*, 28 November 1920, 1; Lynching–Duluth, Minn., Jan.–Nov. 1921, NAACP Administrative File, Box C-359, and NAACP Branch Files, Duluth, Minn., 1915–1920/1920/1921–1925, Box G-103, NAACP Papers.

58. Fedo, *Lynchings in Duluth*, 154, 163–67; Hoffbeck, "'Victories Yet to Win,'" 60, 66, 70–71, 73–74; "Negro's Counsel Quizzes Boy on Phases of Story," *Duluth News Tribune*, 30 November 1920, 6; "Defense Begins Closing

Phase of Miller Trial," *Duluth News Tribune*, 1 December 1920, 3; "Negro Freed on Attack Charge, Off of 'Big Tops,'" *Duluth News Tribune*, 2 December 1920, 1; "Prosecution Foiled by Triple Lynching," *Duluth News Tribune*, 16 December 1920, 1; "The Most Atrocious Crime," *St. Paul Pioneer Press*, 22 February 1998, 6G.

59. Fedo, *Lynchings in Duluth*, 154, 163–67; Hoffbeck, "'Victories Yet to Win,'" 60, 66, 70–71, 73–74; "Negro Freed on Attack Charge, Off of 'Big Tops,'" *Duluth News Tribune*, 2 December 1920, 1; "Prosecution Foiled by Triple Lynching," *Duluth News Tribune*, 16 December 1920, 1; "The Most Atrocious Crime," *St. Paul Pioneer Press*, 22 February 1998, 6G; Warren Greene's Supplementary Statement, accompanying his December 14, 1920, letter to Gov. J. A. A. Burnquist, Correspondence and Misc., Aug. 11, 1920–Nov. 1921, P448, Box 21, Burnquist Papers.

60. "Police to Keep Tab on Risque Modes of Dance," *Duluth News Tribune*, 31 December 1920; Lynching–Duluth, Minn., June 14–29, 1920, Oct.–Dec. 1920, Jan.–Nov. 1921, NAACP Administrative File Box C-359, and NAACP Branch Files, Duluth, Minn., 1915–1920, Box G-103, NAACP Papers.

61. Ida H. Harper, ed., *The History of Woman Suffrage* (New York: J. J. Little and Ives, 1922), 6:320; Heidi Bauer, ed., *The Privilege for Which We Struggled: Leaders of the Woman Suffrage Movement in Minnesota* (St. Paul: Minnesota Historical Society Press, 1999), 118; Spangler, *Negro in Minnesota*, 92; Barbara Stuhler, *Gentle Warriors: Clara Ueland and the Minnesota Struggle for Woman Suffrage* (St. Paul: Minnesota Historical Society Press, 1995), 80–81; Wilkins, *Standing Fast*, 33–35; Barbara Stuhler and Gretchen Kreuter, eds., *Women of Minnesota: Selected Biographical Essays* (St. Paul: Minnesota Historical Society Press, 1998), 347; "Biographies of Black Pioneers," *Gopher Historian* (Winter 1968–69): 20; "Citizens Mass Meeting," *Appeal*, 11 December 1920, 2; "Everywoman Progressive Council," *Appeal*, 1 January 1921, 3; *Appeal*, 25 December 1920, 3; *Appeal*, 9 April 1921, 3; *Appeal*, 7 May 1921, 4; "Francis Rites Hinge on Stimson Decision," *St. Paul Pioneer Press*, 16 July 1929, 18; *Duluth News Tribune*, Supplement, 1 January 2000, 6; NAACP Branch Files, Duluth, Minn., 1920, NAACP Papers, Box G-103; Daniel Paul Mikel, "A History of Negro Newspapers in Minnesota 1876–1963" (master's thesis, Macalester College, 1963), 88.

62. Spangler, *Negro in Minnesota*, 84, 86, 95, 100, 103, 117; "Boost the Drive," *Appeal*, 4 December 1920, 3; "Everywoman Progressive Council," *Appeal*, 1 January 1921, 3; "Everywoman Progressive Council," *Appeal*, 8 January 1921,

2; "The N.A.A.C.P.," *Appeal*, 26 February 1921, 2; *Appeal*, 12 March. 1921, 3; "The Du Bois Address," *Appeal*, 26 March 1921, 2; "Minnesota Legislators Would Prevent Lynching," *Appeal*, 9 April 1921, 2; "Everywoman Progressive Council," *Appeal*, 9 April 1921, 3; "Minnesota Legislators Would Prevent Lynching," *Appeal*, 16 April 1921, 3; "The N.A.A.C.P. Board," *Appeal*, 23 April 1921, 2; "The Anti-Lynching Mass Meeting," *Appeal*, 23 April 1921, 3; "Minnesota Anti-Lynching Bill," *Crisis* 22 (June 1921): 67; "Cretin Residents to Stage Gesture against Negroes," *St. Paul Pioneer Press*, 4 October 1924, 1; Anti-Lynching Measures–Minnesota 1920–1921, NAACP Administrative File, NAACP Papers, Box C-207.

63. *Who's Who among Minnesota Women* (St. Paul: M. D. Foster, 1924), 116; *Who's Who in Colored America* (New York: Who's Who in Colored America Corp., 1928–29), 135; Wilkins, *Standing Fast*, 128–34; "The Story of Afro-Americans in the Story of Minnesota," *Gopher Historian* (Winter 1968–69): 11; "League of Women Voters," *Appeal*, 18 December 1920, 2; "The Race Question," *Appeal*, 16 April 1921, 2; "Body of W. T. Francis to Be Buried in U.S.," *Minneapolis Journal*, 18 July 1929, 3; "Services Sunday for William T. Francis," *Minneapolis Journal*, 9 August 1929, 11; Memorial of William Francis, Memorials: Farnham to Murphy, Ramsey County Bar Association Records, Minnesota Historical Society; correspondence between William Francis and Gov. J. A. A. Burnquist, July 3, 1920, and July 10, 1920, Correspondence and Misc., Aug. 11, 1920–Nov. 1921, P448, Box 21, Burnquist Papers.

64. James Chadbourn, *Lynching and the Law* (Chapel Hill: University of North Carolina, 1933), 13; Fedo, *Lynchings in Duluth*, 142; *Minnesota House Journal* (1921), 1171; *Minnesota Senate Journal* (1921), 1216; Robert Zangrando, *The NAACP Crusade against Lynching, 1909–1950* (Philadelphia: Temple University Press, 1980), 13, 20; Session Laws of the State of Minnesota Passed during the Forty-Second Session of the State Legislature, ch. 401, H.F. No. 785; Hoffbeck, "'Victories Yet to Win,'" 60, 66, 70–71, 73–74; "Minnesota Anti-Lynching Bill," *Crisis* 22 (June 1921): 67; "Father of One Lynched Negro Claims $7,500," *Duluth News Tribune*, 3 July 1920, 1; "Negro Sues Duluth," *Duluth News Tribune*, 4 July 1920, 3; NAACP Branch Files, Duluth, Minn., 1920, NAACP Papers, Box G-103; http://www.kshs.org/people/african_americans. htm#scott (containing biographical sketch of Elisha Scott).

65. James McGovern, *Anatomy of a Lynching: The Killing of Claude Neal* (Baton Rouge: Louisiana State University Press, 1982), 139, 144–47; Spangler,

Negro in Minnesota, 103; Stewart Tolnay and E. M. Beck, *A Festival of Violence: An Analysis of Southern Lynchings, 1882–1930* (Champaign: University of Illinois Press, 1995), 212; Zangrando, *NAACP Crusade against Lynching*, 19, 212; "The Du Bois Address," *Appeal*, 12 March 1921, 3; "St. Paul Honors Mrs. W. T. Francis," *Appeal*, 7 May 1921, 3.

66. Lynching–Duluth, Minn., June 14–29, 1920, Jan.–Nov. 1921, NAACP Administrative File, Box C-359, and NAACP Branch Files, Minneapolis, Minn., 1920–1922, and Duluth, Minn., 1915–1920, Box G-103, NAACP Papers.

67. *State v. Mason*, Case No. 22590 (Minn.), Appellant's Brief, 13, 22, 25, 36; Lynching–Duluth, Minn., Jan.–Nov. 1921, NAACP Administrative File, Box C-359, and NAACP Branch Files, Duluth, Minn., 1915–1920, Box G-103, NAACP Papers.

68. *State v. Mason*, 189 N.W. 452, 453 (Minn. 1922); *State v. Mason*, Case No. 22590 (Minn.), State's Brief, 38.

69. *Mason*, 189 N.W. at 454–55 (Dibell, J., dissenting); Proceedings in Memory of Associate Justices Homer Bliss Dibell and Albert Schaller, 18 October 1934, Pamphlet Collection, Minnesota Historical Society, St. Paul.

70. *Mason*, 189 N.W. at 454–55 (Dibell, J., dissenting).

71. Chadbourn, *Lynching and the Law*, 25–27, 29, 31, 48, 58–59, 86; Fedo, *Lynchings in Duluth*, 155, 171–72; Wilkins, *Standing Fast*, 36, 42–44; "Justice Homer Dibell," *Appeal*, 19 June 1920, 1; "2 Duluth Youths Found Dead in Freight Car," *Duluth News Tribune*, 17 January 1924; *Duluth (Minnesota) Lynching of 1920: An Inventory of the Selected Materials* (St. Paul: Minnesota Historical Society, microfilm publication), 12; Ralph E. Burdick to Charles E. Vasaly, February 23, 1923, inmate case file for Carl John Alfred Hammerberg (Case File No. 5143), Minnesota Historical Society (hereafter MHS), St. Paul; Frank A. Whittier to F. E. Resche, May 19, 1922, inmate case file for Gilbert Henry Stephenson (Case File No. 6598), MHS; H. B. Whittier to C. J. Swendsen, June 15, 1922, inmate case file for Louis Dondino (Case File No. 6614), MHS; L. S. Nelson to H. B. Whittier, April 27, 1925, case file of Max Mason (Case File No. 6785), MHS; Mason M. Forbes to Bertha Wolff, April 14, 1924, Board of Pardons, Application No. 6205, MHS; Mason M. Forbes to State Board of Parole, June 12, 1925, case file of Max Mason (Case File No. 6785), MHS; Discharge Order, September 3, 1925, case file of Max Mason (Case File No. 6785), MHS.

72. MacDonald, *This Is Duluth*, 208; D. J. Tice, *Minnesota's Twentieth Century: Stories of Extraordinary Everyday People* (Minneapolis: University of

Minnesota Press, 1999), 45, 52; Larry Oakes, "Remembering with Shame, Hope," *Star Tribune*, 5 June 2001, B1.

Conclusion

1. Hugo Adam Bedau, ed., *The Death Penalty in America: Current Controversies* (New York: Oxford University Press, 1997), 10–11.

2. LaLonnie Erickson, "Minnesota Homicides 1985 to 1997," Minnesota Planning, May 1999, 3; Daniel Elazar, Virginia Gray, and Wyman Spano, *Minnesota Politics and Government* (Lincoln: University of Nebraska Press, 1999), 148; Dirk Johnson, "Nice City's Nasty Distinction: Murder Soars in Minneapolis," *New York Times*, 30 June 1996, 1A; Raymond Bonner and Ford Fessenden, "States with No Death Penalty Share Lower Homicide Rates," *New York Times*, 22 September 2000, A1; Ford Fessenden, "Deadly Statistics: A Survey of Crime and Punishment," *New York Times*, 22 September 2000, A23; http://www.deathpenaltyinfo.org/deter.html; http://www.disastercenter.com/crime/lacrime.htm; http://www.disastercenter.com/crime/mncrime.htm; http://www.disastercenter.com/crime/txcrime.htm.

3. *Holden v. Minnesota*, 137 U.S. 483, 491 (1890); *State v. Pioneer Press Co.*, 110 N.W. 867 (Minn. 1907).

4. 1893 Conn. Pub. Acts, ch. 137, § 3; 1898 Mass. Acts, ch. 326, §§ 3–4; 1903 N.D. Laws, ch. 99, § 2; 1905 Wyo. Sess. Laws, ch. 11, § 1; 1923 Ala. Acts 587, § 7; 1923 Tex. Gen. Laws, ch. 51, § 1; 1939 S.D. Laws, ch. 135, § 2; 1944 Ky. Acts, ch. 145, § 1; Del. Code Ann. tit. 11, § 4209(f); 1952 La. Acts, ch. 160, § 1; 1908 Va. Acts, ch. 398, § 1; 1909 Wash. Laws, ch. 249, § 209, *repealed by* 1982 Wash. Laws, ch. 184, § 11; Ark. Code Ann. § 16-90-504 (Michie 1987); 1913 Ark. Acts, ch. 55, § 10.

5. John D. Bessler, "The 'Midnight Assassination Law' and Minnesota's Anti–Death Penalty Movement, 1849–1911," *William Mitchell Law Review* 22 (1996): 577, 579, 704, 719–21.

6. Walter Trenerry, *Murder in Minnesota: A Collection of True Cases* (St. Paul: Minnesota Historical Society Press, 1985), 167; "Newspapers Indicted," *Minneapolis Journal*, 3 March 1906, 7; "St. Paul Newspapers Procure Indictments," *Minneapolis Journal*, 4 March 1906, 5.

7. Potter Stewart, "Or of the Press," *Hastings Law Journal* 26 (1975): 631, 634.

8. John D. Bessler, *Death in the Dark: Midnight Executions in America*

(Boston: Northeastern University Press, 1997), 174; Minn. Stat. §§ 244.05, 609.184–.185; "At Death's Door," *City Pages*, 28 February 1996, 10; *State v. Gunsby*, Case No. 84,977 (Fla., Jan. 11, 1996).

9. Minn. Stat. §§ 609.184–.185; Minn. Stat. § 244.05; Patrick McGowan, "The Death Penalty," *Hamline Journal of Public Law and Policy* 14 (1993): 144, 145; Betty Wilson, "Is There an Electric Chair in Minnesota's Future," *Law and Politics* (February 1995): 8–9; "Capital Punishment," *Duluth News Tribune*, 21 June 1920; "Death Penalty in Minnesota," *St. Paul Pioneer Press*, 18 July 1920, 4; "Death for Murderers to Check Wave of Crime in State Urged," *Duluth News Tribune*, 3 December 1920, 1; "Minnesota May Vote on Death Penalty as Murder Penalty," *Minneapolis Journal*, 24 February 1921, 3; "Nimocks Pledged Aid on Death Penalty Bill," *Minneapolis Journal*, 27 February 1921, 9; "Since 1911 . . . Bills to Restore Death Penalty Often Short-Lived," *Session Weekly* (Minnesota Legislature), 28 February 1992, 1, 13; *Briefly: The Minnesota Senate Week in Review* (28 February 1992); *Session Weekly* (Minnesota Legislature), 5 May 1995, 5.

10. Hubert H. Humphrey, *The Education of a Public Man: My Life and Politics* (Minneapolis: University of Minnesota Press, 1991), 77.

Index

John D. Bessler is an attorney in Minneapolis and adjunct professor of law at the University of Minnesota Law School. He has assisted in the pro bono representation of death row inmates in Texas. He is also the author of *Death in the Dark: Midnight Executions in America* and *Kiss of Death: America's Love Affair with the Death Penalty*.